Fouché

The Unprincipled Patriot

FOUCHÉ

The Unprincipled Patriot

Hubert Cole

THE McCALL PUBLISHING COMPANY

New York

ISBN 0-8415-0106-8

The McCall Publishing Company
230 Park Avenue, New York, N.Y. 10017

PRINTED IN THE UNITED STATES OF AMERICA

To an Extraordinary Child

Contents

List of Illustrations

General Brune, from a portrait by Levachez
Reproduced by permission of the Mansell Collection.

Barras, from a portrait by A. Lacauchie
Reproduced by permission of the Mansell Collection.

Sieyès, from a portrait by Levachez
Reproduced by permission of the Mansell Collection.

Hell Hounds Rallying Round the Idol of France, a caricature
published by Ackermann in April, 1815
Reproduced by permission of the British Museum.

Fouché as Minister of Police, *c.* 1799, a portrait by Detarges
Reproduced by permission of Monsieur F. Geffriaud, Nantes.

Louis XVIII climbing the *Mât de Cocagne,* caricature by
Cruikshank, October, 1815
Reproduced by permission of the British Museum.

Fouché, an engraving by Joseph Eymar d'Aix after a portrait
by Mlle de Nanterre
Reproduced by permission of Monsieur F. Geffriaud, Nantes.

Fouché during the Restoration
Reproduced by permission of the Bibliothèque Municipale, Nantes.

Josephine, Comtesse de Thermes, Fouché's daughter
Reproduced by permission of Monsieur F. Geffriaud, Nantes.

PART I
The Executioner of Lyons
c.1760-1794

I

Nantes was noisy, robust. It bulged beyond the girdle of its ancient walls. Its streets were shrill with the squeak of block and tackle for new buildings, the clatter of laden carts over cobblestones, the creak of rope on bollards down at the docks. After half a century of disastrous misrule, France had lost India, Canada, her reputation as a military power and her preponderant voice in Europe. Yet Nantes remained a wealthy city, and to that extent a contented one. The tang of the west wind driving the great Atlantic merchantmen upstream was mulled with the rich scent of the rum and coffee that they brought, with sugar and cotton and indigo, from the great slave colonies of the West Indies.

In contrast to the city, the boy who lodged in the cloisters by the church of Notre Dame, was, though not poor, remarkably unsturdy in appearance. He was frail-jointed, with pale yellow hair and wan skin stretched too tightly over a sharp-featured face. He managed to seem both high-spirited and introvert. At the Oratory School, beside the barracks in the faubourg St-Clément, across the tree-lined cours St-Pierre, his fellow pupils found him good company and admired his talent for practical joking. The Oratory Fathers, who at first 'mistook the gaiety of his character for levity'[1] and 'thought he wanted intellect'[2] because he refused to show an interest in grammar and Latin verses, had since discovered that he had a bent for science. He was stubborn, not to be driven, but, in the opinion of Father Durif, the Director of Studies, a potential scholar within a limited field.

During the holidays he went home to Le Pellerin, a port ten miles down the river where he had been born somewhere about the year 1760. The Fouchés were an affectionate, closely-knit family: the mother, older sister, younger brother and, if he were home from sea, the father, Captain Joseph, descendant of a long line of Breton seamen. The captain was merchant as well as mariner. He bought and sold the cargoes that he sailed back and forth to the Antilles, or on the cabotage trade around the coast to Bordeaux and Marseilles. He had a small estate or two in the neighbourhood of Le Pellerin and a share in plantations on St-Domingue, the richest of the French West Indian islands. By family tradition he would hand on the helm of his ship to his eldest son, just as he had handed on the name of Joseph. The future for the boy seemed secure and prosperous. But they were in a trade where prosperity depended on peace; and peace was hard to come by.

Louis XV died in 1774, when Joseph was in his teens. The *Te Deum* that the choir chanted in the cathedral church for the new king's accession was more heartfelt than most, for there were great hopes that the twenty-year-old Louis XVI would revive the country's finances and repute and give it constitutional reform. Unfortunately, the King put repute before finance. Across the ocean the American colonists, free from the fear of French attack since Wolfe defeated Montcalm in Canada, renounced the English protection that they now found unnecessary and expensive. To the delight of the major-ity of his subjects and the dismay of his advisers, Louis encouraged Frenchmen to seek glory and revenge by serving against the English in support of the rebels.

The undeclared war of volunteers ripened into open hostilities. The British Fleet played havoc with the French West Indian trade. France triumphantly roused almost the whole of Europe against the arrogant English, but Nantes began to feel the pinch. When, after eleven years of marriage, Louis and Marie Antoinette were blessed with their first son in October 1781, the city council confessed that their celebrations lacked 'the magnificence worthy of the occasion . . . our communal income being almost non-existent in time of war', though the meagreness of the festivities was 'supplemented by the intoxication of public joy'.[3]

Shortly afterwards, the lean, pale, courteous, nimble-witted but somehow inaccessible young man left Nantes for Paris. The pros-pects at sea were gloomy; Father Durif had persuaded Captain Fouché that his son had a marked aptitude for teaching and clearly lacked the strong constitution that a master mariner needs. Joseph was on his way to the seminary of the Oratory of Jesus in the rue St-Honoré.

He was also on his way to a seat in the National Convention from which he would vote the death of the no longer popular Louis XVI; to the brutal *mitraillades* of Lyons; to a hazardous career as the most powerful and independent of Bonaparte's ministers. His name was to pass into history as that of the most notorious and powerful chief of

secret police – until the latter-day dictatorships set standards of a
different kind. He was to be the only man to play a crucial part in the
destruction of the two great tyrants of his age. 'Within the space of a
fortnight,' said Robespierre, 'Fouché's head must fall on the scaffold,
or mine will'[4] – and it was Robespierre who went to the guillotine.
'I should have hanged him; that was my intention,'[5] said Bonaparte
over and over again – brooding on St Helena. 'If I had won at
Waterloo, I should have had him shot at once.'

For a century and a half his countrymen have spoken of him with
hatred and contempt. His contemporary, Chateaubriand, described
him as 'a hyena in human clothes, thief, atheist, assassin'.[6] His
first biographer, Martel, referred to his 'cynicism, cold cruelty,
insatiable cupidity and profound hypocrisy' and called him 'one of
the most villainous, most infamous of all the monsters in human
guise of that redoubtable period'.[7]

It is possible, on the other hand, that he was a sincere and
moderately successful patriot. It is not uncommon in France
for egoists to be hailed as patriots, and patriots condemned as
traitors.

2

The Congregation of the Oratory of Our Lord Jesus Christ in France
was founded in 1611, a time when great families gave their wealth to
endow houses of education and their younger sons to staff them. By
the eighteenth century 'vocations were rare; nobility of the sword or
the robe offered other careers than those of the sacerdotal and religious life',[1] and the Congregation was forced to rely more and more
on lay members who had neither a strong enough vocation to dedi-
cate themselves to a lifetime of teaching nor a large enough fortune to
keep them out of it. With the title of Oratorians or Confrères, to
distinguish them from the fully-ordained Fathers of the Oratory,
they were tonsured, took a teaching course at the Seminary, and
served the Congregation on an annual renewable contract. For most
of them this profession was a stepping-stone to a better one. At a
yearly wage that seldom rose above 80 livres, there was no temptation to linger. Meantime they saw a great deal of France; as one staff
emergency grew more acute than another, they were shuttled from
town to town, seldom spending more than a year, as often as little
as a term, in each school.

Fouché hastened home at the end of each term, spurred as much by need as by affection. Writing to his sister Louise from Vendôme, he sent his best wishes to his brother and brother-in-law, both away at sea, and told her he had received the 300 francs sent him by his mother, now a widow. The school speech-day was to be opened by the balloonist, Montgolfier. After that 'I will find out how best to convey my body, or rather my frail carcass, to Le Pellerin. You've never seen me so thin, my bones will soon be sticking out through all my clothes.'[2]

He progressed to fashionable Juilly, a few miles north of Paris, where he took charge of mathematics and physical sciences. The playwright Arnault, who was educated there, described how Fouché, whom his pupils 'regarded as a fine fellow',[3] constructed a montgolfier balloon and, just before releasing it to be wafted by the north-easterly breeze in the direction of Versailles, attached to it an adulatory set of verses addressed to Louis XVI and composed by Father Billaud, who taught Latin and French verse to Class Two. The point of the anecdote is that within a few years both Fouché and Billaud voted the death of the King they now fawned upon. Like many of the stories told about him it is amusing: it presents him as an unprincipled sycophant; and it is quite untrue. When Fouché arrived at Juilly, Arnault had already left.[4]

From Juilly Fouché was transferred to Arras, where he met three men who were to play large parts in his life. One was a round-faced, tight-lipped, priggish Confrère who arrived in the spring from the school at Boulogne – Maurice Gaillard, his lifelong confidant and friend. Another was the nephew of M. Du Rut, the school physician, who was provided with a rent-free house but no garden, and in consequence would often stroll round the school grounds when he felt in need of exercise. The nephew, a sensitive, idealistic, ambitious young lawyer named Maximilien Robespierre, introduced Fouché to the philosophical societies and literary circles of which he was a member (he was a former director of the Royal Academy of Belles-Lettres of Arras) and at one of these, a club called the Académie des Rosati, Fouché made the acquaintance of a clever, pompous, engineer-lieutenant, Lazare Carnot.

Robespierre had already won something of a reputation at the Artois bar. This encouraged him to turn his interest from the arts to the increasingly promising field of politics; and he left no doubt as to the importance of the contribution he intended to make to national life. At one gathering of the notabilities of Arras Robespierre informed the company that 'a great revolution has been long approaching in men's minds'[5] and that he was the man to direct it. Voltaire or Rousseau might have done it, he continued, but Voltaire marred his great talent with grotesque buffooneries, and Rousseau did not know how to use the influence his writing won for him.

'It may surprise you,' he continued, his head back, blue eyes glinting behind tinted glasses, nose tip-tilted at the ceiling and prim, square chin jutting at his audience, 'but I am convinced that it is I who am destined to bring about this revolution. A few more years of meditation and study and I shall have gained more confidence. The march of events will aid me, no obstacles can impede me, success is not in doubt – it will be complete.'[6]

His enthusiasm struck a responsive spark in Fouché. He took to visiting Robespierre at home, where he met the advocate's sister and younger brother. The sister, Charlotte, warmed to the schoolteacher's enthusiasm and admiration for Maximilien and saw in him signs of 'the most ardent patriotism, the most sacred devotion'.[7] He was not handsome, but he had a charming wit and was extremely 'amiable'. She did nothing to discourage him when his visits became more frequent and he began to show her 'that consideration and those attentions which one has for a person in whom one interests oneself in a particular way'.[8]

Her thirtieth birthday was fast approaching. Devoted though she was to her brothers, she would prefer not to spend the rest of her life keeping house for them. The Oratorian laid bare his heart. 'He spoke to me of marriage and I admit I felt no repugnance for that bond, and that I was well enough disposed to give my hand to the one whom my brother had presented to me as a pure democrat and as his friend.'[9]

Was that offer ever made? There is no other evidence to support it. In her *Mémoires* Charlotte post-dated it by several years, to a period when Fouché was already married, as she was well aware. So this was either an invention on her part or, more likely, a misunderstood flirtation exaggerated in retrospect. At the time that, ostracized and embittered, she recorded the supposed proposal, Fouché had for other reasons become one of the men she hated most in the world. 'I did not know that he was nothing but a hypocrite, a swindler, a man without principles, without morals, capable of any action to satisfy his unbridled ambitions.'[10] She was, at least, expressing the general view. And there were no longer any living witnesses to contradict her.

'He so cleverly concealed his vile sentiments and evil passions from my eyes, as from the eyes of my brother, that I was his dupe, as was Maximilien. I replied to his proposal that I wished to consult my brother and also to consult my own feelings, and I asked him to give me time to come to a decision. I did indeed speak to Robespierre, who showed no opposition to my union with Fouché.'[11]

She seems almost to suggest that Fouché seduced her. If so she said nothing to her brother – not even that she was being jilted. For the friendship continued and Fouché was one of those to whom Maximilien turned for money to meet the expense of his trip to Versailles in April 1789 as a Representative of the Third Estate of the Province of Artois. France's financial situation was so grave that the King had been compelled to summon the Estates General to their first meeting in 175 years.

The absence of his mentor did nothing to diminish Fouché's enthusiasm for politics and reform. He was a founder member of the Arras Society of Friends of the Constitution. It was he whom the society chose to write an open letter supporting Robespierre against criticisms from his constituents. He founded and published a *Bulletin of the Patriots of the Oratory*. And in August 1790, on his way home to Nantes for the holidays, he spent a fortnight in Paris as the leader of a deputation of Oratorians who paid their respectful homage to the National Assembly.

He did not return to Arras. It has been suggested that the governing body in Paris removed him because they disapproved of the active part he was playing in politics. The fact is that he was rewarded with the best appointment that he could hope for. He was posted to his old school, in his home town, as Prefect of Studies – responsible for the entire curriculum, under the spiritual direction of the Father Superior.

3

Nantes, because it was Breton and because it was prosperous, had led the agitation for reform. Its burgesses wanted more local autonomy and a share of the power and privilege of the nobility. In November 1788, demonstrators gathered in the streets to demand a new constitution for the Breton Estates. The following January two law students at Rennes were shot dead during riots – and more than a thousand set off from Nantes to avenge them. 'At Rennes they thought; at

Nantes they acted; and the rest of the West Country followed their lead.'[1]

The political ambition of the students and the bourgeoisie produced the first bloodshed, but beneath the surface there were more ominous rumblings from the poor. The winter of 1788–9 was harsh. The prices of wood and flour increased. Some of the workers rioted. The disturbance was put down without trouble, but the municipal officers thought it advisable to set a lower price for bread, even though it meant increasing the subsidy to bakers out of the public funds.

A mild spring and the beginning of a warm summer brought more work and less grumbling, until – on July 18, 1789 – news arrived of the assault on the Paris Bastille four days before. The citizens' militia paraded to the beat of drum and marched on the château, where they successfully demanded the keys from the governor on pain of death. Two days later the town quivered to the rumour that a punitive expedition was being sent against them from the barracks at Montaigu, twenty miles away. The drums beat again; fifty militiamen with axes stood by to demolish the Pirmil bridge; women and children carried buckets of water, stones and broken glass to the upper floors of houses as ammunition against the invaders. But the dragoons never came.

The mayor, in an attempt to harness this energy, formed an Administrative Committee under the Chairmanship of a brisk St Dominican named Coustard de Massy. Coustard appointed himself colonel of a reconstituted and enlarged militia whose companies were named after such modish virtues as Liberty, Equality, Fraternity, Patriotism and Constancy. A few months later, veteran companies were recruited under the banners of Perseverance, Harmony, Wisdom and Prudence. The tide of modernity swept through the town's nine cultural societies: by the end of 1789 four of them had abolished their titles of *Cercle* or *Chambre de Lecture* in favour of the revolutionary *Club* – Club des Capucines, Club de Saint-Vincent, and so on, depending on their meeting places.

The municipal council sent a loyal address to the King, expressing gratitude for his liberal views, and followed this with an appeal to the National Assembly to reject any proposal for the abolition of the slave trade, which would result in 'the loss of our colonies, the annihilation of our maritime commerce, the destruction of our manufacturers'.[2] Nantes had other interests: a considerable trade in grain, a mill capable of grinding eighteen tons of flour a day, an ironworks,

cloth, cotton and hat factories, brushworks and tanneries, two glass-
works, one of them producing half a million bottles a year, and three
breweries to begin where the vintners left off. But the solid found-
ation of the town's prosperity was the commerce with the West Indies
– there were forty vessels employed in the slave trade alone.

The St Dominican slaves were not to strike their first blow for
freedom until the following year; but the Breton peasants claimed
the benefits of the new social order at once. A mob estimated at
between 1,000 and 1,500 marched on the château at Le Fougeray and
burned the records of their land tenures. Similar outbreaks were reported from Blain and Jazé, Gent and Abbaretz. Lacking the means to
take stronger measures, the magistrates addressed a circular letter to
the peasants through the heads of communes: 'If foreign enemies
came and did the same to you, you would not fail to complain . . .
When the National Assembly said that all men are equal in rights, it
meant simply that they should all be equally protected by the law . . .'[3]

In the first week of March the mayor of Nantes found it necessary
to buy a red flag for use when reading the riot act; building labourers
demanded discussions on their pay and hours of work (from five in
the morning until seven at night); three members of the council
were called to the college, where students complained that the Oratory Fathers 'were giving them impositions to write, contrary to the
statutory articles of 1790, etc'.[4] At the May fair in the Place Viarine
the peasants refused to pay tolls on the cattle they brought to market,
claiming that all such taxes should by now have been abolished. The
militia was called out to deal with the ensuing riot, and one unfortunate member was shot dead, by a ball from his own musket.

Yet the general enthusiasm for the new age of reform was undiminished. The masters and pupils of the Oratory School marched in
procession to the town hall to take the civic oath of loyalty to the
Nation, the Law and the King. Father Latyl, the college Superior
who had been elected a deputy for Nantes, presented the National
Assembly with a patriotic offering of 411 livres saved by the students
from their pocket money. Nantes, in fact, was in as great confusion
as any other city of France in this second year of the revolution.
There was enough money in the civic chest to tempt David, *Premier
Peintre du Roi*, down to paint a portrait of the mayor, M. Kervégan
(his fee was 300 livres). But in order to protect the ailing municipal
theatre, Kervégan had to ban a visit from Franconi and Astley's
Equestrian Display in September. And a shortage of wheat (caused
less by lack of money than by bad communications, now that the

road-repairing *corvée* had been abolished) brought the women demonstrating outside the *mairie*, while the men forcibly prevented grain carts from the warehouses leaving the town. Yet the 400 members of the Society of Friends of the Constitution happily offered a great festival of fraternity to the English residents of Nantes in honour of the shared ideals of the two countries.

4

Fouché arrived from Arras and Paris just in time for this splendid occasion. The guests were welcomed by Coustard de Massy, now President of the Administrative Assembly of the Department of the Lower Loire in addition to his many other offices. An immense table was set in the garden of the old Capucin convent in which the Society met. Trees, linked by chains of garlands and crowns, and decorated with banners and shields inscribed with the names of heroes and philosophers, cast a protective shade over the statues of Louis XVI, Liberty, Charlemagne and, somewhat surprisingly, Diana the Huntress bearing the legend 'Abolition of Feudalism'.[1] In the centre of the garden, on the Altar of Concord, lay the globe of the world, surmounted by the Cap of Liberty and flanked by two incense burners.

After depriving the church of its property, the National Assembly's latest enactment of the civil constitution, making the appointment of priests subject to election by their parishioners, met with great opposition in Brittany. In Nantes, as in most of France, the members of the teaching orders accepted the new law, but the parish priests abstained, refusing to take the oath 'to maintain the constitution of the state decreed by the National Assembly and accepted by the King.'[2] The two sides exchanged accusations of *atheist* and *traitor* and grew to believe so fiercely in what they said that the taunts became truth.

In February 1791, Fouché was elected president of the Society of the Friends of the Constitution and became an active agent in the great Jacobin network which an Englishman writing home from Paris described as 'a correspondence from the Pyrenees to the Rhine . . . 287 different clubs of the same kind and for the same purpose . . . The interchange of thought is so immediate and universal that the whole country resembles the whispering gallery of St Paul's Cathedral – all is known in almost the same breath and the same instant that it is uttered.'[3]

The abbé Minée, priest of the parish of St-Thomas d'Aquin in

Paris and a member of the Paris Jacobin club, chosen by the electors
of Nantes to replace their non-juring bishop, was installed on Palm
Sunday. In the villages the people still went to the non-conforming
priests for confession, and pelted with stones the squads of national
guardsmen sent to induct the new conforming *curés constitutionnels*.
In the town, a group of women broke into the aristocratic convent of
Couëts, where the new bishop had been refused admission, and whipped the nuns – 'to save them a job, since this was only what they
inflicted on themselves every day to merit paradise through mortifi-
cation'.[4] They then drove them round the streets in carts, together
with the nursing sisters of St-Charles, who had received the same treatment. The idea was not original. Nantes copied it from Paris where
the Fustigation of Religious Women had, in the spring of 1791,
become a common sport of zealots and perverts.

From Paris, too, came mounting distrust of those politicians who
tried to reconcile the Crown and the Revolution. The memorial service to Mirabeau in April was poorly attended because people 'suspected him of having made an alliance with the court'.[5] Much of this
suspicion, however, came from the working classes and was prompted less by his political activities than by his deplorable morals; the
members of the clubs, better-breeched and broader-minded, held a
ceremony of their own, at which the oration was delivered by
Confrère Fouché.

Nantes was uneasy with class divisions and religious prejudices,
disappointment that the revolution had not brought more benefits,
fear that it might bring unexpected hardships. Women who supported the evicted clergy seized one of the persecutors of the nuns of
Couëts, whipped her in her turn and were only at the last moment
prevented from throwing her into the Loire. Ordinary citizens
insulted national guardsmen; regular troops of the former Poitou
regiment had to be called in to restore order. Whispers grew stronger
that counter-revolutionaries were preparing an armed rising with
the aid of money from the perfidious English. The national guard
confiscated the sails of two British vessels to prevent their leaving
the port.

On June 22 a courier brought news from Paris that the King had
fled with his family. The Nantais deputies in the Assembly sent home
warnings that this might be the signal for foreign invasion or civil
war. Patrols were ordered out into the streets. Officials were summoned
to renew their oaths of loyalty. General Dumouriez, commanding
the 12th military division, handed in his Cross of St-Louis. The

council, unaware that the royal party had been stopped at Varennes, proclaimed: 'The King has gone, but the true sovereign, the Nation, remains; and the French people . . . are more than ever masters of their fate.'[6]

The document was sealed with the cap of liberty instead of the royal arms. The Louis XVI company of the national guard renamed itself the Federation Company (a title that was shortly to be in even deeper disgrace). The guardsmen tore the fleur-de-lys favours from their hats and trampled them underfoot in front of the Altar of the Fatherland in the cours St-Pierre. Mobs toured the town wrenching down and smashing all signs that bore a King's head. Suspects were arrested and thrown into the suffocating Bouffay prison. All members of the national guard were issued with ammunition; the mounted sections rode out to deal with an insurrection at Le Loroux.

Trouble of one kind bred trouble of another. Within a few days there was rioting because of a lack of ready money. Employers had to pay their workers in tokens; the tokens were too high in value for ordinary household purchases, and cautious shopkeepers refused to give genuine money in change. The council issued its own 5-sou tokens. On September 5 a group of workers forced their way into the Hôtel de Ville to protest at being paid in cardboard instead of metal, and rioting broke out again. In the rue du Moulin a detachment of *gardes nationaux* were stoned; in reply they fixed their bayonets and killed one man. The mayor brought out his red flag and read the riot act once more.

The shortage of cash was succeeded by the fear of a shortage of food. Soon afterwards news arrived of the great slave rebellion that had broken out in St-Domingue in the West Indies. 'It meant the extinction of the largest fortunes in the town, afflicted by every calamity at the same time.'[7]

5

Fouché had been busy both inside the college and out. As head of studies he drew up a new curriculum; as a budding politician he served on a deputation that went to Paris late in October 1791 to complain about irregularities in the recent elections to the National Assembly. Socially he was seeing a great deal of Noël Coiquaud, a member of a well-known local family of attorneys, who had for the past year presided over the Nantes District Directory. His first visits to the Coiquaud home were possibly prompted by a decision to quit schoolteaching and try his hand at the law. But as his calls became more frequent, the family perceived that his main interest lay not in law or local government but in the eldest daughter of the house, Bonne-Jeanne, a rather shy and remarkably plain girl who had fallen as deeply in love with him as he had with her. She was to return his affection with a lifetime of devotion.

There was no reason for Noël Coiquaud or his wife Marguerite to disapprove of the match. As a confrère at the Oratory Fouché was perfectly at liberty to marry. As Prefect of the College he had social standing. As the inheritor of his father's interest in several West Indian plantations he had a comfortable private income – even though this seemed temporarily threatened by the mutiny of slaves in St-Domingue. And, in any case, Bonne-Jeanne was already twenty-seven.

In Nantes now the talk was all of war. In August 1791, the month in which the black uprising burst on St-Domingue, the Emperor of Austria and King of Prussia agreed to intervene by force in French internal affairs if other European powers would support them. The Nantais subscribed to buy arms and ammunition for the citizens who volunteered for service in the colony, and simultaneously raised money to equip volunteers to keep guard on the Rhine. They were offering their lives for the preservation of Liberty and Equality in the east, for its suppression in the west. In Paris, loudly protesting its hatred of aggression, the Legislative Assembly enthusiastically talked itself towards war, to unite the divided country and to get its blow in first.

On April 20, 1792, with most of her former army officers emigrated, half of her new army of volunteers untrained and unarmed, one third of her nominal regular army non-existent, France declared war on Austria. The straggling, unaccustomed troops were marched into Belgium. At first sight of the enemy they ran back again. Their cries of betrayal were echoed at home. The Paris mob, screaming that the King was encouraging delay and confusion until help could come to him from abroad, burst into the Tuileries and forced him to put the red bonnet on his head.

In Nantes, on July 18, three years to the day since the news of the fall of the Bastille had arrived, the municipal council published the Legislative Assembly's declaration that the country was in danger, and that in consequence no official would leave his post. The general council of the commune would remain in permanent session. All past and present members of the national guard would stand ready for service at all times. Every person resident in France or travelling through it would wear the tricolour cockade; any who wore a different emblem would be denounced, brought to trial, and, if convicted of bearing such a sign of rebellion deliberately, condemned to death. Before the month was out, the Duke of Brunswick, commanding the enemy troops, issued a threatening manifesto that served to weld all Frenchmen momentarily together, the fainthearts for protection, the patriots from pride.

There were more shocks to come. On August 13 the council received a letter from Coustard – now a deputy at the National Assembly – that began 'Oh God! what a dawn breaks over our unhappy land!' and continued with a description of the second attack on the Tuileries and the massacre of the King's Swiss Guard. 'Two hundred thousand men are under arms and demanding the dethronement of the King . . . blood flows even at the doors of our council chamber. Severed heads are paraded in the street . . . The King and his family have thrown themselves on our protection . . .The forces of order no longer exist . . . The cannonade and musketry fire continue. I conclude. So much horror freezes my heart. Farewell!'[1]

Moved but perplexed by this stirring dispatch, and quite uncertain from which quarters danger now threatened, the city fathers declared themselves in session *night and day*. They instructed citizen Caton, the postmaster, not to provide horses without permission from the municipality; ordered the inspection of all foreigners' passports; and issued a new proclamation: 'Citizens! The country was recently declared in danger. This cry of alarm was the forewarning of counter-revolutionary catastrophes. These have now broken out in the heart of the capital. We are not yet able to discover all the details, but whatever they may be they impose on every citizen the stern duty of unremitting watchfulness.'[2]

On August 18, more details having come to hand, the council met to take the new oath decreed by the Assembly: 'To uphold Liberty and Equality, or die in their defence.' Before dispersing, the councillors, 'feeling the need to be well and promptly informed of events in the capital',[3] agreed to take out subscriptions to the *Moniteur,* the *Feuille du Soir,* the *Thermomètre* and the *Courrier Français.* During the next fortnight they dug up a 75-foot poplar from the garden of the Recollect monastery and planted it as a Tree of Liberty in the Place Egalité (formerly Place Louis XVI); they issued a warning that no soldiers or militiamen were allowed to search houses without

warrants; and they planted a second Tree of Liberty to com-
memorate the primary elections for the next national assembly – the
National Convention that was to decide on France's future form of
government now that the King's authority was suspended.

On August 30, Fouché presided at the college's annual prize-
giving. It was no longer the College of the Oratory, for the Oratory
had ceased to exist in May; and he was no longer Prefect of Studies
but Principal. The violence of the times had reduced the number of
the pupils, and the sequestration of church property had deprived
the school of land and buildings worth half a million livres. Fouché
had been forced to appeal to the town council for financial aid in
March and again in July. At the beginning of August he enlisted the
mayor's support for a project to have the school taken over by the
municipality with a change of staff and another reshaping of the
curriculum in accordance with revolutionary principles – it was, he
pointed out, the only place of secondary education still open in the
whole department. The district council eventually took the responsibility.

It was a day of achievement for the Principal, seated on the platform with the mayor and members of the two councils beside him.
He had reformed his old school and tucked it under the wing of
enlightened authority. Flanked by the senior prizewinners, behind
the military band and at the head of a great procession of citizens, he
marched to the town hall, where the mayor read out the names of the
honoured pupils and ordered them to be inscribed on the register of
the commune.

It was a day of triumph and of parting. Fouché had offered himself
as candidate for the new assembly. A week later, the members of the
electoral body of the Lower Loire chose him as one of the eight
deputies to represent the department. On September 16, 1792, a few
days before he left for Paris, he was married by a constitutional curé of
the church of St-Nicolas to his ugly, adoring Bonne-Jeanne Coiquaud.

6

It was already an act of courage as much as ambition to solicit a seat
in the central government of France. On the same September day
that the electoral college convened at Ancenis, the Paris mob was
running wild once more, dragging suspects from the prisons and
murdering them in the streets. Behind the mob stood the Commune,

FRANCE
PROVINCES IN 1789

illegally set up by the militants of the Paris sections to replace the elected Municipal Council on the night before the massacre of the Swiss Guards. The men of the Commune planned by mob rule to dominate the Convention and, through the Convention, all of France. The initial step towards Government by Terror had been taken.

The newly-married Fouchés began domestic life at No. 315 rue St-Honoré, not far from the seminary where Joseph had completed his training ten years before. The lodgings were handy for the assembly chamber in the Manège, the old royal riding stables, and also for the house of the Duplay family where Robespierre rented two rooms. Several of Fouché's former pupils and colleagues were already experienced deputies, re-elected from previous assemblies – among them Father Billaud of Juilly who, like Robespierre, was a member of the Commune as well as of the Convention. At the opening session the Chamber voted unanimously for the abolition of the monarchy. Next day, September 22, was the first of the French Republic: Ivendémiaire of the year One.

Fouché had come rather late upon the political scene. It did not seem likely that he would make a very durable mark. His appearance was unusual but not impressive – lean, bony, the skin still stretched too tightly over nose and cheeks and chin, his red-rimmed eyes half hidden under drooping lids. His voice, like his general physique, was frail: a handicap in any politician, and never more so than at that time and place. He had little chance of gaining a hearing against the rival shouts of the Montagnards, the wild men of the Mountain high up on the left of the Chamber or of the Girondins, who only so short a time ago were leaders of the progressive faction and had now been carried by events to the centre and reactionary right. So he avoided the tribune, and found work on the committees, where a sharp mind, cool head and steely determination counted for more than high-flying rhetoric and brass lungs. On October 10 he was appointed to the Finance Committee and three days later as a *suppléant* to the Committee of Public Instruction, which he joined as a full member in November. The following year he was elected to the Committee of the Marine and Colonies, in company with Marat, Barras and the ill-fated Casabianca.[1]

There were some occasions when he could not avoid attendance in the Chamber. One, whose consequences were to affect his whole life, was the trial of the King. The unsuccessful attempt at flight and his identification with the enemy had made Louis' conviction for treason a certainty. What remained for the Convention to decide was his punishment: death; death subject to a national referendum; imprisonment; or banishment.

Fouché went to the tribune on January 16, 1793. 'It would be generous,' he said, 'to show indulgence; and doubtless indulgence is the sign of a magnanimous heart . . . But we are judges and must be as impassive as gods. The slightest act of weakness may set off a horrible train of misfortune.'[2]

He argued that a referendum would entail either presenting the people with all the evidence given at the trial – which would mean an interminable delay – or telling them the verdict and thus influencing their decision. In any event to appeal to the people would be 'a manifest violation of the principles of our representative government . . . Let us use the great authority that the nation has vested in us; let us do our duty to the full; and we shall be strong enough to overcome all powers and all events.'[3]

The reforms to which the Revolution was dedicated were endangered by reactionary forces within the country; France itself was threatened with invasion by foreign troops in support of émigré royalists. The future was crystallized in the fate of the King. If he lived he would always be the symbol and rallying point for those who intended the restoration of the old way of life and the destruction of the new.

The hitherto moderate Fouché voted for death without appeal. On January 21 Louis went to the guillotine.

'I meant to strike less at the monarch than at the crown,' Fouché said in later life. 'And it seemed to me then, as it did to many others, that we could not inspire sufficient energy in the mass of the people and its representatives to surmount the crisis except by exceeding all measures, passing all bounds . . . In politics, may not even atrocities sometimes have a salutary effect?'[4]

The argument referred to one man. It could be applied to many. Fouché had taken the first step towards acceptance of the doctrine of Terror. From all the perils that beset her, France was to be saved by fear.

7

The threat of civil war grew stronger. The continued repression of the priests who refused to take the oath; the execution of the King; the decision on February 24, 1793, to raise another 300,000 men for the army – each bred new malcontents by the thousand. The call for Terror seemed to be matched by the need for Terror. On March 10 the Convention established an Extraordinary Revolutionary Tribunal in Paris to deal with all counter-revolutionary acts. On the previous day it had divided the country into forty-one districts, each comprising two departments, excluding Paris and some frontier areas. To each of these districts two members of the Convention were to be sent as special commissioners 'to instruct their fellow-citizens on the new dangers that threaten the country and to assemble sufficient forces to disperse the enemy'.[1]

They were to supervise recruiting, resorting to conscription if not enough volunteers came forward to fill the departmental quota. They were to requisition arms and uniforms, horses and mules not employed in agriculture or essential services. They had full powers 'to take whatever measures they deem necessary to re-establish order wherever it is disturbed; to suspend provisionally or even to place under arrest any officials whom they suspect; to requisition the armed forces if need arises'.[2]

Fouché was chosen as one of the commissioners for the Lower Loire and Mayenne. The appointment was a tribute to the skill he had shown in committee, and also to his tougher qualities, for this was one of the most disturbed regions of Brittany and the Vendée, where royalist-religious reaction was strongest and fiercest. Aristocrats and peasants had joined forces. Throughout the winter they had plotted and prepared their counter-stroke. Now, as the commissioners set out from Paris to drag them or their sons from the land, the peasants marched upon the towns, led by the lords whose yoke they had recently been so eager to throw off.

In Nantes there was fear and consternation. For the influential citizens the aims of the revolution were already achieved; they had got the power they wanted and, like their counterparts in the other great provincial towns, viewed with anxiety and indignation the increasing influence in national affairs of the Paris mob. They would dearly like to call a halt, but nobody would listen to them – neither in Paris nor, more frighteningly, in the surrounding countryside that now seemed to tremble unceasingly under the advancing feet of the peasants. On March 11, one day after the conscripts were due to attend the recruiting centres, the clerk to the departmental council reported that 'there is not at this moment a single spot in the territory of this department which is not a hotbed of insurrection'.[3] In Machecoul, a small town of less than 2,000 inhabitants, the peasants had that morning broken into the houses, seized the prosperous burgesses and cut their throats with hedgehooks or dragged them to the market place to be beaten to death with flails.

On March 12 the members of the Nantes Society of Friends of Liberty and Equality demanded that a guillotine should be set up in the Place du Bouffay, the criminal tribunal go into permanent session, and all suspects be brought to trial and executed without delay. On March 13 the councils of the district and the commune held a joint meeting after which they issued the scarcely encouraging statement that 'the town of Nantes remains intact amid the ruins and smoking debris that cover the region'.[4] They also ordered that all refugees coming in from the countryside were to be given weapons and attached to the national guard. By March 17 there were 'no towns in the Lower Loire, apart from Nantes, Paimboeuf and Ancenis that were not controlled by the royalists'.[5]

Fouché had reached Mayenne, where he gave instructions for the strengthening of the national guard and continued towards Nantes. Finding the direct road cut by royalists he turned westward to Rennes and from there wrote to the Convention urging 'the dispatch of military advisers and muskets'. He wanted authority to set up military tribunals to deal with men taken with weapons in their hands. 'Yesterday, when I passed through Vitry, the people were in a great ferment in this regard. A crowd collected round my carriage and begged me to go to the prisons and act as judge.'[6]

He was not the only commissioner stranded at Rennes. Billaud and Sevestre, who shared responsibility for the Côtes-du-Nord and Ille-et-Vilaine, and Guermeur and Lemaillaud (Finistère and Morbihan), had also been prevented from reaching their posts. They wrote to the Convention on March 23 that five departments were overrun with rebels – 'ill-trained' but 'whom we must quickly confront with good troops to force them to return to their duty before their coalition becomes more formidable'.[7] Two days later Fouché broke through the insurgent cordons and reached Nantes.

Vigorously, incisively, he pulled the town out of its panic. He formed a new battalion of 800 men to keep open the road to Paris. He requisitioned the ships in the harbour of Mindin at the mouth of the Loire. He closed the theatres. He ordered the national guard to carry out military exercises every day (they were now mustered for regular duty, with pay of 20 sous a day for garrison duties and 25 or 35 sous for infantry or cavalry serving outside the town).

He promised protection for children and the aged and called on the able-bodied to 'take action, march to victory – or wait by your fireside for all the anguish and torture of ignominy and death!'[8] To the Convention he reported that 'it is imperative that you send troops . . . You can count on the vigour of the national guardsmen of Nantes; they are full of valour; but they lack leaders experienced in war.' He added proudly, 'this morning we have for the first time formed an army corps of 1,000 men, who are marching to the relief of Paimboeuf'.[9]

He had not forgotten the arm of Terror. When asked whether prisoners brought before courts martial were to be allowed defending counsel, he answered no. 'You would be more lenient than the law [of March 19]. The spirit of that law is to curtail formalities and hasten judgement. The people complain of the delays in justice; the interest of the public weal, humanity itself, demands that it should be prompt and severe.'[10] To representatives of the People's Society of St-Vincent-la-Montagne he preached the necessity to 'keep the strictest watch on the rich, the merchants, the monopolists, the self-seekers, the priests, the aristocrats, those suspects who call themselves moderates. Denounce them on the spot to the nation's justice! . . . A republican needs nothing more than steel, bread and forty crowns a year . . . You have war with the brigands at your doors! Close your ranks, and if you find those among you who are timid or cowardly, run them through with the republican weapon, the bayonet!'[11]

Well might he later excuse himself for having been 'forced to approximate to the language of the period' and protest that 'these commonplace expressions . . . which in calmer times arouse a sort of horror . . . were, so to speak, stock official phrases'.[12] It was true that he saw himself as fighting for the life of the nation as well as the preservation of the republic, but talk of this kind was adding fuel to the flames even though, in practice, his actions did not match the ferocity of his words.

The immediate crisis for Nantes was relieved early in April by the arrival of regular troops under General Beysser. On April 12 Fouché offered a reward of 6,000 livres for the delivery of rebel leaders, dead or alive, but an amnesty to any of their followers who surrendered within twenty-four hours. There was little response.

The general picture was sombre. Industry and commerce was stagnant, hindered not only by the still-erratic communications but also by the daily duties of more than a thousand men in the national guard. To the East and North the armies of the Republic were faring

badly, pushed back by the Prussians on the Rhine, betrayed by Dumouriez in Belgium; to the South the Spaniards were preparing to
invade Roussillon. And closer at hand the struggle against the rebels
showed no sign of ending. 'I have set up my military court,' Beysser
reported. 'Yesterday we cut off the heads of two brigands; the operation was carried out with a sapper's axe on a block of wood; the
speedy dispatch has made the liveliest impression; unfortunately we
shall have many more of the same kind.'[13]

Beysser estimated the royalist forces at 60,000 men, equipped with
artillery and receiving supplies from England, which had been at
war with France since February. They attacked without formation,
often from ambush, 'to the sound of horns and bagpipes . . . uttering
horrible cries in the manner of savages'.[14] Fouché promised compensation to the peasants who had suffered from pillage and burning; he
threatened to confiscate the property of any who did not quit the
rebel bands and return to their homes. But he lacked the power to
carry out either the promise or the threat.

As his two months' mission drew to an end royalist groups con-
verged on the city again. He ordered barricades to be set up in the
streets and armed ships to be stationed in the river. On May 7 he
issued his last proclamation to the citizens of Nantes, urging them to
stop quarrelling among themselves and criticizing the government
in Paris, squandering 'the valuable time that we should devote entirely to the Republic. Let us sacrifice our opinions, our passions; let us
be true to our principles, rally one and all to the Ark of Liberty.'[15] He
was replaced by Coustaud de Massy, whose moderate views recommended him to the city fathers but had no effect on the insurgents
outside the gates.

8

Though Fouché had been away so short a time, he found the temper
of Paris radically changed. After the French army's reverses in Belgium, Robespierre accused the Girondins of betraying the nation by
declaring war and then encouraging Dumouriez's defection in April.
He attacked them in the Convention and at the Jacobin Club. He
summoned the people of Paris to join him in insurrection against
corrupt deputies. After prolonged rioting at the end of May, he had
most of the leading Girondins placed under arrest in their own
homes.

There was nothing in this to dismay Fouché; he was at least as militant as Robespierre, and more extreme in some of his views. But the close friendship of Arras was not renewed. It may be that this was initially Robespierre's choice, a disinclination to admit the still scarcely-known ex-schoolmaster to the court that he now held in the home of the cabinet-maker Duplay.

> 'The salon . . . was furnished with terracotta busts and the walls covered with portraits of the great man, in crayon, stump, bistre, water-colour. He himself, meticulously combed and powdered, clad in the cleanest of dressing-gowns, reclined in a large armchair beside a table laden with the finest fruits, fresh butter, pure milk and fragrant coffee . . . The salon door was glazed; his adorers, advancing slowly and respectfully from the courtyard, did not enter the salon until a sign from the divine man's head or hand, seen through the glass, granted them permission.'[1]

There had been intimations of this apotheosis in Arras. It did not recommend itself to a man of such strong egalitarian views as Fouché. And it may be that his welcome was chilly from more than one quarter, for Charlotte had come up to Paris to join her brother, no doubt bringing with her the memory of her supposed jilting. Fouché later claimed that the first open break came when he entertained Robespierre to dinner and offended him by outspoken criticism. Whatever the cause of the awkwardness, it was resolved – though not forgotten – when Fouché was sent off on a mission again on June 24.

With three other deputies, Méaulle, Philippeaux and Esnuë de la Vallée, he was sent to tour the departments of the Centre and West and 'invite and require the citizens . . . to take arms against the rebels of the Vendée'.[2] The commissioners' powers were wider and stronger than before. They could act independently and co-opt assistant commissioners.

Fouché began his mission at Troyes on June 29. In an address to the local Jacobin club, he denounced foreign agitators who were fomenting civil war, appealed for volunteers to put down the troubles in the Vendée, promised protection for their families and suitable gratuities when they returned, and told them he would be on the main promenade at dawn to swear them in.

Next morning, as promised, he was on the Mall at daybreak, accompanied by the city officials and flanked by the national guard. He set a match to a cannon 'to express the people's joy'[3] and also perhaps to get a hearing for his weak voice. Then he delivered an impassioned speech on the miseries of the civil war in the West, and the dangers that faced the department of the Aube 'if the avengers of Liberty do not take arms to defend it'.[4] His enthusiasm compensated for his lack of oratorical skill. Three hundred volunteers enlisted on the spot. 'Fathers and wives urged their sons and husbands to go.'[5] That evening he led a *marche civique* through every street in the city, whipping up patriotic zeal.

He wrote to the Convention that 'the revolution of the 31st of May [the rioting which culminated in the arrest of the Girondins] has reanimated every heart and renewed every hope . . . It has suddenly transformed into a unanimous concert of praise and homage for the Mountain all the justified complaints that were levelled everywhere against the National Convention . . . In a few days we hope to have raised a battalion, if we do not lack arms.'[6]

His energy and intellectual authority revitalized recruiting. Before his arrival only two companies had been formed, including conscripts, since the emergency legislation three and a half months before. On July 7 he had sent off two more companies; by July 10 eighty gunners were on the way to Paris to collect their artillery and he wrote to the Convention, 'If I had the weapons I should easily find in the town of Troyes 3,000 brave defenders . . . ready to exterminate the brigands of the Vendée and the rebels of Calvados.'[7] On July 15 he reported to the Committee of Public Safety that the first battalion was complete and 'I have been obliged to send back to their work more than 1,500 young men for lack of equipment.'[8]

He left for Dijon and Nevers. His mind was now more occupied by the dangers that threatened from the South. In Normandy, Brittany and the Vendée opposition to the government had come from the peasants and noblemen and arose from religious grievances, royalism and the refusal to be conscripted in a cause that they hated – for they identified the war with the preservation of the government, not the defence of France. In the great towns of the South the grievances were political and economic. The middle classes did not intend sharing their gains from the revolution with the workers. They resented being ruled from Paris – and by the Paris mob. They had dreamed of more autonomy and found themselves with less. They listened to the royalists who promised to bring back better days, and to the remaining Girondins who offered a sort of federalism in place of the iron grip of the Convention and the Committee of Public Safety. Lyons rose in revolt on May 29: Marseilles, Toulon, Bordeaux went the same way.

Fouché arrived in Dijon on July 20. He reported two days later that the national guard were enthusiastic and had screamed with rage when he told them what atrocities the royalists were committing on the Jacobins in Lyons. But the only firm promise he was able to make to the Committee of Public Safety was that 'you can count on 6,000 complete suits, 7,000 yards of cloth suitable for tents or shirts, and a good quantity of cavalry equipment in store at Dijon.'[9] After a frenetic week of drumming up enthusiasm, he was able to promise that 1,500 infantrymen from the Côte d'Or would be under arms within a fortnight, supported by 450 cavalrymen and 342 gunners.

He moved on to Nevers on July 28, and took lodgings at the former Hôtel de France – renamed Hôtel de la Nation (to avoid any suspicion of royalist taint). Custine's troops had surrendered Mainz and lost their foothold on the right bank of the Rhine; that day the Allies captured Valenciennes and were about to invade French soil. Fouché told the Committee of Public Safety that he would send 800 men from Nevers for service in the Vendée, but he proposed to hold the contingents from the Côte d'Or and the Allier ready to repulse any attack from the South. 'The rebels of Lyons, and those of Marseilles may pick whichever of the two roads to Paris they prefer: they will be as firmly repulsed on the one as on the other . . .'[10]

He continued: 'If, as I hope, Lyons submits to the national will . . . the army being formed under the walls of Macon will not be needed; it will be necessary to organize them to march against the brigands of the Vendée. In that case it may be useful for me to be with these men whom I have myself enrolled.'[11] He suggested he should remain at Nevers to see how events turned out, rather than follow the Nivernais troops to Tours or return to Paris.

The suggestion was perhaps prompted by more than a sense of duty. Bonne-Jeanne, who had accompanied him on the fatiguing, roundabout journey, was expecting their first child. The baby was born on August 10 and next day Fouché presented her to the departmental council in the town hall. As a tribute to her birthplace he carried her to the National Altar and named her Nièvre, a ceremony that was terminated with fraternal embraces and a salvo of artillery.

The danger of rebel armies marching from the South diminished, but it was still urgent to recapture Lyons before it made itself impregnable to siege. It commanded the lower course of the Rhône; it could draw small arms from the arsenal at St-Etienne – the largest in France now that Mauberge had fallen into the hands of the enemy

– and it had foundries in which it could cast its own cannon. On August 8, government troops under Dubois-Crancé began the bombardment of the town, while another army under General Carteaux went to face the rebel troops from Marseilles. They drove them back through the Drôme and Vaucluse and eventually vanquished them in a pitched battle on August 25. But this was far from the end of rebellion on the Mediterranean shore. Before the end of the month the people of Toulon opened their port and town to France's enemies; on September 4 the admirals of the British and Spanish fleets, Hood and Langara, called on all republican troops in the South to 'abandon . . . the banners of anarchy and . . . uphold the cause and rights of Louis XVII'.[12]

9

At Nevers Fouché was faced with the food shortage and consequent hoarding and profiteering that was rife in all the cities of France. In Paris, the Procurator of the Commune, Chaumette, successfully demanded that the Revolutionary Army, whose formation the Convention had decreed on June 2, should be mobilized at once and sent into the provinces with a tribunal to judge and punish all speculators, monopolists and other enemies of the nation. The army of 6,000 infantrymen and 1,200 gunners, all volunteers between twenty-five and forty, would elect their own non-commissioned officers and company commanders annually, the senior officers being appointed by the Committee of Public Safety, which included among its members the former Father Billaud and the engineer officer from Arras, Lazare Carnot.

On September 17, the Convention passed the Law of Suspects: 'Immediately upon the publication of the present decree, all suspect persons within the territory of the Republic and still at liberty shall be arrested.'[1] To be suspected was more than a crime: it was a potential sentence of death.

Fouché meanwhile threatened merchants who might be hiding provisions, and invited the affluent to share their wealth. He had enough success to be able to write to the Committee on September 11, 'if you want gold or silver I will send you some: give us weapons!'[2] And he now embarked on a programme that was more extreme than any measures the government had yet proposed.

On September 19 he issued a proclamation in Nevers:

'Whereas begging tends only to degrade the people, causing them to forget their dignity and rights; whereas society owes sustenance to unfortunate citizens, either by providing them with work or by providing the means of existence if they are unable to work; whereas finally the Constitution guarantees public assistance to all Frenchmen,

'The Representative of the People decrees that begging is abolished throughout the department.'[3]

He ordered the public authorities to place all beggars in hostels or have them supported by their own families, who could call on financial assistance from a Philanthropic Committee to be set up in each district 'with authority to levy on the rich a tax proportionate to the number of the poor'.[4]

At Moulins, a week later, declaring that 'riches in the hands of individuals are merely a fund which the nation has the right to dispose of when the need arises',[5] he ordered that all citizens possessing gold or silver in the form of coins, ingots, plate or jewellery, other than clocks, watches and modest trinkets, were to surrender them to the district committee in return for receipts. Those who had not complied within fifteen days would be declared suspects.

He organized a procession through the streets of Moulins in honour of the old people. It was led by a company of workmen bearing picks, hammers, saws and ladders 'to deal with the monuments of fanaticism and feudalism', followed by a troop of cavalry with a banner inscribed 'The French people honours age, virtue and misfortune'.[6] Next came two pieces of cannon, the veterans of the national guard, the drum-major with a naked sword and a copy of the laws, a military band and Fouché surrounded by aged and infirm men and women wearing symbolic crowns of thorns. After them came more patriotic emblems, young women in white carrying bunches of grapes and singing hymns to liberty, those who had adopted children or provided shelter for the indigent, the families of volunteers absent with the armies, munition workers, representatives of other guilds, more troops. The gangs of workmen at the head of the procession destroyed all crosses and religious effigies and emblems that they found in the street; in the main square a pile of feudal documents and some nuns' habits were set alight, a placard with the words 'Only the people is indestructible' rising from the ashes; and then the old people were conducted to the church of the Minimes for a banquet at which Fouché and the civil authorities waited on table.

FRANCE
DEPARTMENTS IN 1790

On his return to Nevers he wrote to the Vigilance Committee of Moulins: 'I am astonished, citizens, at your hesitation. You lack flour? Take it from the rich aristocrats who have it. You lack grain? Mobilize your revolutionary army and put into the pillory the farmers and landowners who resist requisitioning. You lack lodgings? Seize the mansions of those you have arrested – you will return them when peace comes.'[7]

He issued a new decree: 'All rich landowners and farmers possessing grain are held personally responsible for lack of supplies on the market. Any person . . . failing to deliver to market the quantity of grain demanded shall be exposed for four hours in a pillory in the main square on the following market day with this notice: "Starver of the People, Traitor to the Country." For a second offence he will be exposed on two successive market days . . . He will also be declared suspect and imprisoned until the peace.'[8]

To enforce these measures he formed a Revolutionary Guard of two hundred infantrymen, a squadron of cavalry and an artillery company. Their duties included supervising the work of ironmasters and factory owners and denouncing any who failed to maintain full production. They would declare suspect any landowner who sowed less than his usual acreage – and the unused land would be sown at the owner's expense by the poor, who would take the crop.

He preached the right to work, to universal education, to free public assistance, and he proposed that these things should be paid for by a progressive tax on wealth. But his concern was with the practical, not the theoretical. There is no indication that he considered his policies valid or desirable in themselves. He was preoccupied with the details of how best to prosecute the war, to avoid discontent among the workers, to crush treason by the royalists and the rich. They were measures to be enforced 'until the peace'. The argument over principles he left to others.

Chaumette came to Nevers on September 18 to visit his invalid mother. He returned to Paris full of praise for Fouché's energy and success. 'Hemmed in by federalists, royalists and fanatics, the Representative of the People had only three or four persecuted patriots to take council with; yet with this feeble support he has worked miracles: . . . age honoured, infirmity succoured, misfortune respected, fanaticism destroyed, federalism annihilated, production of iron activated, suspects arrested, crime punished in exemplary fashion, monopolists prosecuted and imprisoned.'[9]

Not that Fouché was satisfied. He wrote to the Committee of

Public Safety deploring that 'the region richest in iron, which ought to be the central forge of the Republic, cannot supply one town with weapons'.[10] He ordered that officials who failed in their duty to increase production should be 'treated as bad citizens, discharged from their posts and sent to prison'.[11]

From the rich he turned his attention to the religious. He had spent more than twenty years of his life, as schoolboy and teacher, in a religious institution. When Gaillard first met him in Arras in 1789, it was at the confessional, and next morning at mass, and every day throughout the first year of the revolution. Now 'the ardour of a great Christian faith was completely extinguished. For him, as for many others who were to follow him, the Church was a hotbed of treason.'[12]

He attacked the Church's influence in schools – 'it is more important to be right than to be devout . . . the French people does not want semi-education any more than it wants semi-liberty'[13] – in a written report on national education presented to the Convention in his absence on July 3. Now he launched a head-on attack against the priests, the Church, Christianity itself – a campaign in which he led the rest of revolutionary France.

On September 22 he organized a great parade through Nevers for the installation of a bust of the pagan Brutus in the hall used by the Jacobin Club. He made an anti-clerical speech in the cathedral, which he described as a monument to the enslavement of the people and the tyranny of the great. Three days later, he ordered that 'all ministers of religion . . . resident in this department shall within one month . . . get married, adopt a child, or house and feed an elderly person'; otherwise they would 'be deemed to have renounced the exercise of their functions, and will be deprived of them as well as of their pensions'.[14]

Chaumette, who returned to Paris on September 23, warmly recommended similar anti-Christian action by the Commune, but Paris lagged behind. In October Fouché was stripping the churches of their gold and jewels, using the proceeds of the spoil to pay his Republican Guard and provide food for the aged or disabled poor, and sending the surplus to the Convention to pay for the war. It was not until November that the Commune followed suit. On October 23 Hébert persuaded the Commune to order the destruction of all religious monuments except those within the precincts of churches. Fouché had issued a similar decree a fortnight earlier (and put it into practice at Moulins in September) together with an edict on the conduct of funerals: the coffin was to be draped with a pall bearing the allegorical figure of Sleep and buried in a cemetery whose only emblem should be a statue of Sleep, and whose gates should be inscribed, '*Death is an eternal Slumber*'.[15] The suggestion became popular and was adopted by Commissioners in several other departments.

At Moulins, in the course of one of many orations that he delivered from church pulpits, Fouché had denounced the priests and promised that he would 'substitute for the superstitions and hypocritical cults to which people adhere, that of the Republic and of natural ethics'.[16] He was not, in any strict sense, anti-religious or atheist; at a later period he counted constitutional bishops among his friends and, when the Archbishop of Paris came to call, the Fouché children were always paraded for his blessing. Despite his Oratorian background, he had no religious convictions or loyalties. Having come to believe that Christianity, as practised in France, was anti-republican and unpatriotic, he proposed to replace it with the new religion, both republican and patriotic, that had been germinating in men's hearts since 1789 – 'absolute confidence in the omnipotence of Human Reason, the profound belief in unlimited progress, the vision of a Golden Age set no longer in the past but in the future'.[17] To make the transition simpler, the ceremonial of the new religion was much the same as that of the old; only the symbols were changed.

On October 22, nineteen days before the Convention celebrated the Feast of Reason in Notre Dame de Paris, Fouché organized his own Civic Festival of Valour and Morals at Nevers. In the Plain of Plagny four poplars were planted at the foot of an artificial and highly symbolic Mountain. The sacred fire of Vesta burned beneath their shade and on their branches hung the bow and quiver and torch of Love, the cap of Liberty and the helmet of Mars (the latter with two turtle doves nesting in it). At the far end of the arena stood the column of Liberty and the altar to Valour; at the entrance, the Constitutional Arch was decorated by the Tablets of Law guarded by a Cockerel, and shaded by the Tree of Liberty. A Temple of Love was erected in a small copse to the right of the plain.

Summoned at five o'clock in the morning by five cannon shots from the renamed Place Brutus and the drumming of the general call to arms throughout the town, five hundred men of the National Guard and one hundred of the Revolutionary Guard gave a display of military drill in the arena from 6 a.m. until 11 a.m. They then marched with the People's Representative at their head to salute the Temple of Love, returned to recite the Rights of Man at the

Constitutional Arch, and chanted revolutionary couplets before the Altar of Valour.

At this point a salvo of seven cannon shots announced the arrival of the young couples whose marriages were to symbolize the moral aspect of the occasion. They were accompanied by the Graces, Sport and Mirth, personified by young children dressed in white, crowned with flowers, decorated with tricolour ribbons, trailing long garlands. Escorted by a squadron of cavalry and a military band, followed by nursing mothers and those charitable citizens who had adopted children or elderly people, they entered the arena through a double rank of infantrymen. As they passed 'each warrior piled his arms, so that the image of war vanished to make way for the sports and pleasures of love'.[18] The People's Representative, enthroned on the symbolic Mountain, administered the Civic Oath, to which each couple added a vow to love each other eternally like Philemon and Baucis. This ceremony over, the principals adjourned to one of the 150 tents that had been set up around the perimeter and shared a frugal and republican repast – so frugal indeed, that for several generations afterwards the spot was known as Sharp-set Plain (Plaine de la Fringale).

10

On October 9, Lyons surrendered to the republican forces. On October 10, on the motion of Robespierre's closest adherent Saint-Just, the Convention agreed not to implement the Constitution it had adopted on June 24, because it did not give the executive sufficient power to defend liberty. Instead it passed the law of 19 Vendémiaire under which 'the executive council, the ministers, generals and constituted bodies, are placed under the supervision of the Committee of Public Safety'.[1] Twelve men, meeting in secret, were thus given virtually unrestricted control over France. On October 12 the Convention instructed the Committee to nominate a commission to deal with the counter-revolutionaries of Lyons.

The town of Lyons shall be destroyed; all that part which was inhabited by the rich shall be destroyed; nothing shall remain but the poorhouse, the dwellings of patriots murdered or proscribed, buildings devoted to industry, and monuments consecrated to humanity and education. The name of Lyons shall be erased from the roster of the cities of the Republic; the group of houses that is preserved will henceforth bear the name of Ville-Affranchie. There shall be raised amid the ruins of Lyons a column that shall bear witness to posterity of the crimes and the punishment of the royalists of that town, with this inscription: *Lyons made war on Liberty: Lyons is no more. – The eighteenth day of the first month of the second year of the French Republic, one and indivisible.*[2]

The commissioners appointed to carry out this dreadful sentence were already with the army at Lyons: Couthon, Maignet, Châteauneuf-Randon and Delaporte. Their instructions from the Committee, drawn up by Robespierre, warned them 'Not to yield to the initial reactions of politically inept sentiment . . . the traitors must be unmasked and smitten pitilessly'.[3] They failed to satisfy. On October 30, the Committee ordered their replacement by three other deputies: Collot d'Herbois, an ex-actor, noisy, brutal and often drunk; Maribon-Montaut, who proved to be too ill to make the journey; and Fouché to whom the Committee wrote: 'Revive the flickering torch of public opinion! . . . Complete the Revolution, end the war against aristocracy, let the ruins that it wishes to raise again fall and crush it!'[4]

Fouché showed no eagerness to take up his new assignment. Although he was already more than half-way there, he took a week longer than Collot to arrive, tarrying in Nevers to twist a further knot into the tails of the merchants, the ironmasters and the clergy. He had delivered three cases full of gold and silver to the Convention on October 10. He now sent off seventeen cases of church plate and other items of gold and silver subscribed by the fanatical sansculottes or requisitioned from the rich or noble. 'You will be pleased to see two fine silver gilt crosses and a ducal coronet,' he said. On November 7 the Convention received a letter saying that he was leaving for Lyons, and sending them a further consignment of treasure.

Ten days before, the dapper Coustard de Massy had gone to the guillotine, accused of encouraging federalism at Nantes. He was accompanied by Philippe-Egalité, the former duc d'Orleans whom Coustard had been suspected of secretly supporting, and who had tried too late to take refuge on the Mountain. The following day Madame Roland was executed. Most of her fellow-Girondins had already gone. The Terror was looking inwards for its victims. Gesticulating figures moved frenziedly across the stage of the Convention. The deputy who wished his head to stay on his shoulders kept racing leftwards as fast as his tongue would carry him. In self-defence, the next victim clamoured the loudest for blood.

Fouché arrived in Lyons on November 10. Behind him in Nevers he left a new town clock on the cathedral tower, inscribed with the recently adopted Republican Calendar and the words: *Nature, Reason, Liberty and Equality are the divinities of this country*; and above the town gates the notice: *Here age and misfortune are respected and hospitality is offered*. At Lyons he found rubble, fear, vengeance and the threat of starvation.

The paralysed Couthon had been slow in obeying the Convention's order to reduce Lyons to ruins. It was not until October 26 that, choosing the mansions in the Place Bellecour as 'those which proclaim the most ostentation and which most offend against the austerity of public morals',[5] he had himself taken there in his invalid chair to deliver the first hammer blow against the offending façade. Six hundred workmen with heavier tools began battering and tearing down the fronts of the houses even before the families inside could extricate themselves or their furniture. The number of workmen was increased to 960; 400 soldiers were brought from the garrison to help them. But when Collot d'Herbois arrived to replace Couthon on November 4, he was dismayed at the laggard pace. He reported to the Committee that he intended to use explosives, adding that 'the town is conquered but not converted'[6] and that 'even the executions are not having the effect that one would expect'.[7]

He knew Lyons well, having formerly acted there and directed the municipal theatre. He had since become a member of the Paris Commune, President for a period of the Convention, a member of the Committee of Public Safety since September. Fouché had been chosen by the Committee to rekindle the republican virtues and reorganize the shattered economy of Lyons; Collot's main task was clearly to keep the guillotine of the Revolutionary Tribunal and the firing squads of the Military Court fully employed.

November 10, which would have been a Sunday by the old calendar and was being celebrated in Paris as the Feast of Reason, was marked in Lyons by a ceremony in honour of Chalier, a former procurator who had been executed by the royalists and whom the republicans were in process of canonizing. So the first function over which Fouché presided, in company with Collot, took place at an improvised altar of turf set up in the Place des Terreaux in front of the Hôtel de Ville. A bust of the dead man crowned with flowers, an urn that was understood to contain his ashes, and a dove that was supposed to have shared his prison cell, were carried through the streets by a deputation of Jacobins from Paris, accompanied, in the words of an outraged priest, 'by a horde of clubbists and fallen women crying "Down with the aristocrats! Long live the Republic! Long live the guillotine!"'[8]

They were followed by a delirious mob waving sacramental vessels in the air and leading an ass which had a cope on its back, a mitre on its head, and a crucifix and a bible tied to its tail. On arrival at the altar they bowed their heads while the bust and the urn were placed on it and Collot, Fouché and Delaporte delivered eulogies of the dead man. 'Then a brazier was lighted, the crucifix and the gospel were untied from the ass's tail and cast into the flames. The ass found itself being offered a drink from the chalice; communion wafers, said to have been consecrated, were trampled underfoot; and other profanations, no less horrible, were about to be committed when a sudden storm that Heaven decreed should burst in torrential rain upon that horde of demons interrupted their sacrilegious undertakings and forced them to disperse.'[9]

Fouché, much as he would have enjoyed it, can have played no part in organizing that piece of impiety; but his hand can be clearly seen in the decree that the two representatives issued that day. It set up a Temporary Republican Vigilance Commission of twenty members, divided into two sections, one to remain in Lyons and the other to tour the departments of the Rhône and the Loire. They were to ensure the prompt execution of the Representatives' orders 'for the happiness of the people, the humiliation and annihilation of the aristocracy, the punishment of traitors and the prosperity of the Republic'.[10] They were to direct, activate and purge the local revolutionary committees, supervise all matters of internal security; impose a revolutionary tax on the wealthy for the benefit of the poor and the public interest; and establish, propagate and uphold republican principles. They were paid 18 francs a day, plus expenses, and were, for the sake of reliability, drawn from the Jacobins whom Fouché had brought from Nevers, Moulins and Paris.

Lyons was a city divided by more than ideological differences, by conflicts between royalists and republicans, church and anti-clericalists. There was an economic struggle between workers and employers. There was a strong federalist movement that wished to make Lyons the peer and not the pawn of Paris. And this local pride was shared by many of the town's republicans, who resented the intrusion of Jacobins from outside and their appointment to posts of authority.

The half of the Temporary Commission that was to remain in Lyons established its headquarters at No. 8 rue Ste-Catherine and set about designing its official uniform: steel-grey coat with red trimmings, blue buckskin breeches, tricorne hat with tricolour plume, American boots with bronzed spurs, Spanish gloves, a hussar sabre and a pair of pistols. Their work overlapped with two other commissions that had been set up by Couthon – a military tribunal that dealt with rebels caught with weapons in their hands, and a civil court to judge counter-revolutionary crimes that had been committed during the siege. On November 23 Collot wrote to Robespierre bitterly complaining of the dilatoriness of these two bodies. The same day the Temporary Commission proposed the appointment of General Parein, second-in-command of the Paris Revolutionary Army, to interrogate the hundreds of arrested suspects and decide whether they should be held for trial by the military tribunal, sent to Paris to appear before the Revolutionary Tribunal, or judged on the spot.

> 'Once this operation is under way, at least fifty, a hundred, or even a hundred and fifty muscadins can be put to death every day . . . To make their execution swift and more impressive in the eyes of the people . . . they will be chained together and arranged in lines along which cannon loaded with grapeshot will be fired. Platoons of republicans will be placed at some distance from them, to shoot immediately any who survive the cannon fire. The bodies thus cannonaded or shot will be collected at once and put in a ditch prepared for that purpose with a sufficiency of quick-lime to consume them.'[11]

This form of mass-execution was to be carried out by the Revolutionary Army. When they marched into the city, their commander, General Ronsin, noted that 'terror was written on every brow; and the profound silence that I had taken care to enjoin on our brave soldiers made their march still more menacing and terrible'.[12] They made no secret of the fact that they had come as executioners. 'A new revolutionary commission has just been appointed, composed of true sansculottes; my colleague Parein is its president and in a few days the grapeshot discharged by our gunners will have rid us of more than 4,000 conspirators.'[13]

It is worth noting that the methods that the Commissioners proposed using – the infamous *mitraillades* – were well known to the Committee of Public Safety, the Convention and many others. This does not excuse the Commissioners, but it does justify their plea that they were only doing what they had been told to do. 'The deputy on mission was an automaton,' Fouché argued, 'the mobile agent of the Committees of Public Safety and General Security. I was never a member of these committees of government, consequently my hand was never at the helm during the Terror.'[14]

Nevertheless, it was his signature as well as Collot's which authorized the setting up of the notorious Tribunal of Seven (it in fact never had more than five members) which began its work on December 4 at the Hôtel de Ville, now renamed the Maison Commune. It replaced both the military and civil courts established by Couthon. Its duty was to examine all prisoners awaiting trial, and pronounce immediate verdicts on them.

II

On the first day sixty prisoners were condemned to death and taken to the Plaine des Brotteaux, a pleasant open space fringed with poplars and willows on the east bank of the Rhône. There, ranged between two ditches, they were shot down by three guns charged with grapeshot. Collot, writing to Robespierre's landlord, Duplay, rejoiced at having 'revived the work of republican justice – as swift and terrible as the will of the people . . . What satisfaction there is for republicans in the proper discharge of their duties!'[1]

On the second day the Tribunal passed sentence on 248 accused persons, condemning 211 to death. Three of these were reprieved at the last moment, but when the artillery (there were eight guns this time) and infantry had ceased firing, the burial party discovered that they had to deal with 210 corpses instead of 208. One of the extra bodies was said to be that of a man who came to deliver a parcel to the prison and, despite his protests, was attached to the chain with the others. Nobody knew who the other man – or – woman was.

'Heads falling every day – and still more heads,' wrote one Jacobin enthusiast to a friend serving on the Revolutionary Tribunal in Paris. 'What delights you would have experienced had you seen the national justice dealing with 209 scoundrels the day before yesterday! What Majesty! How impressive! Edifying in every respect!'[2]

At the beginning of each of the three decades into which the republican month was divided, batches of accused men and women were brought from the prisons of the Recluses (a former hospital for prostitutes), St-Joseph (in the fever-ridden marshes to the south of the town), and Roanne, and lodged in the Salle du Commerce, on the side of the Maison Commune that overlooked the rue Puits-Gaillot, to be dealt with during the ensuing ten days. At the front of the building, facing the Place des Terreaux, was the Great Hall of Festivities, its walls and ceiling cracked and scarred by the siege; here prisoners were held for a second interrogation or while awaiting transfer back to prison. In a smaller room between the two, the tribunal sat at a table covered with a green cloth, nymphs disporting on the gaily decorated ceiling above them and a large fire warming their backs. They had rejected the uniform designed a few weeks earlier by the Temporary Commission: each member wore a blue coat, white buckskin breeches, a military hat with a red plume, a broad black bladrick and sabre, and round his neck a tricolour ribbon from which was suspended a miniature axe, the symbol of justice. Behind a wooden barrier, elbow-high, stood the witnesses and carefully-scrutinized spectators, heavily-moustached patriots and soldiers of the Republican Army.

The prisoner was marched in and seated on a stool with an armed guard on each side. Behind him, the turnkey awaited the signal from the judges. On average they dealt with seven cases every quarter of an hour, sitting from nine till twelve in the morning and seven till nine in the evening. They frequently asked only three questions: the prisoner's name, his profession, and what he had done during the siege. They then exchanged glances and each delivered his opinion by 'extending his hand on the table to indicate freedom or further questioning; lifting his hand to his forehead as condemnation to the firing squad; touching the axe hanging round his neck as a sign of death at the guillotine'.[3] For the guillotine had been preserved in the interest of Terror, to impress those who could not or would not witness the executions at Les Brotteaux.

It was believed that a prisoner's chances were better in the morning than at night, when the judges were tired, irritable and sometimes drunk – the President, Parein, 'his characterless face obscured under the mass of plumes in the hat he wore sideways',[4] liked to practise fencing after the morning session, and the exercise increased his consumption of wine. There was also the consideration that in the morning the turnkey's faculties were sharper and he was less likely to make a fatal mistake in interpreting the judges' signals when he tapped the prisoner on the shoulder and led him down the narrow circular staircase to the basement. 'To the left was the good cellar . . .; the accused who were taken there, and would be examined again, were usually acquitted. The bad one was on the right, on the rue Lafont side. There was no spectacle more dismal: a lamp placed in the middle of the vaulted roof cast an obscure light on the blackened walls; one left this cavern only to die.'[5]

Outside, the prisoners' families waited to hear the sentences read from the town hall terrace. Each morning the executioners came in to crop the hair of those about to die. The guillotine, originally set up in the Place Bellecour, had been moved first to a position immediately in front of the town hall, and later, when the ground became sodden and stinking, transferred to the opposite side of the Place des Terreaux; a channel was dug to the fountain to carry away the blood, and the basket into which the heads fell was lined with hide. The work of three executioners – one to send the victim up the ladder, another to strap him to the plank, the third to release the blade – was supervised by two members of the municipal council and two clerks, seated at the first-floor window of Brun's café.

In the early days there were priests among the prisoners, who administered to the spiritual needs of their companions before themselves being executed. When these had all been sentenced and those still at liberty dared not wear their robes, some would gain admission to the prisons disguised as pedlars; two of them, in heavy cloaks, stood in the Place des Terreaux as the victims were taken to the guillotine, or at the Pont Morand as they were marched across to face the grapeshot.

The Terror did not silence all protest. On December 20 a deputation of Lyonnais appeared before the Convention to complain of the severity of the repression. 'We implore France . . . to number us once more among her children. We were French, we were your brothers, your kinfolk, your friends; we are still, we always shall be.'[6]

'Lyons has committed a great crime,' the President of the Assembly replied. 'Lyons is no more. The National Convention will consider your request; its clemency will be as great as its justice.'[7] There seemed room for hope. But the Convention referred the matter to the Committee of Public Safety, and when the Committee made its report next day its spokesman proved to be Collot, recently recalled to Paris. He denounced the deputation and the entire population of Lyons as cut-throats and counter-revolutionaries. The Convention approved the measures taken by the People's Representatives and ordered the Paris sections to make a census of all recently arrived

Lyonnais, who were probably as anti-republican as those who had brought the petition to the bar of the house.

In the Jacobin Club that night Collot developed one of the arguments he had put to the Convention: 'We blasted two hundred at a time and they hold it against ùs as a crime! Do they still not realize that it is a proof of sensibility? When you guillotine twenty criminals, the last of them dies twenty times over, whereas these two hundred conspirators perish together . . .'[8] In his report to the Committee of Public Safety he revealed that 'to spare humanity the deplorable spectacle of so many executions, your Commissioners thought it would be possible to destroy all the conspirators in one day'.[9] But after a three-hour discussion with the leaders of the Revolutionary Army they realized that it was militarily impractical. They decided to make do with a series of smaller executions, using both gunpowder and guillotine. 'Such were the painful duties you imposed on us.'[10]

It has the mad logic of the time, but it was not true. Fouché revealed the true purpose of the mass executions – and the only basis for their justification – when he wrote to Collot that same day, having just heard that Toulon had fallen to the republicans: 'We too, my friends, have contributed to the capture of Toulon, by spreading terror among the cowards who took shelter there, by offering to their view the thousands of corpses of their accomplices . . . There is only one way for us to celebrate the victory; this evening we are sending two hundred and thirteen rebels to face the cannon blast.'[11]

In fact he was doing nothing of the kind. There were 67 executions that day, and none the next. But if the Convention wished to hear of thousands of corpses he was willing to tell them. When the news of the abortive protest at the bar of the Assembly reached him, he wrote – with Delaporte, and Albitte, who had replaced Collot – 'we continue uninterruptedly to strike [the people's] enemies. We annihilate them in the most impressive, the most terrible and most expeditious way.'[12]

He had no interest in punishment as retribution, only as example. As at Nevers and Moulins, his main effort was directed to reform, to creating conditions in which work could be resumed and supplies sent to the armies. By the end of 1793 the rebels had been put to flight in the Vendée and Normandy by the forces he had helped to raise. After the autumn victories at Wattignies and in Alsace, the French armies stood poised for advance northward and eastward in the spring. If he continued to use the guillotine it was not to avenge the past but to ensure the future.

The industrial life of the city had been brought to a standstill. The continued demolition of the houses of aristocrats and wealthy bourgeois provided work for 14,000 men. He had boilers taken to the sites and set firemen to wash out saltpetre from the rubble. He set up a workshop in the Place de la Liberté (formerly des Terreaux) where one man from each section was taught how to extract the precious explosive and then sent back to instruct others. He sent Dorfeuille, the ex-president of the civil tribunal, to harry the small-arms manufacturers of St-Etienne and to send him 'notes on their civism and talents'[13] – a phrase calculated to send premonitory shivers down their backs. The Convention had banned the re-establishment of arsenals or arms manufacture in the rebel towns, so he sent the dispossessed foundry owners to Valence, with workers and tools and orders to set up new factories. He appointed a special commission to supervise the transport of coal down the Loire and the canal at Briare and so to the arms factories of Paris. He still controlled his old territories of the Nièvre and Côte d' Or, and had been given others such as Ain and Saône-et-Loire.

In mid-November, four days after his arrival in Lyons he promulgated an Order for the Suppression of Poverty similar to the one that he had introduced at Nevers. The infirm, the aged, orphans and the poor were to be lodged, clothed and fed by the rich – 'the marks of poverty will be abolished'.[14] So would begging and idleness by the able-bodied under pain of imprisonment. 'Healthy citizens will be provided with work and the tools necessary for the exercise of their trade'[15] and the cost of this, too, would be borne by the rich. As at Nevers, bakers were forbidden to bake different qualities of bread, made from white flour or from bran. Henceforward there would be only one grade – the *Pain d'Egalité*. Struck by this practical application of the dictum that 'wealth and poverty must disappear in a world based on equality',[16] Chaumette brought the decree to the attention of the Convention which ordered its application throughout France.

Fouché's earliest biographer, Martel, saw in these measures clear proof that he was a Communist. There is nothing in the rest of his career to confirm this. The truth seems to lie in a more recent judgement that 'the representatives on mission had not the slightest thought of overturning the social order. They pursued one well-defined objective: to win the war – and, in order to win it, to gain the temporary support of the sans-culottes.'[17]

12

The attack on the Church was widespread. At St-Etienne – renamed Armeville – one of Fouché's predecessors at Lyons, the deputy Châteauneuf-Randon, denounced the priests who had 'used the ignorance of men to make a god out of the sans-culotte Jesus' but proposed that, since he had been 'crucified by the aristocrats of his century',[1] his bust should be placed beside that of the murdered Marat in the Panthéon. Fouché himself, presiding at the Feast of Reason in Lyons cathedral, where a statue of Liberty took the place of the high altar, denounced the intervention of the Church between Man and God: 'The chaste and fruitful breast of a loving and virtuous wife – there is the altar of the honest man, the sans-culotte!'[2]

In Paris Robespierre fulminated against atheism – a predictable reaction from one who found increasing difficulty in distinguishing himself from God. He inveighed against 'men hitherto unknown in the course of the Revolution' who were seeking fame 'by disturbing the liberty of worship . . . Atheism is aristocratic; the idea of a great Being who watches over oppressed innocence and punishes crime is essentially popular.'[3] It was an odd argument; and in any case Fouché was anti-clerical, not atheistic. But the 'hitherto unknown' sneer might have been meant for him; and the attack in general was certainly aimed at Hébert and some of Fouché's close acquaintances, notably Chaumette. Robespierre's hold over the Committee, the Convention and the Jacobin Club was increasing every day; through the Committee or the Club he intended to win back control of the mob from the Commune. Fouché was heading for a confrontation.

There were other, more serious, grounds for dispute. Tightening its grip on the department, the Committee of Public Safety had the Convention pass a decree on December 4 replacing the locally elected procurators by National Agents responsible directly to the Committee. They were to 'ensure the enforcement of the laws and to denounce negligence', and make their reports over the heads of the People's Representatives, who were deprived of many of their powers, notably of raising money and levying taxes.

'We were on the point of seizing all the treasure of the departments confided to us . . . when we received the decree suspending all measures taken in that respect,' Fouché complained to Chaumette. Ominously, the measures he had taken in the Allier were specially referred to in the ban. There was a cold wind blowing from Paris. He replied by protesting at the ineptitude of the order: 'If the movement had not been impeded, the gold and silver would have flowed to Paris as naturally as river water flows to its mouth.'[4]

With two masters to be played off one against the other, the malcontents of Lyons grew more bold. The opposition to the People's Representatives came not from royalists or catholics but from republicans, the local Jacobins who resented their subordination to outsiders. They had remained steadfast in the dark days of persecution, only to find themselves now excluded from honours, authority and the chance of rich pickings. 'Things are at such a point in this infamous Commune,' Fouché wrote to Collot on 5 nivôse An II (which would have been Christmas Day on the old calendar), 'that after having menaced us with daggers . . . they threaten us with the vengeance of the National Convention; they are saying openly that we shall soon be taken before the Revolutionary Tribunal in Paris'.[5]

It was not an idle threat. That day Robespierre presented to the Convention his report on the Principles of Revolutionary Government: 'The revolutionary government owes to good citizens the complete protection of the nation; to the enemies of the people it owes only death . . . The punishment of a hundred obscure and lesser culprits is less useful to liberty than the execution of one leader of a conspiracy.'[6] He nominally spoke on behalf of the Committee of Public Safety, but there were few in the chamber who mistook this for anything but a personal threat. He intended to deal with his rivals one by one. It was a long list: Fouché's name was not at the top; but it was on it. There had been a reference to 'the traitors of Lyons' who criticized as 'ultra-revolutionaries' the 'zealous patriots who, in good faith, committed some error'.[7] Robespierre's tactics were simple: to strike down those ahead of him as Terrorists and then turn and rend those behind him as Moderates.

The disturbances increased in Lyons. Men of the 9th Dragoons and the Revolutionary Army came to blows in the street. At the Jacobin Club there was more talk of denouncing the People's Representatives to the Committee of Public Safety. Fouché ordered a curfew for the soldiers and went down to the Club to deal with the revolt.

He met with a noisy reception. 'There are some among you who seek to demean and degrade the Majesty of the People,' he scolded. 'What opinion do you think others will have of your Society when it is not possible to make oneself heard there?' It was a familiar heart-cry from one whose greatest handicap was a weak voice. 'In a rowdy Society lung-power dominates, hypocrisy triumphs . . . Let equality rule by all means, but it is a long step from equality of speech to unbridled insults . . . I shall appoint two members of the Temporary Commission to be present at your sittings. If this tone continues, I give notice that we shall be compelled to dissolve the Society.'[8]

To Robespierre's veiled threats in the Convention, Fouché replied with open defiance. In January 1794 he protested that the deputy Gouly, sent by the Committee of Public Safety to install the new system of National Agents in the department of the Ain, was intro-ducing 'retrorevolutionary and liberticide measures'.[9] He told the Committee that he had considered putting him under arrest, but had compromised by sending two reliable men to find out what he had been up to and to bring him to Lyons. 'Whatever may be the nature of Gouly's powers, we have the right to know of them, when he presents himself to exercise them in a department which has been placed under our supervision.'[10] Fouché was never a man to accept meekly the diminution of his authority or curtailment of his powers. His protest, supported by Collot, was accepted by the Committee of Public Safety. Gouly, although under Robespierre's protection, was recalled.

As for the law granting freedom of worship that Robespierre had pushed through the Convention, the People's Representatives in Lyons replied with their own decree that the people could not recognize any other cult than that of Public Reason and Universal Morality, any other dogma than that of the Sovereignty of its own Power. 'If, now that the Republic has solemnly declared that it acc-ords equal protection to the forms of worship of all religions, it became permissible for every sect to set up their particular signs in public places, on the roads and in the streets, to celebrate their religi-ous ceremonies, to announce them with the sound of bells or other instruments, the result would be confusion and disorder.'[11] Conse-quently, religious services would be conducted only inside the re-spective temples provided for them. Religious signs were abolished, bells would be broken and sent to be cast as cannon. Religious dress would not be worn outside places of worship. Finally, Fouché's funeral decrees of Nevers were repeated: coffins to be draped with palls depicting Sleep; cemeteries to be stripped of religious emblems; the gates to be inscribed *Death is an eternal Slumber*.

On February 12 Fouché confirmed an order by the Temporary

Commission that 'citizens freed after interrogation . . . or trial cannot be arrested again except for new crimes committed after their release'.[12] The day before he had abolished all revolutionary courts in the departments of the Rhône and the Loire with the exception of the one at Lyons. On February 6 he ordered that no more executions by shooting should be carried out.

13

There were still many prisoners held for trial. The Tribunal of Seven continued its work; the guillotine was not idle. Although it was winter, there were renewed complaints of offensive smells in the Place de la Liberté. The committee set up by the People's Representatives to inquire into this found that the smell 'does not arise from the blood that flows at the moment when the blade strikes the malefactor. This inconvenience was overcome by a large funnel under the grating, discharging beneath the scaffold into a portable bucket. But the bodies, released through a trapdoor, spatter the interior walls of the structure, and especially the earth beneath it, with a very abundant quantity of blood which, soon becoming putrified, gives off an unbearable stench.'[1]

The members of the Committee, 'after having considered the advantages and disadvantages of many measures that might be employed, decided on the following as being the simplest and least expensive: first we had spread beneath the scaffold a moderately large quantity of plaster rubble, known locally as screenings, to mop up the blood which was soaking into the earth. Then, after this had been removed, we had the square swept and tidied as neatly as possible and four tumbrils of fresh screenings put down.'[2] They had given instructions for this procedure to be followed after every execution. 'If to this is added the precaution of whitewashing the scaffold and the interior walls, it may be assumed that these simple measures will suffice.'[3] The work was entrusted to the former churchwarden of St Peter's, who already held the concession of carting the corpses to the burial ditches at Les Brotteaux.

But citizen Bonnet, the churchwarden, was clearly approaching the end of his employment. While Robespierre in Paris increased the fury of the Terror that he had pretended to disapprove, Fouché continued to slacken it in Lyons – to the rage and dismay of the local Jacobin Club, still hungry for reprisals and recompense. On March

11 he reported to the Convention that the citizens of Lyons would soon deserve 'to be numbered among the children of the Republic and to be re-admitted to her laws'. There were still some 'accomplices of the rebellion' to be dealt with, but he and Delaporte and Méaulle (his colleague from Nantes who had replaced Albitte in January) expressed their satisfaction that justice had so soon 'run its course in the rebel city'.[4]

He was swimming against the tide – or against the complex currents in which Robespierre now managed to overthrow within the space of three weeks both Hébert, the spokesman of the Commune, and Danton, once the leading spirit of the Committee of Public Safety. On March 14, the morning after Hébert's arrest, the Lyons National Agent, Fontenelle, wrote to the People's Representatives for advice on a difficult problem. He was required to send to Paris a list of all persons held as suspects. Because the People's Representatives had countermanded some of Fontenelle's orders 'many enemies of the Republic are still walking about with their heads in the air'.[5] The agent did not wish to question the authority of the People's Representatives. On the other hand, he must protect himself. Would they be good enough to instruct him on what he was to report to the Committee?

The threat was as obvious as the impertinence. Fouché and Méaulle answered him bluntly the next day:

> We have never intended or wished to hinder the arrest of suspects; but we do desire that the methods of procedure which protect public liberty should be observed. We desire that there shall be no wreaking of private vengeance; we desire that it shall not be left to the decision of the revolutionary committees to arrest any who happen to displease them, or those whom they have an interest in depriving of their liberty. We desire that the revolutionary committees, purged and reduced to nine in number, shall make a list of suspects and that this list shall be submitted for approval by the People's Representatives.[6]

Fontenelle reported to Paris: 'About 1,800 individuals who were arrested as suspects have been released under an order of the Temporary Commission, confirmed by the People's Representatives. I will not indulge in any comment, but will content myself with observing to you that in one section alone more than seventy ex-nobles and relations of émigrés had been arrested.'[7] On March 24, the day that Hébert was condemned to death, Fontenelle sent a special messenger with copies of the orders he had issued and of those that had cancelled them, and all his correspondence with the People's Representatives. 'A great conspiracy has been discovered as a result of your unflagging zeal,' he said in his covering letter to the Committee of Public Safety. 'According to the reports you have made to the National Convention, it is evident there are ramifications in the departments, and there is every reason to believe the conspirators have not forgotten Commune-Affranchie; perhaps this city may even serve as a rallying point for their accomplices.'[8]

At the Committee's offices in the Tuileries the letter was placed in the file reserved for Robespierre's special attention. 'The scaffold awaits every sort of conspiracy,'[9] he told the Jacobin Club. 'It is not enough to stifle one; we must crush them all; the one that still exists must be attacked with the same fury with which we pursued the other . . . In Commune-Affranchie the friends of Chalier . . . are proscribed at this very moment. I have seen letters from some of them, from those who have escaped from prison and come to beg the help of the Convention.'[10]

Fouché ordered the postmaster, Pilot, to intercept all letters addressed to the Jacobin Club, the mayor, the National Agent and five prominent agitators – not knowing that Pilot was secretly in touch with Robespierre, whom he supplied with silk stockings from the famous Lyons factories. Acting on information from one of his spies, the citizeness Rameau, Fouché had the Jacobin Club's documents sequestered and examined, expecting to find incriminating evidence – but the reports of speeches could not be found, and the secretary maintained that no minutes were ever kept of the proceedings. On March 26 the People's Representatives disbanded the club on the grounds that it had attracted 'a crowd of men who . . . desire to substitute anarchism and federalism for government, audacity, intrigue and depravity for republican virtues'.[11] The members were forbidden to reassemble under pain of being treated as rebels. A new society, its members approved by the Representatives, was installed in a new meeting place, the former Augustinian church.

Robespierre's counter-stroke had already been taken. On March 30 a special courier from the Committee of Public Safety arrived at Lyons with two orders: all action against the Jacobin Society of Commune-Affranchie would be suspended: Representative Fouché would proceed immediately to Paris to provide explanation on the affairs of Commune-Affranchie. His order of recall had been drawn up personally by Robespierre.

Fouché, Bonne-Jeanne and their eight-month-old Nièvre were already on the way to Paris when Robespierre rose in the Jacobin Club to announce his dispatch of a messenger to Lyons. 'He should arrive before it is possible to bring any patriot to trial and sacrifice him. If the Committee's order is not respected, I declare that the innocent blood of the patriots shall be avenged!'[12]

On April 6, the Tribunal of Seven sent 156 people to prison and two to the guillotine. The two were the chief executioners, Jean Ripet and his assistant – who was also his son-in-law – Jean Bernard. They were professionals long employed in the trade; they had decapitated more than 700 royalists and counter-revolutionaries for the republicans, and before that they had performed similar services for the royalists. Among their republican victims had been the martyr Chalier; for this the tribunal condemned them to death and declared its session closed.

The prisons were empty. The Terror in Lyons was ended. 1,682 suspects had been executed, 1,684 had been released; 162 had been sentenced to imprisonment for the duration of the war. Some 300 others had been condemned to death by other courts in the department.

Notes to Part I

Chapter 1

1 *Biographie des Ministres*, 142(1)
2 *Ibid.*
3 Verger, III, 324
4 Despatys, *Ami*, 325
5 Gourgaud, I, 93
6 Chateaubriand, *Outre-tombe*, II, 17
7 Martel, *Fouché*, I, 34/14

Chapter 2

1 Lallemand, 189
2 Caillé, 6
3 Arnault, *Souvenirs*, I, 63
4 Arnault left Juilly in 1783; Hamel says Fouché taught there from 1784 to 1787; Madelin says he first went there in 1787. There is confusion about all his early movements. Madelin and subsequent biographers have placed him at Vendôme from 1784 to 1787, yet the letter quoted above (2/2) contains a reference to 'Wednesday, June 12', which places the year as 1782. Even his date of birth is uncertain: his parents had at least one other son whom they named Joseph and who died in infancy. The correct date is almost certainly between 1759 and 1763.
5 Despatys, *Révolution*, 267–8
6 *Ibid.*
7 *Ibid.*, Robespierre, 261
8 *Ibid.*, 262
9 *Ibid.*
10 *Ibid.*
11 *Ibid.*

Chapter 3

1 Guépin, 399
2 Mellinet, VI, 99
3 Verger, IV, 245–6
4 *Ibid.*, 261

Chapter 4

1 Guépin, 411
2 Verger, V, 114
3 Miles, I, 250
4 Mellinet, VI, 315
5 Guépin, 416
6 Mellinet, VI, 332–3
7 Mellinet, VI, 359

Chapter 5

1 Mellinet, VI, 401–2
2 Verger, V, 276
3 *Ibid.*, 278

Chapter 6

1 He was killed at Aboukir Bay, with his son, the boy who stood on the burning deck in Mrs Hemans's poem.
2 Fouché, *Réflexions . . . Capet*, 5
3 *Ibid.*, 7
4 Fouché, *Mémoires*, 42

Chapter 7

1 *Archives parlementaires*, LX, 9
2 *Ibid.*, 10
3 Verger, V, 323–4
4 *Ibid.*, 325
5 Mellinet, VII, 154
6 *Archives parlementaires*, LX, 556
7 *Ibid.*
8 Verger, V, 330
9 *Archives parlementaires*, LXI, 11
10 Lallié, *Justice*, 14
11 Blanchard, 77
12 Fouché, *Mémoires*, 43/44
13 Mellinet, VII, 206
14 *Ibid.*
15 *Ibid.*

Chapter 8

1 Larévellière, I, 115
2 *Archives parlementaires*, LXVII, 120
3 Babeau, II, 69
4 *Ibid.*
5 *Ibid.*
6 *Archives parlementaires*, LXVIII, 72
7 *Ibid.*, LXIX, 66
8 *Ibid.*, 138
9 *Ibid.*, 486(1)
10 *Salut public*, V, 418
11 *Ibid.*, 419
12 Courtois, III, 118

Chapter 9

1 *Archives parlementaires*, LXXV, 304
2 *Salut public*, VI, 438
3 Martel, *Fouché*, I, 132
4 *Ibid.*, 133
5 *Ibid.*, 175
6 Cornillon, IV, 65
7 Cobb, *Armée révolutionaire*, 19
8 *Archives parlementaires*, LXXVII, 344
9 *Moniteur*, XVII, 762
10 Martel, *Fouché*, I, 195
11 *Ibid.*, 193
12 Despatys, *Ami*, 50
13 Fouché, *Réflexions . . . éducation*, 4/6
14 Martel, *Fouché*, I, 159
15 Fouché, *Première lettre*, 7
16 Martel, *Fouché*, I, 161
17 Mathiez, *Contributions*, 32
18 Fouché, *Fête civique*, 6

Chapter 10

1 *Archives parlementaires*, LXXVII, 317
2 *Ibid.*, 458
3 *Salut public*, VII, 377–8
4 *Ibid.*, VIII, 124
5 Guillon de Montléon, II, 310

6 Saladin, 208
7 Courtois, I, 327
8 Guillon de Montléon, II, 347
9 *Ibid.*, 348
10 La Chapelle, 2
11 Herriot, *Lyon*, III, 136–7
12 *Ibid.*, 142
13 *Ibid.*
14 Fouché, *Mémoires*, 44

Chapter 11

1 Courtois, I, 314–15
2 Saladin, 217
3 Martel, *Fouché*, I, 404
4 Delandine, 192
5 Martel, *Fouché*, I, 404–5
6 *Archives parlementaires*, LXXXIII, 34–5
7 *Ibid.*
8 *Moniteur*, XIX, 26
9 Collot, 9
10 *Ibid.*
11 *Moniteur*, XIX, 37
12 La Chapelle, 174
13 Richard, 110
14 Fouché, *Première lettre*, 10
15 *Ibid.*
16 Soboul, 57(5)
17 Guérin, I, 138

Chapter 12

1 Donot, 57
2 Herriot, *Lyon*, III, 161
3 Aulard, *Jacobins*, V, 528–9
4 Herriot, *Lyon*, III, 215
5 Collot, 17
6 *Archives parlementaires*, LXXXIII, 303
7 *Ibid.*, 302
8 Herriot, *Lyon*, III, 279
9 *Salut public*, X, 76
10 *Ibid.*
11 Gonon, 340
12 *Ibid.*, 351

Chapter 13

1   Herriot, *Lyon*, III, 398–9
2   *Ibid.*
3   *Ibid.*
4   *Archives parlementaires*, LXXXVI, 495
5   Herriot, *Lyon*, III, 443
6   *Ibid.*, 457
7   *Ibid.*, 443
8   *Ibid.*, 484
9   *Moniteur*, XX, 33
10   *Ibid.*, 34
11   Metzger, VII, 97
12   *Moniteur*, XX, 136

PART II
The Giant-Killer
1794-1799

I

Fouché returned to his rooms on the third floor of No. 315 rue Honoré (the saint had been suppressed, he must have been pleased to note) on April 5. The atmosphere in Paris was supercharged with menace and fear. The warmth of peaceful domesticity with Bonne-Jeanne and the child was chilled by the threats that hung over his own head. That evening three tumbrils clattered along the street below, carrying Robespierre's latest victims to the Place de la Révolution. There, beside the statue of Liberty lit by the red glow of the setting sun, they climbed the steps of the guillotine one by one: Danton, Desmoulins, Hérault de Séchelles, Fabre d'Eglantine, Philippeaux – the mounting roll-call of the Revolution itself.

On April 7, he resumed his seat in the Convention. Many of the old faces had disappeared. Some had quite literally lost their heads; some had taken to their beds in fright; others were too frightened to take to their beds. The whole assembly was cowed and cringing. He went to the tribune to give an account of his stewardship but was told to report to the two Committees, of Public Safety and General Security, which now dealt with all such matters. It was an ominous beginning for a man who had hoped to put himself under the protection of the Convention.

At the Jacobin Club, where he boldly presented himself that evening, he heard Dumas, the Vice-President of the Revolutionary Tribunal, attack the counter-revolutionaries of Lyons and denounce those who complained of hard measures. It was the opening shot of the campaign to condemn him as a Moderatist. He reported on his work, protesting that he had acted fairly but firmly. A man in the body of the hall asked permission to speak against him. Robespierre interrupted, stepping cautiously as ever, even faintly praising Fouché's 'incomplete report',[1] but making it clear that his tip-tilted witchdoctor nose was on the scent of a new conspiracy.

There was coldness between the two men but not an open breach. Fouché went to the Duplay house to talk with him and, according to Charlotte Robespierre's highly unlikely account:

My brother called him to account for the blood he had shed, and reproached him for his conduct with such forcefulness that Fouché was pale and trembling. He stammered some excuses and attributed the cruel measures he had taken to the gravity of the circumstances. Robespierre replied that nothing could justify the cruelty of which he was guilty; that it was true that Lyons has been in insurrection against the National Convention, but that was no reason for the mass shooting down of unarmed enemies.[2]

Fouché, always pale but seldom known to tremble, could have replied that Robespierre was perfectly well aware of all that was going on and had tacitly approved it. He claimed that in all his missions he had not signed a dozen warrants of arrest. He could equally claim that, after performing his appointed task of punishing the rebels, he had tried to restore Lyons to normality with as much speed and forbearance as possible. But this was not an argument he could safely advance now (for Robespierre's complaint against him was the reverse of what Charlotte pretends) – and it was not one that would be accepted later. His hands were not as deeply stained with blood as his detractors subsequently made out – but his face was indelibly spattered with it.

Fouché's alleged Moderatism, though it was the crime for which he intended to bring him down, was not his gravest offence in Robespierre's eyes. It was Fouché's attitude to religion and his too-often expressed views on it that made punishment inevitable. Robespierre's confidence in his own divinity was now unbounded. Those who unwittingly held views not in accord with his own were the victims of human error – those who dared knowingly to contradict him were evil creatures guilty of mortal sin. If sinners said something with which he did not agree, he cut off their heads to prevent their repeating it.

Fouché had sinned not once but many times, and must pay the mortal price, but first there were some closer at hand to be disciplined. On April 13, the basket of the guillotine received the severed head of Chaumette who seven months before had so warmly and publicly praised Fouché's measures against the *religious fanatics* of the Nièvre. The warrant for his arrest had been in Robespierre's handwriting. 'The articles of his condemnation were that he had aimed to destroy every kind of morality, stifle every principle of virtue and persuade neighbouring peoples that the French nation had arrived at the most extreme stage of dissolution that it would be possible to reach, destroying even the idea of a Supreme Being.'[3]

From Lyons a stream of denunciations reached the Committee of Public Safety, accusing Fouché of being a supporter of Hébert and a protector of royalists – for with lunatic cogency Hébert had been put to death on a charge of trying to restore the monarchy. Delaporte and Méaulle courageously wrote to Couthon protesting that Fouché had 'spoken great truths' and imploring him 'in the name of God, to get the Committee to tell us how to behave with these "patriots"'.[4] They wrote privately to Fouché, warning him of the plots against him and begging his help in getting them recalled to Paris. The revolutionary committees which Fouché had suppressed were back in control in all thirty-two sections; with their friends they were pillaging shops, storehouses and private dwellings; 'but if you catch one in the act you must close your eyes or you'll have them all screaming about the oppression of patriots'.[5]

2

It was May, the republican month of floréal, when flowers bloom. The Convention echoed to the sound of Robespierre's voice, 'hoarse in the lower range, discordant in the higher notes, and in transports of rage turning into a sort of hyena's howl'.[1] He called for a moral revolution to match the physical one. He denounced the satanic figures of Hébert and Danton, and the counter-revolutionary doctrine of atheism. 'The idea of the Supreme Being and the immortality of the soul is a continual invocation of justice; it is therefore social and republican . . . If the existence of God, if the immortality of the soul, were only a dream, they would still be the most beautiful concepts of the human mind.'[2] The members of the Convention, their master's voice in one ear and the snarl of the hungry, angry streets in the other, decreed that the French people recognized the existence of a Supreme Being and ordained a festival in its honour on 20 Prairial, just over a month ahead.

Robespierre had organized, and taken charge of, a *Bureau de Police Génerale* which kept secret watch on all officials both in Paris and in the provinces, and largely usurped the functions of the Committee of General Security. All revolutionary tribunals throughout the country were now obliged to report daily to the Committee of Public Safety which he dominated with the support of his two principal lieutenants,

Saint-Just and Couthon. Above all, he still held the loyalty of the mob. 'By means of the people he ruled at the Jacobins; by the Jacobins, at the Convention; by the Convention, over all France,' said Meillan, one of the deputies for the Basses-Pyrénées. 'They loved his whims and fawned on his furies; and the tribunal without question struck off the heads of those he specified. His power frightened his accomplices as much as his victims.'[3]

So that he might be qualified to play the leading rôle in his Feast of the Supreme Being on June 8, the Convention unanimously elected him as its President (the office was held for a fortnight at a time) on June 4. But his pleasure was marred by one extraordinary and quite unexpected occurrence – on the same day Fouché was elected to the presidential chair of the Jacobin Club. How he engineered this remarkable victory on Robespierre's own territory is not clear. He had already begun to organize opposition to the man whom he saw was 'aspiring not to a decemviral tyranny [through the Committee of Public Safety] but to a despotic dictatorship'.[4] Some of the leading spirits of the Club, realizing that their prominence would qualify them for inclusion among Robespierre's victims, may have supported Fouché. Some of the moderates who joined the Club for protection but seldom attended may have rallied to vote for him on this occasion. But this would scarcely be enough to secure his election. Some among the rank and file must have wavered in their usual blind allegiance to Robespierre; perhaps because of a burgeoning distrust of his personal ambitions; perhaps because they preferred the Goddess of Reason to the Supreme Being.

Fouché's own actions are interesting, in view of later criticisms that he was never more than an opportunist, always awaiting the turn of events in order to join the winning side. In the first fortnight of June 1794, nothing seemed more certain than that Robespierre would succeed in destroying all opposition and emerge as a dictator – and, indeed, as a popular dictator as far as the Paris mob was concerned. Though Fouché had offended him – as had most of the Commissioners on mission because they enjoyed a certain independence – Robespierre would probably have been ready to overlook this. Fouché was not a rival in the struggle for power in Paris – merely a former provincial satrap who had shown signs of insubordination. From Robespierre's point of view there was no immediate need to strike; from Fouché's there was something to gain by waiting to see if the tide turned against Robespierre, nothing but peril in attacking him now that it was running so strongly in his favour. Yet he attacked.

On June 8, Robespierre led the deputies out of the debating chamber in the Tuileries palace, down the wooden steps to the garden where the Supreme Being was to be honoured. From his old-fashioned powdered hair to his shiny gold-buckled shoes he was the embodiment of self-regarding rectitude. A few voices, Fouché's among them, were raised in protest, but they were quickly drowned by the cheers. Robespierre marched up to the group of allegorical figures designed by David. First the President's torch was to set Atheism and Anarchy ablaze: then Wisdom would rise behind them. But the vices were slow to burn, and virtue overeager. Wisdom's face was blackened with smoke, Robespierre's was pale green with vexation.

On June 10, Couthon presented to the Convention a decree to reform criminal procedure. It had been drawn up by Robespierre but, according to Billaud, never submitted for discussion by the Committee of Public Safety in whose name it was now recommended to the assembly. Henceforth the Revolutionary Tribunal was permitted only one sentence: death. The prosecution was not required to call witnesses; the accused was forbidden to do so. Neither was he allowed counsel. One or two of the deputies were courageous enough to stand up and oppose the bill: Ruamps from Lower Charente, and Lecointre, one of those who had protested against Robespierre in the gardens two days before. Lecointre proposed an indefinite adjournment. Robespierre quit the presidential chair and hurried to the tribune. Alternately cajoling and threatening, he harangued the Convention, 'a nervous trembling passing through his limbs, the familiar tic tormenting the muscles of his face, giving them an involuntary look of pain or laughter, his twitching fingers playing across the lectern as if on the keys of a spinet'.[5] Before the fury of this insignificant yet terrifying figure, resistance collapsed; the Convention meekly adopted the measure.

In the committee rooms in the north wing next morning, Billaud reproached Robespierre for the lack of consultation. He replied with screams of rage that brought spectators trooping to the terrace outside. He strutted away, realizing he could not yet afford to antagonize his fellow committee-men, and returned with tears in his eyes, offering conciliation. While he was away from the main assembly, the deputies introduced a clause stipulating that the Convention must give consent before any of its members were brought before the Revolutionary Tribunal. It was a flimsy defence.

Since the beginning of the year, the monthly total of executions by the Paris guillotine had risen from 61 in Nivôse to 68 (Pluviôse) to 116 (Ventôse) to 155 (Germinal) to 354 (Floréal). Up to the introduction of the new law on 22 Prairial there had been 281; in the remaining eight days of the month there were another 228. Messidor would have 796. From December 1793 to July 1794, the daily average in Paris rose from 2 to 38. One recent examination of the number of victims in the whole of France, from the inception of the Reign of Terror in March 1793 until August 1794, has concluded that 'it is extremely doubtful that the total would reach 17,000'[6] (though the addition of those who died in prison or were shot after capture might increase it to 35,000–40,000). Another suggests a total of 40,000 (including 10,000 who died in prison) but adds that 'the great majority were put to death for alleged participation in civil war. The Revolutionary Tribunal of Paris . . . dispatched no more than 2,639 prisoners.' In contrast with this, '15,000–17,000 *Communards*, almost all Parisians, were shot in May 1871; there were perhaps 40,000 executions after the liberation of France in 1944'.[7]

The difference, of course, lies in the circumstances and purpose of the killings. The Communist and Gaullist executions after the liberation, like those in Paris after the second siege, were primarily local acts of revenge by large groups supported by considerable popular consent; in Paris in the summer of 1794 the guillotine was a weapon of terror used by one ruthless tyrant, with the cowed and reluctant acquiescence of a majority of deputies, to obtain personal domination over the whole of France.

3

In 1789 the Breton deputies to the Estates General formed a club which met in a room on the first floor of Nicolas Amaury's coffee shop in Versailles. Non-Breton members were admitted and, when the Assembly moved to Paris, the club hired the refectory of the Jacobin convent in the rue Honoré for its evening meetings and changed its name to the *Société de la Révolution* in honour of the London club that had just celebrated its centenary. As membership grew, the Society took over the use of the convent library. By February 1790 approximately one third of the deputies to the National Assembly were members of the club, which had again changed its name: to the Society of Friends of the Constitution, though its members were becoming better known as Jacobs, Jacoquins or Jacobins. Deputies were eligible for admission on the proposal of two members, non-deputies if sponsored by five. The president held office for a month (later reduced to a fortnight); the club met to debate at 6 p.m. every day except Sundays and holidays.

Robespierre served his first term as president in April 1790. Mirabeau, who deserted to another club, found it expedient to return but did not achieve the presidency until December 1790. He hoped to tame the leading spirits by appointing them to ministries under the Crown: 'When the Jacobins are ministers, they will not be Jacobin ministers.'[1] But by the beginning of 1791 the composition of the Society had radically changed with only 200 deputies in a total of 1,200 members.

In mid-April, a fortnight after Mirabeau's death, the club took over the former Jacobin church, now become national property. As political rivalries and pressures increased, the divisions were reflected in the positions members took up in the debating chamber: on the right the monarchists, members of the defunct club of '89, soon to establish a new society of their own at the Feuillant monastery; on the left the reformers, who were to give the Cordeliers Club its reputation for revolutionary extremism. After the great schism of April, when the right-wingers quit, Robespierre steadily increased his hold on the Jacobins, although the self-denying ordinance of the Constitutional Assembly kept him out of the legislature for a year. During this period he learned how to appeal to the masses as well as to the members – to the spectators in the public galleries whose interruptions, applause or catcalls could not be controlled by the ushers. The workers and fishwives elbowed out the elegant intellectual ladies who had attended the early debates. Deputations of patriots marched in to salute the president to the sound of *Ça ira!* – even a battalion of volunteers for the Vendée, accompanied by their band. By the time that Fouché reached Paris as a deputy in the autumn of 1792, Robespierre was firmly established at the club.

It was not favourable ground on which to confront him. Yet it was the best available. In the club Fouché had a certain control over events from the presidential chair. In the Convention precisely the same advantage rested with Robespierre – with the added consideration that Fouché lacked the ability to deliver public speeches effectively.

The session of June 11, 1794, began with the customary reading of correspondence and then passed to the *scrutin épuratoire* of Dumont and Javogues. This nightly ritual, begun at the end of November 1793 and still far from completed, consisted in the examination of the true republican principles of members by putting to them such questions as *How much were you worth in 1789; how much are you worth now? If you have increased your fortune how did you do it? What have you done for the revolution?* Robespierre had used it on occasion to have some of his rivals expelled – Anacharsis Cloots, the self-styled Orator of Mankind, for instance. And expulsion from the Jacobins was a long, though not final, stride towards the guillotine.

There was good reason for Robespierre to wish for the purging of Dumont and Javogues, for both had openly opposed his cult of the Supreme Being. Dumont had introduced atheism as official policy during his mission to the Somme; Javogues was equally anti-religious. Fouché had fallen out with him because of the wildly terrorist line he had pursued in the department of the Ain. But Javogues was indebted to Fouché for having protected him against Robespierre's nominee, Gouly; and he hated Robespierre for having sent his lieutenant and friend, Lapalus, to the guillotine at the same time as Chaumette. He was one of the earliest members of the secret group that Fouché was organizing against Robespierre. The scrutiny was concluded; each man was adjudged to be a worthy member of the society.

After this initial triumph, Fouché passed to the next business – the reception of a delegation of Jacobins from Nevers, who had come to answer criticisms of the parent club, and did so by presenting counter-complaints. The president, perhaps over-elated, took it upon himself to reply to them. Anxious to protect himself in public against the charges of moderatism that he knew Robespierre was spreading about him in private, he chided the Nivernais for having been misled – by his old friend Chaumette – into leniency towards suspects and harshness towards honest sans-culottes. Then, switching to what was clearly a direct attack on Robespierre, he urged them to summon up 'the strength and courage to devote yourselves to the defence of patriots and the annihilation of their oppressors. Brutus rendered homage worthy of the Supreme Being when he plunged the steel into the heart of him who was conspiring against the liberty of his country!'[2]

Robespierre took up the challenge – not as one directly involved but as an interested observer of the debate. He was ignorant of what had gone on in the Nièvre, he said. Everybody knew, of course, that Nevers had been one of the principal centres of Chaumette's conspiracies, with the connivance of partisans of foreign powers. 'If the president knows all the details of the Nevers business, it is his duty to explain himself.'

Fouché saw the trap; but his foot was half-way in. To withdraw it he had to offer a little more information, hurriedly adding that he 'had never seen Chaumette except in public'[3] and that was at a time when he was still regarded as a defender of liberty. 'Afterwards he returned to Paris to pursue his abominable trade of assassin of all public and private morality.'[4]

Robespierre was on his feet again. It was astonishing that the president spoke only of trivialities. Since Chaumette had laid his plots in Nevers it was impossible for the representative, and the local Jacobin Society, to have been unaware of them.

'It is not enough to cast mud on Chaumette's grave now, when the monster has perished on the scaffold. He should have been withstood before his death. There are those who have been work-ing evil long enough while speaking the language of republicans; there are those spewing imprecations against Danton today, who were his accomplices a short time ago. There are others who appear to spout fire in defence of the Committee of Public Safety and are sharpening their daggers to use against it!'[5]

The hall rang with applause. Fouché parried Robespierre's further questions and weathered the storm. At the end of the evening he was an isolated figure in the presidential chair.

Robespierre returned to the assault next day in the Convention. He attacked the Representatives who had been recalled from their mis-sions in the public interest and whose pride was being played upon, whose ears were being filled with the poison of calumny, transform-ing them into enemies of the government. These successors of Dan-ton and Hébert were forming a snowball that they hoped would grow larger and larger.

He was well informed. Fouché was canvassing support from others who, like himself, were earmarked for destruction by Robespierre because they had exercised vice-regal powers in the rebel towns – Tallien back from Bordeaux; Barras and Fréron from Toulon. Robespierre's police of the *Bureau de la Surveillance Administrative* had him under observation.

In Lyons the National Agent and the local Jacobins ferreted out 'all the proofs' and sent them to the Revolutionary Tribunal 'so that you may have the sweet satisfaction of judging those individuals whose patriotism has been nothing but a mask'.[6]

On June 13 Robespierre urged the Committee of Public Safety to order the arrest of Fouché, Tallien and others. The Committee, still smarting under the high-handed way in which he had pushed through the law of 22 prairial, refused.

Fouché, warned of Robespierre's request, disappeared from the apartment in the rue Honoré, 'spending more than six weeks away from his home, changing his hiding-place every night, and pursued from refuge to refuge'.[7]

4

Though he dared not sleep at home for fear of being whisked away in a nocturnal domiciliary visit by one of Robespierre's agents, Fouché still made fleeting appearances in the Convention and even in the corridors and cabinets of the north wing of the Tuileries. He had formed a nucleus of opposition from among those immediately threatened: nine deputies, including Legendre, Tallien, Dubois-Crancé, Bourdon de l'Oise, and Chénier, who met secretly at the lodgings of Lecointre. Tallien, desperate to save the life of his imprisoned mistress, Thérèse Cabarrus, as well as his own, confided to Fouché that he intended to stab Robespierre to death in the Convention. Fouché was horrified: 'Robespierre's popularity would have outlived him and we should have been sacrificed on his grave!'[1]

Convinced that his small resistance party needed stronger support, he decided, with typical audacity, 'to go direct to those who shared the control of the Terror with Robespierre and whom I knew to be envious or frightened of his immense popularity'.[2] He spoke separately to Collot, Carnot and Billaud – all old acquaintances from Lyons, Arras and Juilly.

> 'I painted them such a lively and true picture of the danger they were in, that I inspired them not only with distrust but also with the courage to oppose any further decimation of the Convention by the tyrant. "Count your votes in your Committee," I told them, "and you will see that if you are resolute he can be reduced to the impotent minority of [himself], Couthon and Saint-Just. Refuse him your vote and reduce him to isolation by sheer inertia." '[3]

Despite his pleas and warnings, none of them was yet prepared to risk incurring Robespierre's wrath. In the Committee of General

Security he found more readiness to listen. Here, envy and fear were bolstered by resentment. Robespierre's encroachment on their police powers had turned them all against him. And by chance they had a weapon lying close to hand: the Mother of God.

In a third-floor apartment which she shared with the widow Godefroy at No. 1078 rue Contrescarpe, a narrow street on the left bank, between the Observatory and the wine markets, the elderly Catherine Théot had founded a small sect which believed that 'she was the Virgin who would receive the infant Jesus',[4] for his second coming. The apartment was raided in January by the police of the Commune, on Chaumette's instructions, but the meetings continued. The Committee of General Security, which was anti-Christian, maintained a watch on the house, and on May 17 sent their secretary Sénart to arrest Catherine Théot with several of her disciples including a former Carthusian monk, Antoine-Christophe Gerle. On Gerle they found a paper signed by Robespierre, who had known him when Gerle was a member of the Constituent Assembly and also of the Jacobin Club. It certified that he had 'always seemed, although a priest, a good patriot'.[5] For good measure, questioning revealed that, presumably because of his opposition to the anti-clericalists in the Convention, Catherine Théot's followers regarded Robespierre as 'a messenger from heaven',[6] whose name was included in their prayers and adorations.

On June 15, Vadier, the President of the Committee, appeared before the Convention to denounce 'the semi-scholars, doctors, lawyers and idle capitalists who detest the revolution', who had joined the sect. 'There are some who have been discovered to be in touch with *émigré* priests in London . . . This gang is made up of nothing but royalists, usurers, madmen, egotists, muscadins and counter-revolutionaries of both sexes.'[7] He raised a laugh with Sénart's description of the admission ceremony. 'Catherine Théot said to me, "My son, I receive you into the ranks of my chosen ones; you will be immortal." Then she kissed me on the forehead, the ears, the cheeks, the eyes, the chin, and pronounced the sacramental words, "Grace is instilled". Afterwards she passed the tip of her disgusting tongue over my lips and Gerle pronounced these words: "*Diffusa est gratia in labiis tuis.*"'[8]

Vadier admitted that ridicule and pity would be the appropriate response to these fantastic goings on 'were they not linked with the circle of conspiracies which proliferate in so many guises with the intention of leading us back to tyranny'.[9] He therefore proposed that Théot and Gerle and their associates should be sent for trial by the Revolutionary Tribunal.

He made no mention of Robespierre, but pamphlets were circulated surreptitiously, giving the text of a letter found under the Mother of God's mattress in which she referred to Robespierre as 'her first prophet, her beloved minister' and praised him for 'the honours that he rendered to the Supreme Being, her son'.[10] Since Catherine Théot could read but not write, this was evidently a forgery. But Robespierre could not afford to have the affair come to trial. He consulted the President of the Tribunal, Dumas, and the Public Prosecutor, Fouquier-Tinville. Uncertain that their combined efforts could give him security, he called on the Committee of Public Safety to support him. Face to face with him their courage failed. They agreed to a postponement and a new inquiry – which Robespierre would conduct in person.

Distrustful of the Convention and the Committees, Robespierre withdrew temporarily from both. For the conflict that lay ahead he decided to strengthen his position in the Jacobin Club, where he could appeal to the people over the head of the government, and in the Paris Commune, which would provide him with the ultimate argument – the power of its national guard and its armed mob.

He was dependent more than ever on his police bureau. As Messidor, the month of Reaping, drew to a close, one name appeared more and more frequently on the reports he received from his secret agent, Guérin: that of the deputy Fouché of Nantes. From this moment, Barras recorded, 'at the head of those he had marked for death stood Fouché'.[11]

The stifling heat of the unusually oppressive, thunderous July bore down on his nerves. In the Jacobins he attacked the newspapers, complained of a campaign of lies against him, warned of new plots against the republic, and used a speech in praise of the martyred Chalier as a peg to denounce the man who had 'persecuted the patriots of Commune-Affranchie with a skill and perfidiousness as cowardly as it was cruel'.[12] He demanded that Fouché should attend the club to defend his policies and actions. 'I look on Fouché as the leader of the conspiracy we have to overthrow.'[13] Privately he said: 'Within a fortnight Fouché's head must fall on the scaffold, or mine will.'[14]

5

'The Society of Jacobins has invited me to justify myself,' Fouché wrote to his sister, citizeness Broband, in Nantes. 'I have not gone, because Robespierre reigns as master there. That Society has become his criminal court. You will soon hear the result of all this – which I hope will turn out to the benefit of the Republic.'[1] The citizeness was under observation. The letter was intercepted by one of the commissioners in Nantes, Bô, and sent back to Paris for the Committee of Public Safety, to 'strike down the conspirators without mercy'.[2]

Fouché was in a very vulnerable position. The Committee of Public Safety – where he had three certain enemies in Robespierre, Couthon and Saint-Just – was still considering his report on his stewardship at Lyons. He demanded in the Convention that the Committee should pronounce its opinion, but the Committee remained silent. Careful not to set foot in the Jacobins, he sent a written request to the secretary that judgement on him should be suspended until the Convention had received the report.

When the secretary read this to the club, Robespierre had in his pocket another intercepted letter that had just been brought to him. It was from Fouché to his sister, and said, 'Robespierre has only a few more days to reign.'[3] He leaped to his feet: 'I begin by declaring that Fouché as an individual is not of the slightest interest to me. If I have been associated with him it was because I believed him to be a patriot. When I denounced him here it was less because of his past crimes than because he had gone into hiding in order to commit others, and because I regard him as the leader of the conspiracy that we must destroy.'[4]

He denounced Fouché's inexcusable absence. 'Does he fear the eyes and ears of the people? Does he fear that his miserable face will visibly reveal his crimes, that 6,000 piercing glances will discover his true soul in his eyes and read his thoughts there, despite nature's efforts to hide them?' It was a cheap jeer, but it sharply conjured up Fouché's hooded eyes in the bloodless bony face. 'Any man who fears the scrutiny of his fellow citizens is guilty . . . Why does he refuse to appear? . . . I summon Fouché to judgement here!'[5] The members voted to expel him – the man who had been their president a month before.

A deceptive quiet descended on the rue Honoré. The tumbrils no longer jolted their wretched cargoes of the condemned towards the Place de la Révolution, past the Jacobin Club and Robespierre's lodgings and the apartment where Fouché was never at home. The residents had complained and the guillotine was now in the Place du Trône-Renversé, clattering away for longer hours than ever. At two or three o'clock every afternoon the lists of suspects – four or five hundred at a time – were brought to the north wing of the Tuileries and, as Carnot admitted, almost always signed without scrutiny. Robespierre sent his orders for others to sign, and had theirs brought to him in his study at the Duplays.

Guérin reported that Fouché's associates were urging him to make a public statement – and thus a reply to Robespierre – about the Lyons accusations. Fouché answered that they must first close their ranks. 'You are on the list!' he warned them. 'You are on the list as well as me – I am certain of it!'[6]

He had other worries. Each time that he ventured home he found Bonne-Jeanne more concerned about the baby, Nièvre. 'Our poor little girl is in an alarming state of exhaustion,' he wrote to his sister on 3 Thermidor (July 20), 'but we still have hope; we will save her with care and patience. I have nothing new to tell you about my affair, which has developed into that of all patriots . . . A few more days; then truth and justice will triumph resplendently.'

Two days later he wrote to his brother: 'Do not worry, patriotism will triumph over tyranny . . . Today, perhaps, we shall see the traitor unmasked . . . Our little one's condition still worries us. A thousand hugs for Mother and all our friends.'

To the impartial observer his optimism seemed to have little justification. Saint-Just, whom Robespierre had summoned back from the battlefront to help him withstand the attacks at home, was pressing his fellow members of the Committee to sign a report on the Lyons inquiry that would certainly send Fouché to the guillotine. In the Jacobins Couthon denounced the moving of the militia artillery from Paris. Rightly guessing that it was Fouché who had persuaded Carnot to take this step in disarming Robespierre, he accused Fouché and Carnot of corruption, thus echoing Robespierre's attack nine days before on 'men whose hands are full of pillage and crime'.[7] Accusations of peculation and bribery were levelled against each other by all the notable figures of the Revolution. No man could have been less vulnerable to the charge at that time than Fouché, whose 'garret', as Barras described it, in the rue Honoré, indicated the opposite of wealth. The great fortune that he eventually amassed was founded several years later; he was at the moment entering a period of considerable poverty.

On the other hand, it soon became clear that Robespierre's confidence was shaken; that he felt a need to stave off Fouché's attack until he was better prepared to meet it. On July 24 he was at the Jacobins when, towards the end of the session, the president – the same Dr Gouly whom Fouché had evicted from his post in the Ain – invited him to reveal the details of the conspiracies that he had denounced in earlier debates. Robespierre bounded to the tribune and, to everybody's surprise, upbraided the president and successfully called for the session to be concluded.

Next day Fouché was invited to Collot d'Herbois's lodgings and, to his astonishment, found Robespierre awaiting him there. Robespierre said that he did not wish to quarrel with his former friends and was willing to settle the differences between them. Fouché, according to his own account, answered: 'I do not come to terms with tyrants,'[8] and turned on his heel. Despite his deep personal grief – Nièvre had just died – his heart must have leapt at this first clear indication that Robespierre was losing his nerve. It was the seventh day of Thermidor, the month of Heat. He went in search of Tallien. 'The split is complete,' he said. 'We must strike tomorrow.'[9]

His offer of a truce rejected, and unable to bring his opponents to bay in the Jacobin Club, Robespierre was forced to meet them on their own ground: in the Convention. On July 26, his short legs elegant in white silk stockings, an exercise book with notes for his speech tucked under the arm of his sky-blue coat, the fearsome dictator made his way to the tribune for the first time for many days. He realized that fear could be a double-edged weapon now. If they were frightened too much the deputies might turn against him, trample him down in Gadarene panic before he could pick them off one by one.

He began gently, addressing himself to the moderates and the few who remained of the right. He protested his desire to clasp the hand of every upright man. He denounced the whispering campaign against him with the disbelieving horror of a man who would never harm a fly. 'Is it true that they have touted round odious lists, indicating a number of members of the Convention as victims, and purporting to be the work of the Committee of Public Safety, and consequently mine? . . . Is it true that this imposture has been circulated so cunningly and audaciously that a great number of members have not dared stay in their homes at night?'[10]

He attacked the members of both Committees, explaining that he had remained at home for the past six weeks because he felt himself unable to do good or to prevent the evil for which they were responsible. He attacked the Finance Committee, hinting that he had a new fiscal policy that would bear less harshly on earnings and savings. And then he rounded on the 'foul apostles of atheism and immorality'. He harked back to the barracking at the Festival of the Supreme Being: 'Would you believe that the President of the National Convention, speaking to the assembled people, was insulted by . . . men [who] were representatives of the people?' He attacked Fouché directly: 'No, Chaumette! No, Fouché! Death is not an eternal slumber!'[11]

He appealed to the spectators in the galleries and to the crowded turbulent sections of Paris beyond them: 'Remember that if Justice does not rule with an absolute sway in the Republic, Liberty is but a vain name . . . Remember that every man who rises to defend the public interest and morality will be overwhelmed with insults and proscribed by the rogues!'[12] They were silent, hypnotized once more by the endless string of moral pearls that came from the lips of this incorruptible paragon.

He folded his notes and returned to his seat. The applause broke like thunder. There was a motion for the traditional compliment: that the speech be printed at the public expense. Couthon, seeking to drive home the advantage, proposed that a copy should be sent to every Commune in the Republic.

It was a fatal refinement. The victims were given time to realize the danger in which they stood; to recall Fouché's warning that they must unite or be dispatched one by one; to decide to fight before it was too late. Vadier, feeling the sharp edge of Robespierre's revenge for the Théot report already on his neck, sprang to the tribune to protest his innocence. Cambon, the moving spirit of the Finance Committee, leaped to his feet, demanding the right to reply next: 'Before I am dishonoured, I will speak to France!'[13]

Using Robespierre's favourite defence, he turned the weapon on his assailant. Not he but Robespierre was hand in glove with the speculators. Not he but Robespierre was the man responsible for France's ills. 'It is time to speak the whole truth: one man alone paralysed the will of the National Convention. That man is the one who has just spoken. It is Robespierre.'[14]

Suddenly the hall was drowned in uproar and confusion, Billaud demanding that the speech be debated point by point, Robespierre interrupting to claim the right to speak, others shouting him down with 'we all ask to speak!';[15] then fresh denunciations from his associates, his underlings, those who had gladly been his lackeys until now.

At the height of it all, the name of the man who had engineered the great upheaval was tossed into the storm. Panis, the deputy for Paris, accused Robespierre of having included him in the list of victims to be sent to the guillotine. 'I want Robespierre's explanation on that point – and in regard to Fouché.'[16] 'I fear nobody, I have defamed nobody!' Robespierre shouted. 'And Fouché?'[17] Panis repeated. 'I do not wish to discuss him at this moment,' Robespierre shouted back. 'I stand aside from all this. I listen only to my duty . . .!'[18]

They clamoured for him to name the members he was accusing. He refused, and their fear grew. The motion to print his speech and send a copy to every Commune was at last put to the vote – and defeated. It was five o'clock in the afternoon. He had still the Jacobins and the mob to rely on.

At the Jacobins that evening he found Billaud and Collot already in their seats, flushed with victory. Amid a tumult from their supporters, Collot and Robespierre each demanded the right to speak first. It was quickly apparent that here, at least, the Robespierrists were still in the majority. They shouted down all opposition and their champion went to the tribune, 'a smallish man of slender build, narrow-featured, his forehead pinched in at the sides like a beast of prey, his mouth long, pale and tightly compressed'.[19] It was evident at once that he had recovered his composure, and that he had no thought of compromise.

Those who had tried to speak first he dismissed curtly and disdainfully: 'I thank them for identifying themselves so clearly and for having let me the more easily recognize my enemies and those of my country.'[20] Then he read the speech he had delivered in the Convention. Again it was greeted with wild applause. When Collot rose to make his reply he was howled down by members and the spectators in the gallery. Lacoste, the president, himself opposed to Robespierre, tried vainly to restore order. Billaud, attempting to support Collot, was greeted with the chant of 'To the guillotine! The conspirators to the guillotine!' 'I shall expect you at the Revolutionary Tribunal tomorrow!' yelled Dumas, its president.[21]

The crippled Couthon drove the advantage home. 'This is the deepest conspiracy we have yet encountered . . . I demand that we should debate not Robespierre's speech but the conspiracy. We shall see them appear on this platform, the conspirators; we will examine them . . . They will turn pale in the presence of the people. They will be convicted and they will perish!' The motion was accepted with acclamation, members and spectators on their feet, waving their hats in the air and yelling 'The conspirators to the guillotine!'[22]

Since 8 p.m. members of the two Committees had been gathering at the Tuileries, suspiciously eyeing Saint-Just, who sat in one of the offices writing the speech he was to deliver in the Convention and which would certainly be a defence of Robespierre and a sharp attack on his enemies. After midnight, Billaud, Collot and Lacoste returned from the Jacobins, frightened and fuming over their defeat, and relieved to find somebody on whom to release their emotions. 'There is a triumvirate of rogues, Robespierre, Couthon and Saint-Just, scheming against the country!' shouted Lacoste. 'I know you may have us murdered tonight, or perhaps we shall be struck down by your plotting tomorrow,' Collot accused Saint-Just to his face, 'but we are determined to die at our posts. And perhaps before that we shall be able to unmask you!' 'A cripple, a child and a rogue,' sneered Barère. 'I wouldn't put you in charge of a chicken-run!'[23]

They regrouped in an adjoining room. In every man's mind was the memory of June 2 the year before, when the mobs had poured into the streets, summoned by Robespierre, and the deputies had been held captive in their own debating chamber until they agreed to the rabble's demands. Was he ready to call them out again? Could he count on the support of the Paris National Guard or the cadets of the École de Mars whom he had been courting recently? They sent for Lescot-Fleuriot, the mayor of Paris, and Payan, the National Agent to the Commune. Neither man answered the summons; since the end of the debate in the Convention they had been mobilizing the sections, checking arms and ammunition, conferring with Henriot, commander of the National Guard and one of Robespierre's fervent disciples.

The committee-men argued among themselves whether to put the young, energetic, menacing Saint-Just under arrest. When they asked what he was writing in his speech he replied that he had not finished it, but would read it to them at ten o'clock in the morning, before delivering it in the Convention. At 5 a.m. he left, and they still had not made up their minds whether to stop him or not. They gave instructions for Fouché to be fetched – to find out what news he had.

6

The date was July 27, 1794, the ninth day of Thermidor. Fouché arrived at the Tuileries at mid-morning for his interview with the two Committees. The occasion was given piquancy – and robbed of much of its value – by the fact that he was the only man in the room who knew which of the others were his secret allies. He could only assure them that there were now many who had pledged their support. Victory was certain if they would hold firm. Like Robespierre on June 2, 1793, he intended to be absent from the explosion he had set in train, free to take counter-measures if plans went wrong. When he left the palace, before noon, the deputies were already gathering in the great hall.

An hour after the session opened Saint-Just strode to the tribune, confidence clearly written on his long handsome face. Beneath him, as he spread out his notes, sat Robespierre. The two tiers of public galleries were packed. He began to speak.

He had scarcely delivered a hundred words when Tallien began to shout. Hardly a dozen people could have heard exactly what he said, but the sense was apparent: he was denouncing a conspiracy. The heads that had turned towards him swung back in the direction of the tribune. There, unaccountably, astoundingly, Saint-Just had paused. Instead of continuing his speech, talking the interruption down, he stood fumbling for words, visibly bereft of self-possession.

Seizing this unimagined opportunity, Tallien ran to the foot of the tribune and then, seeing Saint-Just still hesitant, leaped up the steps and bustled him aside. As he did so, Billaud entered the chamber, the conference of the committee-men having just broken up. When Tallien paused for a moment, Billaud took his place. Then Billaud made way for Tallien. Saint-Just remained slumped in his seat, exhausted by his long night's work or by the recognition of defeat. From the tribune came frenzied denunciations of a plot against the People's Liberty, a motion that the Assembly, facing dire peril, should vote itself into permanent session.

Robespierre rose from his seat, desperate to stem the flow of accusations and the applause they were arousing, and evidently intent on supplanting Billaud and Tallien by force if necessary. He had no sooner set foot on the tribune steps than the hall began to echo with shouts of 'Down with the tyrant!'[1] He halted, as if not believing his ears; and returned to his place. The shouting died. Above him Billaud called for the arrest of Henriot and the staff-officers of the National Guard. Robespierre got to his feet again. This time he reached the platform, while the roar of 'Down with the tyrant!' grew deafening. His mouth was moving, but his words could not be heard.

Barère appeared beside him, shouldering him out of the way. Robespierre clutched at the lectern, holding on for a moment, then giving ground. Howls and hooting accompanied him as he descended the steps. A jeering speech from Vadier was followed by a new attack on the alleged conspiracy by Tallien. Robespierre tried to interrupt from his seat; but each time his words were drowned by 'Down with the tyrant!' In lulls of the storm he could be heard crying 'Brigands! Cowards! Hypocrites! By what right does the President protect these assassins?'[2]

'Assassins!' screamed Tallien. 'You hear him, the monster, he calls us assassins!'[3] There were answering shouts of 'Arrest him! Arrest him!' Robespierre scurried from one end of the chamber to the other, mouthing pleas and reproaches. In the continuing uproar the motion for his arrest was proposed and accepted. He made for the tribune once more, changed his mind, collapsed breathless in his seat, sprang to his feet, shouted defiance and abuse. Ushers entered and led him out.

Payan, as spokesman of 'the Revolutionary Commune of the 9th Thermidor, destined by the people and on behalf of the people to save the country and the National Convention attacked by base conspirators', ordered the arrest of Fouché and thirteen others, 'to deliver the Convention from the oppression in which they hold it',[4] and sent an armed party to the Tuileries to rescue Robespierre. He was no longer there, having been taken to the Luxembourg prison – where the concierge refused to admit him and sent him to the Mairie on the quai des Orfèvres. He was set free, but refused to leave. It was after ten before he agreed to attend the council meeting of the Commune in the Hôtel de Ville.

Here, despite the opportunity to prepare during the days leading up to the crisis, all was confusion. Henriot, captured while drunk, had recently been rescued by Coffinhal, the deputy president of the Revolutionary Tribunal. Some of the hesitant sections had swung to the Convention, but there was a strong array of armed men drawn up outside on the Place de Grève, awaiting orders from the Commune or the man they had come to save.

No orders arrived. Rain began to fall. The ranks thinned and soon there was nobody to oppose the troops of the Convention who marched into the square and then scattered through the town hall, racing up and down staircases, bursting open doors. As they hunted they heard the sound of a pistol shot, and found Robespierre lying with a broken jaw but still alive. It was an hour or so before dawn.

By dusk, declared an outlaw and thus deprived even of the mockery of a trial, he had perished with monstrous cruelty at the guillotine.

7

The Republic without Robespierre was a vacuum that many rushed to fill. Had Fouché been ready for power he could have joined the closest of his fellow conspirators, Tallien, Fréron and Barras, in their swing to the popular right; or stayed close to Billaud, Collot and Barère, who planned to retain their positions by continuing the Terror. Instead he took up a position between the two, out of any current that could carry him to office. It was not from lack of ambition, though there may have been some lack of opportunity – he was again merely the ex-commissioner around whose neck hung an ugly terrorist record. Almost certainly he was himself confused about his purpose, his future and his past. The triumph of French arms – Tourcoing, Fleurus, the repelling of the Spanish invasion, the reconquest of Belgium – had dispelled the fear of invasion that had justified the Terror. On the other hand, the republican and egalitarian reforms that he had fought for during the past five years were still close to his heart – he could not support reaction. What France needed after this nervous crisis was a period of peace, a smooth middle road, assessment of the changes brought about by the Revolution and conservation of the gains. Always provided, of course, that the gains were calculated on his own left-biased scales.

The Jacobins restored him to membership three days after Robespierre's death. In August, supporting a deputation from Lyons which complained of persecution by the local Jacobins, he pleaded for 'the unfortunate victims of the ferocious brigandage that has reigned [there] for three months in the name of Maximilian the First'.[1] In September he warned that 'any thought of indulgence, of moderatism, is a counter-revolutionary thought'.[2] In November he voted in favour of putting Carrier on trial for the murder of prisoners at Nantes. He supported the restoration of civil rights and its ancient name to Lyons, but asked that the Convention should first take action against those who had robbed their fellow-citizens and municipal funds. And while he tacked moderately along this middle course he watched the leaderless Convention allow 'terror to give way to anarchy, anarchy to reaction and revenge'.[3]

This policy, or lack of one, was not likely to endear him to either side while the struggle for power went on. In January 1795 his former ally, Tallien, denounced him in the Convention for supporting the attacks of the extreme socialist Babeuf. Fouché frankly admitted the association, made pointed allusions to Tallien's scabrous record while on mission at Bordeaux, and got the best of the exchange, scoring one of his rare debating successes. But the time for talking was fast slipping by. The repeal of the control of prices coupled with requisitioning, food and fuel shortage, inadequate wages and almost total loss of confidence in paper money, had brought France to the brink of violence again.

In April and again in May the sans-culottes raged through the streets demanding bread (now rationed to two ounces a day). The deputy Ferraud, guilty of nothing more than having a name that could be mistaken for Fréron (now a great patron of the right-wing *ieunesse dorée*), was seized by the mob and decapitated. The severed head was paraded on a pole into the Convention and under the nose of the President, Boissy d'Anglas. 'Surrounded by pikes pointed at his chest, naked sabres held above his head, grazed by many pistol bullets which struck the wall behind his chair, a target for the most horrifying threats, he bared his breast to the madmen with calm and dignity.'[4] He was bundled aside and a new president and secretaries chosen from the Mountain. It was not until after dark and by the aid of two bayonet charges by national guardsmen that the chamber was cleared.

The shock brought a sharp reaction. In the Convention the Montagnards were forced on to the defensive. Hyde de Neuville, a young royalist sympathizer who had met Fouché in the Nièvre, came across him in the Tuileries gardens a day or two after Ferraud's murder and found him 'downcast' and 'irresolute'.[5] The government set up a military commission to try the ringleaders. The White Terror swelled up in the wake of the Red. In Lyons the members of the Company of Jesus raided the prisons in search of the *matevons* who had pollarded so many royalist heads. They dragged them into the streets, lynched them, and threw their bodies into the river.

Through June and July, one district after another sent to the Convention its accusations against Fouché the former Terrorist. From the Nièvre, Lormes and Clamecy added their complaints to those of Nevers; Grannat and Moulins joined in from the Allier; the many accusations from Lyons were still on the files of the reorganized Committee of Public Safety. It seemed that he would almost have been luckier to have shared the fate of Collot and Billaud and the other Terrorists who had been brought to trial and shipped off to Cayenne, four months before. Finally, in a session that began on August 9 and dragged on into the small hours of the next day, the long-delayed report on his mission to Lyons was debated. Legendre and, surprisingly, Tallien spoke in his defence, describing how he had been the first to make an open attack on Robespierre in the Jacobin Club and how he had kept the conspiracy together and led them to the kill. It was not a strong enough testimonial, and not from a sufficiently pure source. The Convention ordered his arrest.

Next day he was still at liberty. And next week. And next month. He had already developed the inexplicable immunity from constraint which remained with him throughout his life. In an age when arrest was a commonplace, with a habit of taking risks that astounded his contemporaries, treading a line that took him beyond the protection of established parties, he nevertheless spent not a single day in prison. His critics attributed it to blackmail, and corruption. In the autumn of 1795 it was more likely because of his usefulness to the government. Through the intelligence services of his socialist friends he learned what their right-wing opponents were up to. By the time the royalists came out on the streets on October 5, and were scattered by General Bonaparte's whiff of grapeshot, Fouché was working closely with Barras, who was appointed to the newly-created Directory a month later.

He needed employment. His income from St-Domingue had dried up since the English invasion of the island and the abolition of slavery. He had taken Bonne-Jeanne from the lodgings in the rue Honoré and found a cheaper attic for them in the rue de la Convention – an attic that would soon have to accommodate three again, for they were expecting their second child.

Barras rewarded him with the post of government agent to the 10th and 11th military divisions, with the responsibility for 'collecting and sending to the armies, deserters and citizens of the first call-up'.[6] It was no easy task. 'Resources were lacking no less in men than in money, clothing and provisions,' said Barras. 'Firm men were needed, accustomed to deal with difficulties and not to be frightened by them.'[7]

Fouché made Narbonne his headquarters and 'set about his work quietly, without any commotion, without getting himself talked about; in Paris we didn't know what had become of him'.[8] He was wise to lie low. 'Under a government of which I was one of the founders, I was, if not proscribed, at least in complete disgrace.'[9]

He completed his mission in the spring of 1796. With Bonne-Jeanne and his baby son, he moved out to St-Leu in the Montmorency valley, thirty miles from Paris. He was working on a new system of intensive pig-breeding. That he had other employment – probably as a secret agent for Barras – was indicated by a report from the Allier that he had reappeared at Moulins, where he was holding 'suspicious gatherings'.[10] In July there was another domestic tragedy – the baby died. He shared with his wife a great love of children; they had seven, of whom three died at an early age.

He switched from pig-breeding to flax-spinning, without great success. 'I have just learned,' he wrote to his sister in January 1797, 'that in Nantes they credit me with owning fine châteaux. In Spain, no doubt. The wretches! If I were like them I would certainly be rich. In my place they would have made an immense fortune. How would they be able to understand that I have sacrificed everything to my country and am left with only my work and my abilities?'[11] Shortly afterwards, he and Bonne-Jeanne returned to Paris; there was another baby on the way.

He called on Barras, who described him as 'in the direst distress' and 'perpetually pestering me to give him any kind of a place . . . which would provide for the most urgent needs of himself and his wife, an ex-nun as poor as himself'.[12] Barras, waspish as well as inaccurate, reported that Fouché's wife was 'known as "the virtuous woman", because she was hideously ugly, with reddish hair like her husband, even to her eyebrows and eyelashes'.[13] But he fully appreciated Fouché's qualities and was happy to make use of them now that the period of exile had effaced some of his notoriety.

It was probably on Barras's behalf that Fouché had unsuccessfully approached Babeuf, soon after the installation of the Directory, to get him to modify his attacks on the government. His inclination was to placate rather than to agitate. 'When one has power,' he said, 'the sensible thing is to maintain a conservative policy.'[14] Barras obtained from the Minister of War, General Schérer, an appointment for Fouché as one of the contractors to the army that was being assembled for the invasion of England: and in secret attached him to the Ministry of Police that had been formed to take on the work of the defunct Committee of General Security and Robespierre's *Bureau de Surveillance.*

In the first of these jobs – which brought him into contact with several bankers in France and the Low Countries, and with the great contracting firm of the Société de Saint-Ouen, from whose Paris offices he was allowed to conduct his business – he laid the basis of his later fortune, and provided immediate comfort for Bonne-Jeanne and their new baby, whom they named after three of the old saints and one of the republican graces: Joseph-Jean-Etienne-Liberté. In his second occupation he learned the rudiments of how – and particularly how not – to organize confidential police work and found the opportunity to be of further service to Barras – notably in forestalling the uprising of 18 Fructidor (September 4, 1797) which ended with the exile of two of Barras's rivals – Carnot and Barthélemy.

8

In December 1797, Paris celebrated the home-coming of the Conqueror of Italy. 'His complexion was pallid and of almost a yellowish hue, and long, sleek jet-black hair, like that of the *Talapouche* Indians of Florida, hung over both ears.'[1] The general opinion of the appearance of the twenty-eight-year-old General Bonaparte was not flattering. 'He is no more than five feet five,' said another observer, 'his face is pale, his cheeks hollow, his eyes small and lack-lustre; everything points to his being consumptive.'[2] And the verdict on his character was not much more enthusiastic than that on his health: 'His glances reveal profound dissimulation; he wishes to thwart all attempts to penetrate his thoughts, and this excessive reserve destroys confidence.'[3]

On this occasion he did not dissimulate his resentment at not being rewarded for his victories by a seat on the Directory. The article of the Constitution requiring every Director to be over the age of forty he dismissed as irrelevant. He reviewed the Army of England whose command he had been given, stared at the Channel that he would have to cross, then returned to Paris. To Fouché he remarked that the duty of a true patriot would be 'to blow the Directory sky-high',[4] but he did not think this particular moment propitious: 'the pear is not yet ripe'.[5] Instead he began making plans for an expedition to Egypt. With the Directory's permission, and to its profound relief, he sailed from Toulon on May 19, 1798.

The Italy that he had conquered was in turmoil. The French civil officials who had been sent to impose republican institutions and extort taxes were at loggerheads with the French generals whom Bonaparte had encouraged to regard the country as their private reserve and fief. In addition to the exaction of money, the great rape of Europe's art treasures had begun. Fouché's old friend Daunou, one of the civil commissioners in Rome, was at that moment arranging to transport to France '450 to 500 cases [of] books, manuscripts, medallions, antiques, pictures, marbles, statues, engravings and etchings'.[6] Austrian agents fomented discord and Italian patriots dreamed of liberation. In July the commander-in-chief of the French army in Italy, General Brune, went to Paris to complain of the blunders and chicanery'[7] of Trouvé, the French ambassador at Milan, capital of the Cisalpine Republic, and to ask for his recall.

Trouvé, a cousin of Bonaparte's brother-in-law, Leclerc, was also a protégé of the Director Larévellière Lépeaux; Brune, who did not conceal his leftish views and was suspected of favouring the liberation and unification of Italy, had only Barras to support him. He returned to his command with his demand unsatisfied. Learning that Trouvé planned to change the Cisalpine constitution (with French troops occupying the country, the title of ambassador was merely an euphemism for governor), Brune warned the existing government, so that Trouvé was compelled to make his changes by force. Worn down by the bickering, Trouvé resigned.

Barras saw an opportunity to revenge his defeat over Trouvé. Urging that an Austrian attempt to win back her lost Italian provinces was imminent, he persuaded his fellow-Directors to give Trouvé's post to Fouché, 'a man of firm character and strong will'.[8] Fouché arrived in Milan on October 12. Not in the best of health, and fatigued by a journey that had lasted more than a week, he welcomed the suggestion of the new Cisalpine Directors that he should postpone presenting his letters of credence until the tailors had completed their ceremonial uniforms. Trouvé continued in office in the meantime.

During the night of October 18/19 Brune informed the new Cisalpine Directors and 58 right-wing deputies that they were dismissed. Fouché sent a protest to Paris against this military intervention in civil affairs but there was widespread belief that he had connived at it. He was too fond of authority to allow fatigue or a nicety of dress to delay his taking up a post of this kind. The suspicion was confirmed when he made no further protest at Brune's forcible ejection of one of the Directors who refused to quit the Directorial palace. Years later he admitted that he had known of Brune's plan and approved it, since he believed it better to set up an independent government that might become France's ally, rather than a puppet one which would be unreliable in a time of crisis.

Trouvé went off to his new post at Stuttgart after sending Larévellière a warning that the Directors installed by Brune were alarming financiers and causing a flight of money from the Cisalpine Republic. His criticisms were supported by two French civil commissioners of finance: Faipoult and Amelot. Both men were members of the former *noblesse de la robe,* now finding a way back into public employment. In social background as well as political conviction, they were incompatible with the Jacobins Fouché and Brune.

Larévellière levelled his score with Barras by getting Brune posted to Holland and then supported Faipoult's attack on Fouché. 'People have thought him amenable to corruption,' Faipoult reported, using the handiest, least rebuttable and, in Italy, most plausible accusation. 'I cannot vouch for more than the public rumour; but it is my duty to make it known to you.' And Larévellière in turn felt it his duty to make it known to his fellow Directors, charging Fouché with behaving in 'a senseless manner . . . contrary to all reason and propriety'.[9]

Fouché received orders from Paris that the Directors whom Brune had dismissed were to be reinstated. On taking up his post he insisted that all correspondence between the two republics must pass through his hands. He was thus able to prevent these instructions being known to anybody in Milan, while he continued his argument with the French Directory. Here, as on so many occasions, his determination and self-confidence were remarkable. He had just been given the most important post of his career. He had only a year or so before been in great poverty. Yet he had not the slightest hesitation in disputing with his employers, disregarding and suppressing their instructions.

He was supported by Joubert, the general who had taken over Brune's command, but Barras was not ready for an open trial of strength with Larévellière – at any rate not on a minor issue. On November 25, 1798, he agreed that Fouché should be replaced by a special commissioner, Rivaud.

Rivaud arrived in Milan armed with a letter from the Directory ordering Fouché to leave Italy. Fouché 'took no notice of it, being convinced that the Directory had no right to prevent my living in Milan, as a private individual'.[10] Joubert had already left to direct the invasion of Piedmont. On December 7, he warned Fouché that Rivaud had ordered the expulsion of the government – and that Fouché himself was in danger of arrest.

Fouché went into hiding in a country house near Monza, taking with him a carriage, six horses and the embassy towels. From there he made his way to Turin, capital of Piedmont, where he was again in touch with Joubert. 'I have ordered him to leave Piedmont,'[11] Rivaud reported to the Directory on December 16. But the order had no effect. Rivaud told him he had received instructions from the Directory to expel him by force. In the end he was compelled to send a gendarme to Turin with the warrant. Fouché left a little ahead of him and was back in Paris on January 9, 1799.

Far from being abashed at his recall, he made it clear that he still considered himself right and the Directors wrong. 'I felt myself to be in a sufficiently strong position to ask for an explanation in person of their savage treatment of me, insisting on compensation for my dismissal – which I received, but with an urgent request not to make a scandal.'[12] On this last point he was not too careful. At a party at Barras's house he told him: 'The Army of Italy is unhappy at the measures the Directory is taking, which will only result in driving the Cisalpine Republic into the arms of the Emperor [of Austria]; I think it my duty to warn you, and you should certainly bear in mind that an enraged army can be fatal to usurpers like you.'[13] The Prussian ambassador, who reported the incident to Berlin, added that a warrant had been issued for Fouché's arrest. It was never served, perhaps because 'the scene has all the marks of a drama concocted by Barras and Fouché to disparage the other Directors'.

On his own admission, Fouché spent the next six months working on Barras's behalf to get rid of the other four Directors. He was supported by Brune and by Joubert, who had resigned his command and come to Paris, and – for different reasons – by Lucien Bonaparte in the Council of Five Hundred. The May elections produced more Jacobin deputies; by June only Barras remained of the old Directors – now joined by Sièyes, Gohier, Ducos and Moulin.

Fouché did not have long to wait for his reward. In the first week of July he was restored to ambassadorial rank as France's plenipotentiary in Holland, where the Batavian Republic was awaiting an allied invasion. He was teamed with Brune again. His most pressing duty – in which his predecessor, Lombard de Langres, had failed – was to persuade the cautious Batavians to place their troops under Brune's command. He arrived at the Hague on July 11, and presented his credentials on July 14. The following day he was able to report that the Batavians had agreed. It was none too soon. On July 18 news was received that an invasion force of British and Russian troops had already left Kronstadt; another was being assembled in the Thames.

The speed with which he had carried out his task made a striking impression in Paris. With Italy overrun and the Russians and Austrians advancing on the Rhine, the Directory was in as deep disgrace as ever, despite its reorganization. Jacobins, royalists, moderates – all were plotting against it. Nobody knew where trouble would come from, or who was fomenting it – only that it was on its way. Barras complained that the Minister of Police, Bourguignon, was 'not able to cope with the increasing disorder; he hardly sees it, can offer no explanation of it'. He suggested the post should be offered to Fouché who was 'alone capable of dealing the vigorous blow which will undoubtedly be necessary to save the Directory from the wickedness of its bitter enemies'.[14]

Sieyès, who was planning to get rid of Barras, surprisingly agreed. The Foreign Minister, Talleyrand, had pointed out to him that 'at a time when the Jacobins are showing themselves so audacious and so violent against you, none but a Jacobin can . . . knock them down. There is no better man than Fouché.'[15]

On July 21 the ministry was reconstructed with Bernadotte at the Ministry of War, Robert Lindet in charge of Finance, Cambacérès at the department of Justice, and Fouché as Minister of the General Police of the Republic.

Notes to Part II

Chapter 1

1 *Moniteur*, XX, 195
2 Robespierre, 263
3 *Moniteur*, XX, 204
4 Courtois, III, 75
5 *Salut public*, XII, 571

Chapter 2

1 Nodier, *Eloquence*, 26
2 *Moniteur*, XX, 407
3 Meillan, 109
4 Fouché, *Mémoires*, 45
5 Nodier, *Eloquence*, 27
6 Greer, 26
7 Hampson, 250

Chapter 3

1 Mirabeau, II, 228
2 *Moniteur*, XX, 730
3 *Ibid.*
4 *Ibid.*
5 *Ibid.*, 731
6 Courtois, II, 222
7 *Biographie des Ministres*, 143(5)

Chapter 4

1 Fouché, *Mémoires*, 46
2 *Ibid.*, 47
3 *Ibid.*
4 Mathiez, *Hist. rel.*, 108
5 *Ibid.*, 130
6 Levasseur, III, 198

7   *Ibid.*, 191
8   Sénart, 179
9   Levasseur, III, 193
10 Mathiez, *Hist. rel.*, 128
11 Barras, I, 224
12 *Moniteur*, XXI, 201
13 Walter, *Robespierre*, 617
14 Despatys, *Ami*, 325

Chapter 5

1   *Salut public*, XV, 345(1)
2   Rudé, 366
3   Barante, *Convention*, IV, 233
4   *Moniteur*, XXI, 261
5   *Ibid.*
6   Fouché, *Mémoires*, 46
7   Barras, III, 91
8   *Moniteur*, XXV, 454
9   Barante, *Convention*, IV, 233
10 Aulard, *Jacobins*, VI, 251
11 *Ibid.*, 264–6
12 *Ibid.*, 280
13 *Moniteur*, XXI, 329
14 *Ibid.*, 330
15 *Ibid.*
16 *Ibid.*
17 *Ibid.*
18 *Ibid.*
19 Nodier, *Eloquence*, 26
20 Aulard, *Jacobins*, VI, 282
21 *Ibid.*, 283
22 *Ibid.*, 284
23 *Réponses des membres*, 106

Chapter 6

1   *Moniteur*, XXI, 332
2   Walter, *Robespierre*, 433–4
3   *Ibid.*
4   *Réponses des membres*, 101

Chapter 7

1 *Moniteur,* XXI, 575
2 Aulard, *Jacobins,* VI, 402
3 Fouché, *Mémoires,* 49
4 Larévellière, I, 220
5 Hyde de Neuville, 127
6 Debibour, I, 116
7 Barras, II, 18–19
8 Barante, *Directoire,* III, 462
9 Fouché, *Mémoires,* 51
10 Cobb, *Armées révolutionnaires,* 882
11 Caillé, 9
12 Barras, III, 344
13 *Ibid.,* 91
14 Fouché, *Mémoires,* 56

Chapter 8

1 Nolte, 30
2 Girardin, III, 145
3 *Ibid.*
4 Barras, III, 345
5 Fouché, *Mémoires,* 59
6 Larévellière, III, 380
7 Bailleu, I, 228
8 Barras, III, 364
9 Larévellière, III, 476
10 Fouché, *Mémoires,* 65
11 Sciout, 207
12 Fouché, *Mémoires,* 67
13 Bailleu, I, 265
14 Barras, III, 525–6
15 *Ibid.*

PART III
Minister of Police
1799-1804

I

On July 30, 1799, Fouché returned to Paris and called on the Directors at the Luxembourg Palace. Within an hour he had taken the oath against anarchists and royalists and moved into his official quarters in the Hôtel de Juigné and its annexe the Hôtel d'Affry. The offices were at the rear, giving on to the rue des Sts-Pères; the private apartments looked out over the quai Malaquais. They were the most sumptuous lodgings he had ever had. The great salon was reputed to be 'the most beautiful room in Paris . . . a noble apartment, richly decorated'.[1] With a brief interval, this was to be his home for ten years. Here he and Bonne-Jeanne brought up the remainder of their seven children and, except on formal occasions, lived in quiet simplicity.

'His wife, passionately in love with him, as jealous as if he were only twenty years old, preferred this retired life. An aged female relation, Fouché's secretary, her daughter's witty governess, her sons' tutor, a few old Oratorian friends or humble family acquaintances playing a game of cards – that was their only company in the evenings. The children ran about the room; the grown-ups amused them with scraps of nonsense that made Fouché laugh until he cried; he would stroll over to the card table, watch the play . . . and go off to bed at ten, in the same room, it was said, as his wife and three of the children.'[2]

He was very fond of music and his more formal receptions became noted for the entertainment provided by players and singers from the Opera.

He had taken over a ministry that was notorious for its inefficiency. Since its re-establishment in 1798, after having been a subsidiary department of the Ministry of the Interior and subsequently of the two great Committees of the Convention, it had broken the reputation of one minister after another. It was riddled with Jacobin intrigue. It was a tangle of conflicting departmental interests and of corruption.

Fouché ignored the confusion and went to the heart of the matter. 'Within two hours I was acquainted with my administrative duties ... In the current state of affairs I felt that all my energy and skill ... must be devoted to confidential state police work (*haute police*), while the rest could be left without disadvantage to the senior officials. I consequently concentrated solely on seizing with a firm hand all the resources of the secret police and all the elements which constituted it.'[3] He saw himself as having two urgent tasks: 'to bring to light and to disperse the coalitions and legal oppositions against established authority; and to do the same with the sinister plots of the royalists and foreign agents'.[4] But from the latter the danger was much less pressing.

His opening move was typical: he had been appointed to deal with the imminent threat of renewed rioting in the streets. It was clear to everybody, however ill-informed, that the lead in this would be taken by Jacobins and other left-wing extremists. Yet on the third day after taking office he presented the Directory with a decree aimed against the royalists. It proposed that the two or three dozen conspirators who had evaded transportation after the abortive coup of the 18th Fructidor should be declared émigrés.

The Directors looked at each other in astonishment. Sieyès demanded to know why Fouché had come to waste their time over people 'who are to all intents and purposes dead, yet you don't say a word about the Jacobins who are unfortunately very much alive'. Fouché replied: 'If we try a frontal attack our success is doubtful; so we must turn the position . . . We must build up our popularity . . . Strike the first blow against the royalists. All the Jacobins will be with us in that – and next day we come down on the Jacobins.'[5]

He was as good as his word: next day he produced a proposal to control the political clubs which had begun to regain their power after the eclipse that succeeded the end of the Terror. With his usual self-assurance he had issued a personal statement announcing his intention to 're-establish interior calm and put an end to massacres'.[6] In the leading club, the Friends of Liberty, the new Minister of Police was violently attacked.

Sieyès came out strongly in support of Fouché. On the Champ de Mars, where he presided at the annual commemoration of the assault on the Tuileries, he fiercely criticized the Jacobins. As he ended his speech there was the sound of musketry and two or three balls whistled close to his head. Fouché suggested that the army must have been involved, and that the Jacobin-inclined military governor of

Paris, General Marbot, must have been aware of what was going on. An incensed Sieyès persuaded his colleagues to dismiss Marbot that night. A large number of deputies in the Council of Five Hundred claimed that this was the beginning of a counter-revolution, and the clubs took up the same cry. It seemed as if Fouché's proposal to curb the orators was doing more harm than good.

The Club of the Friends of Liberty and Equality, or Constitutional Society, was a recently revived descendant of the discredited Jacobin Club. In the summer of 1799 it was given permission to meet in the Manège, the royal riding school that had been the home of the National Assembly. Its brief existence had been remarkably stormy. Opened on July 6, with a membership of 3,000, including 250 deputies, it planted a Tree of Liberty on July 10, was the scene of a violent confrontation with *muscadins* on July 12, and was deprived of the use of the Manège on July 27. It then moved across the river to the Temple of Peace in the rue du Bac – the former church of St-Thomas d'Acquin which had provided Nantes with its first constitutional bishop. Its debates were fiery and extreme. Members had already put through a motion demanding that the government should declare a state of emergency.

On August 14, Fouché presented himself at the door of the club and, although not a member, insisted on his right to be admitted as a police official. As soon as he was inside he interrupted the debate to announce that the premises were to be closed immediately. The members, who had spent the past week denouncing him with mounting violence, meekly made their way out, leaving Fouché to lock the doors and present the keys to the Directors with a studied absence of drama. He asked them to issue a statement that 'the Royalists would be labouring under a strange delusion were they to see some advantage to themselves in this – the Directory is essentially republican'.[7]

In this post which fitted him like a glove his qualities became more clearly distinguishable; the Minister of Police was also the man: shrewd and sly, courageous and sometimes arrogant, above all confident. He went his own way. Because of that he made many enemies among his ministerial associates, but these were outnumbered many times by the friends he won by kindnesses.

Within a few weeks of taking office he had laid down the principles on which all his later work was based. In a letter to Nantes he defined the function of the police as providing 'security for all; the distinctive character of this ministry . . . is to prevent rather than repress, but to repress vigorously what one has not been able to prevent. Yet vigour must be justice not violence.'⁸

He was aware of criticism though not intimidated by it; and he did not hesitate to control it if he thought it harmful to the national interest. 'Liberty of thought and expression,' he said in September of that year, 'is not the right to incite, at the top of one's voice, passions and resentment against the government and authority; there can be no impunity for those who preach crime and organize revolt when the law punishes those who have been directed or seduced by them.'⁹ A defendable policy at a time when the nation's peace was threatened, it was to be taken to sinister extremes by Napoleon, who transformed it into totalitarian censorship.

As a corollary of his belief that prevention was better than cure, he preferred, when forced to take action, to do so discreetly rather than in a blaze of publicity – again in contrast to Napoleon, who believed that fear was always more potent than reason. In the West the troubles with the *chouans* of Normandy, Brittany and the Vendée had flared again after the Directory's enactment of a vicious and self-defeating hostage law which punished royalists through the property and freedom of their relations. Their capacity for full-scale warfare had long been exhausted, but the iniquity of the new law revived their will to resist. Aided by money and shipments of arms, guerrilla attacks were frequent at the time that Fouché moved into his ministry.

It was a problem that directly concerned the Ministry of War and the Ministry of the Interior. But it was the Minister of Police who took the decisive step – without previous consultation with his colleagues. To the royalist prisoners facing death or long periods of imprisonment, he offered liberty in return for co-operation – and found many ready to accept. 'I arranged means of escape which would not make them suspect by their own party, when they rejoined. Almost all of them gave useful service, and I can say that through them and the information they gave me I later succeeded in ending the civil war.'¹⁰

For those royalists who were tired of the struggle and wished to return to France in peace, he urged that the Directory should lower the barrier by removing their names from the list of *émigrés*. His willingness to recommend the vital *radiation* – the erasure from the roll of outlawry – brought him increasing popularity among the royalist sympathizers who had never left the country. So that by degrees the Terrorist of Lyons emerged as the unexpected lion of the reviving salons in the faubourg St-Germain.

Republican principles and an urbane cynicism protected him from flattery. He never trusted anybody, including his own colleagues and staff. He once remarked to Réal, the Prefect of the Seine, that his police were like stage-coaches: 'they have to do their journey whether they are empty or full. A policeman has to make a report every day to earn his money and show his enthusiasm; if he doesn't know anything he'll invent something; if by chance he discovers something, he tries to make himself important by embroidering it.'[11] He maintained that all French conspirators talked so much that there was really no need for a political police force; sooner or later the conspirators would tell their secrets to one of the minister's friends.

Outside his office he liked to give the impression that his agents were numerous and ubiquitous. He used jokingly to recommend his friends in the faubourg St-Germain to do their conspiring only when he was with them – so that his agents would not bother to report it to him and he would not be obliged to take action. Years later a general complained to him that he wished to give a dinner for twenty people at a fashionable restaurant and the proprietor had told him he must notify the police 'so that they can send somebody to it'. Fouché asked for the list of guests, ran his eye rapidly down it, handed it back with a smile and said: 'There's no need for you to invite anybody you don't know.'[12]

This sort of mystification appealed to his quite childish sense of humour and served to increase belief in the omniscience of the police. Réal, who worked very closely with him, said that in fact 'nobody ever employed fewer agents, yet every day Fouché filled two or three wastepaper baskets with reports which he did not want'.[13] As Fouché himself said: 'You don't do important police work with writings and reports . . . the minister himself must make contact with influential men, with all opinions, with all doctrines, with all the leading classes of society.'[14]

Réal was in the minister's office one evening when Fouché asked him if he was going to the reception at the Luxembourg Palace. Réal said he was not, because he could not stand having the anxious Gohier draw him into a corner and ask him for the thousandth time, 'What's new? Have you a report for me?'

'If that's all you're worrying about,' said Fouché, 'rummage about in that basket – there's a good two hundred reports there . . . plenty to keep him and his counter-police busy for the next week or two.'[15]

They had no sooner got to the palace than Gohier came up to them. His first words were, 'What's new? Have you a report for me?' Réal presented him with the paper he had taken from Fouché's basket, in which an agent reported a gathering of a large number of men in the garden of a house about a league and a half from Paris; he had managed to get quite close but they spoke in such conspiratorially low tones that he could not catch a word they said.

Gohier's face grew more and more serious as he read it. 'This is not the first time I've heard of these meetings,' he said reproachfully. 'I'm astonished you seem so little concerned about such a serious affair.'[16]

Réal, beginning to wonder if he had unluckily lighted on something that should have been investigated more fully, sent one of his own men to check the story. The following evening, he made a special call on Gohier at the Luxembourg. The garden in question, he explained, belonged to a hat maker. 'On fine nights . . . the manufacturer sets his hats out on poles in his garden to dry. Now, if you imagine a hedge at the height of the poles . . .'[17]

2

The unpopularity of the Directory increased. So did the viciousness of street-brawls between the grey-coated royalist supporters, their hair cut *à la victime*, and the blue-coated Jacobins, hair done *à la Titus*. One of the grey coats had recently been upended in a fountain in the Tuileries Gardens and held there until he drowned. Paris was haunted once more by the threat of a total collapse of authority. The lack of confidence included the Directors, but had no effect on them. Three of them clung to office because they did not know what else to do. Barras was determined not to give up a post which brought him soft-living and bribes. Sieyès, as always, had plans. And in these plans Fouché had already played a part.

After his return from Italy he had successfully recommended his friend, General Joubert, for the command of the 17th military division, which controlled Paris. When he heard Sieyès say 'we need two things: a head and a sword',[1] he proposed that Joubert should be the sword, knowing that Sieyès saw himself as the head. Since the sword must be garlanded with laurels if it was to impress the people, Joubert was sent off to Italy to gain glory on the battlefields that had been so rewarding to Bonaparte. But a sniper's bullet killed him at the battle of Novi on August 15.

Since then, Sieyès had been searching for a substitute. He had always regarded it as 'indispensable to place in the government a soldier enjoying the confidence of the army, for without the certainty of having the army on one's side, one can do nothing'.[2] The problem was: which soldier? Moreau leaned too far to the the right, Bernadotte too far to the left; Brune was too hasty and uncouth.

The answer to the problem landed at Fréjus on October 9, 1798: Bonaparte had returned from Egypt. Whether the prime reason for his reappearance was because his brother Louis had brought word from Joseph and Lucien that the pear was now ripe, or because he feared imminent disaster in Egypt, is not certain. He had always a good eye for opportunity; he was never slow in fleeing from failure. But the political situation alone would probably not have induced him to return, for as he said, 'The Directory could have stood up to the opposition at home . . . Abroad, Masséna's victory over Souvarov had freed France from all anxiety. Brune had been successful in Holland. With the arrival of winter there was four months to reform the armies.'[3]

The popular demonstrations of delight that greeted him on his journey to Paris did not represent the opinion of the whole nation. There would have been many to support the comment of Bernadotte, recently dismissed from the Ministry of War, that he would have been court-martialled for abandoning his command had they known of the dispatch sent home by General Kléber. 'He told me to meet him at Rosetta on the 7th,' wrote Bonaparte's unhappy successor, 'but I found nothing there except messages . . . The army has been reduced by half . . . The poverty in arms and ammunition presents as alarming a picture as the . . . diminution in men . . . Bonaparte did not leave a sou in the cashbox . . . on the contrary he has left debts of nearly twelve millions . . . The back pay for the army alone amounts to four millions.'[4]

Fortunately for Bonaparte, France knew nothing of this or of the earlier disasters which he had concealed in his dispatches. He called boldly on Gohier and Moulin and asked their support if he claimed Sieyès's seat in the Directory. They repeated that he would not qualify until he was forty. He called on Sieyès and found him prepared to discuss getting rid of all the other Directors. Sieyès's dream of a philosopher sharing power with a warrior did not immediately appeal to Bonaparte, who saw himself in both roles, but a place in a Dictatorship of two was an undoubted improvement on being one of five Directors.

He avoided committing himself and waited to see what Barras would offer. Relations between the two men were not easy: Barras seemed unwilling to forget the days when Bonaparte was a neglected general whom he befriended; Bonaparte, while admitting Barras's intelligence, suspected that for that reason he would make an awkward partner. While he still hesitated, Fouché and Réal (who had been in communication with him before he left Egypt) persuaded him to have another talk with Barras, whose moderate policy they preferred.

Barras invited him to dinner on 8th Brumaire, October 30. Fouché and Réal went to Bonaparte's house in the rue de la Victoire to learn the result of the discussion, and found two other conspirators, Talleyrand and Roederer, already there. Soon afterwards they heard the general's carriage rattle along the narrow drive from the street and halt at the broad terrace steps. 'Well!' he said, as soon as he came into the room, 'do you know what your Barras wants? He admits that it's impossible to go on in the present chaos; he would like to have a President of the Republic – but he wants the president to be himself . . . And he hypocritically conceals his desires by proposing to give the post to – guess who! – Hédouville!'[5] It was clear that Bonaparte was now thinking in terms of supreme power – and clearer still that Barras's proposal to offer it to a rival general would drive him back into the arms of Sieyès.

Fouché was still only on the fringe of the plot, obtaining most of his information from Réal. Bonaparte later claimed that Fouché was 'entirely ignorant'[6] of the whole affair, but on another occasion contradicted himself by saying that, when he told Fouché and Réal of the conversation with Barras, 'Fouché, who was attached to Barras, ran off to reproach him'[7] – which exactly confirms Fouché's own version. He had known Bonaparte before the expedition to Egypt; he had probably lent Mme Bonaparte money during the general's absence, since the soft-hearted and spendthrift Josephine was quite incapable of living within her allowance. But he was not a member of the inner circle of those who, without being able to define their precise objective, had been planning a radical change of government for the past year.

He now decided to take a more active part – and communicated his decision to the principals by means of a typically ambiguous joke. He invited the playwright Arnault and another of Bonaparte's comrades from the Egyptian expedition, Regnault de Saint-Jean d'Angély, to dinner with him on November 3. Soon after their arrival at the Hôtel de Juigné they found themselves joined by Roederer, by Réal and by the journalist and poet Marie-Joseph Chénier. 'The guest list' they noted with horror, 'seemed to have been compiled from the roll of the conspirators': and they were all in the head-quarters of the Ministry of Police. 'Out of the whole twenty-four, there was scarcely anybody except the minister who was not one of us.' When Bonaparte himself completed the gathering, Fouché greeted him with a smile and the assurance that 'I wanted you to be among the people you find most agreeable.'[8] He could have added that it made a change from the furtive encounters in the rue de la Victoire, or the box at the Théâtre Français, or at Talleyrand's house in the rue d'Anjou. But he had made his point: he knew everything about the plot. They must either let him right into it, or accept the risk of being denounced.

'It would have failed if I had opposed it,' he claimed. 'I could have dissuaded Sieyès, warned Barras, enlightened Gohier and Moulin.'[9] Why then did he support it? Bonaparte's other associates – including Talleyrand, who had lost his post as Minister of Foreign Affairs – could all hope for advancement and public office; Fouché, on the other hand, already had his Ministry. His own explanation was that 'I considered Bonaparte alone capable of carrying out the political reforms that were required by our moral condition, our vices, our shortcomings, our excesses, our defeats and our fatal divisions.'[10] It is the common excuse of those who help to set up dictatorships. There is no reason to believe that Fouché was less sincere than most when he gave it.

The plan for the overthrow of the government was simple, and hinged ironically on what was intended as a protective clause in the constitution. With the past excesses of the Paris mob in mind, the Council of Seniors, if it considered public order to be in danger, was empowered to reconvene the legislature outside the city and appoint a general of its own choice to command the troops of the region. The threat of riots had been present for months; all that was neces-sary was to convince the representatives that the time was now and the general was Bonaparte. He already had wide support among his fellow-officers, led by Murat, who was courting his sister Caroline, and Leclerc who was already married to Pauline. His brother Lucien had been President of the Council of Five Hundred since October 23. Sieyès had won the support of Lemercier, President of the Council of Seniors.

The cabal divided, each fraction forming a new kernel, each group perfecting the details of its own plans: in the barracks, the committee rooms of the Councils, the ante-room of the Directors' quarters, the country house near Bagatelle of Mme Récamier, whom Lucien hoped to make his mistress and from whom he could not bear to be parted. Fouché sent a circular letter to the prefects of all the departments referring to the 'rumours that the government is preparing a change in the constitution', and assuring them that there was no truth in it. Which was strictly true, since it was not the government that was planning the change.

Everybody was ready – except Bonaparte. Nervous, hesitant, spurred on by ambition and reined in by fear of the consequences of failure, he talked, brooded, took to his bed on pretence of illness, tried again to recruit Barras, announced that it was imperative to act at once – and promptly ordered another delay. At last the date was set: the 16th of Brumaire (November 7). To arouse enthusiasm and allay suspicion, the conspirators arranged a subscription dinner by the two Councils in honour of Bonaparte and Moreau for the after-noon of the 15th Brumaire. City officials and deputies of opposing factions gathered in the Temple of Victory (formerly the church of St-Sulpice) and eyed each other suspiciously. The guest of honour, hunched darkly over his plate, resenting having to share the glory with a rival, ate some eggs and a pear, refused to touch any of the made dishes – thus setting off a rumour that he feared he was to be poisoned – and after an hour-and-a-half got up and left.

That evening, Arnault, Régnault and Roederer were at a party given by Talleyrand, waiting for confirmation that all was ready. As time ticked by and no news came they grew increasingly anxious. Finally it was agreed that Arnault should go to Bonaparte's house for information while the others made up a hand of whist, to account for their staying so long.

Arnault found Josephine's circular salon crowded with visitors, notabilities from every walk of life, including the nervous Gohier, currently serving his term as President of the Directory, who was seated on a sofa, sipping a cup of tea. Bonaparte caught Arnault's eye and indicated that he should wait. Presently Fouché came into the room. As he approached Gohier, the Director looked up at him and, as always, asked: 'What is the news, citizen minister?'

'News?' Fouché repeated airily. 'None at all!'

'But surely?'

'Oh, just the usual gossip.'

With Fouché standing, Gohier sitting, and their voices raised above the chatter around them, the conversation had attracted atten-tion.

'About what?' Gohier persisted, certain that something was being held back from him.

'About the conspiracy,' said Fouché.

There was a sudden silence. The incomparable Josephine, momentarily losing her composure, gasped, 'The conspiracy!'

'The conspiracy!' exclaimed Gohier, spilling his tea.

'Yes,' said Fouché. 'The conspiracy.' There was no need, in that company, to say which one. 'But I know where I am,' he continued. 'I know what's going on, citizen director. Rely on me. They'll not fool me.'

He paused again, and then: 'If there'd really been this conspiracy that people have talked about so long, shouldn't we have proof of it by now in the Place de la République or the Plaine de Grenelle [where executions were carried out by guillotine or firing squad]?'

He looked round him and smiled. Josephine chided, 'Fi! citizen Fouché! how can you laugh at things like that?'

But Gohier was soberly appreciative. 'The citizen speaks like a man who knows his business,' he said. 'Calm yourself, citizeness. If one can say things like that in front of the ladies it's a proof that there's no need to do them.' He had a soft spot for Josephine, who was kind to his wife. 'Do as the government does; don't worry about the rumours. Sleep peacefully!'

When the guests had gone and Josephine retired to her room, Bonaparte told Arnault that the coup could not take place next day.

'When the secret is out!' Arnault protested. 'Don't you see everybody is talking about it!'

'It can't be helped,' Bonaparte replied. 'Those idiots in the Council of Seniors . . . have asked for twenty-four hours to think things over.'[11]

There was substance in Fouché's sardonic joke. Discovery was only a matter of time. And if the Paris mob could be roused against them they might well end up on the Place de la République or on the Plaine de Grenelle. On November 8, Fouché went to see Bonaparte, urging – as he had done in the terrifying days of Thermidor, five years before – that the blow should be struck at once. Outwardly he remained as calm and uncommitted as ever. And inwardly, too, perhaps, for when Arnault and Regnault called on him at eight o'clock next morning they found him still in bed.

They had come, on Bonaparte's instructions, to tell him that a hurriedly summoned Committee of the Council of Seniors, packed with his supporters, had voted to transfer both Councils to

St-Cloud, and to appoint Bonaparte to the command of all the troops in the Paris region. The decision would be placed before the full Council of Seniors at 10 a.m. and they were certain to confirm it. The Council of Five Hundred, where opposition was expected, were not due to meet until noon, and would be confronted with a situation that they could not alter. Bonaparte was parading his troops on the Champs Elysées and would march them down to the Tuileries. Fouché was to go to the Luxembourg and test the reaction there.

Of the five Directors, only Sieyès and Ducos were in the plot. At the moment when Fouché arrived Barras had already been warned of what was happening by Madame Tallien – who found him in his bath – and had sent his secretary to see if he could come to some last-minute arrangement with Bonaparte. Fouché went straight to Gohier's apartments and, finding that Barras had been careful not to alert the president, officially informed him that the Legislative Corps was moving to St-Cloud.

'By what strange chance,' snapped Gohier, 'does a minister of the Directory get changed into a messenger of the Council of Seniors?'

'I thought it my duty,' said Fouché, 'to hasten to inform you of such an important decision and to ask for your orders.'[12]

'It was much more your duty,' answered Gohier, his voice trembling with rage, 'not to leave us in ignorance of the criminal intrigues that have led up to such a decision!'[13]

Fouché retorted that he had placed plenty of reports before the Directors – they had not paid sufficient attention to them. In any case, Sieyès and Ducos had already accepted the decision of the Committee of the Council of Seniors.

'The majority still rests here in the Luxembourg,' Gohier replied, 'and if the Directory has any orders to give, their execution will be entrusted to men worthy of confidence.'[14] Fouché retired and Gohier sent for Moulin and Barras. But Barras was busy with other visitors. Bonaparte, having told Barras's secretary that he would have nothing to do with his master, sent Talleyrand and Admiral Bruix to deal with him. They first warned him that if he attempted the slightest resistance Bonaparte would crush him; then promised that if he signed the letter of resignation they set before him, Bonaparte would guarantee him a life of luxury in retirement. Barras signed and left for his estate at Grosbois, accompanied by a squadron of dragoons to make certain that he did not change his mind.

In Gohier's quarters, the Minister of War – Dubois-Crancé, who had conducted the siege of Lyons – was pleading for authority to arrest Bonaparte, Talleyrand, Murat and the other conspirators. The secretary to the Directory, La Garde, who was secretly in the plot, refused to countersign any order that was not confirmed by a majority of Directors.

'In any case,' said Gohier, 'how can there possibly be a revolution at St-Cloud? In my capacity as President I hold the seals of the Republic here.'[15] Moulin added that he was due to dine with Bonaparte at Gohier's table later in the day and they could both then see what Bonaparte had in mind.

At the Tuileries there was no doubt what he had in mind. Backed by a great array of infantry, cavalry and artillery, with a crowd shouting its mindless head off in the pleasantly unseasonable sunshine, Bonaparte was dismissing all protests, announcing that he intended to save the Republic whether it wanted it or not, threatening to put down any opposition by force, inside the building or outside in the streets. There were many who listened to him and recognized the threat of a military dictatorship. Some were among those who had been persuaded to support him and were now changing their minds. None slept very soundly that night, waiting to see what the next day's session at St-Cloud would bring.

The road was busy with traffic from a very early hour: troops on foot, officers on horseback, deputies in carriages taking them to the two council chambers that had been hastily prepared in the Gallery and the Orangery. Fouché remained in Paris, the whole of his police force on duty and special agents stationed at St-Cloud to bring him reports at half-hourly intervals.

'I will take responsibility for Paris,' he assured Arnault. 'The first one who lifts a finger will be thrown into the river. But the general must be responsible for St-Cloud.' And with his usual confidence he sent the general some advice: 'The important thing is to prevent the ringleaders tying the Councils up with points of procedure that will give their partisans outside time to intervene. It would be better to hurry things on.'[16]

There was more than one occasion that day when it seemed that the general, far from hurrying things on, was about to fail to cope with his task at all. The soldiers formed a cordon round the palace, where the deputies had begun an agitated debate on the state of the Republic. Talleyrand, Regnault and other leading conspirators retired to a house they had rented near by. Bonaparte went in to address the Council of Seniors, the chamber in which he could count on the most support, though Fouché's informants reported that during the night there had been a change of heart against him in all quarters. Perhaps intimidated by this, the general stumbled over his words, lost the thread of his argument, and eventually withdrew, leaving the Councillors puzzled and scarcely more favourably disposed than when he began.

His agitation increased, despite the encouraging shouts of *Long live Bonaparte!* from his braver supporters. He knew by now that the Council of Five Hundred, amid cries of *Down with the dictator!*, had agreed that each member should renew his oath of loyalty to the Republic. He crossed to the Orangery, at the head of a platoon of grenadiers. He took four of them with him to the tribune and left the remainder to guard the entrance. This armed intervention brought a new outburst from the Five Hundred, all the members standing, his attempts to address them drowned in screams of *Long Live the Constitution! Down with Dictatorship!* His cheeks turned pale. One deputy, Aréna, drew a dagger and shouted: 'Do you now make war on your country?'[17] Bonaparte swayed, as if about to faint. The grenadiers ran in from the door, formed a protective barrier around him, and bustled him out.

Lucien, seated above the tumult in the presidential chair, repeatedly pleaded for quiet and calm. The confused shouting resolved itself into *Outlaw him! Put it to the vote!* He tore off his presidential robes and ran to the tribune to defend his brother, but another party of grenadiers grabbed him and carried him outside. There he leaped on to a horse and proclaimed that as President he declared the session closed and called on the soldiers to expel those who had 'violated its deliberations, dagger in hand!'[18]

The drums rattled. The tall handsome Murat drew his sabre. The grenadiers advanced at the double, with bayonets fixed. The deputies flew out of doors and windows like clowns in a charade. In the nick of time, Bonaparte had been saved by his brother and his future brother-in-law. He never fully forgave either of them.

Hurriedly shepherding back as many of the fleeing deputies as they could find, the conspirators re-installed them as a rump legislature and pushed through a decree appointing Bonaparte, Ducos and Sieyès members of an Executive Consular Commission to take over the functions of the Directory.

The messengers whom they sent to Paris with the news found the gates closed against them. Fouché had kept this word: he had sealed off the city and not a soul had stirred. He had played a leading part in establishing Bonaparte in a position from which he would lead his countrymen on a fifteen-year rape of Europe, a blaze of glory that would end in the embers of defeat and disillusion. Fouché could at least plead that he was not alone. True to the feminine streak which periodically sets it languishing for domination by men in uniform, the French people, in a free vote, endorsed the new situation by 3,011,107 to 1,562.

3

'The government was too feeble to uphold the glory of the Republic against enemies abroad,' Fouché wrote in a proclamation the following day, 'or to guarantee the rights of its citizens against factions at home. A way had to be found of giving it strength and grandeur.'[1] It was this new strength that he required if he was to reform the police as he had planned.

A centralized police force had long been a key feature of French administration. Louis XIV, wary of any attempt by his captive nobles to gain their freedom, gave it a strong political bias and initiated the practice of having his Lieutenant of Police submit a report to him every day. The office was abolished during the Revolution and the police degenerated into little more than guillotine-catchpoles for the two Committees of Public Safety and General Security. The Ministry of Police that was re-established in January 1798 was invested with wider duties – the maintenance of law and order and the preservation of the internal security of the Republic. But weak government and incompetent ministers reduced it to inglorious debility, distrusted, detested and impotent.

With a strong government under Bonaparte (it was clear from the outset that neither of the two other Consuls need be seriously considered) Fouché at once urged that the iniquitous law of hostages should be repealed. 'Passed in circumstances from which we are already far removed,' he wrote in his report to the Consuls, 'it has been the motive for some, and the pretext for many, of the civil disturbances which trouble the western departments . . . It is in fact merely the proof of governmental impotence.'[2]

In a long letter of instruction to the prefects of departments he outlined the policy of moderation and justice with which he hoped to win the support of the people: a recital of the liberal republican principles which he and most Frenchmen believed Bonaparte would observe.

'No citizen may be held by the police for any longer period than is necessary to commit him to the custody of the law . . . The police must be in a position to produce documentary proof of the precise moment when a citizen was arrested and when he was committed to the custody of the law. The minister of police, prefects and all officials are answerable to every member of society in this respect.

'Never forget' (he warned them) 'how dangerous it is to make arrests on mere suspicion. Remember . . . the number of innocent people who have been sent from the courts to the scaffold only because they were mistakenly brought before the courts.'[3] After Lyons, it was a consideration that he was himself unlikely to forget.

He urged leniency towards prisoners:

'We are guilty if we add in the slightest degree to the rigours indispensible to the execution of the law and the administration of justice; and guilty, too, if we fail to temper those rigours in every possible way. The man on whom sentence has still to be passed is not yet for us an enemy of society; the man who has heard his punishment pronounced is one no longer. He had nothing to expiate before; he has expiated everything after . . . He is no more than a victim that society is condemned to sacrifice; society should weep for him and for itself. The need to punish crimes springs in a great degree from the imperfections of the social system which does not know how to prevent them . . .'[4]

It was a striking new policy. 'Words such as Fouché's had never before been heard for as long as a ministry of police had existed.'[5] They could have been spoken only by a man of great confidence and moral strength. It was a policy destined to waver and sometimes temporarily retreat before Bonaparte's insistence on the simpler efficacies of arbitrary arrest, detention without trial, and torture; but it was never totally subjected so long as Fouché remained at the ministry.

'Every operation of Justice is by its nature dictated by logic and reason,' he wrote to Bonaparte in a report on his proposed reorganization of the police. 'If you introduce the ideas or apparatus of force, then the concept of sanctity conjured up by the name of Justice is weakened or destroyed. The police, as I envisage it, should be established to forestall and prevent crimes, to control and put a stop to those which have not been forestalled. It is a *discretionary* authority in the hands of the Government.'[6]

He made sure that people should know what he was doing. In the *Moniteur* during the following two months he published praise of the improved conditions in the Paris prisons, condemnation of the callous treatment of prisoners in the northern departments – 'none of the measures required by public security calls for inhumanity'[7] – and a ban on the traditional use of prostitutes as police informers. He was emphatic in his refusal to continue using *agents provocateurs*, on practical as well as moral grounds. A new government, he argued, does itself a disservice by discovering and publicizing plots against itself, whether genuine or not, 'because that sort of discovery inevitably calls into question matters that have been accepted as already decided'.[8] The purpose of his police was not to make spectacular arrests but to provide the assurance – or, failing that, the appearance – of order and settled government. Only in that way could the Consulate perform its task of consolidating the gains of the Revolution.

With a victorious general as the Head of State, the principal threat to peace came not from foreigners but from Frenchmen. In a four-thousand-word report to the Directory a month before the *coup d'état* of Brumaire, Fouché, while warning that the authorities should keep a constant watch on the law of 24 Messidor (the law of hostages) so that 'it is never used hastily and never becomes an instrument of vengeance, hatred or private interest',[9] reported that the *chouannerie* had been reorganized. 'Our enemies have agents everywhere. They make use of everything: gold, fanaticism, inflammatory proclamations. The recalcitrant priests give strong support to these disruptive attitudes. The stagnation of business, shortage of money, weight of taxes and conscription–these are their principal means of seduction.'[10] These rebels, armed and financed from England, fought on despite the reverses of the Allied armies supporting the comte de Provence (Louis XVIII) in the East and the reluctance of the comte d'Artois, his younger brother, to cross the Channel and lead their struggle in the West.

In the capital, Barras's swoop upon the royalists in September 1797 discouraged and limited their activities for a time, but during the past year rival groups backed by the comte de Provence and the comte d'Artois had set up secret agencies again in Paris. Their aim was to overturn the government by semi-constitutional means, with the aid of discontented officials, army officers, and members of the legislature, and set in its place a council that would hold France for the royalist cause until the unwieldy Provence or over-cautious Artois arrived in person. Hyde de Neuville and a fellow royalist crossed to London in 1799 and, with the approval of the comte d'Artois, gained the backing of the British Government for their scheme.

The political *coup* in Paris was to be supported by an uprising in the West, and this in turn by an expedition from England. On July 1, 1799, the British Government provided funds for the comte de Plouer to go to St-Malo and 'collect local and political information and arrange communications in the interior which may be useful in the event of an expedition to that coast'.[11] By late autumn British vessels operating from Southampton and the Channel Islands were struggling against high winds to land at various points on the Cherbourg and Brest peninsulas such cargoes as the '600 muskets, bayonets and knapsacks, 30,000 rounds of ball ammunition, 10 half-barrels of powder and 4 kegs of flints'[12] which the sloop *Railleur* delivered to the *chouan* leader Lemercier on November 1. Hyde de Neuville left London on November 12 with assurances of full support, only to discover, on his arrival in Paris, that the Directory had already been overthrown, by Bonaparte.

With little hope of carrying out their project in face of the overwhelming vote approving Bonaparte's seizure of power, Hyde and his two principal associates, Coigny and Crénolle, decided to restrict their activities to propaganda and espionage. In this they had the help of a spy known as Marchand who had for the past year been sending quite accurate information to Dutheil, the royalists' chief of intelligence in London, for a fee of £100 a month. He supplied them, among other things, with an alphabetical list of the secret police agents employed in Paris, which enabled them to keep out of trouble while they prepared their first public demonstration: to mark the seventh anniversary of the execution of Louis XVI.

On that day, January 21, 1800, Paris woke to find the portico of the Madeleine church draped with black hatchments to which were pinned a copy of the late King's will and a proclamation by the comte d'Artois. Other copies were posted up throughout the city on public buildings and monuments. 'A silly spectacle for a few loafers who'll be chased away by a score of dragoons,'[13] sneered the comte de Provence's men, jealous of the stir the trick caused and its association with the comte d'Artois. But there was daring in it, and considerable skill – the statue of Liberty in the Place de la Révolution, for instance, which had one of the proclamations pasted on it, was under permanent armed guard. Fouché, with no evidence, but strong suspicions, had Hyde de Neuville put under surveillance – a fact which was at once notified to Hyde by Marchand. He lay low and in March, when the disillusioned *chouans* made their submission to the government, he accompanied the Breton resistance leader, Georges Cadoudal, back to England.

Behind him, in temporary charge of the so-called English Committee, he left the abbé Godard, whom even the scatter-brained Hyde regarded as a man of 'incredible frivolity'.[14] Within a few weeks Godard was arrested in the street while passing on brochures attacking the First Consul. Fouché did not need a second chance. His police swooped in force on the Committee's headquarters, arrested several suspects including Coigny and Neuville's wife, and discovered that Marchand was in fact a former government spy named Dupérou, who had been getting much of his information from a friend in Fouché's ministry. Fouché published in the *Moniteur* many of the papers that fell into his hands – proposals for new guerrilla bands, the robbing of mailcoaches carrying public funds, attacks on the owners of confiscated church and émigré property. They sent shivers of horror down the spines of most people in the country, yearning for a period of peace and stability after a decade of uncertainty and terror. Copies of a brochure attacking this *Conspiration Anglaise* were concealed in partridge and duck pâtés and sent by Mengaud on Fouché's behalf to Pitt, Grenville, Portland, Dundas and other English politicians.

4

Dupérou was arrested at Calais on May 23, 1800, when returning from a visit to London. Travelling under the name of Dierhoff, he had left Calais with a Saxon passport and come back with a Prussian one, a discrepancy that was at once noticed by citizen Mengaud, Fouché's special commissioner at the port. Mengaud put Dupérou under arrest at an inn. Dupérou got his custodian drunk and escaped, but was recaptured three weeks later. By the end of August he had betrayed many of the royalist conspirators, but Dutheil in London was still receiving reports from an agent code-named Nasica, who revealed that Bonaparte had taken a great interest in Dupérou's conversations with Giraud (Lord Grenville) and that Fouché had had 'a most stormy scene'[1] with Talleyrand whom he suspected of encouraging the leakage of information from the Ministry of Police.

Fouché was still occupied with the reorganization of his department. The secret branch, in particular, had become a refuge for wrecks and wastrels from the successive waves of the Revolution, suborned aristocrats, disillusioned Jacobins, rakes and touts – all under the direction of a highly intelligent and unprincipled ex-priest named Desmarest. Dupérou had indicated the variety of trades and professions from which the police spies were recruited, in the alphabetical list he sent to London: butcher, locksmith, perfumer, wig-maker, Louis Adans in the rue Jean-Saint-Denis who once was *valet de pied* to Louis XVI, Marie-Louise Saint-Huberti who kept a brothel at No. 133 Palais-Royal. These were the workaday informers. On a higher level, paid from secret funds, were such familiar figures as Fréron, who had once been Barras's fellow commissioner in Toulon, and later leader of the royalist *jeunesse dorée*; Wooden-leg Collin, a former friend of Robespierre and Couthon; the Baroness Lauterbourg; Robillard, who before the Revolution had managed the estates of Maurepas, the Prime Minister.

In the lower ranks, informers were divided into three groups, their pay ranging from 1,800 to 6,000 francs a year with expenses 'which usually bring them in more than their fixed salaries'. They kept watch on cafés, theatres, gambling-houses and other public places, the best-paid grade circulating in the higher reaches of society and at more private functions. 'These,' as Dupérou pointed out, 'are rather difficult to identify, because they never report in person to the Ministry of Police. They have a code and transmit their messages, unsigned, through a third person.'[2] There remained, at the very bottom of the scale, the *détaillants*, the retailers who hung about at street corners, waiting for a sign from a police agent to follow a suspect. Women and children took part in this work; the concierges of large houses in the principal streets kept a supply of clothing with which the trackers could vary their appearance.

The country was teeming with spy systems. Bonaparte had his own. His brother Lucien, as Minister of the Interior, had his own. Talleyrand, as Minister of Foreign Affairs, had his own. The generals commanding Paris and other military districts had their own. One spy often worked for more than one master – Robillard, for instance, was on Bonaparte's personal pay-roll as well as the Ministry's – and there were those who found more credit and reward in informing on each other than in keeping watch on the enemies of the state. Fouché's republican principles brought him into constant conflict with the innate aristocratic leanings of Talleyrand and the more recently acquired autocratic views of Lucien. To circumvent Lucien he sent special commissioners to the major cities who corresponded with him directly instead of through the Ministry of the Interior's chain of mayors and prefects. He could not maintain regular agents abroad, but he kept an eye on the comings and goings of Talleyrand's messengers by establishing police commissioners at ports and frontier posts. By August 1800, one English traveller was reporting that 'Fouché and Talleyrand are said to hate each other; indeed I had an instance of it in the refusal of the former to countersign Talleyrand's passport to me.'[3]

His struggle with Lucien was fiercer and more critical. As early as January 1800, Dupérou sent word that 'the split between Lucien and Fouché has reached its utmost extent. Lucien is doing all that is humanly possible to destroy the influence that Fouché has managed to gain over his brother's mind. Eaten up by the most imperious ambition, Lucien is trying as hard as he can to annex the departmental police to the Ministry of the Interior.'[4] His chances of succeeding, however, were not rated high by onlookers. 'Fouché is the only one of all the ministers who seems to enjoy the complete confidence of the First Consul, whose door is open to him at any hour of the day or night. Fouché often calls at two to three in the morning to pass on interesting information'[5].

Side-by-side with his campaign against the English Committee, Fouché was on the track of another important royalist organization, the Swabian Agency. This, though it had begun as an information and action committee responsible to the comte de Provence, had, like the English Committee, come under the control of the English agent, Wickham, who held the purse strings. Its principal objective was to induce uprisings in the East and the South – since Normandy, Brittany and the Vendée were regarded as the special preserves of the comte d'Artois. For the spring of 1800 it planned a great uprising in the Midi, supported by forces landed from a British fleet in the Mediterranean, and led by émigrés who would come in across the Swiss and Italian borders. To these would be added a Free Corps of French deserters and prisoners recruited from the Austrian prison camps.

As usual with the exiled royalists, there was too much talk, too much confusion and too much quarrelling. Acting on information from abroad, Fouché arrested one of the Swabian Agency's men in

Paris. The papers that he carried revealed most of the plot. And, while Fouché hunted out the conspirators at home, all hope of out-side support for them was destroyed by Bonaparte at Marengo and Moreau at Hohenlinden. The Austrians were crushed on two fronts.

Bonaparte returned to Paris at the beginning of July, victorious but in a tearing rage over the so-called Marengo Crisis. In the after-noon of June 20, rumours had circulated in Paris of a serious defeat in Italy. Before a military courier arrived the next morning with the news that Desaix had saved the battle, in the nick of time for Bona-parte, a great many people had openly made plans to 'snatch the imperilled Republic from the grasp of the Corsican', as Fouché him-self put it, and appoint a new Head of State 'who was neither an arro-gant dictator nor a soldiers' emperor'.[6] A favourite candidate was Carnot, the old Jacobin warhorse, now much moderated in his views but again in charge of the Ministry of War. Though he probably knew nothing of the scheme, it cost him his job. Bonaparte dismissed him shortly afterwards and became more wary than ever of the Jacobins and republicans whom he saw as obstacles in his path to supreme power.

There were now sufficient indications of Bonaparte's ambition for it to be clear to all those around him that he intended to be a new Caesar. In February 1800 he had taken up residence in the Tuileries. After Marengo he had presented swords of honour inscribed, 'Battle Commanded in Person by the First Consul'. When the Prus-sian Ambassador, Lucchesini, presented his credentials, Bonaparte was so struck by his uniform and decorations that he exclaimed, 'That's impressive! You need things like that for the people.'[7] There were rumours of approaches to the Pope (which were to result in the Concordat of July 1801) – an alliance with reactionary Rome that symbolized the defection of the leader who had, only a short time previously, promised to protect the harvest of the Revolution.

Fouché opposed this on all fronts. He was particularly dismayed at the thought that an outside authority was again about to control the Church of France. With the decline of the federalist movement, in which the constitutional clergy had been involved, he had mellowed in his attitude towards those priests who were willing to take the oath of loyalty to the Republic. Now, reacting against Bona-parte's anticipated leniency, he insisted on the enforcement of the strict letter of the law.

In June 1800, he published an instruction he had sent to the Prefect of the Gironde and the Commissioner of Police at Bordeaux ordering them to deny rumours that the government was relaxing the observance of the republican, and anti-Christian, calendar. 'The result of this slanderous report is that a law essentially linked with the maintenance of republican institutions is openly violated.'[8] In Belgium, where the unsworn priests were active, Fouché ordered the prefects to take action against them under the law of 14 Brumaire year VII, by which the Directory had condemned most of them to be deported. The order had been only partially carried out, but the lists of the proscribed clergy remained in existence. Fouché did not enforce the sentence of deportation to the colonies, but all those caught performing illegal rites were arrested, passed from one police post to the next and banished beyond the Rhine.

'Let all the cults be free and equal,' he had said in January 1800, 'but ensure that the laws which control them continue to be strictly enforced. Show respect for faith and belief, which are beyond the control of laws and constitutions, but be inexorable against the agitators, whoever they may be, and under whatever pretext they work evil upon earth!'[9]

His efforts to support the republicans, if only as a counterbalance to Bonaparte's increasing partiality for royalists, were often thwarted by the republicans themselves. Their extremists were more numerous and, at the moment, more dangerous than the royalists. Their threats to Bonaparte's position and even to his life, hardened his attitude against them. Fouché continued to receive them privately – there was a welcome for royalists, Jacobins, priests and atheists alike in the *grand salon* at the Hôtel de Juigné (where a new baby, Armand-Cyriaque-François, had recently appeared) – and some of them he managed to befriend: for instance Barère, whom he had known in the Convention and who had been passing through hard times because of his former membership of the Committee of Public Safety. Fouché placed him as a political adviser to the government-controlled newspapers.[10]

In the early autumn of 1800 Barère told Fouché that one of his former employees at the Committee of Public Safety, Demerville, was talking about 'striking down the new Caesar . . . A few brave men will be enough to deliver the people.'[11] Fouché had Demerville put under observation. Meanwhile one of his fellow-conspirators, a retired army captain named Harel, revealed the existence of the plot to Bourrienne, Bonaparte's secretary. Bonaparte, ready to make the most of this Jacobin attempt at assassination, one of whose leading figures proved to be the younger brother of the deputy Aréna who had threatened him at St-Cloud, told Bourrienne to let the affair continue. This was done without Fouché's knowledge. It was only at the last moment, on October 10, that he was told to arrest the plotters, who were waiting at the Opéra to kill Bonaparte when he arrived.

Fouché protested at the trick, and at Bourrienne's bad faith in taking Harel's information direct to Bonaparte instead of to the Ministry of Police. He saw quite clearly why Bonaparte had encouraged the plot: 'Every government in its early days will take the opportunity of a trumped-up danger, either to establish itself or to extend its power.'[12] There was every indication that Bonaparte was ready for the next step – to have himself declared Consul for life.

5

In his determination to make himself the permanent ruler of France – he had been appointed Consul for ten years – Bonaparte had the support of his brothers and sisters and many politicians. Opposed to him were Josephine, who foresaw that he would next attempt to make the succession hereditary and would seek a younger wife to bear him children, and the left-wing men of the Revolution, including several generals of whom the most notable were Bernadotte, Augereau, Jourdan and Brune. Fouché was opposed for very practical reasons. He believed that the Victories of Marengo and Hohenlinden could bring an end to the eight years of war that had cost France so much in men – though not latterly in money. The Emperor Paul of Russia, aggrieved by Britain's seizure of Malta, had swung to the French side. 'England and Austria,' Fouché wrote to one of his agents in Hamburg (the letter was copied by the spy Nasica and sent to London) 'are reaching the end of the road. Albion will no longer be a threat to France.'[1]

Fouché had supported the *coup d'état* of Brumaire not because he saw Bonaparte as a general capable of winning more victories but because he believed him strong enough to impose peace. In his instructions to officials and his secret report to the Consuls in December 1799 he had said that 'in the strength and wisdom of the genius who presided over that revolution . . . the citizens have seen the means of consolidation of the Republic and the return of tranquillity and peace . . . the unanimous cry is for peace'.[2] With peace at hand, he opposed any action likely to stir up strife at home – certainly if its only purpose was to satisfy Bonaparte's ambition.

The most strenuous advocate of the Consulate for life was Lucien – activitated, Fouché claimed, by the belief that if he pushed his brother into a throne he would qualify for the post of prime minister. Lucien was never Bonaparte's favourite brother. His unruly character and his noisy – and all too justified – claim to have been the real hero of the Brumaire *coup d'état* had done nothing to bring them closer together. But in the summer of 1800 he aroused Bonaparte's enthusiasm for a scheme to prepare public opinion for the Life Consulate which he claimed would be effective without directly implicating Bonaparte

His plan was to prepare a pamphlet arguing that the stability and prosperity of France depended on the First Consul's permanent tenure of office. Copies would be sent to each prefect in sufficient numbers for him to distribute one to every leading official in his department. The pamphlets would not be signed, nor would they have any covering letter. They would be sent by the ordinary mail coaches with nothing to connect them with the Bonapartes, yet every prefect, recognizing the way in which they were addressed, would realize he had better distribute them if he wished to retain his job.

The pamphlet was composed by Fontanes, Elisa Bonaparte's literary protégé and lover, under Lucien's supervision and subject to Bonaparte's editing. Its title, *A Parallel between Caesar, Cromwell, Monk and Bonaparte* made its argument sufficiently clear: Bonaparte, the saviour of France, must preside over her destinies as a sovereign. It ended with a plea that the office should be made hereditary – though Bonaparte afterwards claimed that this had been added without his knowledge.

Fouché was aware of what Lucien was up to – and Lucien was aware that Fouché knew. He consequently obtained Bonaparte's permission to have the pamphlets printed at the Imprimerie Nationale, the state printing works which were excluded from police supervision and answerable only to the Minister of Justice. During the afternoon of November 4, Fouché learned that the presses were already running. To avoid a premature confrontation in which Lucien might appeal for help to Bonaparte, he waited until nightfall and then went in person to the Imprimerie Nationale. Despite protests from the guard, he entered the building, had the presses locked, and ordered the confiscation of all the bundles of pamphlets that had not yet been dispatched.

Early next morning he called at the Tuileries. Lucien and Fontanes were already in the ante-room waiting to lodge their complaint as soon as Bonaparte got up. They had overlooked the Minister of Police's prerogative of entering the First Consul's room at any hour of the day or night. Fouché walked past them, knocked on the bedroom door, and entered.

As he explained what he had done he was met with a stream of abuse. He continued unconcernedly. He argued that the pamphlet would produce the opposite effect from that which Bonaparte desired. He predicted that, although anonymous and indeed because of that, it would be taken to have been written by the First Consul himself. He warned that it would divide the people, not unite them. And it would have the same effect in the army, where many generals were jealous of Bonaparte's aggrandisement. He was careful to confine the blame to Lucien and presently had the pleasure of hearing the First Consul agree that the pamphlet must be suppressed and that 'it was in any case printed without his knowledge'.[3] At that moment Fouché had in his pocket a set of proofs corrected in Bonaparte's own hand.

Fouché emerged triumphant from the bedroom and crossed the river to his Ministry where he wrote a circular to all departments ordering the immediate destruction of every copy of the pamphlet. It was his policy to win over his opponents by kindness, never to make an enemy unnecessarily. But there were occasions when he allowed himself a little relaxation. The pamphlets, he told the prefects, well knowing that the letter would be seen by Lucien, were the result of 'a contemptible and criminal intrigue'.[4] That evening he gave a celebratory dinner to thirty guests.

Next morning, squeezing the last ounce out of his advantage, he took Moreau to the Tuileries for an interview with Bonaparte. The Victor of Hohenlinden was no Bonapartist. He detested the Victor of Marengo who had begrudged him recognition. He was contemptuous of his pretentions (later, when Bonaparte created the Legion of Honour, Moreau publicly conferred a Collar of Honour on his dog and a Casserole of Honour on his cook). He curtly warned him that if he did not disavow Lucien the nation as a whole and the republican sections of the army in particular would draw the only possible conclusion: that the First Consul approved the contents of the pamphlet.

Bonaparte retreated without further argument. He packed Lucien off as Ambassador to Spain and gave the Ministry of the Interior to Chaptal. Elisa spent a tearful evening at her mother's house, fretting over her brother's disgrace. Her mother, in a formidable rage, drove to the Tuileries where she 'sought redress against Fouché from the First Consul, in the presence of his wife who' – it is Lucien himself speaking – 'was believed to protect the minister in return, so they said, for a fee of thirty or forty thousand francs a month'.[5] Josephine, always a little terrified of her fierce relations-in-law, burst into tears. But they did not last long. This was for her a fleeting moment of relief from the fear of divorce that was so often in her mind.

On 3 Nivôse Year IX – Christmas Eve of 1800 in the old calendar – Josephine persuaded Bonaparte, with considerable difficulty, to go with her to hear Haydn's *Creation*. By chance – because she lingered to rearrange her shawl and because his coachman, Germain, was a little drunk and drove faster than usual – their carriages became separated in the narrow twisting streets that lay between the Tuileries and the Théâtre de la République et des Arts. A horse-drawn cart with a keg on it stood in the rue St-Nicaise. Just after the First Consul's carriage had passed and just as Mme Bonaparte's appeared at the corner the keg blew up with a terrifying report. The explosion wounded the horse of the last trooper in Bonaparte's escort, shattered the windows of Josephine's carriage, killed a score of bystanders and injured more than fifty others. The First Consul continued to the theatre, showed himself in his box, waited for the orchestra to strike the opening chords of the oratorio, and then returned wrathfully to the Tuileries.

Fouché, who was very fond of music, was also at the theatre that evening, accompanied by Bonne-Jeanne on one of her exceptional sorties into society. He hurried to the scene of the explosion with Réal. They found the street cluttered with debris and the cart completely disintegrated. Of the unfortunate horse, the largest single fragment was one leg. Réal noticed that the hoof was newly shod. He gave orders for all the debris to be collected and taken to the prefecture of police, and then went with Fouché to the Hôtel de Juigné. They had been there only a few minutes when they were joined by the comte de Bourmont, an ex-*chouan* leader who had been employed by Fouché in October 'to discover the two channels of communication with *Monsieur* [the comte d'Artois] and the British'[6] by which the secrets of his ministry were still being sent to England.

When Fouché first met Bourmont after his submission, he said to the small, handsome, quick-witted aristocrat: 'You have sworn loyalty to the Republic. I know about your former relationship with the princes – they do not matter. You may wish them well, but nothing more. If you conspire, you will be arrested and shot within twenty-four hours. You receive payment from England – I will guarantee you the same amount, and half as much again.'[7] But by now, as Fouché well knew, he was also in the pay of Bonaparte and of the royalists.

When Fouché asked him what he knew of the affair, Bourmont replied that the attempt was evidently the work of Jacobins: if Fouché would give him weapons to arm the 300 *chouans* who were in hiding in Paris, he would use them to hunt down the criminals. Fouché answered that all he needed was for Bourmont to tell him where to find two men: Limoëlan and Saint-Réjant, lieutenants of Georges Cadoudal who had come to Paris from Brittany some weeks before. Fouché then hurried back across the river to the Tuileries, where he found Bonaparte's bad temper undiminished.

Fright was at the bottom of Bonaparte's fury. Though he cultivated an air of indifference in public and constantly assured his cronies that he regarded assassination as a commonplace risk that no ruler should allow to bother him, his violent reaction in, for instance, the Enghien and Staps affairs some years later, showed that the fear was strong in his mind. It was known to those who watched him closely and often commented on in secret intelligence reports. In August, Nasica told Dutheil that Bonaparte was 'a prey to the liveliest terrors. He was at the Comédie Française recently (he often goes to the theatre) when he was told that an urgent matter required his presence at the Tuileries. Fouché was waiting for him; they were half an hour together; when he ended the interview, Bonaparte said, "I can see that I shan't die in my bed!" '[8] A month later, in a letter to George Hammond, Under-Secretary of State at the Foreign Office, Nasica wrote: 'Jacobins are still being arrested, on the pretext, according to what Fouché the Minister of Police says, that a conspiracy against the Consul's life has been discovered . . . It is this secret vigilance by the police that makes Fouché very useful and very valuable to Bonaparte, and the means by which he maintains his position against the repeated attacks of Lucien Bonaparte and Talleyrand who cordially hate him.'[9]

Fouché had in fact received information the day before that some sort of plot was planned for Christmas Eve. There were no details, and vague warnings of that kind were commonplace, but he reported it in his nightly bulletin. This accounted for Bonaparte's reluctance to accompany Josephine; he changed his mind only on receiving assurance from his household police that they had searched the theatre and found nothing.

At the Tuileries, the Prefect of Police, Dubois, who had been given the post by Bonaparte in order to keep an eye on Fouché and who saw a chance to step into the minister's shoes, was busily assuring the First Consul that the bomb attempt was the work of the Jacobins. In this he was supported by all the right-wing group, who offered this as new proof of the dangers of Fouché's softness towards them. The argument was all the more readily accepted by Bonaparte because a few weeks earlier, without making any public announcement, Fouché had arrested a Jacobin named Chevalier, who had prepared – and actually tested at the back of the Salpétrière convent – a sort of land-mine stuffed with nails and grapeshot: perhaps a prototype of that evening's infernal machine.

Bonaparte was so incensed that Talleyrand forsook his usual caution and 'openly expressed his opinion in the presence of the First Consul that he should have [Fouché] arrested and shot within twenty-four hours'.[10] Fouché, entering shortly after this, found Bonaparte bearing down on him, his face aflame with anger.

'Well!' he shouted. 'Well! Do you still say it is the royalists?'

'Certainly I say it,' Fouché replied. 'And what's more, I'll prove it.'

'It's your Jacobins who've played this fine trick!'[11] yelled Bonaparte.

'I agree they're capable of it,' said Fouché, quite unperturbed, 'and I'll give orders for some of them to be arrested. But they're not the only ones the police need to keep their eyes on.'[12]

Bonaparte was lusting for vengeance, and only too glad of the opportunity to strike at the Jacobins. He had Demerville, Aréna and their accomplices brought before a court-martial and condemned to death. He ordered Dubois and Fouché to prepare lists of prominent Jacobins. By January 4, 223 suspects had been rounded up and put in the prisons of the Temple, La Force and Ste-Pélagie.

The campaign against the Jacobins was accompanied by attacks on their alleged protector. In the Council of State, Roederer proposed that a petition should be sent to the First Consul, asking for Fouché's dismissal. He failed – and received an even less sympathetic hearing in the Tuileries when he criticized Fouché to Josephine.

'It's not the Minister of Police that Bonaparte should be on his guard against,' she replied sharply. 'The most dangerous men for him are the toadies who persuade him to do things that irritate honest citizens, and try to inspire him with ambitions that he doesn't have!'[13]

Fouché, whose warning to Bonaparte on the night before the explosion had been based partly on the sudden disappearance of Limoëlan and Saint-Réjant from the usual *chouan* haunts in Paris, issued a list of other royalists who had inexplicably disappeared: Joyaux, La Haye Saint-Hilaire, and Carbon, who was known as Little François. 'But the gendarmerie and most of the prefects paid scarcely any attention,'[14] the chief of his intelligence bureau recorded. Chaptal, the Minister of the Interior, let them know that the case was already solved and that the search for royalists suspects was merely another example of 'Fouché's deceitfulness'.[15]

The Council of State, at Bonaparte's suggestion, considered the proposal to deport all the Jacobins whose names appeared on the lists prepared at the Ministry of Police and subsequently augmented by other members of the government. Réal protested that 'certain enemies of Liberty are merely looking for a pretext to proscribe its defenders',[16] and pointed out that some personal scores had been paid off so carelessly that the list included a judge who had been living in Guadeloupe for five years past and a lawyer who had been dead six months.

The list was revised again. Fouché managed to get about 40 deportations reduced to rustication from Paris. But there were still 130 names on the list that Bonaparte presented to the acquiescent Senate on January 5. They were condemned, without trial, to be deported to the Seychelles. 'Do you know why the French army is the most formidable in the world?' Bonaparte said ten years later. 'It is because when the officers emigrated the non-commissioned officers took their places and subsequently became generals and marshals of France . . . The non-commissioned officer . . . has a moral influence over the soldier, leading as well as commanding him . . . After Nivôse I seized the opportunity and had the non-commissioned officers deported.'[17]

Fouché pressed on with his inquiries. The cart was traced to a cornchandler named Lambel, who had sold it to a man answering Carbon's description. The remnants of the horse were pieced together sufficiently for the newspapers to print some details: a bay with a ragged mane, white streaks behind the ears and on the flanks, well-groomed but old, about 14 hands. The description brought no response, but among the blacksmiths summoned to examine the remains there was one who thought the shoe was his work. He had done it for a man about 5 feet 6 inches in height, with a scar under his left eye – Little François Carbon again.

Fouché was satisfied that he was on the right track although his opponents claimed that the incident had been closed with the deportation of the Jacobins, and Bonaparte was reported to have jeered, 'If I were the Minister of Police in such circumstances, I should hang myself in desperation.'[18] Late in the evening of January 6, Fouché learned that Bourmont was at the Tuileries. He went to the palace, presented himself at Bonaparte's private quarters, and was refused admission. He was by now sure that Bourmont was betraying him, and he was ready to inject a little more excitement into the drama in preparation for the climax. When Bourmont emerged at midnight, Fouché had him arrested. At one o'clock he received the expected summons to the Tuileries. Bonaparte was beside himself with anger; he threatened disgrace and even death. Fouché, still quite unruffled, asked for a few hours to complete his inquiries.

On January 8, Carbon was arrested when going to visit his sister, whom the police had under observation. He was sent to the Temple to join Bourmont – still kept under arrest by Fouché, despite Bonaparte's menaces – and within a fortnight a score of minor accomplices were under lock and key. Carbon confessed that the plot was entirely royalist in concept and execution, and was sentenced to death, together with Saint-Réjant who was caught on January 27.

One day when one of Josephine's friends, Stanislas de Girardin, was dining at the Tuileries, Bonaparte took him on one side and, knowing that what he said would be carried back to Fouché, asked: 'Do you know of a man fit to be Minister of Police? . . . Fouché's all right, but I don't think he's sufficiently diligent – he doesn't work hard enough.'[19] With that petulant outburst Fouché's triumph was accepted and, ostensibly, forgotten. In fact, Bonaparte was deeply impressed by the skilled police work that had proved everybody, himself included, to be wrong. The incident increased his strange dependence on Fouché – a dependence that sprang from several causes but certainly included among them the feeling that Fouché could give him more protection than any other man.

'The Consul is entirely in the hands of the Jacobins,' Nasica reported on March 10. 'Fouché and Réal have won his confidence more completely than ever.'[20] And in July:

'Bonaparte should have returned to Paris on the 12th. The horses were already harnessed when a warning from Fouché made him change his mind. Bonaparte is entirely under the thumb of this minister who does what he likes with him by continual scares.

Fear is the only emotion by which you can get at Bonaparte's heart – and that fear comes from Fouché's ministry. In the hands of his minister the hero of Italy and Egypt and other places is like a child in the arms of his nurse. Nurses frighten children by talking to them about ghosts and werewolves. Fouché only has to talk to Bonaparte about Jacobin and royalist plots to terrify him; he's managed to make him frightened of everybody . . .'[21]

6

The year that had begun with such excitement settled to a hopeful jogtrot. The Austrians signed the Peace of Lunéville in February; Pitt's resignation in March brought the possibility of an armistice with England. Despite his tussle with the royalist terrorists, Fouché continued to welcome any who wished to return in good faith, whatever their previous record or principles. Compared with many of those around him, and particularly the master he served, he was remarkably free of rancour. His policy, as the formidable Mme de Staël observed after taking him through one of the intense philosophical discussions that she enjoyed so much, 'was to do as little harm as possible, within the limits of his objective . . . His remarkable sagacity prompted him to choose good as a logical thing, and the light of reason brought him to conclusions which conscience would have inspired in others.'[1]

In June, a week before his wife gave birth to another son, Paul-Athanase, Fouché received the duchesse de Guiche who had been sent by the comte d'Artois to sound out the possibility of persuading Bonaparte to become some sort of perpetual prime minister under a restored Bourbon king. With Bonaparte successful and apparently unassailable, it was a pointless mission, but Fouché felt it as well to underline a few facts that might not have been made clear to the duchess during her conversations in royalist circles.

'The French have become warriors,' he told her. 'They have been brave in all ages; but today they are in love with glory. The Princes should have put in an appearance earlier; now they must keep quiet. It is common knowledge that the comte d'Artois is secretly inciting the British Government against France (and that is scarcely showing love for his country) . . . Does he want to remain in England? He's wrong, he is with his enemies, *our* enemies, and it is he who instigates all these conspiracies against the Consul.'[2]

His own attitude to the Consul was being rapidly modified. 'I was sincerely attached to that man,' he wrote, 'convinced that nobody else in the profession of arms or in civil life had so firm and persevering a character, of the kind needed to rule the state and control the factions. I even flattered myself then that I could mitigate the violence and harshness of that great character.'[3] But in fact it was more than violence and harshness that he distrusted in Bonaparte – it was the direction in which his ambition would drag France.

The Concordat with the Pope, in which Bonaparte recognized him as head of the French Church, made Fouché uneasy and set him in direct conflict with the First Consul again. Without consultation or permission he sent a circular to all prefects on July 20 (less than a week after the Concordat was signed) warning them against the former priests now being reinstated, and recommending the constitutional priests who, 'born of the Revolution, have remained faithful to it; who have no need of pardon; who have linked their fate with that of the Republic'.[4] He ordered them to 'enjoin the mayors of communes where there is only one building consecrated to public worship, to permit it to be used only by the priest who performed there at the period of 18 Brumaire'.[5] This outburst brought him a rebuke from Bonaparte.

More immediate than the preservation of republican liberties was the problem of obtaining peace. The war with England continued through the summer. In August the adventure that Bonaparte had led and deserted in Egypt came to an ignominious end with the surrender of the French army. It was another blow to his pride, a fresh impetus to his envy and resentment. 'I will crush England; France will lay down the law to the rest of the world',[6] he had said to Bourmont.

'Certainly the First Consul will never bring us peace and prosperity!' Fouché said in a typically frank outburst to the royalist abbé de Pradt. 'Just look at the mountebank careering round Belgium with all these feastings and fine receptions that he has ordered for himself.'[7]

It was not the luxury that disturbed him: his own tastes were simple, but he encouraged his wife to dress well (like Madame Bonaparte and other ladies of fashion she was known to have some of her gowns smuggled over from England). What roused his suspicion was the trend towards despotism that he saw in the increased pomp. Bonaparte was preparing to go to Lyons to have himself appointed

President of the reorganized Cisalpine Republic. Fouché, realizing this would cause such resentment and suspicion in Britain that the peace-talks, opened only a few weeks earlier, might break down, did everything in his power to prevent him.

Young George Jackson, brother of the newly appointed British Minister in Paris, went to the opera on December 9. 'Madame Bonaparte was there, and was grossly insulted on leaving. Very obscene language was addressed to her, and, strange to say, the police took no notice of the offenders.'[8] The common opinion, he soon learned, was that 'the insult was a mere stratagem of the police to induce the belief that the commotion among the poorer class, on the increasing price of bread, is of a more serious nature than it really is; it being an object with Fouché just now to keep the First Consul in Paris'.[9] The journey was postponed, but not cancelled; on January 25, Bonaparte became president not of the Cisalpine Republic but of the Italian Republic.

At the beginning of the month, Fouché attended a reception given by the widow of his old friend General Joubert. Chatting with Francis Jackson he turned the conversation to the renewed rumours that Louis XVIII might be restored to the throne.

> 'It would cause a revolution more bloody than any that has taken place . . . The great difficulty that the present government has to contend with is its newness . . . every man is convinced that he has a right to destroy what was, in a manner, his own work. But we will have no more revolutions, therefore we must strenuously oppose the return of Louis XVIII, who could not remain three weeks in power . . . The country is determined to maintain its tranquillity. Even if Bonaparte, with all his glory, tried to crown himself, or crown another, he would be stabbed before the day was out.'[10]

Despite, or perhaps because of, his denials that a change was possible, there were rumours that he was 'concerting with an officer of high standing . . . the best means for giving France another form of government and a new ruler'.[11] It was not difficult to guess that the unnamed officer was Moreau, still smarting under the snubs and churlishness that Bonaparte visited upon him for his victory at Hohenlinden, more than twelve months before. But if Fouché really intended to join forces with Moreau (and not merely sound him out on the conspiracy among the generals that had been rumoured for a year past) the negotiations never went very far. Moreau's moderate views had hardened into a preference for some sort of limited monarchy, with himself as High Constable – a proposition that the Bourbons had already put to Bonaparte.

The winter of 1801–2 was not all rumour and worry. Mme de Staël noted that the period was 'quite pleasant for me because of the readiness with which Fouché granted the different requests I made to him for the return of the émigrés'.[12] With others, the Minister was as benevolent, but only after having his little joke. To Duveyrier, a member of the Tribunate, who approached him on behalf of the elderly bailli de Crussol, he replied that permission for 'the traitor Emmanuel de Crussol to return' would be granted if Duveyrier signed a guarantee. He then dictated a rigmarole in which Duveyrier agreed that, if Crussol was hanged for conspiracy, Duveyrier himself would be hanged beside him. He walked across and looked over his shoulder. 'Good God!' he exclaimed, 'He *has* written it – every last word!'[13] and then burst into laughter.

His straight-faced witticisms were sometimes taken seriously. Dining at the Jacksons' one evening in December he was complimented on the efficiency of his police and replied, 'Oh yes, things are going very well at the moment; but to arrive at it I've had to lop off at least 200 heads!'[14] This remark, uttered 'with that brutal sort of indifference which characterizes him'[15] so shocked the Jackson brothers that Francis reported it in his dispatch to Lord Hawkesbury, while George recounted it again, in almost exactly the same words, to his mother the following February; as did the Reverend Dawson Warren, Jackson's brother-in-law, who had been found a job as the Embassy chaplain. This situation, in which the younger brother and the brother-in-law sent letters home or kept diaries which included extracts from the elder brother's Most Secret messages to Whitehall, was the more surprising because they were conscious of being spied upon and reported (with George this time only a fortnight after Francis) that 'there is not a Family in Paris considered worthy of notice, where one or more of the servants are not in his pay . . . – indeed, this part of his plan is carried on with so little reserve, as to appear likely to defeat its object by putting people so much on their guard.'[16]

It never occurred to them that they were the victims of Fouché's delight in shocking simple souls and practical *mystification* of persuading people that the Minister of Police had a spy under every bed. Fouché evidently shared the joke with Bonaparte: towards the end of February the British Cabinet's secret Paris correspondent reported that the First Consul had described Mr Jackson as 'hare-brained and pig-headed!'[17]

The opinions that most foreigners formed of Fouché were in accord with that of the Jacksons, and of the Reverend Dawson Warren, who found him 'vulgar in deportment, coarse-minded and ferocious in disposition'[18] and, confusing him with Carrier of Nantes, credited him with having 'had the infernal distinction of inventing what he called "Revolutionary Marriages" by tying a man and woman together and flinging them into the water'.[19]

One English tourist, Mary Berry, arriving late for one of the assemblies that the Minister gave on the third day of every *décade*, was greeted by 'a fair, vulgar-looking woman in a yellow wig, with a very fine gold-muslin gown with a border of gold, and a very fine lace handkerchief which fell down like an apron before her . . . The salon is hung in panels with the most exquisite Gobelins, and surrounded with such profusion of carving and gilding in admirable state as I never saw in any palace.'[20] She had no time to speak with Fouché, but dropped him a curtsey in passing. 'His figure is not prepossessing; a little man with a pale flattish face and small grey eyes; his dress that of a Minister of State, blue velvet embroidered in silver, hussar boots.'[21]

One wonders if Miss Berry's escort pointed out the right man. But then where did the Russian Princess Divova, who frequently went to the Hôtel de Juigné for the 'superb concerts' and the singing of Garat and Mme Branchu of the Opera, get *her* information? 'Before the Revolution M. Fouché was a monk and his wife a nun, which certainly gave them no distinction or amiability. After the convents were abolished in France, Fouché and his wife were in the same prison, took a liking to each other and then married in the revolutionary manner, with neither priest nor church . . . He talks little, his wife has a common manner and no idea at all how to receive society.'[22]

During the interval of peace, Paris was full of visitors from other countries. It was about this time that the Spanish Ambassador complained to Bonaparte, at a dinner for the diplomatic corps, that one of his compatriots had been robbed of her diamonds, worth almost a million francs, while staying in Paris. He added that he supposed the burglars would never be found. 'In every country the petty thieves are caught and hanged, but I've never seen those who operate on a grand scale arrested.'[23]

Bonaparte turned to Fouché and asked if he could recover the jewels. Fouché said it was not impossible – but also not easy.

'Well then, get on with it.'

The guests moved to the salon for coffee and liqueurs. Fouché sent for his carriage and left the palace. An hour later he rejoined the company.

'Do you think you'll succeed?' Bonaparte asked.

'Yes,' Fouché replied. 'But I can't guarantee it.'

'Don't spare anything,' Bonaparte persisted. 'That Spaniard has riled me. I'm going to teach him that our police are better than the ones in Madrid. Spend as much as you like.'[24]

By the following evening Fouché had five burglars in prison and the diamonds in safe custody. It had cost him 500,000 francs – more than half the ministry's yearly allocation of secret funds – and a promise that the burglar who had given the information should be allowed to escape after the trial, with a passport, his reward, and free transport to the frontier. He reported his success to Bonaparte that night, and Bonaparte triumphantly announced it next morning at what was rapidly taking on the appearance of his ceremonial levée.

Among those present was Fouché's old enemy Roederer. 'It's another *carmagnole* of the Minister of Police,' he sneered, choosing a word that not only meant a hoax but also recalled Fouché's terrorist past. The remark soon reached Fouché's ears. At two o'clock that afternoon Roederer received a note saying, 'Senator Roederer is requested to come to the Ministry of Police on business which affects him personally. – Fouché.'

He arrived in some agitation, which increased when Fouché produced a key and asked him if he recognized it. 'It is the key of the iron gate leading from my garden on to the Champs Elysées.' 'And this?' 'The key from the garden into the house.' 'And this?' 'The key to my bedroom.'

The senator, a man with a permanent prim, startled look, was trembling with apprehension. Fouché grinned. 'If all this is nothing but a *carmagnole*, Monsieur Roederer, you're getting much too excited,' he said. Then he produced the keys of the two boxes in which Roederer kept cash for household expenses and larger sums of money.[25]

'You've kept me on tenterhooks long enough,' Roederer pleaded ... 'I committed an indiscretion this morning and you have had your revenge ... Please – what is the meaning of this?'[26]

Fouché told him that his house was to be burgled that night while his wife was on a visit to Versailles. If the burglars were arrested before the crime they would get only a few months in prison. If Roederer agreed to let them be arrested while they were actually committing the crime they could be sent to the galleys. 'I will have a squad of sturdy, reliable men hidden in the cupboards and under your bed – you won't run any risk.'

'I must ask my wife before deciding,' said Roederer.

'You're a cry-baby,' said Fouché, dismissing him. 'Anybody else would have let his wife and daughter leave without saying anything to them.'[27]

Two hours later he received a message from Roederer that his wife no longer wanted to go to Versailles and would 'die of fright if the robbers are not arrested before the burglary'.

'The senator lacks backbone,' Fouché replied. 'He ensures protection for the robbers and encourages them in their ugly trade. But I will keep my promise. Madame Roederer may rely on that, and leave for Versailles.'[28] That evening he arrested Roederer's valet whom he had known all the time was the instigator of the plot.

He did not often make himself enemies to satisfy his pride, but he was never loth to show Bonaparte that he was not overawed by him. The First Consul, when in Milan, had been attracted by an opera singer named Grassini. He had her brought to Paris by his chief-of-staff, Berthier, and set her up in a house in the rue de la Victoire with an allowance of 15,000 francs a month. A large and vigorous woman, her appetite far from satisfied by Bonaparte's brusque and feeble attentions, she soon chose herself a lover from among the musicians at the opera. One day, in an ill-tempered mood, Bonaparte sneered that he was surprised that Fouché, 'with all his famous skill, didn't manage the police better, and that there were a lot of things that he didn't know about'.

'Yes,' said Fouché. 'There are things that I didn't know about, but which I know about now. For instance, a short man, dressed in a grey coat, fairly frequently leaves a secret door of the Tuileries at dead of night and, accompanied by a single servant, gets into a covered carriage and goes stoating around the signora Grassini; that man is you, and the singer is betraying you with Rode, the violinist.'[29]

Bonaparte turned on his heel and rang the bell for Fouché to be shown out. Fouché gleefully repeated the conversation, which was widely circulated in Paris and recorded by Gohier, and the wife of General Durand, and (in duplicate as usual) the Jackson brothers and by one of the comte de Provence's agents, who maliciously substituted the name of Bonaparte's sister-in-law and adopted daughter, Hortense, for that of Grassini.

7

It was not surprising that rumours continued to circulate that the Minister of Police was shortly to be replaced. His dismissal would have delighted most of his fellow ministers, who shared Talleyrand's right-wing leanings and were frequently affronted by Fouché's calm interference in their affairs. When three captured *chouan* guerrillas were shot by their military escort while being taken from Auray to Vannes, Fouché wrote to the Minister of War: 'It may be that this incident is attributable simply to the necessity of curbing resistance to the armed forces. It may also be the result of abuses arising from military indiscipline. In the latter event, it is for you to take measures, to remind the various bodies of troops stationed in the West of their duties, and to compel them to respect the laws which guarantee the individual safety of citizens.'[1] A little later, he was lecturing the Minister of War, after another shooting incident, on 'the extreme facility with which the troops get rid of the persons whom they have been ordered to arrest. Any violence by the armed forces against persons whom they are escorting is a crime, and should be punished according to the rigours of the law.'[2]

But he was too useful to be discarded – especially now that he was discovering more plots against the First Consul's position and even his life. There was the one in December 1801. 'According to information from men employed by Fouché, who, they say, has been aware of it for a long time, this conspiracy has its roots in the department of the Vendée, and its object is again the assassination of the First Consul at the instigation of England.'[3] The message received in Whitehall added that, 'nobody believes it yet, but everybody presumes, rightly, that Fouché only brings this plot forward to strengthen the absolute control that fear has won for him over the hero's soul'.[4] The hero, meanwhile, well informed by his own spies of all the rumours that were circulating, sent for Moreau. He 'asked if there was anything he could do that would satisfy him; and on Moreau's answering that he was at present well satisfied, and wished for nothing more than he had, Bonaparte replied, "You are mistaken, Moreau, I can do at least as much for you as Fouché."'[5]

There was always the possibility that Fouché had invented the story of his own plot with Moreau. His startling frankness and apparent indiscretion served as lures. 'It is difficult to believe,' his adjutant Réal said, 'how many people are always ready to tell everything they know, everything they have heard, without any malicious intention; they :hatter for chattering's sake, they recount one item of news in order to receive another which they will have the satisfaction of passing on elsewhere.'[6] Fouché prided himself on doing very little paper work – and reading very little, as his overflowing wastepaper baskets proved. He talked a lot and listened more.

'There are three sorts of conspiracy,' he said, 'by the people who complain, by the people who write, by the people who take action. There is nothing to fear from the first group, the two others are more dangerous; but the police have to be a part of all three.'[7] It was the two more dangerous ones that now concerned him. Mme de Staël and other very articulate opponents of the regime were conferring with Bernadotte, Lannes, Brune and other republican generals on how to prevent Bonaparte strengthening his dictatorship. Pamphlets attacking the First Consul were traced back to Bernadotte's headquarters at Rennes; a member of his staff gave incriminating information to Bonaparte's household police headed by Duroc; Fouché's men reported dinners that were attended only by high-ranking officers and from which servants were excluded. Bonaparte, with the recent murder of the Tsar Paul by his own officers fresh in his mind, realized that this was no time to get rid of Fouché. Fouché as an old friend, and Joseph Bonaparte as his brother-in-law, patched up a temporary reconciliation between Bernadotte and the First Consul.

It was an uneasy truce. In March 1802 the signing of the Peace of Amiens brought Bonaparte a great wave of popularity and glory (France had retained most of her conquests from the war, Britain scarcely any) and gave the obvious cue for his next step. On May 7, Merry, who had replaced Jackson as Minister in Paris a fortnight earlier, sent a cypher message to Hawkesbury, that he had learned 'with absolute certainty, the Existence of a Project for changing the Constitution of France, and for placing General Bonaparte alone, and for Life, at the Head of the Government, with nearly all the Attributes of Sovereignty'.[8] It was the moment of decision for Bonaparte and for France. His establishment of the Empire two years later was a more striking assertion of his personal rule and the final betrayal of the Revolution, but the essential blow was struck when he achieved the Consulate for life.

He prepared the way by a move to win over the army – restless in all ranks now that peace had deprived them of the chance of booty and promotion. He shipped some of the malcontents, particularly those loyal to Moreau, to Saint-Domingue to be killed off by yellow fever. He dispersed Bernadotte's staff. With the creation of the Legion of Honour he succeeded in increasing his own glamour, while at the same time buying the continued allegiance of the army. There were 16 cohorts, each with 7 grand-officers, 20 commanders, 30 officers, and 350 legionnaires. It was 'more richly endowed than any other order of chivalry had ever been: each cohort received an annual income of 200,000 livres from state funds, the allowance for legionnaires was 250 francs, for officers 1,000 francs, for commanders 2,000 francs, and for grand-officers 5,000 francs'.[9]

In the Council of State, Fouché had argued frequently against the proposal that Bonaparte should be given power for life, urging that the time was not ripe, that the First Consul was in danger of losing all his great popularity by one false move. It was clear that nobody agreed. He noticed that his fellow councillors were less open with him. He learned that secret meetings of the council were being held in the rooms of the Second Consul, Cambacérès. He realized that he must act at once, or not at all.

His plan was extremely simple and effective. With the aid of his friends in the Senate, he canvassed support for public recognition of the virtues of the man who had brought France peace and victory abroad and tranquillity at home. What better expression of the national gratitude – and demonstration of the powers of the Senate – than to vote Bonaparte, who still had seven years of his consulate to serve, a further ten years at the end of that period? Fouché spread the word that Bonaparte would be delighted by such a gesture. And on May 8 the Senate informed the Tribunate and the Legislative Corps that it had re-elected citizen Bonaparte as First Consul for an additional ten years.

When Cambacérès called that evening he found Bonaparte 'striding up and down the salon with his hat pulled over his eyes'[10] watched by his mute and despondent brothers. He rounded on the Second Consul, raging about the Senate's ingratitude. Cambacérès waited for him to calm down, and then suggested that the Senate had intended well and might still be led round to doing what Bonaparte wanted. He proposed that Bonaparte should reply that he was flattered but intended to retire from public life now that he had brought back peace to France. If he was to resume the heavy burden of leadership, he could do so only by the will of the people. On May 10, 1802, the Senate received a letter on those lines, with the request that a national referendum should be held on the question: Should Bonaparte be appointed Consul for Life? The voting, spread through June and July, resulted in a resounding 'Yes'.

Fouché had had the table turned on him. He was isolated in the council. His only friend at court – as it could now be fittingly called – was Josephine, herself under constant attack. Bonaparte had been building up her importance as his consort – after the Peace of Amiens the foreign ambassadors were required to go to Madame Bonaparte's quarters to present their compliments before offering them to the First Consul – but this was accompanied by rumours of a plan 'to separate her from the First Consul by a formal Act of Divorce'.[11]

Royalist circles in Paris were convinced that Josephine's patronage would not save Fouché. 'What is quite remarkable,' Provence's spy reported at the end of August, 'is that Fouché's disgrace will seem to some of them to be a misfortune; they claim he had the strength to refuse sometimes to carry out arbitrary measures, and that Dubois [his presumed successor, the Prefect of Police] will oppose nothing.'[12]

The Bonaparte family were Fouché's sworn enemies ever since the disgrace of Lucien – who had only recently been allowed to return from Madrid. Napoleon, as he signed himself from this time forward, was sufficiently enraged by Fouché's opposition to the Life Consulate to screw himself to the point of dismissing his bodyguard. He spent September 13 at his brother Joseph's estate, Morfontaine, where Lucien joined them together with the two other consuls, Cambacérès and Lebrun.

They presented him with a memorandum which, while avoiding a direct attack on Fouché, pointed out that with peace and stability 'the Ministry of Police had become an unnecessary and dangerous power; unnecessary against the disarmed and submissive royalists who wanted nothing better than to accept the government; dangerous as being a republican institution and the shield of incurable anarchists who found protection and employment there. They concluded that it would be inadvisable to leave such great power in the hands of one man.'[13] The next day, Tuesday, he returned to Malmaison and Fouché reported to him to discuss government business, as he did most days.

They completed their work on the documents that Fouché had brought. Napoleon said abruptly: 'Monsieur Fouché, you have served the government well, and it will not stint your reward: from today you are a member of the senior body of the legislature... Under the new arrangements which I have just made, the police will become merely a branch of the Ministry of Justice . . . But be assured that I am not discarding your counsel or your services – this is in no way a disgrace . . .'[14]

Fouché thanked him for his kind words and assured him, slily, that the news did not come as a shock. 'Without being absolutely sure, I was prepared for it by certain indications and whispers that reached me.'[15] He asked permission to present a final report on the state of the nation's morale. He brought it the following morning: a homily on the danger of war and the necessity of establishing the government on the support of 'upright men of good character', neither royalist nor anarchist, but 'the men of 1789 and all wise friends of liberty'.[16] Napoleon accepted the document but did not read it. Fouché produced his accounts of the secret police funds, in which he had a surplus of 2,400,000 francs.

'Keep half of it,' said Napoleon.[17] It was as if, at this moment of parting, he was loth to let him go – or was wary of what might happen if he turned against him. In a message to the Senate he praised Fouché's devotion to the government and the 'talent and activity with which he had responded to every task that confronted him . . . if different circumstances again called for a Minister of Police, the government could not find another more worthy of its confidence'.[18] In bidding farewell to Fouché as a minister he asked for his advice on the reorganization of his private police. 'Give me your views on anything you wish, citizen senator; everything that comes from you will always have my attention.'[19] Bonaparte, when he wanted to be, was as shrewd an observer of human nature as Fouché. He knew that his ex-minister's favourite indulgence was giving advice to other people; his greatest error was in believing that they would listen to it.

8

With more than a million francs in his pocket, he had no immediate problems. He said that he was going to retire to the estate he had recently bought at Ferrières-Pont-Carré but he had no sooner moved out of the Hôtel de Juigné than he sold up his town house at 333 rue Basse du Rempart (the modern boulevard des Capucines) and bought himself a larger one on the left bank at 264 rue du Bac, 'a big three-storey building with a courtyard and outbuildings and a garden in the French style, shaded by fifty lime trees'.[1] The income of 2,000 francs a year that he inherited from his father had been wiped out in the rebellion in Saint-Domingue but he still had his business interests which had brought him in ten times as much before he was appointed to the Ministry.

He was active in the Senate, polishing old friendships and collecting new ones. He was invited to dinner at the Tuileries in November and with his wife attended two formal receptions early in the New Year. (The First Consul was applying himself to the social and ceremonial aspects of his budding court, determined to cure the men of the 'utter disregard of the ordinary decencies of the toilet', which had so shocked the Jacksons twelve months before. It was indeed at one of Madame Fouché's receptions that they had noticed 'more than one pair of spattered boots, and a good deal of linen far from clean'.[2]) In December he was appointed one of the Commission of Four, two senators and two councillors of state, which drew up a constitution for the Swiss Confederation, a task which kept him in Paris until February.

He continued to surprise observers by the ease with which he retained friends in all parties, right and left, even though there was no advantage for them now that he was out of office. 'Mackintosh dined at Barthélemy's the banker – the brother of the ex-director – with a pleasant party,' Creevey wrote in November 1802. 'The ex-director was there, and next to him sat Fouché – now a senator – but who formerly, as Minister of Police, actually *deported* the ex-director to Cayenne. There was likewise a person who told M. he had seen Fouché ride full gallop to preside at some celebrated massacre with a pair of *human ears* stuck one on each side of his hat.'[3]

There were even members of the clergy who regretted his departure from office. The constitutional bishop, Le Coz, who admired him as a defender of the Gallican Church against the foreign authority of Rome, wrote on September 26, 'I have often had the pleasure of expressing my esteem, gratitude and devotion to the *Minister of Police*; permit me to offer them also to the *Senator*. The place has changed but the man is still the same, and that man will always have claims on public recognition and especially on mine.'[4]

It was not entirely out of flattery that the bishop added, 'Already, sir, it is apparent that the trident of the police is no longer in your hands.'[5] Régnier, the Minister of Justice now re-named the Grand Judge, had no flair for police work; Réal, who had been given charge of the department, was too preoccupied with settling the constant quarrelling between Dubois and Desmarest and the feuds with all the private spy systems. Fouché, always ready to demonstrate his superior skills, frequently called in at the Tuileries, providing the First Consul with 'news obtained through the influence he had retained over the police agents, and the secrets that he extracted from them',[6] which always outstripped the reports sent in by the Grand Judge. It was not long before Napoleon decided that he must sooner or later recall him. 'The fear of giving an air of vacillation to his acts of government was the only thing that restrained him.'[7]

It was not so certain that Fouché wished to return. There were many things happening that disturbed him both as a republican and as a patriot. There was the First Consul's approach, in February 1803, to the comte de Provence through the King of Prussia, inviting him to sell the Bourbon claims to the throne of France. There was the new coinage bearing the head of the First Consul and the inscription May God Protect France: the first time for ten years that the French people had seen on their money 'the name of God or the effigy of a man'.[8] Above all, there were the increasing signs of a drift to war, and of Napoleon's appetite for it. He became more stubborn in refusing to honour the terms of the peace treaty. Girardin, observing him from the favoured position of one in Josephine's intimate circle, noted not only that 'his natural leaning draws him towards war', but that he was beginning to see new victories in Europe as a means 'to excuse the fatal result of the Saint-Domingue expedition'.[9]

Lord Whitworth, the British Ambassador, reported on March 21, 1803, that Napoleon 'appears to have made a most dangerous experiment – that of calling to his most intimate confidence those who are his most rooted enemies, and who consequently will advise him to do what they think most likely to lead him to ruin: these are Fouché and Masséna. I have reason to believe they were both for war . . .'[10] This startling misinformation was soon corrected by Huber, the French-speaking Swiss whom Whitworth hired as a spy under the title of confidential secretary. When the rift between Britain and France became so wide that Whitworth asked for his passports, Huber informed the ambassador that Fouché 'stands notoriously high in point of abilities, energy and independence of mind; he has on this occasion been a bold and loud advocate for peace and alone had dared repeatedly to combat the Consul's mistaken pride and ambition'.[11]

Fouché's problem with this man of 'so jealous, so suspicious and so irritable a temper' was to offset the army officers' jeers that 'the little corporal is retreating'. He tried to frighten him with the prediction of civil upheaval, 'You know, my lord, that his private reports to Bonaparte on the State of Paris have always the greatest weight. He has taken measures to put into the Consul's hands in two or three days such a report . . . in consequence of his having made advances towards Peace, and will convey to him the applause and blessings of the common soldiers and of all conscripts . . .'[12]

Huber quoted Fouché as warning Napoleon that he would be 're-opening a trial that has already been decided in your favour. You are yourself, like us, a product of the Revolution, and war will set it all in question again . . . Public opinion in France is entirely against war, there will be no national support.'[13] Despite this frank speaking, or perhaps because of it, Huber believed that the First Consul had offered Fouché his old ministry back if war did come. 'And nobody doubts his being named to it, in spite of all the generals, who dread in him so avowed and so intrepid an advocate of peace, and in spite also of the present ministers, who dread his known influence on Bonaparte.'[14]

He might be named to it, but he was not ready to accept it. His reluctance had nothing to do with the policy of reaction and self-aggrandisement that Napoleon was set on – Fouché never lacked self-confidence and was eager for an opportunity to put all that machinery in reverse. He was delaying simply because he wanted more power.

'I never knew a sounder understanding united to such strong nerves,' Huber reported to Whitworth on May 17, after a long talk with Fouché. 'He remains the same in his wish and expression for peace. He refuses at present to resume the Ministère de la Police *singly*, but that department may shortly be united to the Ministère de l'Intérieure, in which case he would accept.'[15] And, in accepting, become the undisputed master of France while Napoleon was away at war.

Two days later they talked again, and Fouché gave Huber his thoughts on 'the kind of manifesto the English Government must and would produce, and of the course of conduct it should probably steer, just as an enlightened and liberal English character could have done'.[16] But the time for talk was ended. On May 18, Britain declared war on France.

There was no change in the ministry. Fouché was holding out for the double post. Napoleon did not yet want to appoint a man so openly favourable to peace. Hostilities were limited, remote. The

French took Hanover without resistance; the British marauded in the Antilles. Napoleon imprisoned some 10,000 British subjects who had come to France during the peace, and expelled Madame de Staël from the country. He renewed the preparations at Boulogne for an invasion of Britain; the British began to land royalist guerrillas and supplies along the Norman and Breton coasts once more. Towards the end of June, Madame Fouché gave birth to her seventh and last child, a daughter whom they named Josephine.

9

It was not a sunny summer for Napoleon. Blockaded in Europe by the British fleet, he watched the French colonies in the West Indies being captured one by one; the rebellion in Ireland fomented by French agents collapsed almost before it had begun; the army that he had sent to repress the revolt in Saint-Domingue was driven by a rabble of black slaves to seek safety in ignominious surrender to the Royal Navy. War without victories soon brought the discontent that Fouché had predicted. 'In face of this universal change of mood, Bonaparte becomes every day more morose, more choleric and more reserved,' the British informant reported from Paris on August 15. 'Now he is going so far as to flatter the republicans, who he sees are antagonistic to his government. I *perceive*, he said recently to Garat, Fouché and some other senators, *that the republicans seem to be shunning me; but it was with them and for them that I conquered.*'[1]

Certainly it was not from them that he was immediately in peril. The greatest danger lay in the West where, just a week later, the fanatical Georges Cadoudal arrived from England, determined to carry out his long-planned *coup essentiel*: the master-stroke that would rid France of the usurping Bonaparte and restore the Bourbons. Fouché, with his extraordinary network of informants in every region and all spheres of society ('he always had his dirty, ugly feet in everybody else's shoes',[2] Napoleon sneered bitterly on St Helena), undoubtedly knew as much about the plot as anybody – and rather more than the unfortunate Grand Judge who was about to have to cope with it. As an uncommitted spectator he was able to sit back and watch the comedy that eventually turned to murderous tragedy.

The precise nature of Georges's *coup essentiel*, the extent to which he, or the Bourbons whom he served, or the British Cabinet which financed him, contemplated assassination as the final resort has never been clarified. It began as a development of the English Committee's plan to immobilize Napoleon long enough for a party of royalists to declare the restoration of the monarchy, and for the comte d'Artois to claim the throne on behalf of his brother. Uniforms were made so that some of the conspirators could pose as troopers and kidnap him when he drove out to Malmaison or St-Cloud or Rambouillet, perhaps in an ambush, perhaps gallantly challenging the Consular Guard to pitched battle. Or they might steal into the grounds of Malmaison at night, overpower the sentries and whisk him out of his bed. Then they could hurry him to the coast and ship him to England. Or would it be simpler to kill him out of hand? It was a question that nobody posed, and certainly nobody answered.

From August onwards the conspirators were shuttling to and fro across the channel, setting up a chain of houses from the coast to Paris, hiring lodgings in Paris for themselves and for the comte d'Artois, or his son the duc de Berri, in preparation for their arrival on the eve of the great *coup*. So ineffectual had the police become in the twelve months since Fouché's dismissal that Cadoudal – by this time the most famous of the *chouans* and a man of such ox-like proportions that it was almost impossible not to recognize him – openly met two dissident generals, Pichegru and Moreau, in the centre of Paris to invite their co-operation. It was not until the end of January 1804 that the police had any inkling that Georges was in the city. The news galvanized Napoleon into anxious activity. Under his vigorous prodding, Réal and Desmarest managed at last to catch two of the lesser conspirators from whom, on Napoleon's orders, they extracted information by crushing their fingers in musket locks and burning their feet.

On February 15 Moreau was arrested. On February 28 the Senate suspended trials by jury and Murat, recently appointed Governor of Paris, ordered the gates to be closed from 7 p.m. to 6 a.m., and all vehicles to be searched during the day for 'Georges who is still hidden in Paris with fifty of his accomplices, with the intention of assassinating the First Consul.'[3] The curfew and searching went on until March 9, when Georges was captured after a running fight through the streets.

Napoleon had been frightened; he was determined on revenge. Among the papers seized from the plotters there were references to the prince who was to join them for the climax. This unnamed prince was the comte d'Artois or the duc de Berri; (the refusal of either of them to venture into France had caused the delay in the scheme and spoiled whatever chance of success it may ever have had). Napoleon, however, chose to believe, or pretend to believe, that it was the duc d'Enghien, prince of Bourbon-Condé, then living at Ettenheim, in Baden. On March 15 he sent a raiding party across the Rhine to kidnap the duke who was taken under escort first to Strasbourg and then to Vincennes.

Fouché went out to Malmaison early in the morning of March 20 and found Napoleon walking agitatedly in the grounds. 'I can tell what brings you here,' said the First Consul. 'I shall strike a great and necessary blow today.'[4] As Fouché had suspected, he intended to kill the duke. Fouché protested that there would be a great revulsion of public opinion in France and throughout Europe if he took any action without incontestable proof.

'Proof!' shouted Napoleon. 'What need is there of proof? Isn't he a Bourbon, and the most dangerous of the lot?'[5] He refused to listen to argument, growing more and more angry and hurrying with his little strides back to the palace. 'You and your friends have said a hundred times over that I should end up as the General Monk of France and bring back the Bourbons. Well, there'll be no turning back now. What stronger guarantee could I give to the Revolution that you cemented with a king's blood? In any case, I've had enough; I'm surrounded with plots; I must strike terror into them or perish.'[6]

Carriages drew up in front of the portico bringing Talleyrand and the two other Consuls. Fouché drove back to Paris. The duc d'Enghien arrived at Vincennes at 5.30 that evening. His grave had already been dug. After a brief parody of a trial by court-martial, he was taken outside, a lantern was fixed to his chest as an aiming mark, and he was shot. Réal, who was on the fringe of the affair, believed that Napoleon genuinely suspected that Enghien was the prince at the head of the plot against him. Fouché's account points more to his having been inspired by fear. Lavalette, closer to Napoleon than either of the other two, attributed the murder to the Corsican tradition of vendetta which gave him the right, when his life had been threatened, to take the life of a member of his enemy's family, no matter how innocent the victim might be.

Whatever his reasons, his action horrified Europe. 'It is more than a crime, it is a mistake,'[7] said Fouché. He turned his attention to trying to help Moreau, brought to trial with the rest of those involved in Cadoudal's plot. The general was his friend, and also a fellow Breton. Fouché, 'the counsel and centre of relations of the persecuted family',[8] had an easier task than in defending the duc d'Enghien, for Napoleon was well aware that he could not go too far in what many would consider to be the persecution of a rival general. Indeed, he had difficulty in compelling the court to condemn Moreau, who was banished, while the death sentences on several of the well-born conspirators were commuted at the request of Josephine.

The Jacobins jeered that it was only non-aristocrats who were sent to the guillotine. The royalists distributed caricatures showing Napoleon sprinkling blood from the severed head of Enghien over Joseph, Louis and Murat while proclaiming 'I create you princes of the blood'.[9] For Napoleon had taken the final step and appointed himself to the imperial throne. 'We have done better than we hoped,' said Cadoudal in the death cell. 'We intended to give France a king and we have given her an emperor.'[10]

The Emperor's subjects received the change of title coldly. Horror at the murder of Enghien drew the Emperors of Russia and Austria together. Pitt, newly returned to Office in England, began negotiations to draw them into a third coalition against France. On July 18, 1804, the long-expected announcement appeared in the *Moniteur*:

'Senator Fouché is appointed Minister of Police . . . The Ministry of Police is re-established.'[11]

Notes to Part III

Chapter 1

1 Warren, 187
2 Chastenay, II, 40–1
3 Fouché, *Mémoires*, 79
4 *Ibid.*
5 Barras, III, 560–1
6 Fouché, *Mémoires*, 82
7 Barras, III, 561
8 Mellinet, X, 204
9 Aulard, *Hist. politique*, 621
10 Fouché, *Mémoires*, 86
11 Réal, I, 1
12 Stendhal, 24
13 Réal, I, 2
14 Fouché, *Mémoires*, 79–80
15 Réal, I, 4–7
16 *Ibid.*
17 *Ibid.*

Chapter 2

1 Fouché, *Mémoires*, 81
2 Talleyrand, *Mémoires*, I, 270
3 Bertrand, I, 163
4 Gohier, I, 182
5 Fouché, *Mémoires*, 101
6 Bertrand, II, 278
7 Gourgaud, I, 469
8 Arnault, IV, 351–2
9 Fouché, *Mémoires*, 99
10 *Ibid.*
11 Arnault, IV, 355–6
12 Gohier, I, 237
13 Fouché, *Mémoires*, 108
14 *Ibid.*, 109
15 *Ibid.*, 110
16 Arnault, IV, 394
17 Fouché, *Mémoires*, 115
18 Arnault, IV, 394

Chapter 3

1 Picard, 34
2 Iung, I, 370–1
3 Fouché, *Mémoires de la publique*, 36–8
4 *Ibid.*
5 Desmarest, xxxix
6 Fouché, *Rapport au Ier Consul*, 104
7 *Moniteur*, Il frimaire an VIII, p. 281
8 *Biographie des ministres*, 146(18)
9 Aulard, *État de France*, 16
10 *Ibid.*, 1–2
11 PRO, FO 27/54
12 *Ibid.*

13 Daudet, II, 410
14 Hyde de Neuville, 320

Chapter 4

1 PRO, FO 27/56
2 Fortescue, VI, 291
3 Bord, 54–5
4 Bord, 54–5
5 *Ibid.*
6 Fouché, *Mémoires*, 139
7 Carnot, II, 237
8 *Clef du Cabinet*, No. 1235, 21 prairial an VIII
9 *Annales de la Religion*, X, 236
10 This did not inhibit Barère from savagely attacking Fouché after his death. At this period Fouché also made Charlotte Robespierre an allowance from his secret police fund. From his private income he set aside 2,000 francs a month for charity. His hand was extensively and frequently bitten by those he fed. *See* Baudot, 36, and Dautry.
11 Desmarest, 37
12 Fouché, *Mémoires*, 150

Chapter 5

1 PRO, FO 27/57
2 Fouché, *Ministre de la Pol. Gen.*, 1
3 Despatys, *Ami*, 77
4 Fouché, *Mémoires*, 152
5 Iung, II, 294
6 PRO, FO 27/57
7 Pingaud, *Bourmont*, 845
8 PRO, FO 27/56
9 *Ibid.*
10 Pasquier, I, 155
11 Fouché, *Mémoires*, 161
12 Gohier, II, 118
13 Roederer, III, 356
14 Desmarest, 55
15 *Ibid.*
16 *Ibid.*, 60
17 Barante, *Souvenirs*, II, 72
18 Fescourt, 19(2)
19 Girardin, III, 225
20 PRO, FO 27/58
21 *Ibid.*

Chapter 6

1 Staël, 8–9
2 Guiche, 789
3 Fouché, *Mémoires*, 169
4 Boulay, *Docs.*, III, 446
5 *Ibid.*, 447
6 *Buonaparte et Bourmont*, 165
7 Vitrolles, I, 188
8 Jackson, *Diaries*, I, 25
9 *Ibid.*
10 *Ibid.*, 54–5
11 Jackson, *Diaries*, I, 28
12 Staël, 31
13 Duveyrier, 122–3
14 Jackson, *Diaries*, I, 62
15 *Ibid.*
16 PRO, FO 27/61
17 *Ibid.*, 27/70
18 Warren, 230
19 *Ibid.*, 56–7
20 Berry, II, 151
21 *Ibid.*, 152
22 Divoff, 114–15
23 Despatys, *Ami*, 94
24 *Ibid.*, 95
25 *Ibid.*, 97
26 *Ibid.*, 98
27 *Ibid.*, 99
28 *Ibid.*, 100
29 Fouché, *Mémoires*, 169

Chapter 7

1 Chassin, *Pacifications*, III, 627
2 *Ibid.*, 724
3 PRO, FO 27/58
4 *Ibid.*
5 *Ibid.*, 27/61
6 Réal, I, 350
7 PRO, FO 27/70
8 *Ibid.*, 27/62
9 Molé, 208–9
10 *Ibid.*, 205
11 PRO, FO 27/63

12 Remacle, 100
13 Fouché, *Mémoires*, 200
14 *Ibid.*, 201
15 *Ibid.*
16 *Ibid.*, 203
17 *Ibid.*
18 Nap., I, *Corresp.*, VIII, 34 (6326)
19 Fouché, *Mémoires*, 201–2

Chapter 8

1   Montarlot and Pingaud, III, 252
2   Jackson, *Diaries*, I, 23
3   Creevey, 7
4   Le Coz, 49
5   *Ibid.*
6   Méneval, *Mémoires*, I, 284
7   *Biographie des Ministres*, 146(20)
8   Molé, 377
9   Girardin, III, 301
10 Browning, 210
11 PRO, FO 323/4
12 *Ibid.*
13 Browning, 210
14 *Ibid.*, 211
15 *Ibid.*, 269
16 *Ibid.*, 270

Chapter 9

1   PRO, FO 27/70
2   Las Cases, I, 502
3   Murat, II, 51
4   Fouché, *Mémoires*, 215
5   *Ibid.*
6   *Ibid.*, 216
7   *Ibid.*, 217
8   Chastenay, I, 464
9   Sarrazin, 211
10 Cadoudal
11 *Moniteur*, 22 Messidor an XII, p. 1315/1317

PART IV
Minister of Police
1804-1810

I

He had not come back on his own terms, for he had failed to get the Ministry of the Interior. On the other hand, the re-establishment of his ministry and his recall were an admission of the Emperor's urgent need of him (despite Napoleon's bitter denials later: 'He has a face like a cat and is crafty as a cat . . .[1] I only reappointed him the second time because I considered him a nonentity but familiar with the routine of the job').[2] He had four councillors of state to help him, one for each of the three *arrondissements* of the Empire and one for the district of Paris. They were responsible for supervising the work and reports of prefects and special commissioners and met regularly in conference with Fouché usually on the fourth day of each decade, or on Wednesdays after the Gregorian calendar was reintroduced in 1806. There was a rumour that the Emperor had appointed them to keep an eye on the Minister, but the Minister showed no sign of inconvenience or resentment. Indeed, their interests and allegiances were so conflicting that Fouché had no difficulty in playing off one against the other: Réal, who was an old friend but coveted his job, against Dubois, who also coveted his job and was an old enemy. Miot de Mélito, the henchman of Joseph Bonaparte, against Pelet de la Lozère, the creature of Cambacérès.

Confident that he could control them, Fouché was happy to leave the routine administration to the four councillors while he concentrated on the direction of his secret police, still with Desmarest as the divisional head. He increased the number of general commissioners in the major cities, working independently of the prefects. He controlled the gendarmerie, all state prisons and the issue of passports. The fees for passports – and more importantly the taxes on gaming houses and brothels – provided his secret funds.

His policy remained the same: 'to control more by warning and alarming than by repression and coercion. I revived the old police maxim: that three men should not be able to meet and talk indiscreetly without the Minister of Police learning about it next morning.'[3] Napoleon believed in bullying, publicizing the trials and executions of spies and rebels 'in order to create fear'.[4] Fouché preferred to make light of the opposition, to hush up the reprisals, though he made no secret of them in private. On the night of the explosion of the infernal machine in the rue St-Nicaise, when he was trying to convince Bonaparte that the real culprits were royalists backed by English money, he said: 'I use the same methods to deal with dangerous men in the Vendée. When I want a man killed, I say to one of my fellows, "There's two hundred or three hundred louis. Bring me so-and-so's head." Why shouldn't the English do the same?'[5]

The Vendée was quieter than it had been for twelve years past; but royalist agents were still secretly entering the country. Though civil war was now unlikely, the risk of another attempt at the *coup essentiel* remained. Dubois, as Prefect of Paris, issued an instruction that all returned émigrés were in future to report to a police officer once a week and sign a register. Delighted to find an opportunity of demonstrating his policy and at the same time delivering a snub to Dubois, Fouché promptly ordered him to withdraw the instruction, as 'ill-advised and pointless'. In that day's Bulletin to the Emperor he gleefully expounded his reasons: 'ill-advised because, such a measure not having been thought necessary even at a time when a conspiracy was on foot against the State, it would now be seen as the result and sign of serious misgivings; pointless, because any surveillance of which one is warned is useless. The only efficacious means are those that are invisible; the others offend everybody and succeed against nobody.'[6]

These bulletins sent every day except Sundays and public holidays to the Emperor whether he was in Paris, at Malmaison, touring the country or abroad with the army, were the lineal descendants of reports that had been submitted by lieutenants and commissioners of police under Bourbons, the Convention, the Directory, and Consulate. But only under Fouché, and particularly during the first six years of the Empire, did they reach such a peak of accuracy and sensitivity, at once comprehensive and concise. To consult them is to see how much more efficient Napoleon's police state was than those that succeeded it, thanks to the network of informers, the conscientious clerks of the Hôtel de Juigné, and one man of intelligence, endowed with memory and insight and untrammelled by any of the sensual vices – His Excellency the Minister.

The raw material for the report was provided by the prefects and general commissioners. This was digested by the confidential clerks in the bureaus of the four *arrondissements* and submitted to the central

Joseph Fouché, by Dubufe

Reproduced by permission of the Musées Nationaux, Château de Versailles.

Fouché as a young man, by Martin Knoller

Reproduced by permission of the Landesmuseum Ferdinandeum, Innsbruck.

Demolition in the Place Bellecour, Lyons, an unfinished sketch by Bidault

Reproduced by permission of the Musée Historique de Lyon, photo: J. Camponogara

Demolition in the Place Bellecour, Lyons, an unfinished sketch by Bidault

Reproduced by permission of the Musée Historique de Lyon, photo: J. Camponogara

Le Seize septembre mil Sept Cent quatre vingt
Douze, après la publication d'un ban canoniquement faite
aux prônes des grand'messes de cette paroisse et de
celle de St Clément de cette ville sans opposition ni
empêchement venus à notre connoissance, vu le
certificat de la dite publication et la dispense
des deux autres accordée par Mr l'évêque de ce
département en date du douze, de Cernois; Nous
Curé soussigné avons fiancé et épousé en cette
église Joseph Fouché, citoyen françois, Député à
la convention nationale, fils majeur de feu
Joseph Fouché, Capne de navires, et de Dame
Marie françoise Croizé sa veuve consentante
par écrit; natif de la paroisse du pellerin,
district de paimbœuf en ce département et domicilié
de celle dudit Saint Clément d'une part, et Delle
Bonne-Jeanne Coiquaud, fille Majeure de Noël
françois Coiquaud, président de l'administration du
district de Nantes, et de Dame Marguerite
Gauthier, son épouse, présents et consentants;
native de la paroisse Ste Croix de cette ville,
et domiciliée de celle-ci, Rue de gorges d'autre part
ont été témoins du présent mariage du côté de
l'époux, Jean-Julien Fouché Capne de navires, Son

père germain, et pierre louis Troband, ancien Capne
de navires son beau frère et du côté de l'épouse Noël
françois Coiquaud son frère, notaire public et pierre
françois, lesquels signent ainsi que les époux

Bonne-jeanne Coiquaud J. Fouché Gauthier Coiquaud
Coiquaud Fouché Coiquaud L.B.Troband
pierre françois

Coby vicaire de St nicolas: Lefeuvre curé de St nicolas.

The entry in the marriage registry of Fouché's marriage to
Bonne-Jeanne Coiquaud

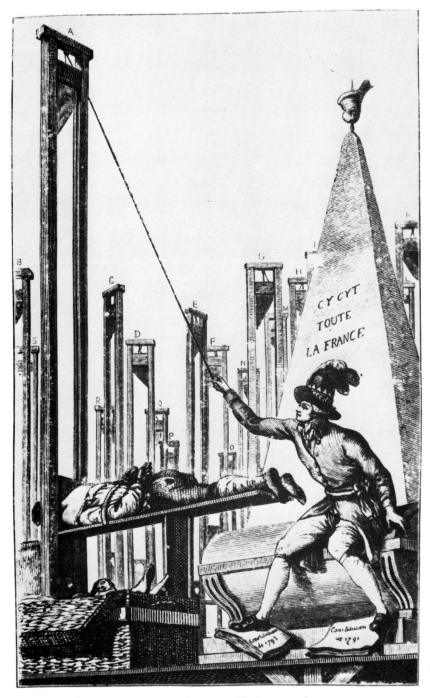

Robespierre operating the guillotine—a caricature

Reproduced by permission of the Mansell Collection.

General Brune, from a portrait by Levachez

Reproduced by permission of the Mansell Collection.

Barras, from a portrait by A. Lacauchie

Reproduced by permission of the Mansell Collection.

Sieyès, from a portrait by Levachez
Reproduced by permission of the Mansell Collection.

Hell Hounds Rallying Round the Idol of France, a caricature
published by Ackermann in April, 1815

Reproduced by permission of the British Museum.

Fouché as Minister of Police, *c.* 1799, a portrait by Detarges

Reproduced by permission of Monsieur F. Geffriaud, Nantes.

Louis XVIII climbing the *Mât de Cocagne,* caricature by Cruikshank,
October, 1815

Fouché, an engraving by Joseph Eymar d'Aix after a portrait by
Mlle de Nanterre

Reproduced by permission of Monsieur F. Geffriaud, Nantes.

Fouché during the Restoration

Reproduced by permission of the Bibliothèque Municipale, Nantes.

Josephine, Comtesse de Thermes, Fouché's daughter

Reproduced by permission of Monsieur F. Geffriaud, Nantes.

bureau to be combined into a single report by a clerk named François – an ex-barrister and royalist agent whom Fouché had released from prison and given employment in December, 1799. The report was passed to Desmarest and from him to Fouché; each made corrections and two copies were then prepared, varying in length from fifteen to twenty folios. One copy was placed in the files, the other was returned to the Minister, who made his final annotations and marginal comments, to be seen by the Emperor's eyes only. Tied with green ribbon and sealed by Fouché, it was carried direct to Napoleon by a courier of the State Secretariat or of the Military Governor's staff.

It dealt with every facet of the nation's life, its thoughts and gossip: a storm at sea off Boulogne; the arrest in the Lower Pyrenees of two Milanese deserters from the Walloon Guard; the birth of triplets and two sets of twins in one night at the Paris Maternity Hospital; a riot that gendarmes quelled with their sabres when they arrested a young man at Viabon; the arrival of the chevalier de Péronne, a royalist agent, in Guernsey; highway robbery at Lamballe; seditious words or actions by the newly-returned non-constitutional priests; the public reaction to the opera *Ossian*; reports of British ships off Fécamp, possibly looking for new landing places for agents; watch kept on a Frankfurt banker visiting Paris and believed to be acting as British paymaster to royalist spies; a complaint from Cologne booksellers that they do not know which books they are forbidden to sell; an unfortunate grenadier, awarded the cross of the Legion of Honour and stabbed to death the same day by a jealous comrade; the King of Prussia's chamberlain's loss of all his ready money plus an I.O.U. for 40,000 francs in Livry's gaming house; two priests in St-Malo falsely accused of intending to murder the Emperor; names of suspects whom the Minister has ordered to be detained, to be banished fifty miles from Paris and the coasts, to be sent home under surveillance or to be released. These were among more than a hundred separate items reported on in the first ten days of Fouché's return to the ministry.

He used the bulletin to support his own campaigns. 'The most absurd rumours are circulating in Boulogne,' he noted just before Napoleon's visit there in the second half of July. 'The Emperor came as far as Amiens but went back to Paris, because he was greeted on the way with cries of "Long live the Emperor – but peace!"'[7] Miot de Mélito, Joseph's nominee who controlled the Eastern *arrondissement*, became an easy mark for Fouché's sniping at the beginning of August when Bourmont escaped from prison at Besançon. 'The Minister notes that, having received a letter from Besançon on the 11th [of Thermidor] in which it was said that Bourmont could escape whenever he wished, he communicated that warning the same day to the Councillor of State Miot . . . From the 11th to the 14th [August 2] no orders were issued by the Councillor of State in accordance with that warning. In the Bulletin of the 7th of this month there is an account of the instructions given by the Minister to the Councillors of State . . . as well as the gendarmerie, for the surveillance and security of all fortresses containing prisoners of state.'[8] And then back again for a jab at his solitary reader: 'Paris, Rumours. – For several days there have been rumours of war . . . Yesterday they changed completely . . . It is peace, even with England . . . It is remarkable that this idea of imminent and universal reconciliation in Europe is generally accepted. But the businessmen from selfish motives, and the military from their personal interests, support war to a finish, include all the nations.'[9]

Fouché was greatly concerned over the need for peace. Because of the Enghien murder, 'the Empire had been improvised under such horrible auspices and public opinion was so ill-disposed and recalcitrant' that he believed it might totter under the impact of war. For the same reason 'the state of Europe called for caution, not arrogance' yet 'a fit of anger on the Emperor's part almost ruined everything'.[10] Napoleon decided on another adventure in kidnapping.

2

After the renewal of the war with Britain, a Frenchman named Méhée de la Touche arrived in London via Guernsey. He approached the comte d'Artois on behalf of a Jacobin Committee in the east of France which proposed co-operation with the royalists in order to overthrow Bonaparte. Méhée's credentials as a Jacobin were impeccable: as Clerk to the Paris Commune he had signed the order for the massacres at the Abbaye prison in September 1792. The comte d'Artois recommended him to the Foreign Office, who sent him to Munich to confer with Francis Drake, ambassador to Bavaria and head of the British East-European spy network. Drake supplied Méhée with codes, invisible ink and the names of British agents and sent him back to France. There Méhée reported his adventures to the police, who continued the deception and during the next three or four months, through another agent sent to Drake and his colleague Spencer Smith, at Stuttgart, collected more than £150,000 for the work of the entirely fictitious Jacobin Committee.

To cover and excuse the Enghien atrocity, Napoleon had details of this hoax published in the *Moniteur*, with much righteous denunciation of the British abuse of their embassies in neutral countries as centres of espionage against France. Lord Hawkesbury replied on April 30, 1804, with a note which did little to still the laughter in Europe. Napoleon, however, was determined, as always, to have the last word. On October 7, he wrote to Fouché: 'Immediately after the Drake affair, Lord Hawkesbury had the stupidity to compose a circular justifying that minister's conduct in the eyes of the cabinets of Europe. My intention was to send to those same cabinets the circular and a reply underlining the ridiculousness and atrociousness of the principles put forward in it. I have since thought better of it.'[1]

His second thought was to capture a live British diplomat, seize his papers and show that the same sort of espionage was still going on; (though in fact Hawkesbury had freely admitted this, contending it was quite legitimate practice in a neutral country against an enemy). The diplomat chosen by Napoleon was Sir George Rumbold, British Minister to the Circle of Lower-Saxony, stationed at Hamburg, which, with the neighbouring Altona, was a centre of anti-French activity. 'His Majesty the Emperor's express order,' Fouché wrote to Marshal Bernadotte, commander-in-chief of the army of Hanover, 'is that M. Rumbold shall be seized and that all the papers in his house shall be impounded'.[2]

Around midnight on October 24, a party of French soldiers crossed the Elbe from Harburg, landed between Hamburg and Altona and made their way to Rumbold's house in the village of Grindel, arriving there about one-thirty. They knocked on the door and, when Sir George sent his servant, Fraser, to find out what was going on, told him that they brought an express message from Hussum (the port in Schleswig through which official correspondence was directed). Rumbold cautiously told Fraser to open a window protected by an iron grille and take in the letter. The French soldiers, seeing they could not get in peacefully, broke down the door, ordered Sir George to get up and dress, collected all the documents in the house and bundled them up in a sheet, and made off with their captive and his papers.

Rumbold was held at Harburg next day in the house of the garrison commander, General Frère, and Fraser was allowed to join him.

On October 26, he was taken to Hanover with an escort of four officers, hussars and gendarmes and kept at the outlying village of Neustadt for three days, with two gendarmes in his room day and night. Travelling only by day, Rumbold reached Paris at noon on Friday November 9 and was taken to the Hôtel de Juigné. He stayed there until six that evening, growing more and more anxious.

'I suffered under the apprehension,' he told Lord Harrowby, Hawkesbury's successor, 'that to palliate this outrage I was to perish by secret means which would have been ascribed to my own state of Despondency',[3] a common fear since news had reached the outer world of suspicious alleged suicides in Bonaparte's prisons. He was so frightened when he was taken to the notorious Temple prison that he asked the gaoler for a quarter of an hour's grace to write to his wife. In the morning, though relieved to find himself still alive, he refused to eat any breakfast unless the gaoler joined him. On meeting a refusal, he insisted on being served only a raw egg.

In this state of trepidation he was taken back to the Hôtel de Juigné to be interviewed by Fouché, who opened the conversation by assuring him that he was perfectly safe. He politely 'lamented the Prejudices of England against the French Government'[4] and hinted that he would begin serious questioning the following day, to probe this new plot against the Emperor's life. Sir George protested that there was no such plot and 'endeavoured to set at rest such suspicions by desiring him to reflect on the unblemished Christian and Moral virtues of my Sovereign, on the high characters of his Ministers, on the Loyalty of my Countrymen'.[5]

Fouché, on the other hand, reported to Napoleon that 'M. Rumbold said that for eighteen months he had been disgusted with the dirty business, but that the interest and advancement of his children forced him to keep at it'.[6] Their talk ended shortly afterwards. 'M. Fouchet behaved to me with great civility, hoped I was as well taken care of as the nature of my confinement would allow, said I might have books, and suffered my servant to accompany me to the Temple . . . I determined to have confidence in his promise and ordered a dinner and wine which I ate and drank heartily.'[7]

He assumed he was to be kept prisoner for a long time. This was probably Napoleon's original intention, but that day he received, through Talleyrand, so strong a letter of protest from the King of Prussia that he changed his mind. As Director of the Circle of Lower Saxony, the King was incensed at the kidnapping and its brazen reminder of the Enghien outrage eight months before. Napoleon perceived, a little late in the day, that he was on the verge of pushing Prussia into the threatened English-Russian-Austrian coalition. Aided by a nudge from Fouché in that day's Bulletin, 'Some persons are trying to argue that the arrest of M. Rumbold will be the signal for a general war',[8] he ordered the Englishman to be set free.

Fouché saw Sir George at 9 a.m. on Sunday morning, told him that he was to be released and then went to St-Cloud for an audience with the Emperor. On his return he told Rumbold that he would first have to give his parole not to reside anywhere within fifty leagues of the French army for the duration of the war. When Sir George hesitated, Fouché said, 'It's better than the Temple – you have the choice.'[9] Rumbold signed the paper that Desmarest put before him. Just before he left at 5 p.m. he asked for his documents to be returned, but Fouché refused.

Rumbold was escorted to Cherbourg and taken out under a flag of truce to a British ship, the *Niobe*, which landed him at Portsmouth before dawn on November 17. He travelled directly to London and sent a note to Harrowby asking if he would find time to see him on Sunday – 'tomorrow being the only day on which I can attend your lordship without any humiliating apprehension'.[10] His statement to Fouché that he would have liked to give up his post at Hamburg but could not afford to was only too true – in London the duns were lying in wait for him.

He received a very chilly reception from Harrowby, who would not forgive him for having given his parole and thus admitted to a crime, nor for having left his papers in Fouché's hands. Rumbold denied that 'they contained any public matter that could give me a moment's anxiety'.[11] Fouché had already issued orders for the arrest of the baron de Haletz, Mme de Stane and a man named Larrazet – 'Rumbold's spies, according to his papers'[12] – followed by the Bylandt brothers, Guyot-Lagrange, Sandillaud, Boecklin and Henoul (who was enlisted as a double-agent). Dossiers were revised, ripples spread out to Holland, Hanover, Brunswick . . .

3

In September the Emperor Alexander I had broken off diplomatic relations with France. In December, within a few days of Napoleon's coronation as emperor, Britain entered into alliance with Sweden, and Spain declared war on Britain. With the Spanish fleet joined to his own, Napoleon was now in a position to launch his great Army of England across the Channel from Boulogne. But he distrusted the sea and decided to deal with Europe first. On January 1, 1805, he sent a letter to 'His Majesty the King of England' beginning 'Having been called to the Throne of France by Providence and by the suffrages of the Senate, the People and the Army, my first sentiment is a wish for peace . . .' and concluding 'your good brother, Napoleon'.[1] The attempt to divide his adversaries was too obvious and the snub came promptly. 'His Majesty has received the letter addressed to him by the Chief of the French Government', Lord Mulgrave wrote to Talleyrand, assuring him that there was no object closer to the king's heart than peace; but since the peace of Europe was concerned, he must first 'communicate with those powers on the Continent with whom he is engaged in confidential intercourse and connexion'[2] – and in particular with Russia.

In March, Napoleon proclaimed himself King of Italy. In April, Russia signed the Treaty of St Petersburg with Britain. In July, Napoleon was back from his coronation in Milan, inspecting his great army and waiting to hear that Villeneuve had successfully lured Nelson to the West Indies. But Villeneuve failed; Napoleon swung round to face eastward; the Grand Army left Boulogne in August and by the end of September was in Bavaria. On November 13 Murat led his cavalry into Vienna; on December 2 Napoleon crushed the armies of the two other emperors at Austerlitz – a victory dazzling enough to blind his subjects to the October catastrophe at Trafalgar.

Her fleet destroyed, France was locked in Europe with a leader whose lust for power was boundless and whose military reputation was without equal. 'The army was henceforth entirely won over to him. Every day witnessed the entry into military service of the sons of the best families, those who had held aloof until now. It was difficult indeed to see such a great harvest of glory, to be young, and not to want to take part.'[3]

The royalist jibe after the murder of Enghien was fulfilled in earnest. The Bonaparte family became not Princes of the Blood but Kings: Joseph in Naples and then Spain; Louis in the Kingdom of Holland that had been the Batavian Republic; Jerome a year later in the patchwork realm of Westphalia; Murat a Grand Duchy in Berg and Cleves followed by the Crown of Naples, handed down from Joseph.[4] Now it was *Sir, my brother* indeed in writing to crowned heads, and *My cousin* to our newly created princes.

There was a whole new nobility to adorn the imperial court; and an imperial adjustment to the tricolour that had symbolized the revolution's fury and failings and noble ideals: the blue, white and red were replaced by blue, red and white, with the white slightly larger than the others. A spreadeagle clutching a thunderbolt replaced the fasces crowned with a cap of liberty; and beneath the eagle-tipped standards the battle honours clustered as the years marched by: Jena and Auerstadt, Pultusk and Eylau; Friedland and a pause to reach temporary peace with Russia at Tilsit; Portugal and the beginnings of the folly of Spain.

Fleeing from the disasters of Spain as he had from Egypt ten years before, he set off to face the threat of a revived Austria, 'with my little conscripts, my name and my long boots':[5] Abensberg, Landshut, Eckmühl, Ratisbon, Aspern and Essling and Wagram. Victory upon victory; the name of Napoleon daubed in glory across the breadth of Europe with the blood and flesh and bones of the little conscripts.

With the Emperor almost as often out of France as in (from his departure for the Austerlitz campaign in 1805 to his return from Wagram in 1809, he spent 742 days abroad and exactly the same number at home), Fouché bore almost the sole responsibility for the security of France. The Ministry of the Interior was reduced to routine administrative tasks. It was Fouché, from the Hôtel de Juigné, who issued orders for arrest and release, supervision and the dreaded trial by court-martial which usually meant death within twenty-four hours.

In February 1805 he was awarded the decoration of Grand Eagle of the Legion of Honour. Five months later he was sadly informing Murat, who provided the courier to carry the daily bulletin, 'I have just lost one of my children. It breaks my heart. Watch over the health of your own. The loss of a child is a terrible thing.'

Each time the Emperor embarked on a new campaign the royalists saw a fresh opportunity to instigate trouble at home. Since the discovery of the secret route that Cadoudal had set up across the Channel and through Normandy, the coastguard service had been strengthened and was itself constantly under surveillance. 'For several days past the enemy had been coasting closer to Fécamp. It is thought he was trying to land spies.[6] The Prefect of La Manche reports that enemy cutters approach the coast every night . . . it is urgent to increase [the numbers of coastguards] by at least forty.'[7] Night fishing from boats had been forbidden since 1800, the Prefect proposed to make shore-fishing at night illegal except with a special licence. There was anxiety at St-Valéry over the communication between neutral ships and the British patrols. By the spring of 1805 it seemed that despite all precautions – doubling the guard and removing the handropes leading from cliff-top to beach – Cadoudal's old route through Biville was being used again. In October, with the local garrisons depleted for the Austrian campaign ('the 112th regiment of the line is still at Cherbourg, but is almost entirely composed of foreign deserters'),[8] three separate landings of *chouan* leaders were reported by the Prefect of Rennes.

In September 1806, before leaving for the campaign against Prussia, Napoleon set up a mobile force under General Boyer, and placed it under the orders of the Minister of Police. Three flying columns, each divided into nine platoons, combed the villages, woods and lonely houses of the Morbihan and Finistère. In the first nine days they rounded up thirty deserters but found the peasants too frightened of *chouan* reprisals to be willing to give information. Fouché urged the general to look more closely and gave him more names and addresses from the files. By December some of the *chouan* leaders had fallen into the net; the catch was not great but the fear inspired by Boyer's men kept the West pacified for some time. Those royalists who remained active turned their energies to simple highway robbery and kidnapping.

There remained the internal conspiracies, supported by money and agents sent from London through the Channel Islands and Spain. In these Fouché had complete mastery. Aided by double-agents, by spies in every capital, and by the daily increasing information in his ministry files, he tracked down one conspirator after another and sent them to the firing squad. Dubuc and Rosselin were arrested in Paris in May 1805 and their correspondence with the baron d'Imbert, formerly naval commander at Toulon and now chief of the comte d'Artois's espionage service, seized together with nearly 30,000 francs. From them the trail led to Laa, another of Imbert's men, arrested at Bordeaux in June and shot in July. (Two years later Imbert was deported from Britain to Hamburg, where he promptly offered his services and knowledge of the network to France.) It was in October 1804 that Fouché first put out a warning to watch the baron d'Auerweck, who organized infiltration from the East, but not until July 1807 that he was finally arrested in Baden, whose ruler was then linked to France through the Confederation of the Rhine. La Haye Sainte-Hilaire, who had been involved in the bomb-plot of Christmas Eve 1800, was captured in September 1807 and condemned to death in

October. In June 1808, Prigent, who had made more than 200 expeditions from England to Brittany in fifteen years, was hunted down in a field of rye. He turned his coat, swearing hatred to England and fidelity to the Emperor.

Among La Haye Sainte-Hilaire's many exploits had been the kidnapping of the Bishop of Vannes, appointed by Napoleon and not recognized by the royalists. In August 1806, La Haye Saint-Hilaire held up the Bishop's carriage at pistol point, forced him to get out with his secretary, and sent a message to Vannes saying that the Bishop would be killed if two *chouans*, captured a month before, were not set free. After the two men were released, La Haye Saint-Hilaire sent the Bishop back but retained the secretary as hostage, to be freed only on receipt of the Bishop's ring, his cross of the Legion of Honour, and 24,000 livres in gold. La Haye Sainte-Hilaire's capture and execution did little to discourage the robbing of private carriages and stage-coaches. In Normandy, a group led by Armand le Chevalier, and Chevalier's mistress, Louise Acquet who took part in hold-ups dressed as a dragoon, made several raids on coaches carrying public funds with the intention of forming a local army to join with the English and Russo-Swedish who they were convinced would land at any time. The local gendarmerie tracked them down; several of their companions were arrested; Le Chevalier took refuge in Paris.

By the time the arrested men had confessed and named Le Chevalier as an accomplice he was already in custody. Fouché, suspicious of his visit to Paris, the amount of money he was spending, the fact that his name appeared on the ministry's list of suspected *chouans* and that he had not presented his passport for a week, had him brought in for questioning. When sent back to Caen for trial he pleaded an alibi in Paris. Brought back to Paris he was lodged in the Temple and police interrogation began again; both there and in Caen. 'The Minister will make a detailed report to His Majesty on the whole of this affair,' Fouché noted on the bulletin of October 16, 1807, 'it is very important and very interesting.'9 A fortnight later, at the end of a long summary of new evidence obtained in Normandy, he wrote, 'The Minister, in a general report to His Majesty, will make known all the public officials who have been negligent or culpable.'10

It was all the more humiliating to have to begin the bulletin of Monday, December 14 with the news that 'Chevalier escaped from the Temple prison tonight . . . He made a hole measuring one foot by two, in the outer wall of his room, and lowered himself with sheets and torn clothing to a courtyard outside the wicket, and from there reached the main gate used by people having business in the main buildings.'[11] A general alarm was sent out, and Fouché, with typical practicality, noted at the end of the report, 'Le Chevalier can be recognized; he can only use one arm.'[12]

The sequel was briefly told:

Wednesday, January 6, 1808: Le Chevalier, escaped from the Temple in the night of December 14, has been arrested by agents of the Ministry of Police. His sister-in-law, Madame Thibout, who has Le Chevalier's child living with her, was taken into custody on the day he escaped and watch was kept on the house; some anonymous letters were sent to her through the post, but Le Chevalier did not call, nor anybody on his behalf. The Senator Minister considered that if the woman Thibout was released and all apparent surveillance withdrawn, Le Chevalier was more likely to venture there. In fact she was freed on Saturday, the 2nd, and yesterday evening Le Chevalier turned up; his beard was excessively long, as with a man who has been shut up for a long time, or perhaps as a disguise. The porter went immediately to alert the inspector-general of the ministry who took all the appropriate measures to carry out His Excellency's orders.[13]

Saturday, January 9, 1808:

Le Chevalier, accused of brigandry and plotting against the State, was today brought before the military commission. He refused to reply to questions put to him regarding the names and lodgings he had used but acknowledged the letter he addressed to His Excellency the Senator Minister of the general police, in which he described his activities; he admitted to the judges that he had planned to stir up new troubles in an attempt to overthrow His Majesty's government. The thefts which he caused to be committed were intended for the execution of his plans and to pay the persons taking part in them. He was condemned to death. The sentence was carried out at four o'clock.[14]

4

In a world of single, double and treble agents, there was always the risk that the senator minister himself might fall into a trap. On February 13, 1805, he ordered the Prefect of Police to release from the

Temple a Swiss printer and publisher named Louis Fauche-Borel who had been arrested two and a half years before on a charge of espionage. Fauche-Borel, who had certainly been spying for the British Government in 1800, was a man fascinated by intrigue and the opportunity it gave him to meet people in high places. He was stupid and indefatigable and monotonously unsuccessful. He earned his release in 1805 by promising Fouché that he would act as a double agent. He was so hard up at that time that instead of being escorted to the frontier by 'an officer of the gendarmerie who will travel in his carriage with him as far as Munster',[1] as Fouché had ordered, he in fact left on foot 'for reasons of economy',[2] being passed from one brigade to the next until he reached the frontier.

He reached Wesel on March 6, and wrote to say that he was going to Berlin; from there he would send news to the ministry through his brother, Pierre-François, who had been given permission to remain in Paris. He sent nothing of interest until late December, when he obtained copies of the manifesto that the comte de Provence and the comte d'Artois had drawn up at a meeting in Sweden, condemning Napoleon for the murder of Enghien. Shortly afterwards, printed copies of this denunciation began to reach France, together with news from other agents that the royalists had set up a secret press in Berlin. On checking the wrappers, the police discovered that, although sent from Hanover and Frankfurt as well as Berlin, all the addresses were written in Fauche-Borel's hand – he had changed sides again and become the comte de Provence's publisher.

In January 1806, he went to London as agent for Prince Pignatelli, who was offering to raise a force of 10,000 Italians to fight the French, if the British Government would pay him £600,000. Fauche-Borel failed to get the money but embarked in high spirits on a new conspiracy – the most important and most promising in which he had yet been involved. He reported to the comte de Provence that he was now in secret correspondence with a man named Bourlac, who lived in Paris and was closely connected with a new Royalist Committee which had enlisted many senior officials in a plot to overthrow the emperor. The comte d'Avaray sent new ciphers from Mitau to be used in exchange of information. The success of the plot depended on finding a sympathetic general who could bring a large part of the army with him. By October 1806, it seemed that such a man had been found: Marshal Berthier, Napoleon's Chief-of-Staff. In January, Fauche-Borel's nephew, Charles Vitel, arrived in Paris by way of Hamburg, for talks with Bourlac and the Royalist Committee.

To Bourlac he revealed that he had conferred with Lord Howick, the Foreign Secretary, before leaving London; and that the purpose of his mission was to confirm the British Government's support of the Committee and to arrange for the necessary funds to be provided. He talked with the greatest freedom, unaware that Bourlac, whose real name was Perlet, was a police spy who had been recruited by Inspector Veyrat, of Dubois's staff, while the Royalist Committee was the invention of Desmarest. After allowing him to roam freely in Paris for a few days to see whether he had any other contacts, Fouché ordered his arrest early in March. On being questioned he claimed that he had come simply to ask for permission for his two uncles to return to their birthplace at Neuchâtel. The police knew better than this. They persisted with their questioning and Vitel at last admitted that he carried a written message from Fauche-Borel to a person of great importance. He unscrewed the bamboo cane that he carried and produced a note addressed to – the Minister of Police.

Thus, without warning, Fouché found himself implicated in a plot against the Emperor. Without his knowledge Veyrat, presumably on Dubois's instructions, had told Perlet to name Fouché as the leader of the disaffected senior officials in his correspondence with Fauche-Borel. The letter that Vitel brought could not have been better worded for this purpose. Fauche-Borel asked for a passport so that he could come to Paris 'to discuss an important matter intimately concerned with the welfare of the State and the minister's personal interests'.[3] The implication was very clear.

Too many people were aware of what had happened for Fouché to be able to hush the matter up; even to attempt to do so would redouble suspicion. He suspected that Perlet was working for Napoleon as well as for Dubois, since Perlet's brother-in-law, Fiévée, was one of the Emperor's secret informants; he probably knew that Veyrat was Napoleon's principal spy within the ministry. He reported the affair in the Bulletin, but added in his own hand, 'It is conceivable that a wretch such as Fauche-Borel might invent an intrigue to get himself money, but it is extraordinary that the Cabinet in London should be so taken in by such a rascal that it is willing to believe the most shocking improbabilities. It is sheer blindness.'[4]

It was perhaps protesting too much. Certainly, as Fouché himself realized, 'it was impossible that such an affair would not leave some shade of doubt in Napoleon's mind'.[5] It was also an indication of the impression abroad: he was regarded as one of the few men in France who could, and perhaps would, engineer a royalist restoration. A strange metamorphosis for the regicide monster and terrorist.

5

It was a mistaken impression. He did not want the Bourbons back: he realized they could never be reformed. Yet his doubts about Napoleon grew greater.

There had been a time, early in 1806, when it looked as if peace with Britain might again be a possibility. On February 18, 1806, Fox, who had recently taken over the Foreign Office, sent a personal letter to Talleyrand, warning him that he had been approached by a man named Guillet de la Gevrilière who 'had the audacity to tell me that to bring peace to the Crowned Heads, the leader of the French must be killed'.[1] Talleyrand replied to this friendly gesture with a copy of Napoleon's speech to the Legislative Corps on March 2 and a note pointing out that 'you will see from it that our intentions are peaceful, as always. I do not ask what they are with you, but if the advantages of Peace are appreciated there, you know on what bases it can be discussed.'[2]

There was no doubt about Fouché's attitude. Fiévée, in a secret letter to the Emperor, commented on the fact that rhymed couplets in favour of peace had been inserted in the strictly-censored plays on the Paris stage – which could not have been done without permission.

> 'The police is loudly for peace. What are its intentions? Does it fear that victories would free the Emperor from the tutelage in which the revolutionary party claims to hold him? . . . The Emperor knows of my distrust for a minister who can make and unmake public opinion, who has the department of plots and conspiracies, money for which he does not account, and who boasts that he can take care of the revolutionary party, which is as good as saying he controls it . . . the more I study the Ministry of Police the better I understand why the English bear it no ill will.'[3]

As before, the British Government was ready to begin negotiations but only if Napoleon's aim was peace, not a truce, and if the negotiations included Russia. Napoleon refused to talk with the

Russians, on the grounds that this would 'imply the continued existence of a war which he has brought to a glorious conclusion'.[4] At
the end of May, Lord Yarmouth, a prisoner on parole from Verdun,
was allowed to return to England; three weeks later he was back in
Paris, authorized by Fox to open discussions on 'various Points regarding the Basis of Negotiation for a Treaty of Peace'.[5] Fouché at
once set a close watch on him, reported that the whisper of peace had
brought rising prices on the stock market, and noted in his own hand
that 'In case the peace negotiations succeed, Lord Yarmouth is trying
to get a corner in brandy, which would bring him 300 per cent
profit.'[6] Lord Yarmouth was also paying frequent visits to the Hôtel
Grange-Batelière, giving a great deal of extra work to the police
agents who had to discover whether this was for the purpose of talking
with the Russian Minister, Oubril, who was staying there, or for
business of a different nature with Madame Saint-Armand, his mistress, recently arrived from Verdun.

Napoleon, protesting that he had no more territorial demands
provided he could keep his spoils, strengthened his position by the
formation of the Confederation of the Rhine: a new assault line,
threatening Prussia and Russia beyond. Fouché optimistically
reported at the end of July and the beginning of August: 'In Paris they
talk of nothing but peace. Everybody is setting out the terms; some
people even assert that the preliminaries are already signed.'[7] 'Public opinion and hope are for peace, which is believed to be certain and
very near.'[8] On August 5, Lord Lauderdale arrived 'to sign the peace
treaty prepared by Lord Yarmouth',[9] said the gossips; but Fouché
knew the truth, that Lauderdale had been sent to try to save the
talks from breaking down.

Lauderdale brought a British offer to recognize all of Napoleon's
conquests and the kingdoms and principalities that he had set up in
Europe. Britain would also surrender to Louis Bonaparte, King of
Holland, all the captured Dutch colonies with the exception of the
Cape of Good Hope.

'If there are still difficulties on the part of the French Government,'
Fouché commented bluntly in the Bulletin of August 6, 'the conclusion must be that it does not desire peace. The public expects the
quickest and happiest results; it is already looking forward to associ-
ating the benefits of peace with the Emperor's birthday.'[10] It was
to be disappointed. On August 8, Napoleon rejected the British
proposals as dishonourable. On August 15, Lauderdale made his
round of farewells. An attack of fever detained him in Paris until

October 10; on that day Napoleon was at Schleiz, having won the first battle of the Prussian campaign. Iéna lay four days away; by October 26 he was in Potsdam filching the sword and decorations and battle standard of Frederick the Great from his tomb. At Berlin on November 21 he declared a blockade of the British Isles, forbidding any trade or communication with them. He marched on into Poland, to spend January 1807 in Warsaw; in February he beat the Russians at Allenstein and Eylau. He sat out the late winter and early spring in Osterode and Finckenstein; on June 14, he broke the Russian army at Friedland; on July 8, at Tilsit, he signed a peace treaty with Russia and Prussia.

6

'When he returned to St-Cloud on July 27,' wrote Fouché, 'he was the object of the most mawkish and extravagant adulation . . . Each day I saw progressive intoxication changing that great character.'[1] The madnesses of Spain and Moscow still lay in the future. He was now at the zenith of his career. His grip on Europe seemed unshakeable. Yet France could at any moment be plunged into confusion and civil war – by an unlucky shot in battle or an assassin's knife or bomb. There was no heir to the imperial throne. A son, even though only a day old, would serve as a focus of loyalty for the mass of the people. Without that son, the politicians and the marshals would fight out their claims to a finish.

Until a few months before, the problem had been a little less acute. The eldest son of Louis Bonaparte and Hortense de Beauharnais – whom gossip and Louis himself pretended to believe was Napoleon's child – had been marked down as the Emperor's successor despite Louis's refusal to allow him to be legally adopted. But the boy, less than five years old, died in March of a sudden attack of croup. The question had to be faced again: how could France find security without a divorce that would free Napoleon to find a younger wife?

Fouché had long been convinced that there was no other solution. Until the establishment of the Consulate for Life he had been Josephine's ally in opposing divorce and blocking the Bonaparte family's plans for setting up a dynasty. But once Napoleon was made virtual king, Fouché reversed his view. 'It is much to be hoped,' he said to Bourrienne, 'that the Empress will die: it would remove many difficulties. Sooner or later he will have to take a wife who can bear children. For as long as he has no direct heir, there is the danger that his death will be the signal for an upheaval. His brothers are disgustingly incompetent and we shall see a new party spring up in favour of the Bourbons – and that is what must be prevented.'[2]

Josephine remained in good health. Fouché requested a private interview at which he read the Emperor a note setting out the necessity for a divorce. 'Without indicating anything positive . . . Napoleon let me perceive that, from the political point of view, his mind was already made up in favour of a dissolution of his marriage.'[3] Unfortunately, the Emperor was a moral coward. He could not bring himself to broach the matter to Josephine. Fouché was ready to perform Napoleon's duties for him. At Fontainebleau one Sunday, when the imperial family returned from Mass, he drew Josephine into a window embrasure and began to speak of 'a separation which I depicted to her as the most sublime and at the same time most inevitable sacrifice'.[4]

Of all the betrayals into which his policy led him, this was the saddest. Coming from her former champion, the only man of substance who had supported her in the long and bitter battle against her relations-in-law, the blunt suggestion that divorce was unavoidable brought Josephine to the brink of a nervous crisis. When Fouché showed her the draft of a letter that he suggested she should send to the Senate, her flushed cheeks turned deathly pale. Her lips swollen, her voice breaking, she asked if he had been instructed to make the approach. He said that he had not – and made an excuse to leave her.

She found the courage to confront Napoleon and ask if Fouché had spoken on his behalf. He denied all knowledge of the business. He talked of getting rid of Fouché. 'If it would not have seemed like eliminating the idea of a divorce, I would have dismissed him for having dared peep into my bed,'[5] he said to Bertrand. But that was on St Helena, and he was weaving his legend. At the time there was widespread belief that Fouché 'acted in that way only by command of the Emperor',[6] and that 'he would not have ventured so far had he not been sure of pleasing the one in whose name he had to some extent spoken'.[7]

Hortense was relieved to find her mother and step-father on better terms than for some time past: 'he was just as he had always been towards her, and the project appeared to be forgotten'.[8] But not by Josephine, or Napoleon, or Fouché. 'It was clear to me that if he had not already decided on a divorce, he would have sacrificed me instead of restricting himself to a simple disclaimer of my action.'[9] Despite Napoleon's embarrassment over Josephine's tears, the Minister of Police continued to circulate rumours of divorce and to preach it openly to his friends and visitors.

'It is time for you to stop meddling directly or indirectly in a matter which is no concern of yours,' Napoleon wrote to him on November 5. 'This is my will!'[10]

Fouché's reply came in the opening paragraph of the Bulletin for Tuesday November 17: '*Paris* . . . There was surprise at not seeing Her Majesty the Empress at the performance of *Trajan*. Some said that she was unwell; the majority spoke of the dissolution of the Emperor's marriage and his alliance with a sister of the Tsar Alexander. This news has become the topic of conversation of all classes in Paris, and the truth is there is not a single person who has not welcomed it as proof of peace and the continued tranquillity of the State.'[11]

On November 19, he was at it again: 'There is only one opinion in the Imperial Family: it is unanimous for divorce. In Paris circles there are no two opinions among people attached to the dynasty: they seem to be firmly convinced that only children of the Emperor can assure its continuance.'[12]

On Monday, November 30, Napoleon again told Fouché to mind his own business. On the following Friday the Bulletin began with a report on Madame Hamelin and other fashionable ladies 'who take it upon themselves to comment upon, provoke and exaggerate the complaints and afflictions of the Empress'.[13] The virtue of these gossip paragraphs in the Bulletin was that in the daily process of re-writing, editing and annotating, Fouché could say precisely what he wanted, yet claim that he was only passing on public opinion. And so he continued, 'They claim to know that the Empress's sterility is not her fault; that the Emperor has never had children; that the liaisons His Majesty has had with several women have never had any results, though these women, when they were married, became pregnant almost at once.'[14] The Minister, of course, had warned Madame Hamelin 'that if she ever happens in future to utter the name of the Emperor or the Empress, he will have her arrested on the spot and taken to the Salpêtrière'[15] – the hospital-prison for prostitutes.

In the Bulletin of September 21, 1807, Fouché preached his master a long sermon on public opinion and the need for enduring peace:

'The people fear war because it is a state of discomfort; they ardently desire peace because peace means commercial prosperity, industrial activity, reduction of taxes and of conscription. For them it is the sole augury of abundance. It is clear to anybody keeping a close watch on the shades of public opinion that the Emperor is more or less praised according to whether his sword is more or less thrust home into its scabbard. If the people pause for an instant to consider political institutions they do so in order to examine them in relation to peace or the duration of peace. If they are told of union between the present dynasty and foreign powers, they express joy because they see it as a guarantee of peace; and the stronger the foreign power the greater their joy.'[1]

Fouché saw marriage with a Russian princess as a stabilizing factor for peace; Napoleon saw his newly-formed friendship with Alexander as an insurance against trouble in the East while he dealt with the West. He could crush liberty throughout Europe, yet it still flourished stubbornly in the small island across the Channel. Wary of another attempt at invasion, he determined to plug the gaps in the continental system and starve his enemy to submission. There was the Pope, insufficiently subservient and with an independent State untidily situated half-way down Italy; there was Portugal, traditional ally of Britain, with a great port wide open to the Atlantic; there was Spain, a slavish ally too weak to resist.

He took Portugal first, sending in Junot with French and Spanish troops and supporting him with more French units that were shortly to be used against Spain. In February 1808 he ordered the invasion of Rome. In April he went south, through Bordeaux to Bayonne, where he took the throne of Spain from His Catholic Majesty Charles IV and his lecherous old wife and simple son, and gave it to his brother Joseph. 'Remember that the sun never sets on the immense heritage of Charles-V,' he said to Fouché. 'I shall hold the Empire of the Two Worlds!'[2] Instead, he had lit an unquenchable fire of rebellion in a fierce, cruel and implacable people; and provided the British with an opportunity to get their army on to continental soil in comparative safety.

In January Fouché had brought up the divorce again, indirectly by a reference to comments in the English newspapers, then a snippet of gossip from the wife of Isabey the painter that Josephine 'wants a divorce but dares not admit it', and finally: 'There is little talk of the divorce at the moment; but people think about it, since they believe it is certain that the Empress can no longer have a child. It is generally believed that there are only two of the Emperor's brothers (the King of Westphalia and Senator Lucien) who would have the courage to reign. It is said that the two others are on their thrones despite themselves.'[3]

In February 1808, David's vast picture of the coronation went on exhibition. 'It is setting all the rumours of divorce in circulation again,' Fouché reported. 'Some people commiserate with the Empress on her situation; but this feeling of sympathy does not prevent them from expressing their desire to have heirs to the Empire. The most short-sighted and stupid are now sufficiently enlightened on this point to say openly that the dynasty can be only temporary, so long as the Emperor has no children.'[4]

In March he used the return of Joseph Bonaparte's estranged wife, Julie, as the pretext for a homily on the lack of male heirs in the Bonaparte family. 'For in the succession to thrones, especially at the beginning of a dynasty, only children can become settled heirs and continue them . . . There is no security in our present prosperity –we should have proof of it if by misfortune the Emperor was ill and had to keep to his bed for a few days. The public funds fall at the mere news of his departure for Spain.'[5] Within a week he was taunting him with the gossip that 'the Emperor says the divorce is a political fairy tale to deceive Russia – if he wanted one, he would have been done with it in twenty-four hours'.[6]

He returned to it in May. 'Everybody here believes in the divorce . . . The need for such an event is deeply engraved on every heart . . . There is not a single individual in France or abroad who is not convinced that the duration and prosperity of the dynasty are dependent on the fruitfulness of a marriage by the Emperor.'[7] A reproof was already on its way from Bayonne: 'All this talk about a divorce is doing dreadful damage: it is both harmful and indecent. The police have a thousand methods of preventing it; I do not understand why they don't use them.'[8] The nagging ceased for a while: a more serious subject for discord had arisen.

General Malet, a former republican firebrand, smarting under the indignity and hardship of having been dismissed from his post in Rome, had pondered on the question that so exercised Fouché's mind – what would happen to the country if Napoleon died – and had arrived at a satisfactory answer: he would assume power himself. Moreover, he saw no reason to wait for the event – he believed it would be sufficient for him to proclaim the Emperor's death and take a firm hold on the reins during the ensuing confusion. It was a more venturesome version of the old royalist dream. It might just have had a chance of success had he not discussed it with so many people: among whom sooner or later there was bound to be a police informer.

On June 8, the Prefect of Police began a series of arrests: General Guillaume, who admitted that Malet had proposed setting up a dictatorship of himself and four others; Démaillot, an anarchist whose real name was Eve, who denied all knowledge of any plot but later accused the generals of being cowards; and Malet himself, in whose home was found nearly 10,000 francs in gold and silver. Fouché told Napoleon that he had ordered the Prefect 'to investigate this affair with all the care and rigour demanded by the contemptible and odious character of most of the accused'.[9] The Prefect Dubois, whom Réal described as 'a mediocrity who thought himself a genius' and 'never went to bed without praying for a small conspiracy on which to demonstrate his rare ability',[10] went to work with such a will that he soon convinced himself he had uncovered a vast plot, involving many members of the Senate and Fouché himself, whose name was included in a list of ministers drawn up by Malet. Fouché thought it as well to add to the Bulletin of the 12th a note in his own hand: 'The Malet affair is still being investigated. Your Majesty will not find in it any but the most miserable scoundrels, without backing, credit, soldiers or followers.'[11]

Meanwhile, however, Napoleon had become anxious. There was an unexplained gap in the Bulletins, and they were arriving nearly a week late. He wrote from Bayonne on June 13, 'You don't send me any clear account of the anarchist conspiracy. It is certain that Malet . . . and other generals . . . have been hatching a plot; I was informed of it a month ago.'[12] On the same day he ordered General Clarke, the Minister of War, to set up a special section of military police to keep watch on all retired senior officers in the Paris district.

The information that the Emperor received might have come

from his own secret police; but it was also possible (and this later proved to be the fact) that Dubois had been corresponding with him directly, over the Minister's head. Fouché went straight to the point in the first paragraph of the June 16 Bulletin:

'Paris is peaceful . . . The arrest of a few discredited generals has made only a slight impression. Nobody believed for a minute that anybody in his right mind would have joined their conspiracy. The Prefect of Police is making too much noise and talking too much about this affair. He tells everybody that many members of the Senate are involved in the plot. The members of the Senate then complain of the irresponsibility of the Prefect who wants to make out there is a big fire so as to claim the credit for extinguishing it. The Minister has taken charge of all the documents . . . and will make an exact and detailed report to His Majesty in a few days.'[13]

It crossed two letters from Napoleon. One to Fouché: 'The examination of Jacquemont and Florent-Guyot [two of the accused senators] has surprised me very much. I am far from seeing nothing new in it, as you do; I see clear evidence of a conspiracy.'[14] And to Cambacérès: 'This business needs to be followed up . . . Send for the Prefect of Police and convey to him my satisfaction with the energy he is bringing to the inquiry into this plot. Tell him to keep you informed every day, independently of what he writes to me.'[15] On June 21, he wrote to Dubois: 'I am far from considering that you arrested Jacquemont without good reason . . . Continue to pursue this affair with the utmost energy.'[16]

Fouché replied with another attack on Dubois: 'It is remarkable that in every little political crisis the Prefect of Police has always exaggerated or distorted the facts. He could have drawn the government into false and dangerous moves if his reports had been believed.'[17] And, since Napoleon had complained in his last letter about continuing references to a divorce ('this sort of talk disturbs public opinion and breeds trouble in the most peaceful country in the world – if everybody set the example of doing his duty, and nothing but his duty, lots of things would never happen'[18]), he snapped back: 'It is being said that divorce is discussed in the Minister of Police's salon. His excellency has not held a circle since his wife's illness which began with a miscarriage five months ago. It is not always from malice that divorce is talked about – more often it is with the best of intentions.'[19]

The bickering continued into July. Fouché sent a two-thousand-word analysis of Dubois's report, argued that it was nonsense, and said he had ordered the three other Counsellors of State attached to the ministry to open a new investigation. Napoleon wrote to Cambacérès, 'I could not be more dissatisfied with the Minister of Police who is indulging his hatred of the Prefect of Police, instead of supporting, encouraging and guiding him.'[20] A fortnight later, 'Send for Fouché. Ask him what he means by his letter of the 10th, which I enclose . . . Tell me what Fouché is up to in all this. Is he mad? Who's he getting at? Nobody's attacking him.'[21] Again more ominously: 'I begin to fear that Fouché, who has had his head turned, is favouring these madcap schemes that he hopes to make use of, and doesn't wish to discourage people who foresee death and accidents, since he's got his own eyes so much on the future – witness his proposals for a divorce . . . There's feeling and behaviour in all this business that I don't understand.'[22]

Fouché managed to get the last word with a paragraph that he inserted in the Bulletin for July 14 of once glorious memory. 'The members of the Senate continue to complain of the Prefect of Police's chatter. The Minister has assured them that the Emperor has rejected any sort of imputation in their respect.'[23] Napoleon let it drop, but did not forget it.

He was reacting more sharply now to Fouché's nagging about peace and divorce. In the Bulletin of August 26, Fouché noted that Kuhn, the American Consul in Genoa, had returned from a visit to England wearing the Cross of Malta and that the American Minister in Paris, General Armstrong, had expressed surprise at his having accepted a foreign decoration. From Rambouillet, Napoleon ordered Kuhn's arrest and the seizure of his papers. 'What is more, I am displeased that you have communicated with the Ambassador of the United States. My police does not recognize ambassadors. I am the master here. When a man is suspect in my eyes I arrest him. I would even arrest the Austrian Ambassador if he was plotting something against the State.'[24] The symptoms of mania were strong in him that day. He had learned that two actors dressed in French uniforms had been hissed by Prussian officers in a Königsberg theatre. In a letter stuttering with repetitions he ordered his Foreign Minister to send for the Prussian representatives in Paris, to demand that two of the officers be shot, and to tell them that 'if these scoundrels, as cowardly on the field of battle as they are arrogant in the wings of a theatre, continue to behave like this, the Prussian monarchy will have a brief destiny . . . If I do not receive satisfaction the country will not be evacuated, and if there is any delay I will declare war on Prussia.'[25]

8

In June the Austrian Ambassador, Metternich, had protested to Fouché about French-inspired rumours of imminent war with Austria (a threat intended by Napoleon to keep the Austrians quiet while he first dealt with Spain). Fouché denied any knowledge of the Emperor's intentions but added that all the military men were for war. 'Since the marshals have been made dukes [with Napoleon's institution of an imperial nobility a few weeks earlier] they wish to be archdukes, and so on.' He made no secret of his fears that Napoleon's thirst for blood would eventually bring ruin to France. 'Where will this scourge stop? When war has been made on you, Russia would remain, and then China . . .'[1]

Russia for the moment was still a firm ally. Before going to Spain to take command of the armies, following Junot's defeat in Portugal, Napoleon hurried to Erfurt for a conference with Alexander. One result of this was a joint letter to the King of Great Britain, suggesting peace talks. Canning replied coldly that His Majesty assumed that in any 'Negotiations for a general Peace, the Relations subsisting between His Majesty and the Spanish Monarchy have been directly taken into Consideration.'[2] Not for the last time, Britain chose to stand alone against tyranny.

Napoleon returned to Paris, and then went on to Spain, taking with him 80,000 veteran troops from Germany 'to punish that heap of *canaille* and chase out the English'.[3] By December 9 he was in Madrid, writing to Fouché to send him a good chief of police, and assuring him that the 'Spaniards are no more dangerous than any other nation'.[4]

Assassination was again on Fouché's mind. This time he decided to seek some insurance against the disasters that might follow it. Surprisingly, he took as his associate a man whom he disliked and with whom he had almost nothing in common: Talleyrand, the Grand Chamberlain, who had lost his post as Foreign Minister after Tilsit. The two men had conducted a spasmodic feud against each other ever since they first met to support Bonaparte at Brumaire; but they shared a desire for peace and a conviction that the war policy would eventually ruin France. They were brought together by Hauterive, the quiet, scholarly archivist at the Foreign Office who had known Fouché when they were both Oratorian teachers at Vendôme and who had spent three years with Talleyrand in America as an émigré.

They met first at Hauterive's country house at Bagneux; then at Suresnes, in the home of the Princesse de Vaudémont, one of Fouché's most devoted – and outspoken – aristocratic admirers ('My God, little Fouché,' she said one day, taking him by the chin and turning his head towards a looking-glass, 'don't you look like a weasel!');[5] later at the town house of the Rémusats (he the Emperor's First Chamberlain and Master of the Wardrobe, she one of the Empress's ladies-in-waiting and Hortense's oldest friend). All these encounters were discreet, casual and unnoticed. Suddenly the whole of Paris society was startled to learn that Fouché had attended one of the brilliant soirées that Talleyrand gave at his house in the rue Saint-Florentin. It was the first time Fouché had ever been seen there. 'Nobody could believe their eyes . . . especially when they linked arms and strolled from one room to another all through the evening.'[6]

News of this extraordinary alliance was sent to Napoleon by Lavalette, the Postmaster General and head of the *cabinet noir* by which letters were intercepted and copied. Shortly afterwards more light was shed on the mystery by Eugène de Beauharnais, who intercepted a letter to Murat, the new King of Naples, and sent it to the Emperor. Fouché and Talleyrand proposed that, in the event of Napoleon's death, Murat should rally the army in support of the new government and possibly occupy the vacant throne himself. Murat, the brave and brilliant cavalryman, was as likely as any man to win over his jealous fellow-marshals: he had a whiff of legitimacy from his marriage to the Emperor's sister Caroline; he was already a king.

On receiving the information from Eugène, Napoleon returned so swiftly that he covered the 700-odd miles between Valladolid and Paris in six days. To explain his haste, he had the rumour put about that he was preparing to counter a possible attack by Austria. But, as Fouché remarked, 'Napoleon had another three or four months in hand, and he knew as well as I did that if Austria was stirring she was not yet ready.'[7] To Fouché, the Emperor's aides confided that he had been impressed by the minister's warnings and had come back to avoid being assassinated. But to Cambacérès he denounced Fouché and Talleyrand as traitors.

Fouché knew very well why he had returned. Yet on the first

occasion that he went to the Emperor's study to work with him, there was no mention of Murat or of meetings with Talleyrand. Napoleon spoke of the Legislative Corps's refusal to accept a clause in the new criminal code he had set before them. He had told them they had no claim to speak for the people: 'the supreme representative of the nation is the Emperor, with his ministers who are the instruments of his decisions'.[8] He asked Fouché what he thought of this dictum.

Fouché replied that he entirely agreed with it. 'If Louis XVI had behaved like that he would still be alive and on the throne.'

Napoleon raised his eyebrows, not certain how the remark was intended. 'Yet I fancy you are one of those who sent him to the scaffold?'

'Yes, Sire,' said Fouché. 'It was the first service that I had the good fortune to render to Your Majesty.'[9]

Napoleon could not afford to lose Fouché when he was about to be involved in war with Austria as well as Britain and Spain. But Talleyrand was dispensable. In the throne-room, before an audience of ministers and court officials, with the indecent abuse that sprang easily to his lips when he was enraged, he upbraided his Grand Chamberlain as a thief and a coward, filth in a silk stocking: 'You deserve to be shattered like a glass; I have the power, but I despise you too much to take the trouble.'[10] The impassive Talleyrand ('if he got a kick in the backside while he was talking to you, his face would never give you a sign of it'[11]) bowed and retired.

'Since Sunday evening [Fouché reported in the Bulletin of January 30, 1809], they are talking in the salons of nothing but the disgrace of the Prince of Benevento [Talleyrand]. It is generally attributed to his jibes about the army bulletins and against the war in Spain. M. de Montesquiou, the new Grand Chamberlain, is well spoken of. They say that during the Emperor's absence the Prince of Benevento and the Minister of Police formed an alliance for political reasons and often met at Madame de Rémusat's house: that Her Majesty the Empress showed uneasiness at that association. A man of sense remarked that if the Minister of Police did have any personal views he would have allied himself with the Legislative Corps rather than with the Prince of Benevento.'[12]

Having brought the subject into the open he took the opportunity to defend himself against another criticism which he suspected

Cambacérès might have passed on. 'The police is much criticized in the Archchancellor's salons. His Highness has confided to many people that the Minister of Police told M. de Romanzow in the Emperor's salon that His Majesty was applauded at the Opera thanks to the skill and attention of the police. The intention was simply to throw the blame for an indiscretion on the minister and an insult on M. de Romanzow.' To this Fouché added in his own hand, and certainly with his tongue in his cheek. 'All this salon tittle-tattle proves that the most useful things can be denigrated and that the position of a Minister of Police is delicate and could become dangerous if the minister did not have the security of the Emperor's heart.'[13]

Josephine, enraged by Fouché's betrayal over the divorce and indignant at the plan to put Murat on the throne at the expense of Hortense's children (a third son, the future Napoleon III, had been born the previous year), urged the Emperor to take some action against Fouché. But Napoleon had spent his immediate fury. He saw now that there had been no plot against his person, merely a project to be put into operation after his death – to somebody else's disadvantage no doubt, but not to his.

Fouché probed the sore spot three or four times more. On February 1:

'The faubourg St-Germain and the faubourg Saint-Honoré are still talking about the Prince of Benevento's disgrace. In some circles they insinuate that this disgrace is the result of relations that became intimate between the Prince and the Minister of Police ... The sensible ones are of the opinion ... that there cannot have been complete confidence between two men so different in outlook, character and position; that they can have combined only for the real and evident interest of the Bonaparte dynasty.'[14]

On February 3: 'It is said . . . that the Emperor has asked the Minister of Police for his portfolio. General Savary affirms that the Emperor is displeased with this minister, that he showed this displeasure at Valladolid, because he had connections with the Prince of Benevento and the faubourg Saint-Germain.'[15] On February 7: 'The dismissal of the Prince of Benevento is generally attributed to the unfavourable view taken by the Emperor of his recent liaison with the Minister of Police ... In all the gossip about ministers and ministries, that of the police has been brought into question, though lightly.'[16] On

February 9: 'They're beginning to spread a rumour that relays were established between Naples and Paris so that the King of Naples could arrive more quickly, and that the Minister of Police knew the secret of this arrangement.'[17]

At last Napoleon spoke. When they were alone together one day he suddenly shot at him: 'What would you do if I were killed by a cannon ball or an accident of some other kind?'

'Sire,' Fouché replied without hesitation, 'I should seize as much power as possible, so as to control events instead of being swept along by them.'

Napoleon remained silent for a moment. Then he nodded. 'Very well,' he said. 'It's the rule of the game.'[18]

9

In March 1809 Austria began to mass troops along her western frontiers, hoping that an early success, while half the French army was tied down in Spain, would encourage the restive German states to join her. Splitting her forces, handing their command to princely incompetents, she scored a few minor successes before collapsing under the rapid blows struck by Napoleon. He left Paris on April 13 and slept at Schönbrunn on May 10.

There still remained a large force of Austrians on the north bank of the Danube. Napoleon tried to put his troops across, and failed. A tremor of hope ran through Europe. Fear gripped him and he lashed out wildly. To General Andréossy, Governor of Vienna, he wrote on June 25, 1809. 'The town of Vienna is badly governed. The insolence of the people springs from negligence in repressing the excesses they have indulged in for the past month. These are of such a nature that there is not one that should not have been punished by the death of several men.'[1] To Berthier, Prince of Neuchâtel, Chief of Staff of the Army of Germany, July 3: 'Write to General Laroche that as soon as he can return to Nuremberg, he is to arrest the six leaders of the riot and have them hanged in the main square.'[2] To Marshal Lefèbvre, Duke of Danzig, commanding the 7th Corps of the Army of Germany:

'Order 150 hostages to be handed over to you . . . Make a law that any house where a musket is found will be razed to the ground; that every Tyrolean found in possession of a musket will be put to death. Clemency and pity are out of place with these brigands. You have the power in your hands, be terrible, and act in such a way that part of your troops can be withdrawn from the Tyrol without fear that they will begin all over again. Six large villages must be pillaged and burnt – and in such a manner that not a vestige remains and that it shall be a monument to the vengeance employed against these mountaineers.'[3]

There had been a time when the peoples of Europe believed that the armies of France would release them from bondage to their rulers. That was long past; now they thought less of overthrowing their kings than of asserting their national dignity and independence. In his fury Napoleon turned not only patriots but Catholics against him. The Papal States had been occupied by French troops since February 1808. Held a virtual prisoner at Rome, Pope Pius VII at last grew tired of protests and, on June 10, 1809, excommunicated both Napoleon and Murat. The Emperor's reaction was immediate. 'No more kid gloves,' he wrote to Murat. 'He is a raving lunatic; he must be locked up.'[4]

At four o'clock in the morning of July 6 the Pope was arrested in the Quirinal and carried off with Cardinal Pacca in a carriage which 'locks with a key and is very solid . . . I've got them as if they were in a cage', the general of the gendarmes reported. 'The older one [the sixty-nine-year-old Pope] is very tired and broken up after such a rapid journey over so rough a road in so much sun and dust; he has dysentery and fever.'[5] He had been carried off so hurriedly that he had not got his glasses or even a change of shirt.

On the day the Pope was abducted, Napoleon met and defeated the Austrian Archduke Charles at Wagram. He had waited six weeks to build up an army that was half as strong again as the Archduke's. In the ensuing carnage the French lost 30,000 men, killed, wounded or missing, and the Austrians 25,000. The Austrians retreated, but in good order. 'Wagram retrieved Napoleon's fortune but did not restore his prestige; he was still victorious, but he no longer seemed invincible.'[6]

During the six tense weeks before Wagram, the Minister of the Interior, Cretet, became so ill that Napoleon was forced to replace him. On June 29 he gave Fouché temporary charge of the ministry, making him indisputably the most powerful man in France. It was an extraordinary tribute to his ability from a man who was in no mood to pay him compliments. It was a post in which he faced many problems.

As so often happened, the new war had encouraged a fresh outbreak in the Vendée – the royalists recruiting support from conscripts and deserters. Belgium was seething with unrest, ready to spring into rebellion if Napoleon met with a decisive defeat. From England came news that 40,000 British troops were being embarked for an invasion of the Low Countries. At the end of the month they were sighted off the coast of Zeeland, making for the Scheldt estuary and Antwerp. By the time this news reached Paris they had captured the island of Walcheren.

The Council of Ministers met on July 31. Fouché, supported by Decrès, the Minister of Marine, proposed calling out the National Guard to face the enemy. The other members of the council, terrified of taking a decision of any importance in the Emperor's absence, rallied behind Clarke, the Minister of War, who said he could find 30,000 regular troops, and these would be enough. Fouché demanded a second session of the council but still could not persuade his timid colleagues.

'What will the Emperor and the army say,' he demanded, 'if France allows her own soil to be dishonoured while they are defending it far away?'

'As far as I am concerned,' said Cambacérès, who presided, 'I have no desire to have my head cut off. I have sent a courier to the Emperor; we must await his reply.'

'And as far as I am concerned,' said Fouché, 'while we are waiting, I shall do my duty.'[7]

As Réal said of him: 'He had one virtue that was very rare during the Consulate and Empire. He made up his mind, had the courage to stick to his opinion in the face of a master who seldom brooked contradiction, and acted in accordance with his convictions.'[8] As for the other ministers, 'they were no more than clerks, expert at executing and transmitting orders, but never daring to take an important step on their own responsibility'.

On August 2, despite the decision of the Council, Fouché wrote to the prefects of the northern departments, ordering them in the Emperor's name to mobilize the National Guard. The mayors of the Paris *arrondissements* he exhorted to 'Prove to Europe that though the genius of Napoleon can bring lustre to France, his presence is not necessary to drive back her enemies!'[9] – a dictum that greatly displeased the Emperor when he heard it, though it no doubt accurately represented Fouché's attitude. His disillusioned soul flamed with the old passions now that the country was in danger; the proclamations and adjurations that flowed from his pen glittered with the fervour of sixteen years ago. As for Napoleon: 'Stick him in a bag and drown him in the Danube and everything can be settled quite simply!'[10] he told the messenger who brought the news of Essling.

He chose his old republican friend and opponent, Marshal Bernadotte, Prince of Ponte Corvo, to be commander of the National Guard. Clarke and Cambacérès, knowing that Bernadotte had been sent home in disgrace for having offended the Emperor, uttered more cries of horror and protest. Fouché paid no attention. Napoleon, now back at Schönbrunn but several days in arrears with the news, wrote to Fouché: 'You did well to prepare the prefects to provide national guards. I've written to tell you that I have ordered the calling out of 30,000.'[11] A week later he gave Fouché the title of Duke of Otranto, with estates in the Kingdom of Naples that would bring him 60,000 livres a year. This was in addition to two annuities of 20,000 livres each which he had been given in March and August the year before. He had been made a Count of the Empire in April 1808, but never used the title; he attached so little importance to the foreign decorations conferred on him that he had difficulty in naming them. But his friends noticed that the dukedom pleased him immensely. Pride permitted him to covet only the fruit at the top of the tree.

When Napoleon's letter authorizing the raising of the National Guard arrived in Paris, Bernadotte was already at Antwerp exercising both military and civil command, and very soon horrified by the levies who were being sent to him: 'more than half have already deserted; those that remain are badly armed, without cartridge pouches, without uniforms.'[12] Napoleon, aware of their quality, told Clarke that there must be 'no offensive, no attack, no boldness[13] . . . unless they are four to one, and in a good position, protected by redoubts'.[14] Fouché warned the Emperor on August 16 that the English were shelling Flushing and would probably capture it. By the time Napoleon's reply reached Paris – 'Flushing is impregnable as long as it has bread, and it has enough for six months'[15] – the town had fallen.

On August 30, Fouché received reports that the British intended a landing on the Mediterranean coast. He immediately ordered the Prefect of Marseilles to hold his national guard on twenty-four hours notice, and a week later warned all prefects in the Midi to prepare for mobilization. Clarke, furious at losing control, complained to the Emperor that Fouché was even ordering uniforms and paying for them out of the Ministry of Interior funds.

'The mobilization of the National Guard,' Fouché claimed, 'has consolidated the Emperor's position more than the Coronation. Then he was Emperor solely by military right – now it is the civil power which consecrates him.'[16] A similar thought was beginning to form in the Emperor's mind, though in different terms: 'whether a mere minister should have the authority to organize such resources as, in a moment of defeat, might be directed against the unlucky sovereign'.[17] There was also the vexation of Bernadotte in the role of defender of the homeland, with Fouché as the organizer of victory. He sent Bessières to replace Bernadotte, and changed the tone of his letters to Fouché.

'You were wrong to disquiet the whole of France and even as far as Piedmont, writing everywhere to "prepare" the National Guard. "Prepare" means nothing; it alarms the whole Empire for no reason. You never speak to me about Paris. I don't know what this mounted guard is.'[18] It was, in fact, an escort that the Minister of Police and the Interior had provided for himself: a troop of *chevau-légers* that accompanied him to the races at the Champ de Mars on September 24, and about which Clarke at once complained to the Emperor.

The military situation in the north had at first seemed critical. The French levies too old, too young, too unfit, too ill-equipped, had since the damp days of early September been falling sick by the hundred every day. In the first week of October there were 79 officers and 12,918 other ranks in hospital. To compensate for this, the British commander (Pitt's elder brother, the Earl of Chatham) wasted so much time on capturing Flushing and advancing up the Scheldt that Antwerp had ample time to prepare its defences. After some cautious and cursory probing, Chatham withdrew his men to the fever-ridden island of Walcheren and both armies settled down to a war of attrition by disease.

Meanwhile, Napoleon had ordered the National Guard to stand down and had appointed a more biddable Minister of the Interior – Montalivet, until then Minister of Bridges and Roads. Fouché remained invigorated by the recent flurry and eager for more action.

The old alliance between Royalists and Catholics had been revived by the Emperor's brutal treatment of the Pope. Not yet daring to resort to violence, the conspirators, working through lay congregations of the Virgin, set up secret cells throughout the country for disseminating anti-Bonapartist propaganda. In September a member of the Paris cell was heard to boast that 'he had counted the trees in the boulevard from the Madeleine to the Bastille and had found there were exactly enough to hang the Emperor, his family, his ministers, the members of the Senate and the Legislative Corps'.[1] Fouché's men raided his home and found his son, a senior clerk in Dubois's prefecture, making copies of the Pope's Excommunication of the Emperor.

Fouché, who had been attacking the Church and Cardinal Fesch during the summer, made the most of this in his bulletins. But when Napoleon returned to Fontainebleau on October 26, Fouché contented himself with maliciously reporting that at the time of the Emperor's defeat at Essling the wits of the faubourg St-Germain 'had spread the ridiculous rumour that he had gone out of his mind'.[2] He begged him though to pay no attention 'to this violent cackling . . . It is only to be expected. Who was more maligned than Julius Caesar?' He wanted his imperial master in a calm mood to consider two projects that he put before him. They were, once more, peace and divorce.

Peace with Britain, he argued, was possible on favourable terms. If Napoleon agreed to leave Portugal undisturbed and took the army of occupation out of Prussia, the British would let him retain Spain, Westphalia, Holland and Italy, the four countries where his brothers and brother-in-law ruled. The argument for ensuring the succession was strengthened by the attempt of the German student, Staps, to kill Napoleon a fortnight before. 'It was a brilliant destiny to have given rebirth to the Empire of Charlemagne; but the Empire must be given security for the future; for that purpose it was urgent, as I had indicated, for him to divorce Josephine.'[3]

Napoleon listened more readily now. The thought of marrying into one of the great reigning families overcame his superstitious fear of parting from Josephine, his Lady of Victories. He told Cambacérès to discuss with Fouché the means of preparing public opinion. But his hatred and envy of Britain made peace less likely than ever. 'When I reappear on the other side of the Pyrenees,' he bragged to the Legislative Corps, 'the terrified leopard will make for the Ocean, fleeing from shame, defeat and death.'[4]

Ever since Tilsit, Fouché had been arguing that when Napoleon remarried he should choose a Russian princess. He was supported by Cambacérès and Murat, partly because, as Talleyrand said, 'they believed the revolutionary interests would be better guaranteed by a Russian alliance',[5] and partly because, in Murat's words, 'we shall have war against the power that we do not marry, and I would rather have war against the Austrians than against the Russians'.[6] Unfortunately the Tsar showed a strong reluctance to marrying his sister, the Grand Duchess Anne, to Napoleon, and Napoleon found it impossible to resist the glamour of a union with the Archduchess Marie-Louise, of the same house and blood as Marie-Antoinette. When the Austrian alliance was finally decided upon early in the New Year, Fouché remarked with a wry smile, 'There's nothing left now but to pack my bags.'[7] Before he went, however, he intended to bring off one last triumph.

In the brief moment of euphoria that accompanied his marriage and admission to the ranks of the truly royal, there might be a last chance of Napoleon's forgetting his envy of Britain and discussing a genuine peace. Fouché had begun to prepare for this possibility, choosing as his intermediary a royalist ex-officer of Irish descent, François Fagan, formerly captain in Dillon's Regiment. Fagan had met Lord Yarmouth while visiting his eighty-four-year-old father, who still lived in exile in London. Two of his cousins had served in India under the new British Foreign Secretary, Lord Wellesley, elder brother of Sir Arthur, recently created Viscount Wellington.

Fagan left Paris on December 5 but illness and the difficulty of getting across the Channel delayed him. Posing as an English officer he landed on the Thanet coast on January 21, 1810, and went straight to London, where he had no difficulty in obtaining an interview with Wellesley. Wellesley made it clear that the new government, formed by Perceval on the death of Portland, would not agree to any terms which did not assure the independence of Holland and Spain (where he had recently been ambassador to the patriot *junta*).

'We have just heard,' he told Fagan, 'that Napoleon has given orders for the invasion of Holland; that does not look like making dispositions for peace.'[8] However, he said that the British Government was ready to receive any proposal provided that its allies were included in the negotiations. Fagan fell ill again and did not reach Paris until March 12. Fouché was by then occupied with a more promising approach, through Louis Bonaparte, King of Holland.

Louis had arrived in Paris on December 1, 1809, summoned by his brother to account for his unsatisfactory stewardship. The Dutch, whose survival depended on commerce, were continuing to trade with Britain despite Napoleon's blockade. In reply to the Emperor's reproaches, Louis retorted, 'If Your Majesty had given kings the rank of electors and had appointed himself Emperor of all the allied states, as your brother I should have been one of the first to submit with good grace', but since he had in fact been placed as monarch 'at the head of a nation composed of men who prefer independence to life, I can only struggle ceaselessly between my feelings and my duty to Holland'.[9] This was the rub: Napoleon could not promote his family to less than kingship, because of his pride; they could not behave as less than kings, because of theirs.

Louis stayed with his mother in the faubourg Saint-Germain. He would not go to his own Paris house because he was hoping for a legal separation from Hortense; Napoleon forbade him to lodge at the Dutch legation for fear of gossip. Fouché called on him several times, offering his services as mediator between the two brothers, but was suddenly struck down with cerebral fever. Napoleon, showing unusual solicitude, called to see him and found that he was desperately ill. He ordered him to be examined by the senior physician of the Hospital of the Imperial Guard, Dr Sue, who had a reputation for unorthodox methods.

Sue, unable to break the fever but knowing that Fouché was devoted to music, sent for the entire wind section of the orchestra of the Opéra. He seated them round the bed and gave them the signal to play. 'At the end of a quarter of an hour of this singular improvised concert, Fouché's eyes filled with tears and a copious sweating occurred. The delighted doctor thanked the players and declared his patient saved.'[10] Within a few days Fouché resumed his talks with Louis and nurtured, perhaps implanted, in Napoleon's mind a plan whereby France could obtain advantageous peace terms from Britain without appearing to make the first approach.

The scheme was simply to threaten to incorporate Holland in the French Empire if Britain refused to negotiate. Since the British would not respond to a threat put so bluntly, the information would be conveyed in confidence through the Dutch Government. Louis hesitated at first, but gave way when Champagny, the French

Minister of Foreign Affairs, told him that he could never expect a reconciliation with his brother until he 'gave incontestable proof of his intention to follow blindly the will and policy of the Emperor'.[11]

Louis sent to his Council of Ministers the letter that Napoleon had drawn up for him, pointing out that 'there is but one hope for us – that a maritime peace may be negotiated ... Take the necessary measures yourselves without mentioning my name; but you must act at once. Send a safe and reliable business man to London.'[12]

Roell, Louis' Foreign Minister, carried these instructions to the Hague. With him went Pierre-César Labouchère, a senior partner in Hopes, the Amsterdam banking house; he was the reliable business-man whom Fouché had decided should carry out the mission.

Labouchère, 'a man of great intelligence, distinguished manners and appearance',[13] and at this time approaching forty, was Dutch-born but French by extraction – his father's family were well-to-do Protestant wool merchants at Orthez in the Lower Pyrenees. As a young man he was sent to London on business. He dined with Sir Francis Baring, the banker, fell in love with Sir Francis's daughter, Dorothy, asked her father's permission to marry her, and was refused.

'If I were a partner in my bank, instead of an employee, would you still reject me?' he asked.

'The situation would be very different,' Sir Francis replied. 'It might be considered.'[14]

Labouchère went back to Amsterdam, pointed out the advantages of a family link between the two houses, was given a partnership and at once returned to London where he successfully claimed Miss Baring's hand. The story was well known. His skill as a negotiator recommended him to Fouché; so did the fact that his father-in-law, Sir Francis, who was a director of the East India Company, had long been a friend and adviser of Lord Wellesley; so did his business relationship with Ouvrard, the French banker, who first introduced him to Fouché.

Ouvrard had known Labouchère for about five years. He had been associated with him and Baring in a project to develop the South American silver mines which were suffering from the effects of a long blockade by the Royal Navy. With Fouché his connections were both older and more recent – they had met when Fouché first became an army supplier during the Directory; their latest enterprise had been only a few months before when they tried to help Murat (faced, like Louis, with the impoverishment of his kingdom because of

Napoleon's blockade) to open up trade with England through Malta. Labouchère was to arrange the purchase of the English goods that would be exchanged for Neapolitan silk, grain and oil, and it was probably this business which had brought him to Paris. On Fouché's recommendation Napoleon and Louis accepted him as the man to carry the appeal from the Dutch Cabinet.

II

Labouchère sailed from the Brill on February 2, 1810, and landed at Yarmouth on February 5. He arrived in London on February 6 and at once sent a message to Sir Francis, who was at his country house at Lee. When Sir Francis met his son-in-law in Hill Street the following morning, Labouchère produced his authority to talk on behalf of the Dutch Council of Ministers and told him that French annexation of Holland and the Dutch fleet, with the consequent threat to Britain, could be avoided only if the Cabinet rescinded the Orders in Council with which they had set up a counter-blockade to Napoleon's Continental System. Baring immediately sent a note to Wellesley, who called at midday and invited Labouchère to dine with him.

The two men talked from 5 p.m. until 11 p.m. without making any progress. From Wellesley's point of view, the new proposal was even less inviting than that brought by Fagan (who was still lying ill in London). There was no mention of Spain; Holland was being used for coercion. Wellesley gave Labouchère a noncommittal reply, leaving the door open but making it clear that any future discussions would have to be wider-based. Labouchère returned to Holland on February 21.

Napoleon had become impatient. On January 24 he ordered Champagny to send a long note to Roell, inveighing against the British Orders in Council, protesting his own desire for peace, and upbraiding the Dutch for being influenced solely by 'miserable mercantile considerations, thus forcing His Imperial Majesty to resort to rigorous measures'.[1] Unless the British Government gave proof of a change of policy in speeches in the new parliament, the Emperor proposed 'to recall the prince of his blood whom he had placed on the throne of Holland . . . and to occupy all points of access to Holland and all ports by French troops'.[2]

Louis, in ill-health, unhappily married, tired of his kingship but committed by conscience to the service of his people, cold-shouldered by his brother yet refused permission to return to Holland, desperately groped for some solution that could satisfy Napoleon's rancour without entirely destroying Dutch freedom. He leaned heavily for advice on Fouché, whom he rather touchingly thanked in a letter of February 5 for 'the interest you take in my sad situation. Accept the assurance of my esteem, and of my gratitude'.[3] He enclosed a note of the proposal they had discussed – that France should occupy Holland only as far as the left bank of the Rhine. Fouché passed this on to Napoleon who, after adding a few humiliating touches, told Champagny to confront Roell with the document and insist on a prompt acceptance.

But on February 22, intending to prod the British into a decision, he had Champagny's note of January 24 published in the *Moniteur*. Two days later Louis received Labouchère's report on his talks with Wellesley and at once passed it on to Napoleon. Seeing that Wellesley promised nothing about the Orders in Council, Napoleon lost his patience and ordered the annexation of all Dutch territory south of the Waal, the lower arm of the Rhine, and the occupation of the whole of Holland by 18,000 French troops.

He did not sign this order until March 16; and on March 20 he changed his mind again. Before setting out for Compiègne, where he was to welcome his bride, Marie-Louise, he told Louis to send Labouchère back to England. He gave him a note of the terms Labouchère should discuss but insisted that he 'should have no title, no official character, and that in no circumstances should he show any signed document or one written in a known hand'.[4] The note said that if the Orders in Council were withdrawn, French troops would immediately quit Holland and possibly the Hanseatic towns as well.

Labouchère wrote to Baring the following day, assuring him that 'there never was a more favourable moment . . . I hardly know any point that would not meet with serious consideration – Malta, Sicily, Naples – the Ionian provinces, the Hanseatic towns, Hanover – Holland – Portugal'. There was a real chance that Napoleon was ready 'to replace the System of Conquests by a System of Consolidation of Power'.[5]

The vast difference between the terms of this letter and those of Napoleon's note was due to a communication Labouchère had received that day from Ouvrard: 'It appears that he is now, though only on the occasion of his marriage, ready to yield on the following points: Malta, Sicily',[6] etc. Labouchère rightly guessed that Ouvrard was writing on behalf of Fouché; he wrongly assumed that Fouché was speaking on behalf of Napoleon, just as Louis had been his brother's spokesman in the other note. In an enclosed letter which he asked Baring to pass to Wellesley, he even put forward the proposal that the British Cabinet should solicit French co-operation 'to destroy the United States of America [and make them] again dependent on England'.[7] This was purely Ouvrard's suggestion; indeed, he sent a similar memorandum to Napoleon, with the modification that France should ask for Cuba as her share of the adventure; from Cuba she would conquer North America; and Britain, threatened from west and east, would be forced to accept a dictated peace.

Baring acknowledged receipt of Labouchère's letter but, seeing that this time he apparently represented nobody, not even the Dutch Government, he hesitated to pass it on to Wellesley. The acknowledgement did not reach Labouchère until April 10. By then Ouvrard had sent him a note from Fouché, written on the 5th, saying that the copy Labouchère submitted of his letter to Wellesley 'has met with approval . . . the reply is waited for impatiently'.[8] The implication was clear – that it was the Emperor who was waiting.

Labouchère sent a reproachful letter to Baring, asking for an answer 'by the very first opportunity . . . if the present moment is suffered to escape perhaps it will never again occur as favourably'.[9] He enclosed another letter to Wellesley, which he asked Baring to read and deliver. These arrived in London in the evening of April 17 and Baring at once notified Wellesley that he had a communication 'from a very old friend which I would send or deliver in person'.[10] Wellesley, about to retire to bed with a bilious attack, sent his servant for the letter but found nothing in it on which he could take action. He had an hour's talk with Baring at Hill Street on April 20, and Baring called on him on April 27 when they had another discussion lasting an hour and a half. The Cabinet was wary of any move which Napoleon might be able to misrepresent in the *Moniteur* as weakness, or which might infuriate the long-suffering Britons by raising hopes of peace only to dash them again. After a final discussion with Baring on May 8, Wellesley sent him a note of his conclusions:

'No advantage can be derived from receiving in London any person whose authority to act shall not be clear and indisputable.

'No advantage can result from opening a negotiation unless it shall be understood that certain indispensable points can be settled by the parties in the progress of the Treaty.

'It would be useless and even dangerous to open a negotiation with the certainty or even the apprehension that unsurmountable obstacles must occur in its first stages.'[11]

Baring, passing this on to Labouchère, added that he had asked Wellesley whether an accredited representative would be received. 'Yes,' replied Wellesley, 'he would certainly be received in accordance with his powers, provided that they allowed us a reasonable hope of a satisfactory conclusion.'[12] But by the time this message reached Labouchère the position had completely changed.

12

Napoleon married Marie-Louise on April 1, 1810. At the end of the month he paraded her as his latest trophy in a tour of the Belgian towns that had once been Austrian possessions. He had apparently put the thought of peace out of his mind, ordering Fouché to press on with the manufacture of forged English banknotes ('I expect great and powerful results from this measure'[1] – which he had originally planned to use against Austria). At Antwerp on May 5, Louis was officially received by the Emperor. He told him that Labouchère's latest talks seemed promising. Napoleon, who thought the negotiations had faded away, asked for details. Ouvrard's name was mentioned and he probed deeper. In a letter to Louis he spoke of his 'extreme displeasure that he has taken it upon himself to act in an affair of this importance at the instigation of a wastrel and intriguer such as Ouvrard'.[2] Louis defended Labouchère as 'a man who is as honest as he is well-informed',[3] and Napoleon concentrated his mounting wrath on Ouvrard.

Ouvrard, however, was so dazzled by his plans to get at the Mexican silver that for three weeks after the inquiry began he was still urging Fouché to continue with the negotiations. To Napoleon he protested that, having received no reply to his memorandum, he assumed that the Emperor approved of it. But his claim that he acted in all good faith and innocence sounded less credible when it turned out that some of his correspondence with Fouché had been in invisible ink, through an accommodation address.

By the time he returned to St-Cloud, late in the evening of June 1, Napoleon was in a thundering temper about Holland, the last straw having been added quite fortuitously by a brawl in Amsterdam during which the comte de la Rochefoucauld's coachman was maltreated by the Dutch mob. Claiming that this attack was a calculated affront to France, Napoleon wrote to Louis that he was recalling La Rochefoucauld. At the end of the letter he added in his own hand: 'This is the last letter I shall write to you in my life,'[4] a promise that he kept for three years until the perverse, tortured, faithful Louis offered to come to his aid in the dark days of 1813.

There remained Fouché. Looking back on the affair, Ouvrard attributed much of the Emperor's rage to the mere fact that Fouché was at the bottom of it.

> 'Fouché had rendered him great services, but he was none the less an object of distrust to him. Napoleon seemed to fear that his minister thought himself indispensable. He was always inclined to think he interfered too much in the conduct of government. He deeply resented the English papers representing him as always acting according to the views and inspirations of Fouché. Finally Fouché was a representative of the Revolution and had retained certain associations which made his loyalty suspect.'[5]

There was a great deal of truth in this analysis. The fear was perhaps not that Fouché thought himself indispensable but that Napoleon himself might find him so. The Minister of Police treated his instructions with a coolness not far short of contempt, acting as no other Minister would dare, yet receiving no more than a scolding. He had almost completely elbowed aside the Minister of the Interior, and was always itching to get his hands on Foreign Affairs. And, since the new marriage, the vote that he had cast for the death of Louis XVI returned to condemn him. 'The more the Emperor departs from the principles of the Revolution,' Girardin observed, 'the more he will discard those who are accepted as having been its authors.'[6]

Fiévée harped on this in one of his reports to Napoleon that month. The function of the Ministry of Police, he said, was 'to provide protection against dangers that might threaten the State . . . If the Duke of Otranto had been willing to confine himself to that, all would be well; but he has also tried to provide protection against dangers that might threaten the old spirit of the Revolution.'[7]

Napoleon still hesitated. Working with his secretary Méneval, he suddenly said: 'I want to dismiss Fouché!' Méneval, who heartily disliked the Minister of Police, replied: 'Sire, I expected it. I am astonished at only one thing, that you've not dismissed him already.'[8]

The Emperor got up from his perch on the corner of Méneval's desk, walked up and down the study with his hands behind his back, then changed the subject. To other people he complained of Fouché's past attempts to drag him to the divorce – 'one day he's prying into my bed and the next day into my private papers',[9] Nesselrode, the Russian diplomat, reported him as saying. But when the Council met he seemed to be taunting him into offering an acceptable excuse.

'You think yourself clever,' he jeered, 'but you're not. Talleyrand's the clever one; and this time he's played with you like a child. He's made you his cat's-paw.'[10] Fouché, quite unperturbed, replied that Talleyrand had nothing to do with it; and he himself had been inspired simply by the conviction that he could render a great service to the country. Then Ouvrard was the evil genius of the affair, said Napoleon. Fouché replied that it was he who had told Ouvrard to probe the attitude of the British Government, through Labouchère.

'Ouvrard went much farther than that,' said Napoleon. 'He made overtures, put up detailed proposals. If he was not acting with your authority, he should be arrested as a dangerous and guilty man.'[11] Fouché protested that Ouvrard was well-intentioned though perhaps overzealous. Napoleon insisted that he should be arrested. Fouché replied that he would refuse to sign the warrant. Napoleon passed a note to Savary, the general commanding his military police, who sent a colonel and a squad of gendarmes to take Ouvrard to prison.

In the council chamber the row continued. 'It's not enough for that man to interfere in my family affairs without my permission,' Napoleon said to Maret a few days earlier, 'now he's making peace without me!'[12] His accusation to Fouché's face was more revealing: 'So it's you who decides peace or war!'[13] Fouché's mobilization against the British invasion the year before still rankled.

'You deserve to lose your head on the scaffold!' he raged. Turning to the Minister of Justice, he demanded: 'What does the law decree for a minister who treats with the enemy without his sovereign's knowledge?' 'Your Majesty has just pronounced it,' was the reply; 'the law is precise on that point.'[14]

On that menacing note the Council broke up.

When it convened next morning, July 3, Fouché was not present. When it rose he was no longer Minister of Police: his post had been given to Savary.

That evening at dinner, the Emperor informed the Empress that he had dismissed one of his ministers.

'Which?' asked Marie-Louise.

'The Police,' said Napoleon.

'What!' exclaimed Marie-Louise. 'When I left for France, my father said to me, "If you find yourself in any difficulty, take the advice of Fouché – he is the one who will be most useful to you." '[15]

Notes to Part IV

Chapter 1

1 Bertrand, II, 127
2 *Ibid.*, 117
3 Fouché, *Mémoires*, 228
4 Nap. I, *Corresp.* X, 414(8742)
5 Gohier, II, 118
6 *Bulletins*, I, 59(197)
7 *Ibid.*, 5(16).
8 *Ibid.*, 35–6(117).
9 *Ibid.*, 261(824).
10 Fouché, *Mémoires*, 228

Chapter 2

1 Nap. I, *Corresp.*, X, 17(8100)
2 PRO, FO 33/26
3 *Ibid.*
4 *Ibid.*
5 *Ibid.*
6 *Bulletins*, I, 168(525)
7 PRO, FO 33/26
8 *Bulletins*, I, 168(526)
9 PRO, FO 33/26
10 *Ibid.*
11 *Ibid.*
12 *Bulletins*, I, 175(548)

Chapter 3

1 PRO, FO 27/71
2 *Ibid.*
3 Pasquier, I, 231
4 Murat, III, 453
5 Roederer, *Oeuvres*, III, 541
6 *Bulletins*, I, 6(18)
7 *Ibid.*, 38(124)
8 *Ibid.*, II, 120(370)
9 *Ibid.*, III, 395(1078)
10 *Ibid.*, 411(1111)
11 *Ibid.*, 468(1236)
12 *Ibid.*
13 *Ibid.*, IV, 5(11)
14 *Ibid.*, 9(20)

Chapter 4

1 *Bulletins*, I, 291(910)
2 *Ibid.*, 298(931)
3 *Ibid.*, III, 173(453)
4 *Ibid.*
5 Fouché, *Mémoires*, 248

Chapter 5

1 PRO, FO 27/72
2 *Ibid.*

3 Fiévée, II, 180–1
4 PRO, FO 27/72
5 *Ibid.*
6 *Bulletins*, II, 409(1276)
7 *Ibid.*, 444(1394)
8 *Ibid.*, 445(1397)
9 *Ibid.*, 451(1416)
10 *Ibid.*, 453-4(1421)

Chapter 6

1 Fouché, *Mémoires*, 252
2 Bourrienne, VI, 296
3 Fouché, *Mémoires*, 264
4 *Ibid.*, 264–5
5 Bertrand, II, 80
6 Avrillon, II, 127
7 Pasquier, I, 369
8 Hortense, I, 336
9 Fouché, *Mémoires*, 265
10 Nap. I, *Corresp.*, XVI, 140(13329)
11 *Bulletins*, III, 433(1166)
12 *Ibid.*, 437(1174)
13 *Ibid.*, 455(1216)

Chapter 7

1 *Bulletins*, III, 370(1023)
2 Fouché, *Mémoires*, 255
3 *Bulletins*, IV, 35(69)
4 *Ibid.*, 54(111)
5 *Ibid.*, 106(227)
6 *Ibid.*, 114(245)
7 *Ibid.*, 194(412)
8 Lecestre, I, 194(280)
9 *Bulletins*, IV, 222(455)
10 Réal, I, 223–4
11 *Bulletins*, IV, 228(466)
12 Lecestre, I, 199–200(289)
13 *Bulletins*, IV, 232(445–6)
14 Lecestre, I, 205(297)
15 *Ibid.*, (296)
16 *Ibid.*, 207(300)
17 *Bulletins*, IV, 243(479)
18 Lecestre, I, 205(297)
19 *Bulletins*, IV, 243(497)
20 Lecestre, I, 212(310)
21 *Ibid.*, 215(315)
22 *Ibid.*, 220(322)
23 *Bulletins*, IV, 277(565)
24 Lecestre, I, 109(173)
25 *Ibid.*, 108(171)

Chapter 8

1 Metternich, II, 214
2 PRO, FO 27/77

3 Fouché, *Mémoires*, 260
4 Lecestre, I, 257 (381)
5 Norvins, 69
6 Pasquier, I, 352
7 Fouché, *Mémoires*, 267
8 *Ibid.*, 268
9 *Ibid.*
10 Pasquier, I, 358
11 Las Cases, I, 500
12 *Bulletins*, IV, 521(1034)
13 *Ibid.*, 522(1035)
14 *Ibid.*, 524(1041)
15 *Ibid.*, 526(1047)
16 *Ibid.*, 533–4(1060)
17 *Ibid.*, 535(1064)
18 Desmarest, 219

Chapter 9

1 Lecestre, I, 319(463)
2 *Ibid.*, 322(467)
3 *Ibid.*, 337(492)
4 *Ibid.*, 317(459)
5 Despatys, *Ami*, 175
6 Sorel, 182
7 Réal, I, 238
8 *Ibid.*, 237
9 Fouché, *Mémoires*, 273
10 Las Cases, II, 148(3)
11 Lecestre, I, 342(500)
12 Lanzac de Laborie, II, 153
13 Nap. I, *Corresp.*, XIX, 351(15667)
14 *Ibid.*, 382(15698)
15 Lecestre, I, 352(513)
16 Chastenay, II, 98
17 Artaud de Montor, 260
18 Lecestre, I, 363(526)

Chapter 10

1 Bertier de Sauvigny, 44–5
2 Fouché, *Mémoires*, 276–7
3 *Ibid.*, 278
4 Nap. I, *Corresp.*, XX, 50(16031)

5   Talleyrand, *Mémoires*, II, 9
6   Barante, I, 313–14
7   Fouché, *Mémoires*, 283
8   Coquelle, 203
9   Rocquain, 243
10 Despatys, *Ami*, 160
11 Louis, *Documens*, III, 199
12 Coquelle, 208
13 Louis, *Documens*, III, 200
14 Labouchère, 429

Chapter 11

1   Louis, *Documens*, III, 223
2   *Ibid.*, 224
3   Rocquain, 248
4   Nap. I, *Corresp.*, XX, 275(16352)
5   Northbrook, A.20
6   Coquelle, 221
7   *Ibid.*, 223. It has been suggested that Aaron Burr, then taking refuge in Paris from the wrath of Jefferson, proposed this North American adventure. This seems most unlikely. Burr first asked for an interview with Fouché on March 21, 1810; he was still vainly applying on April 24. Ouvrard's memorandum was dated Amsterdam, March 22 [Martel, *Historiens*, III, 284]
8   *Ibid.*, 224
9   Northbrook, A.20
10 *Ibid.*
11 *Ibid.*
12 Coquelle, 228

Chapter 12

1   Chuquet, *Inédits*, II, 49
2   Rocquain, 270
3   *Ibid.*, 271
4   Louis, *Documens*, III, 268
5   Ouvrard, I, 159
6   Girardin, IV, 388
7   Fiévée, III, 65
8   Méneval, *Mémoires*, II, 387
9   Nesselrode, III, 264
10 Pasquier, I, 393
11 Desmarest, 224
12 Ernouf, *Maret*, 282
13 *Ibid.*
14 Desmarest, 224
15 Despatys, *Ami*, 199

PART V
Disgrace 1810-1815

I

The Emperor of Austria was not the only aristocrat to hold a high opinion of Fouché. The faubourg St-Germain was shocked and resentful at 'this thunderbolt ... Everybody is dejected, gloomy, eyes downcast, already seeing themselves locked up or exiled'.[1] As soon as the news was known, 'Fouché's salons were crowded ... Some came from gratitude, others to show their dissatisfaction with the Emperor's decision ... They were not unaware that police agents were preparing lists of those who came in person or sent to have their names put in the visitor's book.'[2]

Napoleon himself was having speedy second thoughts, according to Nesselrode: 'He said the other day that Ouvrard and Labouchère deserved to lose their heads for having set him at odds with his best friend. Indeed, he must be feeling acutely the loss of a minister who rendered him such brilliant service and watched so carefully and energetically over the peace of France and the protection of his life, which must be regarded as less secure since the Duke of Otranto's disgrace.'[3]

Nesselrode had more personal reasons for regretting Fouché's dismissal. Napoleon's jibe about Talleyrand had had more truth than either he or Fouché knew. Nesselrode warned the Russian Imperial Councillor, Speranski, that one of his best sources of information was dried up now that the Legal Expert could no longer obtain news from the President. (In the Embassy code, Napoleon was Sweetheart, My Friend or Sophie Smith; Fouché was Natasha, the President or Bergien; Talleyrand was My Cousin Henry, Ta, Anna Ivanovna, Our Bookseller, Handsome Leander or the Legal Expert.) Talleyrand had been supplying Nesselrode with secret information since his arrival in Paris two months before.

'His moderation,' Nesselrode wrote of Fouché later in the month, 'proved by so many examples, must have won him great popularity. He succeeded in effacing the odious role he played during the Revolution, and it is certainly not inappropriate in this bizarre century that one of the most fanatical pillars of the Committee of Public Safety should be accompanied into disgrace by the sympathy of the whole nation. But it is precisely this popularity, his force of character and superior ability, that constitute his true offence in the eyes of the Emperor.'[4]

Despite his ruthless war against their friends and relations in the Vendée and elsewhere, despite his opposition to the authority of the Church and to any hint of restoration, the royalists and returned émigrés admired him for his fairness, his lack of malice, his eagerness for reconciliation. They revived the scores of anecdotes about his love of practical jokes and schoolboy mystifications and showing off the apparent omniscience of his police system. The two émigrés who asked for passports to leave Paris and go to the south of France, whom he astonished 'by relating to them the names of the towns, the streets, and names of the people with whom they had lodged at various times, during their emigration in England'.[5] Or the woman who came to plead for her husband to be given permission to return to France and was upbraided by the stern-faced Fouché: 'It well befits you, madam, to come here and flaunt your sorrow and your love for your husband when I know that for the past two years your children's tutor has occupied his place with you and enjoyed all his rights!' The woman turned pale and protested her innocence. Fouché grinned and said: 'Don't worry, madam, I know that the tutor is in fact your husband'[6] – and gave her the certificate that legalized his clandestine return.

Fanny Burney, wife of the long-exiled d'Arblay, who admitted that she had always regarded the Minister of Police as a monster, found to her surprise that he was 'a man of the mildest manners, the most conciliatory conduct, and of the easiest access in Paris. He had the least glare of the new imperial court of any one of its administration; he affected, indeed, all the simplicity of a plain Republican.'[7] She often saw him strolling under the trees in the Champs Elysées, 'muffled up in a plain brown rocolo and giving *le bras* to his wife, without suite or servant, merely taking the air, with the evident design of enjoying also an unmolested tête-à-tête.'[8] Cardinal Maury, shortly to be Archbishop of Paris, praised him 'as a man of great talent . . . moderate, gentle, accommodating . . . very simple, very amiable, very honest.'[9]

He was all things to all men, suiting himself not to their tastes but to his own whim and sardonic humour. So that where the Jacksons had found him 'coarse-minded, vulgar and brutal',[10] to Madame d'Arblay 'his person was the best fashioned and most gentlemanly of any man I have happened to see belonging to the government'.[11] To Méneval he recalled 'the physiognomy of Marat'.[12] For the actress Ida Saint-Elme he had 'something invincible in his face ... I saw him often, and in private or in public he retained the same authority ... In favour or in disgrace, he never lost his terrifying impassiveness.'[13] While the Fürst von Clary-und-Aldringen merely remarked that 'he has the hollowest cheeks I have ever seen'.[14]

Pasquier, who shortly afterwards became Prefect of Police, found him 'without affection for anybody, false and perfidious to an extent that has perhaps never been equalled'.[15] Fauriel, the writer who served briefly as his secretary, accused him of 'combining falseness with indiscretion, wit with ignorance ... regarding the absolute principles of justice and truth as nonsense'.[16] And Napoleon's mouthpiece, Montholon, described him as 'by nature restless, muddleheaded and double-dealing, no less dangerous to the party that employed him than to the party from which he was excluded. Without principles or passions or political scruples, perhaps without definite purpose, this bizarre personality seemed to practise intrigue for its own sake, as the Stoics practised virtue.'[17]

He had always been thought of as a leader of the Jacobin faction, and he still had a great deal of support there, but it was from the aristocratic comte de Narbonne, presumed illegitimate son of Louis XV and one-time Minister of War under Louis XVI, that his most eloquent defence came. Narbonne was invited to a reception at the Hôtel de Juigné about a month after Fouché's disgrace. All around him Fouché's former retainers were running down their dismissed benefactor. Savary, the new Minister, asked Narbonne why he was so silent.

'Because I do not share these gentlemen's opinions at all. The Duke of Otranto was a man who was of value to France and of value to the Emperor; his removal is a public misfortune. He rendered me great services – as he did to others. I shall never hear ill spoken of him without defending him, when I can do so without violating the rules of politeness; and I shall not enter any house where I do not have the right to speak my mind about the former Minister of Police.'[18]

2

When the official letter of dismissal from the Emperor arrived it was accompanied by another, friendlier in tone, appointing Fouché Governor of Rome. 'I've been made Pope,'[1] he joked to Réal's mistress, Madame de Chastenay; but he made no secret of his chagrin at losing the ministry, nor was he in any hurry to give up his official quarters. When Savary called at the Hôtel de Juigné in the evening of June 3, 1810, Fouché explained that his dismissal was so unexpected, and the records in such confusion, that he felt he must put them in order before handing over. Savary gratefully accepted this friendly offer.

Fouché sent for Gaillard, the colleague from his Oratory days to whom he entrusted his closest secrets. He gave him the key to his confidential files and told him to destroy anything that might at a later date embarrass himself or his acquaintances. For the next three days, Fouché passed on to Savary what he described as the most important secrets of the department in his study on the ground floor, while in the *cabinet noir* next door Gaillard stripped the files.

On June 5, Napoleon wrote to Savary, 'The Ouvrard affair is becoming serious. It must be rooted out.'[2] He ordered Ouvrard to be held incommunicado at Vincennes until one of his secretaries, Mounier, had interrogated him: 'There has never been a State criminal of a worse kind.'[3] On June 6 Maret sent Fouché the Emperor's instructions to leave the Hôtel de Juigné at once and to be on his way to Rome by June 15.

Gaillard had extracted two groups of confidential documents: those of possible historical interest, and those which gave the Minister authority for various measures that he had taken. 'Burn them all,'[4] said Fouché. Gaillard protested that he might later need the protection of the second group. Fouché answered that in the event of a change of régime 'they would deny the right of the Directory, the Consulate, the Emperor himself to have given me the orders that you consider to be a safeguard. Burn them!'[5] Nor was he persuaded by Gaillard's argument that the first group were of interest to later generations and would be useful for the memoirs that Fouché would no doubt write. 'Most of them contain family secrets that no minister with decent feelings would think it right to publish,' Fouché replied. 'We've no time to go through them again. Burn them!'[6]

He left for his estate at Ferrières-Pont-Carré on June 7. Three days later he received an urgent note from Maret: 'Return to His Imperial and Royal Majesty your personal correspondence for the whole period of your ministry.'[7] He answered that he had considered it his duty to burn all the Emperor's orders and personal letters. Maret repeated the request next day; and Fouché sent the same reply, but this time with a long commentary: He had not handed back the First Consul's letters on leaving the Ministry in 1802 and consequently had not expected to be asked for them this time. Indeed:

'His Majesty honoured me with such trust that if one of the princes, his brothers, aroused his displeasure he charged me with recalling him to his duty ... in such circumstances, everybody confided his grievances and complaints to me ... Furthermore, His Majesty's sisters are not secure from calumny; the Emperor graciously informed me of all the rumours that came to his notice ... He gave so much warmth to his mode of expression and his complaints that, if I had not known the princesses so well, I should have been tempted to believe there had been certain lapses on their part. I immediately burned all these letters and nothing in the world would cause me to regret such prudent actions.'[8]

It was a reasonable explanation, even though couched in impertinent terms. Was it a threat as well? If Fouché had hidden the letters instead of burning them, he could reveal many murky Bonaparte family secrets whenever he chose – and other matters, more weighty, more shameful. The threat, it is clear now, was a real one. Whatever important papers Gaillard may have destroyed at the quai Malaquais, Fouché must have retained others – or copies of those destroyed – for when his *Mémoires* were published in 1824 they contained excerpts of letters reproduced word for word from the originals. That he should have thought the threat necessary is explained by the fact that he had just learned that Napoleon's inquiries had led him beyond the unauthorized briefing of Labouchère to the hitherto unsuspected mission of Fagan.

'I beg you to send me the note which was conveyed to you by Fagan, whom you sent to London to sound out Lord Wellesley, and who brought you back a reply from that lord, which I have never had knowledge of,'[9] the Emperor wrote on June 17. He sent

Mounier to Ferrières with the letter and strict instructions not to come back empty-handed. But Fouché blandly replied that he had burned the documents connected with Fagan's journey because they were 'insignificant'.[10] Exactly a week later Maret renewed the demand for 'all the letters His Majesty has written to you during your ministry . . . He has had a chronological list made by his archivist, and regards them as the property of the ministry.'[11] Fouché replied once more that he thought the contents private between the Emperor and himself and, as their only use would have been to cover his own responsibility, he had burned them.

He could not carry on this dangerous game for ever. He had already overstayed the time-limit set by Napoleon and should have been in Rome by now. He calculated that the Emperor would not take violent measures against him until he was sure what papers existed, and where, but the messages he received from friends in Paris indicated that he might be placed under arrest while the château was searched. A little before dinner-time on Thursday, June 27, when he was going over the estate books with Dumont, a former Oratorian whom he intended to appoint as his steward, a servant announced the arrival of Dubois, the Prefect of Police.

Fouché's old rival and opponent greeted him with unexpected warmth. He was, in fact, the wrong man to have been sent on this errand. His envy of Fouché had died with his loss of the ministry and was now directed at the new occupant, Savary. His indignation at not having been given the vacant post was buttressed by the well-founded suspicion that he would shortly lose his own job, and by resentment of his treatment at the imperial court, where he was constantly snubbed since his recent marriage to the actress-daughter of a chambermaid. Dinner was put back, the two men chatted amiably until 8 p.m., and Dubois assured Fouché that he entirely believed that all the documents had been destroyed. He would report that he had found none of the sort that he had been sent for. However, since his instructions were to search and seal, 'if you put any papers you choose in a suitable piece of furniture in a room that nobody uses, I will seal it'.[12] They dined and he returned to Paris, promising that if all went well he would return the next day to remove the seals.

June 28 passed without news from Dubois. That night Bonne-Jeanne wrestled with her fears and at last broke down, imploring her husband to get out of Napoleon's reach, if only for a few days. Over and over again she harked back to Napoleon's vindictiveness, to the Enghien murder, to the new danger that – if the Emperor did believe Dubois's assurance that there was nothing left to hide – there was equally nothing to hinder his having Fouché put to death. In the morning she enlisted Dumont, who put the same argument to Gaillard. But Gaillard warned that sudden flight and concealment would be a virtual admission of guilt. He went to the Duchess's room and talked her into accepting a compromise – that the Duke should leave the château but not the neighbourhood, at any rate until that evening.

Gaillard proposed that they should drive out together on the pretext of inspecting two newly acquired farms. They would cut through the forest of Armainvilliers and dine at Combreux with some friends of Gaillard. If Dubois returned to Ferrières with good news, a horseman would be sent over immediately. If nobody arrived, Fouché and Gaillard would leave at nightfall, heading back towards Ferrières, but would turn off to Chaumes where Gaillard's wife had a cousin living in a house without servants. Fouché would remain there for two days while Gaillard sought for news. If the position was bad, he would then make for England.

The escape route was reminiscent of many that his agents had tracked down in the past, but leading in the opposite direction: from Chaumes to a surgeon at Crécy-en-Brie who shared Gaillard's interest in horticulture; to a former Benedictine monk at Montceaux whom Gaillard had defended during the Terror; up the valley of the Ourcq to a notary at Lizy; to the Duchastel de Montrouge family at Monthoury; to a former Oratorian at Compiègne; to two others, the Petit brothers, at Saint-Pierre just outside Amiens; to another, living in retirement in a village between Abbeville and Montreuil. While the Duke hid there with Father Caroulle, Gaillard would go to Boulogne to arrange with the commissioner general, Fouché's former secretary Villiers du Terrage, to send a boat to Etaples to carry him to England. He had always rewarded his supporters; seldom persecuted his opponents. All over France and in the territories she controlled he had an astonishing number of friends and even mere acquaintances ready to help him now.

They set out in warm sunlight and after a leisurely drive called on the Jaucourt family at Combreux. After dinner, while the comtesse de Jaucourt was strolling in the grounds with Fouché, Gaillard slipped away to a hill overlooking the road to Ferrières. Just as dusk was falling, Fouché's architect, Lemaistre, came riding up with news that a visitor had arrived – the duke's old associate and protégé,

Réal. He had orders to remove the seals and to ask once more for the return of the Emperor's letters. Fouché stood his ground – they had all been burned, he said.

By now there were many people in Paris who knew what had been going on. They watched in astonishment. Ouvrard commented: 'The resistance had been stubborn, victorious. The negotiations with Fouché had been conducted as if between one power and another, by ambassadors. The ambassadors obtained nothing. They returned empty-handed from Pontcarré to inform the Emperor of a refusal which more than one king would not have dared to permit himself.'[13] But there was a limit to the extent to which even Fouché could carry defiance. On July 1 the Emperor cancelled his governorship and ordered him to leave for his senatory 'within twenty-four hours'.[14] To Savary, Napoleon said that Fouché must live in Nice, but he could go to Italy or Naples if he desired, provided he informed Savary of his route.

He recognized defeat. Desmarest provided him with a passport that evening, and next day he set off with his eldest son and the boy's tutor, Antoine Jay. He made for the Franche-Comté and then up into Switzerland, over the Simplon and down into Tuscany. Here he had friends and letters of introduction that he had obtained from the Grand Duchess Elisa earlier in the year, when he saw disgrace looming. Elisa, once his sworn enemy because of his quarrel with Lucien and support of Josephine, had since become indebted to him for his protection of some of her many lovers against Napoleon's wrath. Her Chief of Police, who owed his job to Fouché, gave him blank passports and he went to Leghorn, where the Commissioner-General, Oudet du Crouzot, was another of his protégés.

The prefects and the army were spying on him. He could still count on the support of most of the police, but it was only a matter of time before Savary purged them. He began to wonder if his flight had been a mistake. Distant from friends, yesterday's minister forgotten today, he was haunted with the fear not of death but of imprisonment and oblivion. He obtained letters of credit payable in London and Naples, hired a ship and set sail from Leghorn, saying that he was making for Naples and from there would return to Rome.

His true intention, according to an intercepted letter from Jay to his wife, was to make for the United States and prepare the way for bringing over the rest of the family; he said the same in a letter he wrote to Elisa Bacciochi: he had made up his mind to throw in his hand and begin a new life in exile. But they were scarcely out of harbour when this scion of a long line of sturdy Breton mariners collapsed with sea sickness. 'It tore at my chest and twisted my entrails.'[15] Finally he fell unconscious and was brought back to shore, vowing never to set foot on a ship again.

One fear had driven out the other. Or had his erratic wanderings in Italy been a cover for the disposal of the papers that Bonaparte so much wanted to lay his hands on? He knew he was being watched, knew that his and Jay's letters would be intercepted. Too closely observed by land, had he passed on the papers at sea during the mysterious voyage that began when he went aboard the *Elisa* at Leghorn before dawn one morning and was landed fifteen miles down the coast next day?

Whatever the reason, he suddenly decided to return to France and on August 13 arrived in Lyons, where he lodged with the Commissioner-General of Police, his former secretary, Maillocheau. He wrote to Napoleon, quite in his old form, denouncing 'the subordinates who . . . have for a long time been intercepting my wife's letters . . . Recalling that at the time I left France I was given the option of installing myself in my senatory, I am going to Aix where I am confident my family will be able to join me.'[16]

Napoleon seemed almost glad to hear of his return. 'I think we should pay no attention to the Duke of Otranto,' he wrote to Savary. 'I think he is going to his senatory; write to him to that effect.'[17] And when the apprehensive Bonne-Jeanne begged him with tears in her eyes to let her join her husband, he treated her 'with great benevolence'. The only indulgence he allowed himself was to order the dismissal of Maillocheau, 'for having received in his house an exile returning to France without authorization',[18] and of Oudet du Crouzot in Leghorn.

The Duke arrived at Aix on September 5 and took up residence in the rented Hôtel de Forbin, where he was joined in October by the Duchess and their other children. For six or seven months he played the part of a contented exile, giving 'an occasional reception for the local authorities, busy with charities, taking care not to get involved in public affairs, and restricting his correspondence to the administration of his properties'.[19]

Having built up this picture of the politician in permanent retirement, drained of all interests in affairs of state – though, in fact, he had managed to place Jay in Savary's office and was informed by secret correspondents of most of what went on at court and in the council – he asked permission to return to Ferrières for the benefit of his health and so that his children could receive better education. Napoleon replied through Savary on August 11, 1811, that he was 'at liberty to spend the autumn at his country estate'.[20]

During the past twelve months Napoleon had poured men into Spain in an attempt to drive out the British troops and crush the Spanish regulars and guerrillas. Three hundred and seventy thousand French soldiers were deployed through Spain and Portugal, across the Sierra Morena to Seville, through Ciudad Rodrigo to Almeida; but at the end they found Wellington still facing them from behind the lines of Torres Vedras, waiting for winter and hunger and extended supply lines across bitterly hostile territory to do his rough hewing for him. In the spring the birth of a son to the Emperor distracted attention from Masséna's disastrous retreat from Portugal. In the summer, Spain settled down to another bloody stalemate, while those near the Emperor perceived the portents of a new war. As Fouché and his fellow opponents of the Austrian marriage had predicted, Napoleon was preparing for battle against Russia.

At the end of the year the Duke of Otranto received the final token of forgiveness – an interview with the Emperor. Napoleon made no secret of the campaign he was preparing, nor of his confidence of winning it. To the Russian envoy, Prince Kourakin, who mentioned his country's manpower, Napoleon replied: 'But can your master afford to spend 25,000 men a month, as I can?'[21] He asked Fouché his opinion of the approaching war; but since Fouché was still firmly in favour of peace he was not consulted again. In January 1812 he was invited to resume his seat in the Senate, with the implication that he was now free to return to Paris and the two houses that he still had in the rue du Bac and the rue Cerutti.

Napoleon continued to mass troops in Saxony. In June he crossed the Niemen. Through the bludgeoning heat of July and August he marched his men eastward, stretching his supply lines to breaking point, ceaselessly pursuing the elusive Russians and the mirage of world-domination. At Smolensk they turned, made him fight for the town at bitter expense, then set it on fire and disappeared eastward again.

Fouché had seen him set out gleaming with confidence. 'He had never enjoyed more perfect health; I had never seen such vigour in his looks.'[22] But now he was showing weariness: 'He has put on a lot of weight and has more difficulty in mounting. The Master of the

Horse has to give him his arm to get him into the saddle.'[23] The legend of the tough, alert, self-driving soldier genius was rubbing thin; he spent most of his time in his carriage, dozing, and appeared before his troops on horseback only when the day's march was over. 'There he is, flat out on his couch, gorging himself with lemonade,' complained one of his staff, 'and tonight he'll torment us.'[24] His bulletins reflected his fantasies: Russian morale was low, the Cossacks would all desert if they could.

In France the scourge of conscription fell again on the flinching and at last resentful people. The Prefect of the Lower Seine reported that 'young men have had all their teeth extracted to avoid military service; others have managed to rot them with acids or by chewing incense. Some have blistered their arms and legs and made the wounds incurable by bandaging them in arsenic. Many have induced hernias; some have applied such violent caustics to their generative organs that the doctors doubt if they can escape death.'[25] Even so, they were perhaps better off than the wounded who lay untended in the fire-gutted streets of Smolensk, or the hundred men in the military hospital who were forgotten for four days, unfed, untended, while the Emperor jogged along the dusty roads to Borodino and to Moscow.

There was sleet in Moscow on October 9. It had been falling, on and off, for ten days, twinkling in the glare of the fires started in the shopping quarter nearly four weeks before. The Emperor, dejected, deflated, could not bring himself to decide whether to stay or go. In the château at Ferrières the Duchess of Otranto lay dying; and Fouché was sunk in grief.

Bonne-Jeanne, whom some had found vulgar, and others a figure of fun with her red hair or her yellow wig, had for him been 'the faithful companion of good days and bad, an impeccable wife, a tender and devoted mother'.[26] His friend Gaillard, who never really liked her, admitted that 'this woman, despite her ugliness, her shyness and her cantankerous temper, had exercised a considerable influence over her husband. Her loss left an indelible scar on Fouché's life.'[27] Among her clothes, Fouché found a hoard of 300,000 francs in gold, witness to her well-known tight-fistedness and to the fear of poverty that had stayed with her since the attic in the rue Saint-Honoré.

With Napoleon farther away than he had ever been before, and the country more sunk into foreboding, General Malet conceived the time ripe for another attempt at his favourite plot, despite the fact that he was still in prison. Having bribed a warder, he escaped during the night of October 22, 1812, announced the death of Napoleon and his own appointment as Governor of Paris, took command of the 10th cohort, arrested the Minister of Police, Savary, and the Prefect of Police, Pasquier, and put them in prison, and only by bad luck failed to take over the 1st military division. Next day he and thirteen accomplices were shot.

Whether Fouché had any hand in the conspiracy is not clear, though he must have greatly enjoyed the discomfiture of Savary, whom he disliked, and Pasquier, whom he despised. (For weeks afterwards, the wags greeted their friends with : 'Do you know what's going on in Paris?' 'No.' 'Ah, then you must be in the police.')[1] He defended the plot in his *Mémoires*, claiming that if the conspirators had been a little more ruthless they could have held Paris long enough to purge the Senate and depose the Emperor, and would have received wide popular support – as Malet said when asked by the President of the Court-martial whether he had any other accomplices, 'yes, the whole of France and you too, if I had succeeded'.[2] In that case, as Fouché pointed out, 'it would have been easy to form a government that could reconcile us with Europe . . . what future calamities France would have been spared!'[3] It is likely that Fouché had an inkling of the plot – as he still had of most that was going on – but was never invited to play an active part. Certainly Gaillard, still closer to him than anybody else at this time, did not believe him to be involved.

On the Thursday night that Malet attempted his *coup*, the Emperor was asleep at Fominskoye on the Kaluga road. He had begun the retreat from Moscow on October 19. In increasing misery from cold and neglect, his men stumbled westward, pillaging their supply wagons, stealing from their officers, drifting off to find their own way to safety since they faced only starvation if they stayed with the colours. On December 5, the Emperor cut and ran, leaving Murat to fend off the pursuing Russians. (It is a tenet of the Napoleonic fable that he dashed back to Paris to deal with the Malet crisis – in fact he had received news of it on November 6, almost exactly a month before he deserted his troops.) On December 18 he arrived in Paris to prepare his revenge.

He was living beyond his means. Although he had drawn heavily on foreign troops for the Russian campaign, he had exhausted the French class of 1813 by September 1812. For the new holocaust that he planned he must take next year's conscripts – the young men of the class of 1814 – and add to them those who had escaped the dragnets of 1809, 1810, 1811, 1812. The army that he formed was almost entirely composed of infantry; of the 80,000 cavalrymen who had crossed the Niemen in such fine array – 'no French army ever possessed so many or so fine'[4] – none was now fit for service. His artillery he had abandoned in flight. On April 15, 1813, he left St-Cloud to put down the War of Liberation that had blazed up almost spontaneously in Prussia. At Lützen on May 2 and at Bautzen on May 21 he beat the armies of Prussia and Russia, but for lack of cavalry was unable to follow up the advantage. On June 4 he signed a two-month armistice.

From Dresden on May 11 he wrote to Marie-Louise, Regent in his absence, sending her a letter which she was to hand immediately to the Duke of Otranto. It was an order 'to come secretly and incognito to Dresden. You can pick three or four reliable persons of whose loyalty I can have no doubt ... Don't let any word of this leak out in Paris. You must be thought to have left for your country house and you must arrive here while they still think you are there ... I am very pleased to receive fresh services from you, and new proof of your devotion.'[5] He intended to make Fouché Governor of Prussia as soon as he had conquered it.

Méneval commented that 'the Emperor thought it prudent not to leave this personage in Paris in the present circumstances',[6] and Fouché mischievously perpetuated this story that Napoleon 'feared my presence in Paris'.[7] But it seems more likely that he was sent for because he was needed. The King of Prussia had been forced into the war by a wave of nationalism that sprang from the mass of the people (it was distrust of this proletarian fervour that kept Austria neutral). To hold down a conquered Prussia in this mood needed a man of authority and skill in police work – and his old Jacobin feeling for liberty and patriotism would help him to come to terms with those he governed.

Fouché found Dresden 'both a capital city and a vast fortified camp. The near-by forests were toppling under the sappers' axes.

Everywhere on my arrival I saw earth being dug, trees being felled, ditches and palisades being constructed.'[8] Napoleon was preparing for his next advance while trying to persuade Austria to continue neutral. Austria was willing to discuss terms – the return of her conquered provinces: Illyria; perhaps more of Italy; certainly ten or twenty million pounds sterling to compensate for a similar sum that Britain had offered her to join the alliance of Russia, Prussia and Sweden. Metternich, setting himself up as an honest broker, offered to mediate at a conference in Prague between France and her opponents. He journeyed to Dresden where Napoleon, believing that Austria was bluffing, refused to make concessions. Metternich warned him of the possible consequences. He replied: 'It may cost me my throne, but I will bury the world beneath its ruins.'[9]

The Illyrian provinces which Austria wanted had since January been governed by the duc d'Abrantès, the once-handsome General Junot, now a shambling wreck, three times wounded in the head, his brain further damaged by venereal disease and the cold of the Russian campaign. He had taken to riding on the coachman's seat of his carriage and using the whip indiscriminately on horses, postillions and escort. On June 27 he took a squad of gendarmes to search the town of Goritz for a servant girl who had failed to obey his order to come and sleep with him; he dossed down that night on straw laid across a row of chairs in a suburban inn, and the following morning had some sort of seizure. Eugène Beauharnais, Viceroy of Italy, begged Napoleon to send a replacement for his embarrassing neighbour who now proposed to make peace with the English and divide the world between his friends. 'I appoint you King from the Adige to Cattaro,' Junot wrote to Eugène. 'I give you all that the Turks possess in Bosnia. I give you an island in the Adriatic, one in the Black Sea, one in the Red Sea, one in the Mediterranean, one in the Ocean, one in India . . .'[10]

Since there was no governorship for Fouché until Prussia had been conquered, Napoleon sent him to replace Junot. He had organized some police work in Dresden, intercepting Austrian dispatches, and had tried to win back Bernadotte, now Crown Prince of Sweden and the most active opponent of Napoleon in the Confederation of the North. He had also pressed for peace with an outspokenness that the Emperor had not encountered for some time. The country had supported the latest war against Prussia, he said, as a matter of honour, since the Prussians had made the first move. But now that Napoleon had again proved the superiority of French arms at Lützen and Bautzen his subjects had a right to expect peace. Her enemies would not dispute her right to establish her frontiers on the Rhine and the Alps. If Napoleon did not take the opportunity to conclude peace on those terms, France would feel she was being sacrificed to Napoleon's personal policy: 'a senseless policy, and one that she detested as much as Europe, because she suffered as much from it'.[11]

He arrived in Prague in the evening of July 19. Next day he talked with Metternich, on Napoleon's instructions. He had last met him as Austrian Ambassador in Paris in 1809, and had sheltered him from Napoleon's order that he should be ignominiously expelled. There was little for the two men to discuss. Napoleon was set on his path of destruction. All that Fouché could do was to try to interest Metternich in support of a regency. For he had by now decided that the only solution of France's problem was to dispose of the Emperor and set up in his place 'a monarchy tempered by a reasonable aristocracy and a representative democracy'. This alone, he believed, 'could preserve France from the double danger of invasion and dismemberment'.[12]

He left Prague at dawn on July 21 and went by way of Vienna to Gratz, taking his children and their tutor with him, for even in this desperate situation he remained the devoted father and family man. The journey through Bohemia gave him a taste of the unconcealed hatred with which the French were regarded by the rest of Europe. There was trouble over post-horses and with the peasants who, according to the plainclothes agent whom Metternich sent to keep an eye on him, shouted, 'Here comes that rascal Fouché, the biggest thief in Paris and the biggest police spy. And the other scoundrels with him are nothing but wastrels, thieves, bloodhounds and spies who ought to be whipped out of the country.'[13]

From Gratz in the summer sunlight he drove down the Mura, crossing on wooden bridges from side to side, climbing over the snow-capped mountains, rattling down to the orchards above Maribor and along the willow-lined roads to Laybach (Ljubljana), capital of Carnolia and the Illyrian provinces of Carinthia, Istria and Croatia that Napoleon had jumbled together four years before to make a barrier between Austria and the sea. He took up residence in the Governor-General's palace on July 29 and gave an inaugural ball the following evening. In supreme control of both civil and military affairs, he would have greatly enjoyed his position in happier times, but all his energies for the moment were concentrated on reviving the morale of a country anxiously peering in two directions at once – to the north where the Austrians might at any moment attack by land, and to the south where the British had a few weeks earlier assaulted Fiume from the sea.

Charles Nodier, the editor of the *Télégraphe Illyrien*, who had never seen him before, was struck, as were many others, by the extreme pallor of his face. 'It was a cold but living tint like that which time gives to monuments. But very soon the power of his deeply sunk eyes prevailed over all other first impressions. They were very pale blue but entirely lacking the sparkle that comes from feeling or even the play of thought. There was something formidable, that still makes me tremble at times in retrospect, in their strange demanding, deep yet lustreless fixity.'[14] He was in his early fifties, lean as ever 'and even a little bent with age, when he allowed himself to succumb to tiredness or boredom. His bony, sinewy, knobbly body did not lack vigour, but neither did it have the exuberant health that marks the fortunate ones of this world, the selfish, the idle and the rich. There was not a single feature of his face on which work or worry had not left its imprint.'[15]

After the pomp and panache and unpredictable frenzies of Junot, the natives of Illyria were pleasantly surprised to find their new ruler behaving with a friendly simplicity 'that had been regarded until then as incompatible with the French character'.[16] He strolled about Laybach in a grey coat, round hat and thick shoes, 'surrounded by his children, usually hand in hand with his pretty little daughter, returning every salutation, without affectation, arrogance or formality, and whenever he was tired sitting himself down without ado on a promenade bench or the steps of a building'.[17]

He was presiding over the dissolution of one of the provinces of the Empire. His duty was to delay it as long as possible and to make things as difficult as he could for the Austrians. It was for this reason as well as because of his natural moderation that he began by trying to make things as easy as possible for the Illyrians. Conscription, 'which in the last analysis was merely organizing battalions for the enemy',[18] lost its urgency and severity. Entirely master in his own province, he treated instructions from the Emperor and the Regency with the same contempt as of old. Ordered to arrest the notorious bandit known as Sbogar he asked Nodier what was known of him. Nodier replied that he was said never to have killed except in self-defence and was very popular with the people. 'In that case,' said Fouché, 'he may well be more useful to us than the imperial court,'[19] and tossed the dossier into his wastepaper basket.

On August 12, 1813, Austria decided. News of her declaration of war sent Fouché hurrying to Udine to concert plans with Eugène, then back to his capital to resist the inevitable invasion, pausing on the way at Goritz to celebrate the most unfestive of fêtes: the Emperor's 44th birthday on August 15. With false newspaper reports of his own strength, of the enemy's weakness, of the support that was coming from Eugène, of an imaginary lightning advance by Napoleon on Vienna, the Governor-General desperately strove to encourage a people who were as willing to welcome the Austrians as to oppose them. But by August 26 he was forced to begin transferring his seat of government to Trieste, and from there to Goritz.

'I am in a difficult position here,' he wrote to Gaillard on September 20. 'The Austrians and English are closing in on us from all sides. Since I arrived in Illyria I have been with the advanced posts all the time. If the enemy were bolder I should have been a prisoner long ago.'[20] The excitement appealed to him and no doubt encouraged a little exaggeration, though a member of his staff writing to Gaillard the same day said 'the Duke ... is doing marvels here'.[21] He was facing an Austrian army of 100,000 men. He fell back to Udine. On October 7 – the day that Wellington crossed the Pyrenees into France – Fouché was on his way to Venice, his province totally overrun by the invaders.

4

In Paris, Marie-Louise appeared in person before the Senate to ask for a further 280,000 men. From January to October 1813, Napoleon had demanded 840,000 men from France alone. 'Someday,' said the horrified Prefect of Police, 'when all the laws are examined – all the decrees and all the regulations which were deemed necessary to ensure the annual levy of human beings torn from their homes – we shall recognize that the intoxication of glory must be powerful indeed, since it served for so many years to make a highly civilized nation submit not only to so dreadful a sacrifice but even to the odious means needed to effect it.'[1]

During the four days of the battle of Leipzig, Napoleon inflicted 54,000 casualties on the enemy and sustained 40,000 on his own troops. And in the end he had not enough men or ammunition to pound his way to victory. By November 2 he had led his defeated army back across the Rhine, and a week later the Allies offered him peace. He would retain his throne; France would keep not only her natural territory within the Rhine, the Alps and the Pyrenees, but Savoy, the Rhine provinces and Belgium as well. The offer was overgenerous, yet not enough to satisfy his pride. At the end of the month the Allies resumed their advance. The Germans had hesitated because of the belief that France was a difficult country to invade. Thanks to Napoleon they were about to disprove this for the first time.

On November 21 Fouché received a letter from the Emperor instructing him to remain in Italy to advise Eugène and Elisa and to rally Murat, who had hurried south after the catastrophe of Leipzig to try to save his own kingdom. Fouché was to take up the duties of Governor-General of Rome. There was no doubt this time that Napoleon was deliberately keeping him away from Paris. 'I have to take precautions for my absence,' the Emperor said to Roederer a few days before. 'Everything has been very peaceful this year . . . There have been no plots like those that Fouché and Talleyrand got up to three years ago.'[2]

So Fouché wrote to Murat, went to Florence to encourage the Bacciochis to resist, then decided to go to Naples to talk to Murat in person. If Neapolitan troops were sent to reinforce Eugène's North Italians along the line of the Po, Fouché believed the Austrians could be held at bay through the winter while Napoleon came to terms. He did not know that an offer of peace had already been rejected.

He still had his children with him, and was still unmindful of appearances – as the startled Minister of Police, Norvins, discovered on the morning after his arrival in Rome. Norvins, calling to receive instructions on presenting the members of the Government of the Roman States to him, found him lodged 'in a mediocre apartment composed of a small ante-room, a small salon and a bedroom'.[3] The Governor-General was in the ante-room, wearing his nightshirt 'under which was visible a flannel vest flapping loosely around his scraggy neck, and a pair of faded cotton trousers tucked into frayed greenish slippers'. His night-cap lay on the chimney-piece beside a scrap of soap. 'The red soap box was next to the washbowl. He himself was sharpening a worn razor on a strop . . . and was about to shave . . . in front of a little mirror hung on the window.'[4]

He hurried on down to Naples, preceded by the beautiful Mme Récamier, on her way to visit the Murats and unwittingly stealing all Fouché's relay horses until he caught up with her at Terracino, and they travelled on together across the flooding Garigliano. He remained in Naples for three weeks while Murat – King Joachim of the Two Sicilies – wrestled with his problems and his conscience. His kingdom was threatened, as it had been ever since he took it over from Joseph Bonaparte five years before, by a British-led invasion from Sicily. He had identified his interests with those of his people, as Louis had in Holland. He believed, mistakenly, that the Italians accepted him as a leader. He had asked both Napoleon and Metternich to declare Italy independent and had made it clear that he would support the first one to do so. Meanwhile he was moving his troops northward: thirty infantry battalions, sixteen cavalry squadrons, fifty guns.

Neither he nor Fouché can have doubted that Napoleon was prepared to sacrifice him to the Austrians if it served his purpose. Fouché hoped to persuade Murat not to forsake France. There was a clear distinction now between the Emperor and the nation. If Murat came to terms with the Austrians it would lessen France's chances of a favourable peace. On the other hand, if he led a successful campaign for Italian independence it would diminish Napoleon without aiding the Austrians; it would incidentally revive for Fouché his forgotten republican dreams of fifteen years ago. They parted without any decision or agreement. Fouché merely advising him 'to increase his army and make sure of his troops',[5] so as to defend himself against all comers.

On his return to Rome, Fouché wrote to the Emperor, detailing Murat's temptations and possible moves. A week later, at Christmas, Murat himself sent a last plea to Napoleon, begging him to declare Italy independent: 'Make peace, and at any price; gain time and you will have gained all . . . if you refuse to listen to the entreaties of your subjects and your friends, you are lost – and so are all your friends.'[6]

On December 27 Fouché wrote to Napoleon again, this time about the speech the Emperor had made to the Legislative Corps on the 19th in which he had protested his good intentions and demanded their support. 'It would have made a deep impression on Europe and touched every heart,' said Fouché, 'if Your Majesty had added to the desire he has shown for peace, a magnanimous renunciation of his former policy of universal monarchy. So long as he does not make a pronouncement on that point, the coalition powers will believe or will say that this policy is merely deferred, and that you will revert to it as soon as events permit.'[7]

On the last day of the year, a handsome fairhaired young cavalry officer with a patch over one eye arrived in Naples – Count Adelbert von Neipperg, the future lover of Marie-Louise. He brought a letter to Caroline Murat from Metternich, once one of her keenest admirers. It warned her that Napoleon was about to come to terms with the Allies, agreeing that they should do as they pleased in Italy, provided Eugène's interests were protected.

It was a lie. Napoleon was farther than ever from accepting peace terms. At the Council of Ministers on December 1, when he presented a decree calling up another 300,000 conscripts, he had broken into a wild denunciation of the treachery around him. Screaming for revenge against Eugène's father-in-law, the King of Bavaria, who had changed sides, his eyes bloodshot, he repeated again and again: 'Munich must burn! Munich shall be burnt!'[8] His ministers were apprehensive of the reprisals to come, but none had the courage to oppose him. On New Year's Day 1814, he told the Legislative Corps: 'I am one of those men who can be killed but not dishonoured . . . Within three months we shall have peace; either the enemy will have been driven from our soil or I shall be dead.'[9] He left Paris on January 25 to direct what was now the Battle of France.

Murat did not hesitate any longer. On January 11 he signed a formal alliance with Austria; on January 17 he announced he was taking possession of Italy up to the line of the Po; on January 23 he assumed command of his army at Ancona; and by January 31 he was at Bologna. Fouché left Rome for Florence on January 5, wrote a letter on behalf of Elisa to Murat and supervised her departure from the city on February 1. He joined her in Lucca and from there wrote to Napoleon on February 5 pointing out that 'Italy will become the home of insurrection and brigandage. Your Majesty will perhaps consider that my services would be more useful to him elsewhere. I fear neither difficulties nor dangers, but I desire employment in which I may have hope of success and of giving your Majesty fresh proofs of my devotion.'[10] He was itching to get his hands on the controls of State, now dispersed between Marie-Louise as Regent, Joseph Bonaparte as Lieutenant-General of the Empire, and the Emperor close at hand in the field.

Napoleon's new conscripts marched unwillingly to the slaughter. He ordered Savary to send execution squads of the élite gendarmerie from Paris 'to arrest the stragglers and decimate them, that is shoot one in every ten in accordance with my order of the day'.[11] He wrote to Fouché on February 13, 'The conduct of the King of Naples is infamous, that of the Queen is beyond words. I hope I live long enough to avenge myself and France for such an outrage and such atrocious ingratitude. Go to Lyons or Marseilles, according to the direction you are coming from, and make for Paris.'[12]

Fouché was meanwhile tidying up the dismal retreat. At Lucca he signed a treaty with Murat's representative, General Lechi, surrendering Tuscany. He sent orders for Rome to be handed over, then crossed into Emilia, where Murat and Eugène confronted each other, and urged them to delay fighting, since Napoleon's collapse was now inevitable and imminent, though he still seemed determined to sacrifice every Frenchman and every French town. 'There is only one way to save ourselves,' Fouché told Elisa: 'To kill the Emperor out of hand.'[13]

He went once more to Eugène, at his headquarters at Volta, and begged him not to sacrifice more men by answering Napoleon's call to march his army into France. Then he set off on the long, winding road up into the Alps and down to Lyons, where his path was blocked by the Commissioner-extraordinary, Chaptal, formerly Minister of the Interior. On Savary's orders, and perhaps in accordance with Napoleon's second thoughts, Fouché was kept away from Paris while the curtain came down. Headed off at every attempt to turn northward, he drove through Valence to Avignon and as far west as Toulouse before he could make his way up through Limoges and Orleans. He reached Paris on April 8, to find the allied troops in occupation and Talleyrand at the head of a provisional government.

On April 6 the Senate had proclaimed the comte de Provence King of France as Louis XVIII. A fortnight later, Napoleon set off from Fontainebleau to take possession of his new kingdom of Elba. As he drove south he found the people dancing in the streets. Between Montélimar and Avignon his carriage was held up by crowds shouting, 'Long live the Bourbons! Long live Louis XVIII! Down with the tyrant! Down with the butcher of our children!'[14] Their relief at having thrown the monstrous jockey who had ridden them for fifteen years took an ugly turn. At Orgon he was hanged in effigy while the women screamed, 'Give us back our sons!'[15] By the time the party reached La Calade, the man who could be killed but not dishonoured was riding as a courier disguised in Austrian uniform while one of his servants crouched behind the shattered windows of the filth-bespattered coach.

The events in Paris during the week before his arrival dealt Fouché a double blow. He had foreseen Napoleon's defeat as the opportunity to set up a Council of Regency – 'the only way to provide a safeguard for the Revolution and its principles'.[1] The proclamation of a monarchy destroyed this hope; and the return of the Bourbons made the future uncertain for all those *votants*, like himself, who had condemned Louis XVI to death. Belatedly, he tried to prise a way back into government and within two days saw his opportunity.

Monsieur, the comte d'Artois, presented himself at the gates of Paris on Easter Sunday, April 10, 1814, to assume the Lieutenant-Governorship of the realm on behalf of his elder brother who was still making his unwieldy way from Hartwell. He had not accepted the constitution drawn up by a committee of the Senate and the provisional government; nor had he replaced his white cockade – so long the symbol of France's enemies on the battlefield – by a tricolour one. The provisional government told his emissary, the baron de Vitrolles, that acceptance was essential. *Monsieur* still refused. France was confronted with a constitutional crisis even before the King was back on the throne.

As a temporary measure, Talleyrand suggested *Monsieur* should take his place at the head of the provisional government. The comte d'Artois accepted this and entered the city on the 12th. But the King's brother as head of government was no substitute for the king as head of State. On April 14 Talleyrand invited Fouché to be present at a meeting of the Council of Ministers; and there he propounded a way out of the impasse: the government could not accept Artois's appointment by the King as Lieutenant-Governor until he or the King accepted the constitution, but why should not the Senate confer the Lieutenant-Governorship on Artois, thus establishing the Senate's superior authority until the King arrived? The solution was accepted by both sides. Fouché made no secret of his liberal principles but impressed Artois by his desire to find a compromise – and even more by his refusal to be a member of the deputation that formally received the prince on the grounds that 'it was necessary to avoid confronting him with persons who might remind him of painful memories'.[2]

But if they did not confront him they could at least communicate with him. A fortnight later, Artois received through Talleyrand a letter from Fouché. It was accompanied by one that he had just written to Napoleon which 'I believe it my duty to communicate to Your Highness' since 'tranquillity ... can never be fully enjoyed as long as the Emperor Napoleon is on the island of Elba'.[3]

The enclosed letter began: 'Sire, when France and part of Europe lay at your feet, I always dared to let you know the truth; today, when you are in misfortune, I am more worried at speaking to you frankly, but I owe it to you to do so.' He pointed out that neither his title nor his kingdom were worthy of Napoleon's past and 'would serve only to make your regrets more bitter; they will seem not the remnants but the vain mockery of so much vanished grandeur'. So long as he remained in such close proximity to France and Italy and Spain, 'a genius such as yours will always inspire suspicion among the great powers. You will be accused without being guilty, and though guiltless you will do harm, for fear greatly harms both governments and nations!'[4]

He therefore urged him to give up his crown. 'There would be more glory and more consolation for you in the life of a private individual – and today the safest and most suitable refuge for a man like you is the United States of America. There you will begin life again among people who are themselves still young, who will be capable of admiring your genius without fearing it ... You will prove to those people that if you had been born among them ... you would have preferred their virtues and their liberty to all the dominions of the world.'[5] He received no reply from either the Emperor or Artois.

Louis XVIII arrived in Paris at the beginning of May, 'uncomfortably corpulent and seemingly infirm on his feet',[6] well-intentioned but hopelessly blinkered by upbringing and the rancorous environment of exile. He refused the constitution, substituted a charter given in what he insisted on calling the 19th year of his reign, and soon showed that, whatever liberal tendencies he might have himself, he was quite incapable of controlling the reactionary mania of his followers, full of their rights and oblivious of their duties, an alien horde for whom the gains of the Revolution had been losses and the victories of the Empire had been defeats.

Led by the duc d'Angoulême and his wife, daughter of the guillotined Louis XVI and Marie Antoinette, reinstated by foreign troops, tolerated only because of the agonizing need for peace after so much bloodshed, the extremists had the insane effrontery to treat with contempt the sole consolation left to the defeated French nation – pride in the recent glories of her army. 'Every salon in Paris abounds with stories of the insults and the vulgar pleasantries of the Duke of Berri,' wrote one English observer. 'Does he learn from [one soldier] that he has served twenty-five years? *Vingt-cinq ans de brigandage* is his reply. Do the old guard displease that great commander the Duke of Angoulême in performing some manœuvre? They are told they must go to England and learn their exercise. Lastly, is a colonel to be degraded? The Duke of Berri tears off his epaulets with his own hand.'[7] At court the imperial guard was being replaced by musketeers and gentlemen of the household in fancy uniforms with superior rates of pay. Place-seekers were descending to such offensive servilities as Jérôme Bonaparte's late Court Chamberlain who paraded the streets with his Cross of the Legion of Honour tied to his horse's tail.

'We shan't have them for more than a year,'[8] said Fouché. He went to Ferrières for a few weeks, 'buried away to avoid even the suspicion of ambition,'[9] he said to Gaillard. But it was quite impossible for him to stay peaceably out of things. 'He had *governomania*,' said Barère. 'Nothing seemed beyond his intelligence and ambition.'[10] Even if he was not able to control affairs he was still a compulsive giver of advice. He returned to the house in the rue Cerutti (shortly to revert to its former name of rue d'Artois) on the old pretext of finding tutors for his children. His outspoken views on the necessity to remove Napoleon from Elba and for the royalists to moderate their conduct soon came to the ear of Sir Charles Stuart, the British Minister in Paris, who wrote to Castlereagh that Talleyrand had recommended the King to give Fouché a post in the government, 'a resolution which I much doubt if the King will adopt . . . though the acknowledgement of his Talents had already induced the King to seek the opinions of that Individual'.[11]

The first step towards this reconciliation of the King with one of the men who had condemned his brother was made by Fouché himself. He asked the Corsican-born Russian ambassador, Pozzo di Borgo, to arrange a meeting with the King's favourite, the comte de Blacas. They met on Sunday, June 20, at the duc de Dalberg's house; Blacas was sufficiently impressed by Fouché's views to ask him to put them into writing for submission to the King. Fouché could have wished for nothing better.

He protested that he had no desire except to remain in retirement, though he regretted he was not allowed to take a seat in the Chamber of Peers which the new constitution had substituted for the Senate. He realized that the sight of some senators was painful to Louis, but it would have been easy to discourage them from attending the sittings without publicly excluding them. He pointed out the simple truth, so obvious to 'a monarch enlightened by his studies, his observations and his misfortunes' that 'princes who have been absent for twenty-five years do not suddenly become the object of the affections of a people who ... have been educated in feelings and maxims so opposed to the monarchy'.[12] Even the enthusiasm shown for the King on his return was already diminished because of 'imprudent acts, or at least acts imprudently committed'.[13]

He listed the principal causes of public anxiety: fear of the return of feudal rights; fear of being deprived of property purchased from the *domaines nationaux* (and previously confiscated from the émigrés); fear of persecution because of past services to the Republic or the Empire; disappointment among the democrats that the constitutional charter insisted on the King's *hereditary* rights; and dissatisfaction among the army – the most dangerous section of the population – at the loss of prospects of promotion and fortune. As one officer said: 'This tranquillity of Europe is a fine thing – but will it not keep me always a captain?'[14] Fouché urged above all that the King should make clear that 'every Frenchman is assured of finding support and protection beneath his throne',[15] and to curb the royalist extremists. 'One knows where reaction begins, but not where one can bring it to a halt; it drags everything with it: above all, the Sovereign Power. And the resistance to the Sovereign Power is not felt or seen until it is stronger than that Power itself.'[16]

He sat back to await the King's reply, reasonably confident that he was on the road to rehabilitation and re-employment. The royalists were coming round in his favour. 'It was accepted,' according to Pasquier, by those, 'who prided themselves on their broad views, that M. Fouché was the most able man to have emerged from the Revolution.'[17]

'The ex-minister Fouché, despite his quiet exterior, is very active in trying to force the King to make use of him,'[18] Pozzo wrote to St Petersburg on July 11. The same day, but better informed, Stuart sent a dispatch to Castlereagh telling him that Fouché's suggestions had been turned down, to his great annoyance. Stuart was disappointed, too. Fouché's appointment to the ministry he said, 'would in every way contribute to the tranquillity and good government of this country'. Now, on the other hand 'the

Negotiation has been broken off under circumstances which leave a feeling of ill-humour that it is to be feared may be materially prejudicial'.[19]

He was right. Fouché retired to Ferrières and sulked. In readiness for the inevitable collapse of the new régime he asked Corvisart, formerly the Emperor's physician, to propose him to Marie-Louise for the post of Governor to the infant King of Rome. Under cover of a commercial code he entered into correspondence with Eugène. He alarmed Gaillard by receiving mysterious messengers from Jérôme, who assured him that exile in Elba had 'produced its inevitable effect; Napoleon will not be as despotic, he will listen to his ministers and particularly to one to whom he owes his return to France'[20] – if only Fouché would join in the plot to bring him back.

6

Late one evening in August a gendarme, who had lost his way and clattered for hours around the neighbouring villages, rode up to Ferrières with a request that the duc d'Otrante should be at the office of the Chancellor, the vicomte Dambray, at eight o'clock the following morning. Fouché had his carriage prepared, set off shortly after midnight, and, travelling as fast as the darkness would allow, arrived at 5 a.m. in the rue du Cherche-Midi outside the lodgings that Gaillard used when his work in the criminal appeal court brought him to Paris. Fouché tugged at the bell; the concierge refused to stir out of bed; the door was eventually opened by Gaillard himself. Fouché apologized for rousing him so early and told him of Dambray's message. 'I didn't want to seem feigning reluctance,' he said, in explanation of his wild dash through the night. 'Those fellows must be at their wits' end if they want me as a minister. I'm going to have a job straightening out all their blunders.'[1]

Gaillard answered sharply that far from being appointed to office, Fouché was to be questioned on his dealings with the Bonapartists. He had just learned that a letter from the Duke to Eugène had fallen into the hands of the King's police. 'The walls of my apartment have ears,' he said, while he hurried with his dressing. 'We will go to the Luxembourg – they open the gates about now.'[2] As they strolled through the gardens Gaillard nagged his friend on his lack of prudence – the likelihood that the extremists would seize this opportunity to charge him with treason. 'No doubt,' he concluded portentously, 'they will not make a final decision until they see your answers to the questions the chancellor will put to you.'

'If he's really been told to interrogate me,' said Fouché briskly, 'I'll give him such a fright that he'll not bother with drawing up a report.'[3] It was half past seven. They left the Luxembourg, walked down to the river and across to the Tuileries Gardens. Gaillard waited on the Feuillants terrace; Fouché continued up the rue Castiglione to the Chancellor's office in the Place Vendôme. An attendant in full livery, plumed hat, baldrick, sword and halberd conducted him to the ushers' ante-room; from there an usher escorted him to a large salon and, throwing open the double-doors to the Chancellor's study, revealed Dambray ceremonially robed and carrying his cloth-of-gold cap.

Dambray offered him a chair and opened the conversation nervously, apologizing for bringing him up from the country at such short notice. His Majesty wished the Duke to enlighten the Chancellor about some correspondence. Fouché expressed surprise. 'Correspondence?' he repeated.[4] Had he been invited here to discuss a mere correspondence – at a time when the government was in desperate need of winning 'the love of the people, the confidence of the army'?[5]

The Chancellor halted, pondering on this interruption. When he seemed about to reply, Fouché spoke again. In his dry, harsh voice he recited the government's blunders: the failure to allay the fears of purchasers of the *biens nationaux*, to strengthen the national morale so enfeebled by the humiliation of defeat. Why were they not repairing the roads, broken down by military transport; reviving agriculture, ruined by taxes and requisitioning; restocking stud farms instead of filling other nations' pockets every time a man needed to buy a horse? Anything that came into his head was a bludgeon to beat the astonished Chancellor with. 'Don't forget that every day you fail to increase the confidence of the people in you is another day by which you increase the difficulty of establishing your authority over them.'[6]

The Chancellor rose to his feet. Fouché followed suit.

'Monsieur le duc,' said Dambray, 'the King —'

'– The King,' interrupted Fouché, 'is too wise not to appreciate that if just one letter – which never even received a reply – occupies his ministers for a quarter of an hour, the *cabinet noir* will take up so much of their time that they will be unable to deal with a single piece of business or remedy a simple abuse.'

He raised his voice and began making for the door. 'I fear, Chancellor, that you do not understand your true position. You are sitting on kegs of gunpowder; the slightest spark may set off the most violent explosions anywhere in the kingdom ... Honour and conscience demand that you should warn the King that His Majesty is suspended over an abyss, and at this instance I see only a thread preventing his plunging into it. I do not wish to keep you longer from your affairs – please, Chancellor, do not hesitate to call on me at any time that you have anything to communicate to me.'[7]

Dambray, 'tripping over his gown and trembling like a leaf, his forehead covered with sweat', according to Fouché's gleeful and no doubt exaggerated account, rang for the double doors to be opened and conducted his visitor to the ante-room in silence. The Duke made off down the rue Castiglione and joined Gaillard outside the Tuileries railings. Roaring with laughter, he gave him a highly-coloured résumé of the interview, whose basic veracity was later confirmed by the Minister of Finance who heard Dambray confess to the King: 'I didn't *dare* interrogate that man.'[8]

But it was not at all certain that the King and his other ministers would let the matter drop. Fouché took Gaillard – who had a week free from duty – back to Ferrières with him, setting off early that afternoon. As they were finishing dinner, a servant brought Gaillard word that a member of his family had called to see him. He went out to find a man he had never met before, who introduced himself as one of Jérôme's aides-de-camp. He brought a warning that the man who had last visited Fouché on Jérôme's behalf had been questioned by Beugnot, the Director-General of Police. Another of Jérôme's men had been summoned for interrogation that evening. Gaillard arranged for him to return with more news the following day and to meet in a copse on the way to the château de Combault, where Fouché would go on the pretext of calling on the Duke of Danzig. They kept the appointment and learned that neither man had been detained but that the first was badly frightened and intended to leave the country. Fouché sent an urgent warning that to do so would confirm the suspicion against them all.

The emergency passed. Fouché continued to offer advice to the King by roundabout ways. He also continued to keep in close touch with the many conspiracies now on foot – most of them concerned not with the unnecessary task of toppling the Bourbons but with deciding who should succeed them, in what constitutional framework. Pozzo di Borgo reported towards the end of September that 'the regicides are agitating because they want Fouché in the Council';[9] but his own more modest ambition to be admitted to the Chamber of Peers was thwarted by the duchesse d'Angoulême who was said to have 'resorted to a fainting fit to obtain from the King his exclusion'.[10]

He found life tedious in the country, despite the company of his children, the boys' German tutor and the girl's governess Mademoiselle Ribou. He invited the pretty, witty Madame de Custine to 'come and spend a few days here with your son. My children will arrange some shooting and fishing parties for him.'[11] He could have the run of the library too. 'We don't neglect education; we know it is necessary under all governments – even in countries where they don't govern at all.'[12] His letters to her were sprinkled with bitter little comments on the follies of the Bourbon administration despite his protests that 'the door is closed here to all serious follies, all human ambitions; henceforward I consider myself emeritus in public affairs, I have resigned my active life to others'.[13] But knowing that she had many friends at court he continued to drop hints and complain that the letters he sent to the King were probably left unread. Meanwhile he encouraged other guests to stay for weeks on end at Ferrières, such as Jullian, one of his former police lieutenants, with whom he spent hours walking in the grounds of the large estate.

He came back to Paris in November and spent a few days in the rue d'Artois, where the police kept a sharp eye on his doorkeeper's list of the visitors the Duke was willing to receive. In December he was back again. This time the Prefect of Police, Anglés, made a note that 'he has taken fright, following the way in which public opinion has shown itself against the *votants*. He announces his intention of selling his property and retiring to England with his children, but wishes, he says, to obtain formal authorization from the King'.[14]

It was a wise precaution to prepare for flight, now that he knew so much about so many secret schemes; but his letter to the King that prompted Anglés's comment was in terms of admonition, not fear. 'The Duke of Otranto would have left France on the day he realized that all the King's promises would not be fulfilled, had he not been stayed by the hope, given him by His Majesty, that the Constitution would not be violated. If, however, the Constitution is to continue to be binding only on the Nation and breached with impunity by all the agents of the government, the Duke of Otranto petitions the King to permit him to choose another country for himself and his sons.'[15] In fact he had not the slightest intention of dropping out of the game at this stage.

In January 1815 he received an unexpected inquiry from Metternich, who wanted his opinion on what form of government would be most acceptable in France if the Bourbons fell: Napoleon I, Napoleon II, a Republic, or a Monarchy under the duc d'Orléans. Fouché, true to his preference for a regency in which he hoped to play a leading part, answered that 'the moment was never more favourable for establishing the regency of the Empress; the new government had caused so much disillusion that if the Emperor's son appeared at Strasburg accompanied by a peasant on a donkey, the first regiment to which he presented himself would lead him without hindrance right to Paris'.[16]

Though many of the groups with whom he was in contact believed that experience had taught Napoleon a lesson, Fouché's attitude to him had not changed. He considered King Log was doomed, but did not welcome the return of King Stork. He continued to send his warnings to court and in January received a visit from André, who had recently replaced Beugnot as Director-General of Police. André had been sent by the King, despite opposition from Blacas; he told Fouché that he had come for lessons in police work.

Fouché smilingly suggested they should for the moment confine themselves to 'the question that no doubt occupies you day and night: what is going on and being said on the island of Elba, what visitors go there, what agents leave it, the packages that are smuggled in and those that slip out'.[17] André suggested they need not devote their valuable time to such details; whereupon Fouché gave him a lecture on the value of minutiae in police work. 'How many ships have you got on day and night patrol in the part of the Mediterranean that separates Elba from the Continent? How many soldiers have you posted along the coast – soldiers who can be relied on to fire on anybody, no matter who, trying to land in secret?'

'Repeat to M. de Blacas before this night is out,' he urged André, 'that if our coasts are left for a few more months in the same state of neglect, the Emperor will be back with the swallows and the violets.'[18] There was a sinister ring to this reminder of the name the soldiers gave to Napoleon – *Le Père Violette*. Doubting whether André would pass on all he had said, he put it in writing and sent it to Blacas. 'Napoleon's return to France would be a great calamity,' he said to Gaillard, whom he had asked to be present at the interview. 'We must prevent it.'[19]

He saw that there was little chance of success with a government which 'tries to be clever and only manages to rouse distrust',[20] egged on by returned émigrés who 'act and talk as if they'd taken France by assault, where they only came back at the enemy's coat-tails. Why print insults about Napoleon every day? It keeps him in mind the whole time. I strictly forbade any mention of the Bourbons in the newspapers, good or ill. And half France forgot them.'[21]

It had not forgotten Napoleon. In the evening of February 26, 1815, he set sail from Porto-Ferrajo under a full moon. On March 1 he set foot on French soil between Cannes and Antibes. Keeping eastward of the royalist country that had given him such a frightening reception ten months before, he took the post-road to Grasse, making for the lower slopes of the Alps where resistance was less likely.

7

It was Sunday, March 5, before news of Napoleon's return reached Paris, carried by a courier from the coast to Lyons and sent from there by telegraph. The government kept it quiet, believing or just wishing that it was false. Fouché knew within a few hours, and was not comforted by it. As he said: 'Up to the very last moment I had continued to seek some compromise, some means of reconciliation which would have avoided resorting to the desperate measure of the Emperor's return.'[1] Even now he hoped the bulk of the people, the National Guard, and perhaps some of the army could be rallied against Napoleon by a liberal government, in which he saw himself, Lafayette, Benjamin Constant and others.

The news took many of the conspirators by surprise. There had been a plan to kidnap Marie-Louise and the King of Rome and bring them back into France; another to march the troops of the 16th military division from Lille to Paris and arrest the King and his brother. Both went off at half-cock. Paris learned officially about Napoleon's reappearance in the *Moniteur* of March 7, when the King ordered him to be hunted down as a traitor and a rebel. On the 8th the capital was without information because of the heavy rain that obscured the telegraph signals. The Russian envoy mentioned Fouché as one of the notabilities who were hourly expected to be arrested, and next day was of the firm opinion that Bonaparte would be shot – indeed, 'they say a battle has already occurred in which Bonaparte has been taken prisoner'.[2]

'It is strange not yet knowing where Bonaparte is,' Fouché wrote to Delphine de Custine on March 9. 'Up to now Paris is quiet and in good heart, we have nothing to worry about if a close watch is being kept throughout the kingdom and, above all, if the immediate chiefs of the soldiers can be relied upon.'[3] At ten o'clock next morning he told her he was still without any firm news. 'There can only be one side for people of sense and enlightenment. Everybody wishes for tranquillity and liberty, and Bonaparte cannot seem to anybody the way to attain them. But I admit I fear the blindness of the soldiers.'[4] Late that night he sent another brief note. 'It is probable that Bonaparte is at this moment at Lyons. I pity the King for having been so badly served.'[5]

A wave of cheering like an unbroken *feu de joie* accompanied the imperial eagles northward. The tricolour flew high once more. Higher still rose the assurances that the same Bonaparte who had returned from Egypt to save the principles of the Revolution had now come back from Elba to restore them. And so disgusted were the people with ten months of Bourbon rule that they were ready to believe him.

The Allies gathered in congress at Vienna outlawed Bonaparte. The two chambers in Paris were assured by the King that he had no fears for himself, only for France: 'At the age of sixty, how better can I end my days than dying in her defence?'[6] He renewed his consultations with Fouché through Blacas, André and the Minister of the Interior, the abbé Montesquiou, who had proposed in September that Beugnot should be dismissed and the Ministry of Police restored under Fouché. When Louis had told his niece the duchesse d'Angoulême that he was contemplating reinstating the man who had voted for the death of her parents, she had replied: 'I will, if necessary, forget that I am their daughter; but do not you forget that you are the King.'[7] Louis had given way to her then; but he was desperate now.

Fouché continued to try to reassure his friends, telling them to 'rely on me. Old ministers have prophetic powers, like old women'.[8] He took tea with Delphine on the afternoon of March 11 and was unfavourably impressed by the false optimism in court circles that he found repeated there. But he urged her not to flee from Paris. 'You have friends here; we will look after each other. Believe me – the military government that is about to overrun us will not last long.'[9]

On March 13 Louis sent Dambray to Fouché. The Chancellor asked for his advice on 'what may best be done to stop Bonaparte's mad and criminal enterprise, whose unexpected success is beginning to give the King some anxiety'.[10] Fouché read him a lecture on the Bourbons' lost opportunities and told him the King had only one hope of survival now – to appoint a new ministry composed of men who were known to stand for the ideals of the Revolution and would guarantee their preservation.

It sounded as if he were proposing himself, as he almost certainly was, with Lafayette and the others as co-ministers. He was pessimistic. 'They are wasting their time asking me for advice – and making me waste mine,' he wrote to Delphine. 'Because they don't believe it is sincere. No doubt they have reason not to.'[11] He mentioned the news that Macdonald's troops had refused his orders and gone over to Bonaparte. 'The same thing will happen to the other marshals.'[12]

The King swallowed his pride and sent Dambray back next day to tell Fouché that he accepted his suggestion and wished him to name the ministers who would unite the nation behind the King. But the dawdling had gone on too long; there was no time left; Bonaparte was between Macon and Chalon, less than 250 miles away. Fouché replied coldly that he did not know which men would gain the King's confidence; he had indicated the sort of men – it was for the King to make his own choice.

'Sir,' said Dambray sternly, 'your King asks you in a moment of extreme crisis for your advice and you refuse it . . . I had thought you were a better Frenchman.'[13]

'I am more devoted to the King than most of those he brought back from exile,' Fouché retorted. Then in a sudden flood of impatience and resentment: 'If I had been Minister of Police, Bonaparte would never had set foot in France. Today, no power on earth can prevent him reaching Paris . . .'[14]

Dambray protested that he was not allowing for the resources the King could still call on: 'the universal love that his qualities have inspired in the nation, the courage of the princes and nobility around him, the strength of his household troops, the genuine devotion of those generals and regiments who have remained loyal to him, the Paris National Guard and the regular troops who are being concentrated at Melun and outnumber Bonaparte's rebel followers three to one.'

'I know it all down to the last detail,' said Fouché, 'and it is entirely illusory. If the King could count on six regiments of cavalry he could make Bonaparte his prisoner. But as soon as that man appears at Melun, the regular troops will join his colours, the National Guard will be drawn in with them or will disperse, the princes and the household troops will have no choice but to take to flight – and he will enter Paris on the 21st or 22nd of this month.'[15]

He told Dambray he would talk with complete frankness, enjoying playing the oracle and proving how right he had been. 'I am neutral,' he said, 'because I was rejected when I could have been useful, when I could have prevented the misfortunes that have so suddenly descended on the Royalist party (which, by its foolish conduct, has led to the collapse of the throne). I do not belong to the faction that is bringing back Bonaparte to supreme power; on the contrary, my party is greatly opposed to that ferocious tyrant, and I am his irreconcilable enemy because I know that he detests me and wishes to ruin me. But the connections between his group and ours are close enough for all the moves in his favour to be known to us.'

'But if you are so much his enemy,' said Dambray, 'why don't you join the King's loyal servants in preventing his success?'

'Our position is quite logical,' Fouché replied. 'Resistance is useless. I will be even more frank with you. We shall join forces with the tyrant. I whom he detests, I who abhor him, I shall resume the Ministry of Police under him two days after his return. He cannot do without me. When he thinks himself strong enough he will try to destroy us; but we shall not give him enough time. Within three months from now we will bring him down.'[16]

His refusal prompted some members of the council to demand his arrest, and André dropped him a hint that Bourrienne, newly appointed Prefect of Police, would like nothing better. A rumour that the King was reshaping the ministry – with Richelieu at the Interior, Fouché at the Police, Argenson or Molé in Dambray's post and Carnot as Minister of War – steadied the price of government bonds. And instead of a warrant from one of Bourrienne's policemen, Fouché received an invitation from the comte des Cars, to call on him at nine that evening.

Des Cars, the fair-haired aristocratic aide-de-camp of the duc d'Angoulême, took his visitor for a talk with the comte d'Artois. It lasted from ten until midnight. It was scarcely to be expected, if he could not reach agreement with the King, that he would find any more in common with his more reactionary brother. He again refused office but repeated to *Monsieur* what he had said to the marquis de la Maisonfort five days before: 'You save the monarch; I will save the monarchy.'[17]

On Thursday, March 16, shortly after his carriage had turned out of the rue d'Artois into the boulevard des Italiens, eight plain-clothes policemen armed with pistols pulled up the horses. The carriage door was flung open by a police agent, Foudras, who had been keeping watch on him for several weeks past. Foudras pushed a piece of paper under his nose. It was the warrant for his arrest.

'One does not,' said Fouché, 'arrest a former minister in the street.'[18] He pushed Foudras away, slammed the door and ordered the coachman to drive him back home. The police, taken by surprise, failed to hold the horses, but followed on so closely that they reached the Hôtel d'Otrante at No. 9 rue d'Artois before the great gates could be shut. They trotted at the tail of the carriage through the entrance flanked by stables and domestic offices and out into the colonnaded courtyard. The Duke mounted the steps to the large vestibule with Foudras at his heels. He swung left into the dining-room, where his children were at lunch. To Mademoiselle Ribou he whispered: 'They've come to arrest me – have somebody go to the National Guard post.'[19]

The third battalion of the second legion of the Paris National Guard had its headquarters at the corner of the rue Lepelletier and the rue de Provence. The infantry and cavalry commanders – Voisins, a lawyer, and Tourton, a deputy governor of the Bank of France – came hurrying round with a squad of twenty-five men. They found the Duke refusing to leave and threatening any police-man who dared search the house.

'Gentlemen,' said Fouché. 'The police have just arrested me on the authority of an alleged warrant signed by Bourrienne, the Prefect of Police. I have reason to believe this to be a false warrant. I request you to set a guard on this house with orders to prevent anybody entering or leaving until we have tested the validity of the warrant. I spent part of the night in conference with the comte d'Artois – there is something wrong about this.'[20]

The National Guard officers posted their men in the courtyard and rushed off to the Tuileries, where Tourton made for Artois's lodgings in the Pavillon de Marsan while Voisins went to the main building to send in a message to the King's ministers. Artois con-firmed that he had talked with Fouché and indignantly denied that he had ordered his arrest. But Louis's reply to Voisins's inquiry was brief and uncompromising: 'I know about the warrant – let it be executed.'[21]

In the Hôtel d'Otrante, Fouché strolled from room to room, followed by Foudras clutching his piece of paper. Suddenly the Duke whisked open a door and disappeared into an unlit corridor that ran beside his bedroom. He turned through a second door, into the bedroom, before Foudras had got the first door open. Stumbling along the corridor in the darkness, Foudras eventually found himself in one of the two lavatories at that corner of the house. He turned and made his way back, again failing to find the bedroom door, which Fouché had bolted behind him. Arriving at the door leading back into the salon he could not find the catch hidden in the ornamental carving. While he groped at the woodwork, wondering whether to raise the alarm and risk making a fool of himself, his prisoner had stepped out of the bedroom window on to the terrace at the rear.

The garden was about 100 feet wide and slightly less in length. On the right was the Hôtel de Rovigo, home of his old enemy, Savary; at the bottom of the garden was the wall dividing it from No. 34 rue Taitbout; on the left was the Hôtel de St-Leu, whose mistress, Hortense de Beauharnais, had already fled to avoid arrest. Unlike the Hôtel d'Otrante it had a gate giving access to the rue Taitbout, and secured by a padlock. Fouché, who was fully prepared for a hurried escape, had borrowed a key from Hortense and had also provided himself with a light ladder which he now set up against the wall. He climbed it, straddled the wall, drew the ladder up and set it on the other side, then descended it and made for the garden gate.

At this point he realized that he had left the key of the padlock in his bedroom. Hurrying back up the ladder he grabbed a piece of coping stone from the wall, then ran with it to the gate. He cracked open the padlock and peered out into the rue Taitbout. There was no sign of any policemen. He crossed to the west side of the street, walked smartly down the rue du Helder and disappeared into a house on the other side of the boulevard. With his usual talent for foreseeing crises and retaining faithful friends he had already arranged to spend a few days if need be as the guest of Lombard-Tarradeau, formerly Secretary-General at the Ministry of Police.

He sent a note to Madame de Custine, regretting that he would not be able to call on her that afternoon, as he had hoped. He was indignant at being arrested on suspicion. 'Why didn't they ask me for an explanation? I would have left them in no doubt about the purity of my motives and the sincerity of my feelings.' He added a typically shrewd postcript: 'If I had anything to reproach myself with, I should have accepted the ministry.'[22]

That afternoon the King addressed the two chambers, wearing for the first time the star of the Legion of Honour and receiving from the comte d'Artois public and totally unconvincing protestations of democratic fervour. Napoleon was on the road from Autun to Avallon, 145 miles away. Next day, at Auxerre, he was joined by Marshal Ney, who had left Paris promising to bring him back in an iron cage.

On Palm Sunday, March 19, the National Guard replaced the regular troops, now considered unreliable, on duty at the Tuileries. The two chambers met in secret session. At midnight the cumbersome King climbed into the *berline* that awaited him under the porch of the Pavillon de Flore and drove off rapidly in the direction of Lille. Fouché, whose concealment was discreet rather than absolute, had a word with Bourmont, now a general, before the royal household fled. 'Napoleon is mad,' he said. 'We shall not let him throw France into the abyss again.'[23]

Napoleon was at Pont-sur-Yonne, sixty-five miles away. He found the troops that he had sent on in barges from Auxerre waiting for dawn to light them past a dangerous stretch of water ahead. He jeered at them, asking if they were afraid of getting wet, and they shamefacedly set off down the river again. Later, through the darkness there came a rending crash as one of the boats struck a bridge-pier and sank. A great cry of *Vive l'Empereur!* pierced the night as thirty men drowned. If it was an omen, nobody was yet in a mood to heed it.

Napoleon left in the very early hours for Fontainebleau. There, at midday, he received a message from Lavalette, who had already resumed his office as Postmaster-General, that the King had gone and there was no obstacle to his entry to Paris.

A crowd had been collecting outside the Tuileries since seven in the morning. Some half-pay officers under General Exelmans argued their way through the gates and doubled the guard duty with the National Guardsmen who still wore the royal badges. Shortly after noon the tricolour was flying over the Hôtel de Ville and the Tuileries, where the former imperial officials were arriving in uniform, accompanied by their wives in court dress. The ladies drifted through the state-rooms, glittering with diamonds, their gowns gay with violets, laughing, chattering, suddenly settling like a cloud of butterflies on the carpet of the throne room, unpicking the royal lilies that had been thriftily stitched on top of the imperial bees.

The hero's welcome was ready, but the hero, awaited since midday, did not arrive. Dusk came, and mist over the river, and full darkness. The diamonds still twinkled under the chandeliers but the glitter began to fade from eager eyes. The wonderment of this return to the scene of past glories, the rapture of fresh rewards to come, the climax of all the pent-up excitement engendered by the miraculous three-week march – slowly they could be seen to dwindle and the fears peep through, the anxieties, the forebodings, the suspicion of some great catastrophe that had betrayed them.

Then, with the clock approaching nine on the evening of Monday, March 20, the Emperor drove up in a travel-stained post-chaise and was at once seized and borne bodily into the palace and up the stairs to his study.

Notes to Part V

Chapter 1

1　Clary, 311
2　Despatys, *Ami*, 199–200
3　Nesselrode, III, 266
4　*Ibid.*, 275
5　Carr, 216
6　Girardin, IV, 388–9
7　Burney, VI, 62
8　*Ibid.*
9　Marmottan, *Elisa*, 408
10　Jackson, *Diaries*, I, 47
11　Burney, VI, 63
12　Méneval, *Mémoires*, I, 156
13　Saint-Elme, III, 69
14　Clary, 343
15　Pasquier, I, 242
16　Fauriel, 164
17　Montholon, *Récits*, I, xxxiii
18　Despatys, *Ami*, 200

Chapter 2

1　Chastenay, II, 124
2　Lecestre, II, 38(623)
3　*Ibid.*
4　Despatys, *Ami*, 203
5　*Ibid.*
6　*Ibid.*
7　*Ibid.*
8　*Ibid.*, 204
9　Nap. I, *Corresp.*, XX, 417(16567)
10　Ernouf, *Maret*, 282
11　Chuquet, *Inédits*, II, 50
12　Despatys, *Ami*, 206
13　Ouvrard, I, 162
14　Lecestre, II, 47 (641)
15　Fouché, *Mémoires*, 308

16   Despatys, *Ami*, 214
17   Lecestre, II, 62(669)
18   Despatys, *Ami*, 214
19   *Ibid.*, 215
20   Lecestre, II, 157(862)
21   Chaptal, 341
22   Fouché, *Mémoires*, 363
23   Castellane, I, 112
24   *Ibid.*, 110
25   Lanzac de Laborie, II, 405
26   Despatys, *Ami*, 250
27   *Ibid.*

Chapter 3

1   Ménière, 52
2   Billard, 142
3   Fouché, *Mémoires*, 371
4   Pasquier, II, 50
5   Chuquet, *Inédits*, II, 167
6   Méneval, *Napoléon*, II, 137
7   Fouché, *Mémoires*, 388
8   *Ibid.*, 390
9   Metternich, I, 191
10   *Souvenirs et Mémoires*, III, 214
11   Thiers, *Consulat*, XVI, 168
12   Fouché, *Mémoires*, 407
13   Dostal, 167
14   Nodier, *Souvenirs*, II, 307
15   *Ibid.*
16   *Ibid.*, 308
17   *Ibid.*
18   *Ibid.*, 310
19   *Ibid.*
20   Despatys, *Ami*, 255
21   *Ibid.*

Chapter 4

1   Pasquier, II, 90–1
2   Roederer, *Oeuvres*, III, 582
3   Norvins, 70
4   *Ibid.*, 71
5   Fouché, *Mémoires*, 429

6   Weil, III, 293
7   Fouché, *Mémoires de la vie publique*, 49
8   Pasquier, II, 99
9   Durand, 331
10   PRO, FO 27/122
11   Brotonne, 531(1319)
12   Nap. I, *Corresp.* XXVII, 157(21239)
13   Desmarest, 269(1)
14   Fabry, 32
15   *Ibid.*, 36

Chapter 5

1   Fouché, *Mémoires*, 455
2   Pasquier, II, 353
3   PRO, PRO30, 43/29
4   *Ibid.*
5   *Ibid.*
6   Shepherd, 209
7   Hobhouse, I, 84–5
8   Despatys, *Ami*, 269
9   *Ibid.*, 268
10   Barère, IV, 211
11   PRO, FO 146/1
12   *Ibid.*
13   *Ibid.*
14   Scott, 45
15   *Ibid.*
16   PRO, FO 146/1
17   Pasquier, III, 55
18   Polovtzov, 35
19   PRO, FO 146/1
20   Despatys, *Ami*, 275

Chapter 6

1   Despatys, *Ami*, 276
2   *Ibid.*, 277
3   *Ibid.*, 278
4   *Ibid.*
5   *Ibid.*, 279
6   *Ibid.*
7   *Ibid.*, 280

8 *Ibid.*
9 Polovtzov, 93
10 Chastenay, II, 372
11 Bardoux, 205
12 *Ibid.*, 206
13 *Ibid.*, 417
14 Firmin-Didot, 183
15 Sotheby, 50(212)
16 Méneval, *Mémoires*, III, 383
17 Despatys, *Ami*, 301
18 *Ibid.*, 302
19 *Ibid.*, 305
20 Firmin-Didot, 252
21 *Ibid.*, 253

Chapter 7

1 Fouché, *Mémoires*, 468
2 Polovtzov, 159
3 Bardoux, 215
4 *Ibid.*, 217
5 *Ibid.*, 218
6 *Moniteur*, 17 March 1815, p. 301
7 Ferrand, 125
8 Bardoux, 418
9 *Ibid.*, 219
10 Despatys, *Ami*, 312
11 Bardoux, 223
12 *Ibid.*, 222
13 Despatys, *Ami*, 314
14 Ferrand, 126
15 Castlereagh, X, 338
16 *Ibid.*, 339
17 Fouché, *Mémoires*, 470
18 Despatys, *Ami*, 318
19 *Ibid.*
20 *Ibid.*
21 *Ibid.*
22 Bardoux, 226
23 Pingaud, *Bourmont*, 866

PART VI
Minister of Police
1815

I

Fouché made his own entry at the Tuileries an hour or two later, greeted with unusual warmth by the throng of imperialists still celebrating the great return. They all knew of his rejection of office under the Bourbons, the warrant for his arrest, his evasion: he was a hero in a small way. There was scarcely a person present who doubted that he would be recalled at once to his old ministry. Napoleon later said that he reappointed him only because he was overpersuaded by those around him. Fouché perpetuated this myth to ingratiate himself with the royalists. But Napoleon was not the man – nor was this the time – to bow to persuasion; he gave Fouché the job because he needed him. He needed him for his administrative ability and he needed him as a Republican figure, a guarantee of the new liberal regime that he had announced in Lyons on his way to the capital. For the same reason he put Carnot at the Ministry of the Interior.

If Fouché had even for a moment been tempted to believe in Napoleon's strange new passion for peace and individual freedom, his first interview quickly disabused him. He could read the Emperor's true disposition better than most. 'Napoleon has come back more of a despot than ever,' he told Gaillard next morning. 'He talks of nothing but vengeance, of courts-martial to punish traitors.'[1] Walking with Pasquier in the garden of the Hôtel de Juigné on the Friday of that first week he said: 'That man has not been reformed in any way and has come back as despotic, as eager for conquest and, in short, as mad as ever.'[2]

He told Pasquier that he was prepared to see the Bourbons return. 'But this time things must be arranged a little less stupidly than they were last year by Talleyrand; we mustn't leave everybody at their mercy. We must have a sound agreement, good solid guarantees.'[3] He said he would need Pasquier to take over the Prefecture of Police from Réal, whom Bonaparte had set to watch him, together with Savary at the head of the *gendarmerie d'élite*.

He talked so openly about the future that even the Counsellor at the Austrian Embassy, packing for departure, knew all about it and on arrival in Vienna told Metternich that 'it is probable that within two months either Bonaparte will be struck down or Fouché and Carnot will be shot'.[4] It was typical of the unreality of the situation that Carnot was the recipient of Napoleon's confession: that he intended to deal with Fouché but must have victory first.[5]

Meanwhile, there were the reins of the ministry to be picked up, tranquillity to be preserved, and the violence of Napoleon's vindictiveness to be guarded against. At the end of March Fouché sent a circular to all departments, warning the prefects 'not to extend your supervision beyond the demands of public and private security . . . I do not ask from you, and do not wish to have, anything other than facts, collected with care, presented exactly and simply . . . We must discard the fallacies of the *aggressive police* which . . . menaces without assuring, torments without protecting. We must confine ourselves to the limits of a liberal and positive police, that *police observation* which . . . watches over the happiness of the people, the work of industry, for the peace of all.'[6]

On April 4 Napoleon addressed letters to the sovereigns of Europe announcing his return to the throne amid the love of his people, and his determination to 'requite such great affection by the maintenance of an honourable peace'.[7] The letters never got beyond the frontiers. His couriers were refused recognition. France was in quarantine. He needed to persuade the Allies not to attack before he was ready for them. The 120,000 men whom he found in the army on his return must be doubled at once and quadrupled within a year. The munition factories roared into life again and the streets were full of artillery on the move, trucks laden with weapons, soldiers rejoining their units.

To rally the people behind him the Emperor announced that he would shortly hold a great public ceremony – the Champ de Mai – at which the departmental electoral colleges would meet to modify the constitution. On April 23 he published an *Acte Additionel* (to the laws of the Empire which he implied had never been abrogated by the Restoration) prepared for him by Benjamin Constant, the liberal politician, which predictably disappointed everybody. It was too progressive for the Bonapartists, too reactionary for the Jacobins.

That same day Fouché sent a written warning to Napoleon against revenging himself and his supporters on the public figures who had served the King. Immediately on his return he had ordered many of them to live at least seventy miles from Paris; since then he had prepared a list of men who were to be tried – mostly in their absence – and their property confiscated.

'I am far from wishing to minimize the faults of those who betrayed the cause of the Empire,' Fouché wrote. 'But at the moment when that cause is triumphant, is it not in its interest, and to its dignity, to disregard all this in applying an unswerving policy of clemency and forgetting?' Then, in what could be taken as an apologia for his own past: 'Political revolutions, whatever their principles or results, are not produced by the combination of a few ideas, nor the work of a few individuals. Those who are harmed by them were often their authors, those who seem to direct them do no more than follow the current.'[8] Who then was to judge, and by what standards? Where would the accusation end?

He was striving for the preservation of harmony at home. He did not want Napoleon overturned by civil war, even if it were feasible. He planned for him to be driven out by the other powers of Europe. But this time he wanted, as he had said to Pasquier, to have things better arranged than they were last time. It was this that he was privately engaged on.

2

On April 29, Napoleon sent a note to Réal: 'Fouché spoke to me about this man yesterday; he supposed it was a hoax. It appears that this man brought him a letter in invisible ink under the address of a banker to whom he delivered another at the same time. Interrogate this individual. He may have delivered other letters to other persons.'[1]

It was not a hoax. The Emperor knew it was not a hoax. He was pretty well convinced that Fouché knew it was not a hoax. But he could prove nothing.

The incident had begun with the arrival of a representative of the Austrian banking house of Arnsteiner and Eskeles at the private residence of the French banker, Laffitte, at No. 19 rue Cerutti (which had so briefly reverted to rue d'Artois and today bears Laffitte's own name). The man, Franz Christian Koeckh, brought remittances to the value of 150,000 francs. It was a moderate sum – not, Laffitte considered, large enough to warrant being sent by special messsenger. Though the French frontiers were closed, bankers were finding no difficulty in conducting business through Switzerland. He sent for the man and asked bluntly: 'Bringing 150,000 francs is not the real purpose of your mission: is there something diplomatic involved?'[2]

Koeckh replied by asking to be put in touch with the duc d'Otrante. When Laffitte asked him why, he told him he had a letter in invisible ink inviting Fouché to go to Basle for talks. As credentials he produced from inside his watchcase a piece of card bearing the signatures of the Austrian, Russian and Prussian ministers: Metternich, Nesselrode and Hardenberg.

Laffitte, not at all pleased at finding himself mixed up in so dangerous a business, hurried off to inform his neighbour at No. 9. Fouché was out. Laffitte left a message, giving the address of Koeckh's lodgings but suggesting that Fouché should talk with the man at No. 19, if he preferred. He heard no more from either of them; and after two days of anxiety went to Caulaincourt and asked him to tell the Emperor the whole story.

Napoleon had Koeckh arrested and brought to the Elysée Palace, where he had moved from the Tuileries on April 17, believing that he could there be more safely guarded against assassination. Koeckh was taken out into the grounds, where the Emperor told him: 'I know all about your tricks. If you confess at once, I will pardon you. If not, you will only leave this garden to be shot.' The Austrian needed no further encouragement. He confessed that he had been sent by Metternich to invite Fouché to send a man for talks at Basle. He was to ask for Herr Heinrich Werner at the Three Kings Hotel.

'Did you pass the message to Fouché?'

'Yes.'

'Has he sent his representative?'

'I don't know.'[3] He had talked with Fouché twice, each time entering the ministry building by the garden gate in the rue des Sts-Pères.

Napoleon had heard enough. He had Koeckh taken away and locked up, and then sent for Fouché, with whom he discussed routine affairs, giving the Minister plenty of time to report the remarkable approach from Metternich. Fouché did not mention a word of it. Napoleon said he had heard that a man had called on Laffitte with a secret message for Fouché. Fouché, completely unprepared, replied without blinking an eyelid that it was no doubt a hoax. As soon as Fouché had left, Napoleon sent his instruction to Réal for Koeckh to be interrogated more closely. Convinced that Fouché was deceiving him, he sent his secretary, Fleury de Chaboulon, to Basle posing as Fouché's messenger.

Next morning, exercising his privilege as Minister of Police, Fouché entered the Emperor's study without formality and blandly announced that, having been overwhelmed with work for the past few days, he had 'forgotten to show Your Majesty this letter from M. de Metternich. It is for Your Majesty to decide whether I should send him an agent, as he asks. I wonder what he can be up to?'

'Leave your letter there,' said Napoleon. 'We will talk about it tomorrow.'[4] He was fuming at Fouché's effrontery. The contents of the letter infuriated him still more. Dated from Vienna on April 9, it said:

'The Powers will not have Napoleon Bonaparte. They will make war against him to the last, but they do not wish to fight France. They desire to know what France wishes, and what you wish. They make no claim to meddle in national affairs, or with the wishes of the nation concerning its government, but they will in no circumstances tolerate Bonaparte on the throne of France. Send a person who possesses your exclusive confidence to the place which the bearer will indicate to you. He will find there a person to whom to speak.'[5]

During the course of the day, Fouché learned of Fleury's departure for Basle. Realizing that he must bring matters to a head at once, he returned to the Elysée that evening. 'I have come for Your Majesty's instructions on the reply to be made to M. de Metternich,' he said.

Napoleon boiled over. He snarled accusations and abuse at him. Fouché stood calmly. 'You are a traitor!' the Emperor shouted. 'I ought to have you hanged!'

Fouché bowed. 'I do not,' he said, 'share Your Majesty's opinion.'[6] The waves of imperial anger continued to break over him. Eventually he persuaded Napoleon to accept, if not to believe, that the communication from Metternich was merely the logical outcome of a mission to Vienna on which the comte de Montrond had been sent with his knowledge and approval.

For three-quarters of an hour the Postmaster-General, Lavalette, had been waiting in the ante-room, listening to the sounds of fury that came through the partially open door. They died down and the door opened. He was astounded to see Fouché stroll out in apparently high spirits 'wishing me a cheerful good night, and telling me the Emperor had gone back to his private rooms'.[7]

Fouché was not out of the wood yet. It was true that Montrond, a middle-aged dandy and close friend of Talleyrand, had been sent with Napoleon's knowledge to try to arrange an exchange of letters with Marie-Louise and to persuade Talleyrand, still in Vienna as a delegate to the Allied Congress, to return to the service of the Emperor. But he also had secret instructions from Fouché to interest Metternich in talks, while another of Fouché's secret emissaries, Saint-Léon, had the specific mission of discovering whether the Allies would regard the duc d'Orléans as a suitable candidate for the throne. It was in answer to these approaches that Metternich had sent the baron von Ottenfels, under the name of Heinrich Werner, to the Three Kings Hotel at Basle.

Ottenfels, accepting Fleury as Fouché's representative, talked to him in accordance with the instructions he had received from Metternich. These were that, though he was to commit nothing to writing, he should reveal that he spoke on behalf of the Austrian Cabinet. He should repeat that the Allies had no wish to interfere with the internal affairs of France, but that they could not permit Bonaparte to remain on the throne. He would inform Vienna of the Duke of Otranto's choice for a successor; on the Allied side it was tacitly assumed there could be no question of a republic: Fouché's proposals 'can only reasonably refer to the following: Louis XVIII, the duc d'Orléans or a Regency'.[8]

They had no marked preference, but Austria was not enthusiastic about a Regency because it would involve her too closely in French affairs, thus risking suspicion from the other powers, and a long minority would lay France open to greater risk of disorder. The two men parted, agreeing to report to their sponsors and to meet again in a week's time.

When Fleury returned to Paris, Napoleon sent him to repeat his report to Fouché. Fouché suggested sending messages to deceive Metternich – having already warned Metternich that the correspondence had been discovered. This time, when Fleury arrived in Basle, he found Ottenfels noncommittal. The negotiations ended.

It had been a close shave, but it had in no way shaken him. Receiving a royalist who wanted a pass to leave Paris and sit out the stormy days ahead on his estate at Le Mans, Fouché said: 'Why are you going? You should always stay in the game. Isn't it amusing and instructive to watch?' He took him into the garden where they could not be overheard. 'That man has come back more insane than he went,' he said. 'He's making a lot of fuss, but he'll not be here for more than three months ... There are 750,000 men marching on

France as a first instalment, to say nothing of those in the Vendée –
I've asked them to wait, while discreetly letting them know it won't
be long . . . He'll wait for the enemy on the frontier, or perhaps he'll
go to meet them just outside in Belgium . . . He may gain one or two
battles . . . but in the end he can't win . . . While he's rummaging
around the arsenals, beating to arms, changing the numbers of the
regiments, we're preparing a chamber of representatives where, by
God, he'll have a bit of everything.'[9]

It was a strange double-bluff. He talked freely and often at the
top of his voice. Some was lies, but a great deal was truth, and three-
quarters of it went straight back to the Emperor – as Fouché knew
it would. When Ballouhey, formerly Josephine's Keeper of the
Privy Purse, brought Napoleon a warning from Eugène that Fouché
was intriguing against him in Vienna, he simply replied that he knew
it already. When Méneval, devoted to the Emperor and a sworn
enemy of Fouché, returned from a year in Vienna, Fouché pressed
him to call and give him all the news. Napoleon ordered him to do
so but 'to listen rather than reply'.[10]

After the initial courtesies, Fouché, 'with his usual self-assurance
when speaking of the Emperor, said: "Well, there he is; we didn't
want him, but you can't take him off like a pawn from a chessboard.
We'll see what we can do to keep him."' Méneval repeated the
conversation to Napoleon who 'merely gave a shrug of contempt'.[11]
He seemed to be as deeply under Fouché's spell as ever, distrusting
yet dependent, not knowing how to handle this man who showed no
fear of him.

On May 22 the frontier police intercepted a letter to Fouché from
Austria. It said: 'Do not trouble to write to us because we now believe
nothing that comes with your signature. Send Gaillard.' Napoleon
flourished it under Fouché's nose and shouted: 'So Metternich is
determined to arrange a correspondence with you!'

'You see treason everywhere,' said Fouché. 'Metternich must have
some handsomely paid spies on your staff. Through them he will
have learnt that the agent sent to Basle wasn't picked by me. So he
suspects the letter that agent carried wasn't from me. And the result
is he wants to find a reliable intermediary in case he ever needs to
write to me.'[12] The Emperor handed him the letter and dropped the
argument.

In addition to his contacts with Metternich, through Montrond,
Saint-Léon and Bresson, whose tasks were to sound the support for
the duc d'Orléans or a Regency by Marie-Louise, Fouché had sent

messengers early in April to Ghent, where they assured Louis of Fouché's support, but also informed Wellington that 'calling the Duke of Orléans to the throne is the only acceptable middle term between Bonaparte, the army, and the Jacobins on the one hand, and the King and violent émigrés on the other', as Wellington told Castlereagh on April 11. Wellington himself was of the opinion that the royalists had lost a great deal of sympathy by scampering out of the country and he pointed out that the Tsar now 'detests and is decidedly against the Bourbons'.[13] Castlereagh replied that the British must publicly support Louis so as not to discourage the royalist risings in the south and west but, 'our hands must not be tied in the matter of future decisions'.[14]

In mid-May Fouché sent Chiappe, a Corsican whom he had known since they both sat in the Convention, to Sweden to learn Bernadotte's choice for the succession. Chiappe, who passed through London on his way, made no secret of Fouché's 'desire to bring about some change in the state of affairs' nor that 'the interests of that party will be given to the highest bidder'[15] in terms of constitutional concessions.

3

The risings in the South and West did not fulfil Castlereagh's hopes. The duc d'Angoulême was quickly defeated in the South. His wife was unable to hold out in Bordeaux. Vitrolles was captured and imprisoned in Vincennes. Fouché, promising Madame de Vitrolles that he would save her husband's life, enlisted her as a go-between to the king through the comte d'Artois. In the West, the duc de Bourbon raised the royalist standard during the last days of March only to find the people too scared of reprisals; but as Napoleon began to withdraw troops to face the threats from north and east, the guerrilla forays broke out in the Vendée again, and developed into widespread revolt by the second week of May.

Fouché was determined that, though Bonaparte must go, France should not again be torn by civil war. It was for this reason that he had urged Louis XVIII to quit. This had, indeed, been the purpose of his policy for more than fifteen years. He asked the Emperor to be given complete control and promised to restore tranquillity by negotiation. Napoleon, only too glad not to be called upon for troops, readily agreed.

Fouché sent for the comte de Malartic, a former *chouan* leader. The two men had always been on opposite sides, but trusted each other.

'Your friends are mad! Fouché said to him. What are they hoping to do? Vanquish Bonaparte? They'll never do it ... They'll be crushed before war begins on the frontiers. It'll take a few days, and at the end of it Napoleon can call back the troops he's sent into the Vendée and transfer them to Belgium. Do you think that's good politics? Napoleon's fate can't be decided in the west. Only in the north. Wouldn't it be more sensible to avoid the spilling of French blood and to preserve for the King resources he will be very pleased to have on his return, and for France arms capable of defending her?'[1]

Malartic agreed and was dispatched to preach this gospel of patience to the Vendéan leaders. Three of them accepted it. The fourth insisted on fighting, and was killed.

The drama was approaching its climax – more quickly than anybody really believed, despite Fouché's earlier predictions that Napoleon would be finished within three months. Having ensured that there would be as little civil upheaval as possible, Fouché set about organizing a body of support in the newly-elected chambers. It was among the moderate liberals that he found them (he was himself elected one of three representatives of his native department, the Lower Loire). To lead them he chose his son's former tutor, Antoine Jay, and a brilliant young lawyer he had first met during his exile at Aix, Jacques-Antoine Manuel.

In the new chambers, as Pasquier noted, most of the members 'did not have the time to get to know one another; when the critical moment came, it turned out that the only influence in a position to take advantage of it was that of Fouché'.[2] He had one other great advantage: despite the small number of his committed supporters – and despite his enemies' accusations of trickery – he retained the trust of a great many people. 'He is decidedly the *best head*, so they say, in France,' an English observer reported, 'and at the moment is in possession, unaccountable as it may seem, of the confidence of all parties, if perhaps we except the very decided imperialists attached to the person of Napoleon.'[3]

On June 1 the repeatedly delayed ceremony of the Champ de Mai was staged in the Champ de Mars, where workmen had been busy for six weeks building tiers of seats, tribunes and a dais for the imperial throne. In the space between the seats and tribunes, troops were massed rank upon rank. Around the sides and in the narrow streets two hundred thousand spectators sweltered under the fierce sun.

At eleven a salvo of guns announced the departure of the Emperor's procession on the other side of the river. At twelve another salvo and a roll of drums heralded his arrival in a gilded glass coach. When he got out and walked to the steps that led to the throne his costume could be clearly seen for the first time: not the familiar and still beloved blue jacket of the *grenadiers de la garde* or the green topcoat of the *chasseurs* but an orange-red tunic and short spanish-style cloak, white satin breeches, rosettes on his shoes and white feathers in his wide black velvet cap. Charlemagne had returned in the robes of a pantomime prince.

At the altar the Archbishop of Tours celebrated Mass, unseen by most, unheard by almost all. The loyal speeches of the deputations were lost in the mounting buzz of chatter. The presentation of the *Acte Additionel*, the Emperor's oath to observe the Constitution, the *Te Deum*, the drumming and trumpeting and firing of guns, and at last the distribution of the eagles – it all went on too long, the tawdriness and vulgarity obtruded. All of them, bystanders as well as participants, seemed figures of the imagination locked in the perverse fantasy world of this malignant little man in the odd clothes. The dream was turning to nightmare, but it was too late for them to get out.

That day Davoust, the Minister of War, sent Napoleon several intercepted reports from royalist agents, all indicating 'the hopes that the party reposed on the Minister of Police'.[4]

On June 2, Fouché was appointed to the newly-constituted Chamber of Peers. Many saw in this Napoleon's desire to get him out of the Chamber of Representatives, where he could do most harm. Few took it to be any sort of reward, for the Emperor's outbursts against him had become more frequent and more public. Fouché, evidently suspecting an attempt to muzzle him, declined the honour. At a meeting of the Council of Ministers Napoleon suddenly burst out: 'You are betraying me – I know it – I have proof!' Then, picking up an ivory-handled knife: 'Why don't you take this and plunge it into my chest? It would be more honest than what you are doing. If I sent you to be shot everybody would applaud it as an act of justice.'[5] But he did not have him shot. Perhaps he did not want to. Perhaps he did not dare to. Even those closest to the two men could not tell what part fascination played in their relationship and what part fear.

The moment was approaching when he must take command of the army that he was massing along the northern frontier, leaving behind him a Minister of Police who had placed himself within reach of every lever of civil power. His stomach pains and other disorders grew worse.

On the first Sunday in June he held a great reception in the Louvre for nearly 10,000 guests. For the mob in the Champs Elysées there was free entertainment that included bread and circuses and fountains of wine. On the following Wednesday he opened the first session of the two new chambers.

At the end of the week Bertrand, his most trusted military aide, brought a messenger into the Elysée Palace by the back stairs. In Napoleon's study he produced intercepted letters which Fouché had sent to the Allies. Hobhouse, to whom Bertrand told the story later, asked why Napoleon 'did not do what he might with Fouché. "He was not strong enough," said Bertrand.'⁶

4

At 4 a.m. on Monday, June 12, Napoleon drove away from Paris to join his army. Behind him he left a Council of Government composed of his two brothers, Joseph and Lucien, four Ministers of State, and the eight Ministers with Portfolio – including the Minister of Police. Next day, Carnot, as Minister of the Interior, presented to the two chambers the Report on the State of the Empire which Napoleon had ordered him to draw up to allay public alarm. All the ministers contributed to this optimistic review, with the exception of Fouché.

By the evening of June 14, Napoleon had concentrated most of his army near Charleroi. His strategy was the same as always: to bring his full strength against the weakest point of the enemy's front, break it, and attack the disjointed segments piecemeal. He aimed at the junction of the British and Prussian armies, put his advance troops across the Sambre on June 15 and on June 16 was fighting at Quatre-Bras and Ligny.

With the news of the Emperor's departure the revolt in the Vendée flickered into life again. On June 17 Fouché sent to the assembly his own Report on the State of the Empire, nominally addressed to the

Emperor but more evidently aimed at him. He spoke of a nationwide network of conspiracy, of great cities such as Marseilles, Toulouse, Bordeaux on the edge of rebellion; and he asked for increased powers to curb the Press and control all activities. He could scarcely have made his purpose clearer had he gone into the tribune and stated his two objectives: to demolish faith in the Emperor and to strengthen the control of the Council of Government.

Later that Saturday evening news reached Paris of the Prussian defeat at Ligny. At that moment the French army was coming into position along the Belle Alliance ridge on each side of the Charleroi-Brussels road. Facing them in front of the crossroads at Mont St-Jean were the British under Wellington. The rain was falling in torrents. It was the eve of Napoleon's sixtieth pitched battle.

At 11.35 on Sunday morning he ordered an attack on Wellington's right at Hougoumont. Half an hour later the brutal roar of the guns that he loved so well announced the main assault on the centre of the British line at La Haye Sainte. Hour after hour, wave after wave, his cavalry and infantry broke on the British squares. By four o'clock in the afternoon the arrival of Prussian forces on the French right was beginning to relieve the pressure on the British centre. At 8 p.m. Wellington ordered the whole line to advance. The French army crumpled and dispersed in panic flight, led by its commander-in-chief and pursued with savagery by the Prussians.

He must have known that he had run away from defeat once too often, that this time his reserve of glory was exhausted. But, whatever black despondency accompanied him on the first day of his headlong flight towards Paris, when he reached Laon he was again planning to hold on to power by force and terror. 'If I return to Paris and dip my hands in blood,' he said to Bertrand when they halted at the posthouse in the lower town, 'I must plunge them in up to my elbows.' His valet, Marchand, who overheard the conversation, noted that Fouché was mentioned immediately afterwards, 'and seemed to me to be marked down for his vengeance'.[1]

Despite the speed with which Napoleon had fled from the battlefield, the news of the disaster outstripped him. That evening it was communicated by his brother Joseph to the Council of Government. Carnot and Davoust urged that the fight against the enemy should be continued; the others knew that the country would have no more, of war, or of Napoleon. As Fouché said: 'The patriots had agreed to give him their support on condition that he emerged victorious; he had been beaten and they considered the contract broken.'²

Fouché's problem, in a crisis which had befallen the country more rapidly than even he had predicted, was to force Napoleon's abdication so that the peace negotiations could be conducted by a Provisional Government which he intended to control. Only by getting rid of the Emperor first could France hope to avert humiliating and crippling conditions from the Allies, who now saw that they had treated her too leniently in 1814, and to prevent the return of the Bourbons in a more reactionary mood than ever.

Boulay de la Meurthe, one of the four Ministers of State, said:

'He had to divorce the Chamber from the Emperor, present his cause as contrary to the interests of the country, and oblige him to put off his crown for the second time. So Fouché set about circulating by himself and through his adherents, the most alarming rumours best calculated to turn opinion against Napoleon. They said he was returning with the determination to dissolve the Chamber, to set up a dictatorship and to use it to carry on a desperate struggle against Europe, sacrificing France to his ambition – so it was essential to forestall him, to deprive him of the power of action and to save the country without him, since he was the only obstacle to the return of peace.'³

It was almost dawn on Wednesday morning when Napoleon arrived at the Elysée. His nerve had gone again. Blaming Ney, Grouchy, everybody except himself, he had to be helped from his carriage by Caulaincourt. 'I can't do any more!' he said. 'I am suffocating! Have somebody prepare a bath for me!'⁴

He had fought his last battle, expended his last man. One eminent Frenchman estimated that, reckoning only from the time when he crowned himself Emperor in 1804, 'Napoleon had brought about the death of 1,700,000 Frenchmen born within the ancient frontiers of France, to whom must probably be added two million men born outside those frontiers and killed for him as allies or by him as enemies.'⁵ Subsequent research suggests that this is an exaggeration. It was probably no more than a million men that he killed.

He lay in the bath for an hour, regaining confidence as the warmth of the water soaked into his plump, womanish body. He got out, had his valet sponge him with cologne, and went to meet the Council. 'All is not lost,' he told them. 'Give me money and men and I guarantee to save France.'⁶

Fouché sent word to Lafayette that there was talk in the Council of dissolving the two chambers. In the Palais-Bourbon Lafayette proposed, and the Chamber of Representatives accepted, a motion that a state of national emergency be declared, that the two houses remain in permanent session, that any attempt to dissolve or prorogue them be treated as an act of treason, and that the Ministers of War, Foreign Affairs, the Interior and the Police report to them immediately. It was an open challenge to the Emperor's authority, perhaps itself an act of rebellion. Across the river, in the Luxembourg, the Chamber of Peers adopted a similar motion. Fouché had gained the initiative.

When news of the Chambers' defiance arrived at the Elysée, Napoleon seemed for a moment to summon up the courage to act – to govern with the support of the army 'and all the rabble of Paris'.[7] He would purge the Chambers 'and hang seven or eight of the members – Fouché above all'.[8] It may be that he had already tried to deal with Fouché. Earlier that morning two of his most loyal officers, Flahaut and his cousin Labédoyère, had burst into the house in the rue Cerutti and demanded to see Fouché. When told that he had already left for the council meeting, Labédoyère bellowed at the footman: 'The traitor is hiding! He's frightened of me! But I'll find him!'[9]

In the Council Napoleon renewed his bluster. 'The nation didn't elect them to depose me but to support me. I've no fear of them. Whatever they do I shall always be the idol of the people and the army.'[10] But he knew the truth in his heart, as did the uncommitted onlookers. 'The effect of this fifth retreat from his armies ... is an entire abandonment of him and his cause. Even in the army he has lost his best partisans ... He cannot be forgiven by the brave men who have seen themselves deserted.'[11]

The deputies sent a message repeating their demand that the four ministers should report to them. Lucien harangued his brother, trying to stiffen his spirit, trying to snatch victory from defeat for him as he had done at St-Cloud more than fifteen years before. He pleaded with him to declare a state of siege, proclaim a dictatorship, summon all patriots to the defence of France, and drive out the unruly deputies. He spoke with the fire and fervour of Brumaire, but today there was no Murat to force home the argument with the bayonets of his grenadiers; there was no brilliant young general returning from Egypt with promise of peace and prosperity – only a bankrupt warlord, stripped of honour by his own hand.

The most Lucien could get from Napoleon was permission to accompany the four ministers when they obeyed the summons to the Palais-Bourbon. But there he did more harm than good, alarming the representatives with his appeals for loyalty to the Emperor, stirring their resentment with his talk of oath-breaking.

Lafayette, white-haired, egoistic, idealistic, a figure from a more heroic past, stepped to the rostrum. 'You accuse us of failing in our duty to the nation's honour and to Napoleon,' he said. 'Have you forgotten all that we have done for him? Have you forgotten that we followed him into the sands of Africa, into the wastes of Russia, and the bones of our children and our brothers bear witness to our loyalty everywhere? We have done enough for him – our duty now is to save our country!'[12]

Fouché sat impassively on the Ministers' bench. His protégé and spokesman, Manuel, took up and elaborated Lafayette's theme: the interests of the country must not be confused with those of the man who had misruled and misled it. Another delegate proposed the election of a Commission of Five, from each chamber, to deal with matters of public safety. While the motion was put to the vote and accepted, the Ministers left.

There had as yet been no open talk of abdication. Though time was short, Fouché wanted this act to come from the Emperor, not be forced on him. When Molé found him during the evening and suggested the Paris Municipal Council should send an address to the Chambers, demanding Napoleon's deposition, Fouché asked him to wait. Such direct tactics, he said, would force people to take sides, and the Emperor's supporters in Paris and in the army 'to commit themselves to engagements which it would be impossible for them to go back on later. Let me deal with it, don't hurry things, and rely on me to tell you when it is time to act.'[13]

It had been a day of great tension. 'That devil frightened me this morning,' he said. 'I thought he was going to begin all over again.'[14] But the danger was fading. Throughout the night he kept up the nervous pressure at the conference of ministers with the Parliamentary Commissioners. 'The Chambers,' said Napoleon, 'felt themselves supported and guided by him. It was he who brought in Lafayette, who inspired everything, encouraged everything . . . I ought to have had him shot.'[15]

The conference in the Elysée, presided by Lucien, sat until three in the morning. It was agreed that the Chambers should nominate another commission charged with negotiations with the enemy.

That the Chambers should appoint it was an admission that Napoleon had ceased to govern. Pressed still further by Lafayette, who called for an immediate abdication, Lucien answered that, if the need arose, the Emperor was prepared for any sacrifice.

When the Chamber of Representatives reassembled on Thursday, June 22, Paris was buzzing with the rumour that Grouchy, at the head of his own corps of 30,000 men and an equal number of survivors from the main body that fought at Waterloo, was marching on the capital to support the Emperor. After a brief, stormy debate, the Chamber decided to demand Napoleon's immediate abdication.

Suddenly all opposition collapsed. Lucien and Joseph assured their brother that he had no other choice. Recognizing the true victor, Napoleon turned to Fouché and said, 'Write to these gentlemen and tell them to keep calm. They shall have their way.'[16] Fouché took a sheet of paper and wrote to Manuel, while Napoleon dictated the Act of Abdication to Lucien.

Two copies were prepared. Fouché took one of them to the Palais-Bourbon and read it to the deputies. 'I have no need to urge upon an assembly of Frenchmen,' he added, 'the consideration due to the Emperor Napoleon or to remind them of the feelings which his misfortune must arouse. In the negotiations which must open shortly, the representatives of the nation will not forget to insist upon the interests of the man who presided over the destiny of our country for so many years.'[17] The Chamber resolved to send a deputation to Napoleon Bonaparte to thank him for his past services, and to elect three members of the Chamber of Representatives and two of the Chamber of Peers to act as a provisional government.

'We've got the abdication!' Fouché said triumphantly to Pasquier. 'You must admit that's a reasonably big job to have completed in twice twenty-four hours.'[18] He entertained sixty guests at the Hôtel de Juigné that evening, a celebration which turned a little sour for him when he learned that, though he had been elected to the Provisional Government, Carnot had received more votes than he had, and of the other three members only two, Caulaincourt and Grenier, were likely to support him, while Quinette would join Carnot in opposition.

He was not depressed for long. Carnot that night sent a note to his four colleagues, inviting them to meet at the Ministry of the Interior next morning. Fouché, feigning not to have received this, circulated his own invitation for them to gather at the Tuileries. It was at the Tuileries that they met. He had won the initial, silent trial of strength.

He had little difficulty in persuading the others to appoint him as president of the *commission de gouvernement provisoire*.

5

During the night, Lucien and the more extreme Bonapartists tried to persuade the Chamber of Peers to proclaim the Emperor's son as Napoleon II. Fouché was in difficulties here. He had favoured a regency until now, but during the past few days it had become clear that Lucien saw his brother's abdication as an opportunity to set himself up as regent. Yet to deny the possibility of a regency at this point would deprive Fouché of a bargaining counter; it would also increase the danger of civil disturbances, for the Bonapartists were now bringing the Emperor's *canaille* on to the streets; armed mobs from the faubourg St-Antoine were parading up and down the avenue de Marigny, cheering every time Napoleon came out on the terrace to wave to them.

Napoleon himself was dreaming of a counterstroke: to set up the same court that condemned the duc d'Enghien, to arrest Fouché, 'have him tried in a couple of hours, placard his sentence all over Paris, proscribe or arrest a dozen members of the Chamber of Representatives . . .'[1] But it remained a dream. From time to time he walked out on the terrace, bowing, 'pointing to his heart, leaning over to give them his hand, while his chamberlains and equerries threw money to the crowd, stimulating their enthusiasm.'[2]

Fouché countered by having Manuel, who was his guest in the Hôtel d'Otrante, move in the Chamber of Representatives a resolution that 'Napoleon II has become Emperor of the French by the fact of the abdication of Napoleon I and by virtue of the Constitutions of the Empire'.[3] It served to quieten the Bonapartists and, since the Empire had already ceased to exist and been replaced by a Provisional Government, it was quite meaningless.

Napoleon's continued presence in Paris was, however, an evident danger. Among the troops falling back on the city before the advancing Allied armies were some who were still ready to support him. Fouché began to play on his fears, warning him of the danger of assassination, sending massive reinforcements for his guard in the middle of the night, constantly urging him to move out to Malmaison.

Meanwhile he had to negotiate, to sound out the Allies and

discover which hand he could play most profitably against them: the regency, the duc d'Orléans, or the discredited Louis XVIII. At this moment his inclination was probably towards the duc d'Orléans, son of a *votant* regicide, former soldier in the Republican army, and not tarred with either the Bonaparte or the Bourbon brush. Unfortunately, all this was speculation in a vacuum. Fouché was unable to get any information back from the Allies.

Neither had he been able to bring the fighting to an end. At its first session the provisional government put Davoust in charge of the defence of Paris with authority to call men to the colours, and appointed a deputation of five politicians to negotiate peace terms. The Five – Lafayette, Argenson, Sébastiani, Pontécoulant and Laforest – were given two specific objectives: to maintain France's national independence and the integrity of her territory. They were to insist on the succession of Napoleon II and the exclusion of the Bourbons, a family that 'has become estranged from our way of life, and is still surrounded by men who have ceased to be French'.[4] They left immediately, in the direction of Laon.

Fouché ordered Vitrolles to be released from Vincennes and early on Saturday morning, June 25, received him at the house in the rue Cerutti. He assured him that he intended to restore Louis XVIII, knowing that Vitrolles would pass this on to the members of the major royalist group in Paris – Pasquier, Girardin, Barante, Royer-Collard and Molé – who would see that it was conveyed to Ghent.

Having dismissed Vitrolles, he had Gaillard brought in. He handed him a safe conduct signed by Davoust that would carry him through the French lines, and another for the royalists that Vitrolles had just written. In addition there was a letter to the comte d'Artois from Vitrolles and another to the King from Fouché: both of which were sewn into the collar of Gaillard's jacket. There was one other mission: Gaillard was to call at the Duke of Wellington's headquarters, ostensibly for a safe-conduct, but secretly to ask the Duke what the Allies thought of the duc d'Orléans as a candidate for the throne.

His interviews and letter-writing made Fouché late for the eleven o'clock meeting of the provisional government. When he arrived, unaware that the man whom Carnot had set to watch his house had reported Vitrolles' visit, he was greeted with the blunt accusation from Carnot of having 'deserted your post to confer with Louis XVIII's agents!'[5] He replied that he had spoken to Vitrolles with the aim of getting the best possible terms for the country in the event – which seemed probable and imminent – that they would have to come to some arrangement with the foreign powers who were supporting the Bourbons.

'And who entrusted you with that mission?' Carnot asked indignantly. 'Do you think the provisional government is you alone? Are you in such a hurry to hand France over to the Bourbons? Have you promised it to them?'

'And you,' Fouché snapped back, 'do you think you are doing the country a service by all your harping on useless resistance? I tell you – you don't comprehend a thing!'[6]

At midday on Sunday, June 25, Napoleon gave way to Fouché's pressure and left the Elysée for Malmaison. The following morning the walls of the city were placarded with the announcement that 'the decrees and judgements of courts and tribunals, the acts of notaries, shall provisionally be intituled, in the name of the French people'.[7]

'Thus,' noted Hobhouse, 'Napoleon the Second, after a reign of three days, has been replaced by the French people . . . This confirms what I before said, that the Duke of Otranto will not be embarrassed in his communications with the Allies by any premature adoption of a sovereign . . . To whatever *men* he may incline, there is no reason to think that his wishes or opinions respecting *things* are different from those of the great majority of the nation, or unbecoming the great part which he is called upon to perform in this momentous juncture.'[8]

The Deputation of Five that had been sent in search of peace terms arrived at Blücher's outposts. In answer to their request to see him to discuss an armistice, the Prussian Field Marshal sent 'a verbal answer that he should suspend hostilities when he should arrive at Paris, provided Bonaparte were given up to him, and the Château de Vincennes and various territories and forts on the frontiers'.[9] On June 26, Wellington received a copy of the letter they had sent to Blücher and a request from the provisional government for a passport to permit Bonaparte, his brothers and his suite to sail for America. In reply Wellington refused a truce on the ground that Bonaparte's abdication was not a sufficient guarantee of peace; and refused a passport because all the Allies must be consulted on Bonaparte's fate. In this he was supported by both the Minister of War, Lord Bathurst, and the Foreign Minister, Castlereagh, who wrote to him: 'I earnestly trust that nothing that has passed at Paris will induce the Allies to relax their operations . . . We must not leave our work imperfect a second time.'[10] So the British and the Prussians moved on; Wellington slowly, Blücher eager with fire and sword.

Gaillard saw Wellington the same day, learning from him that the Allies were extremely unlikely to favour the choice of the duc d'Orléans as king (none of the monarchs was eager to encourage the junior branch of a royal family usurping the throne of a senior). He was in Cambray on June 27, where the king had already arrived. Left without news, Fouché sent off another representative, Colonel de Rigny, the nephew of baron Louis, to discover what terms the King would accept for his return. He had no sooner done so than a messenger arrived from the Deputation of Five. On the strength of a conversation with the officers of the Prussian outposts and before receiving Blücher's reply, they reported that they did not believe the Allies would insist on Louis's restoration.

If this were true, there was room for bargaining. Since the British seemed to favour Louis, whom they were again bringing back in their baggage wagons, he wrote to Wellington that 'the French nation wishes to live under a monarch, but it also wishes that the monarch should reign under the rule of laws. The Republic has acquainted us with all the evils of excessive liberty; the empire with the evils of excessive power.' He said that France had its eyes on the English constitution: 'we do not aspire to be more free than she; we will not consent to be less so.' And that the French Government was drawing up a new charter: 'As soon as this has been signed by the Sovereign who shall be called to govern France, this Sovereign will receive the sceptre and the crown from the hands of the nation.'[11] He sent the letter by the hand of Colonel Maceroni, one of Murat's former aides-de-camp whom he had met in Naples in 1813.

The chances of bargaining would have been stronger had not Davoust lost his nerve at this point. In face of the Allied advance and widespread dissension among the French troops who were split between Bonapartists and anti-Bonapartists, the Minister of War warned the enlarged Council – the five members of the Provisional Government, Ministers with Portfolio, Ministers of State, Presidents, Vice-Presidents and Secretaries of the two Chambers – that the military situation was desperate and there was 'not a moment to be lost in making submission to Louis XVIII'.[12]

He sent Fouché a letter next day, repeating that the situation was critical. 'We should proclaim Louis XVIII, we should beg him to make his entry into the capital *without foreign troops*, who ought never to set foot in Paris.'[13]

This was precisely the sort of impulsive blundering that Fouché was trying to avoid. He replied that same night that he was convinced they must negotiate for an immediate armistice, but before entering into wider, political commitments 'we must find out what the enemy wants. A badly calculated step would result in three evils: (1) having recognized Louis XVIII without any engagement on his part; (2) having to receive the enemy in Paris nevertheless; (3) failing to get any concessions from Louis XVIII later. I take the responsibility of authorizing you to approach the enemy outposts and conclude an armistice, making any sacrifice compatible with our duty and dignity.'[14]

Since none of his messengers had returned he decided to go himself. On June 28 he sent General Tromelin to Wellington's headquarters, repeating the request for a passport for Bonaparte and telling the Duke that Fouché was anxious to communicate with him personally, if possible. Wellington repeated that he had no authority to issue a passport, and the Allies would certainly demand that Bonaparte should be surrendered to them. He was willing to see Fouché whenever he liked.

Writing to Sir Charles Stuart at Cambray that day, Wellington told him that he expected 'the Jacobins will give [Bonaparte] over to me, believing that I will save his life. Blücher writes to kill him; but I have told him that . . . if the Sovereigns wished to put him to death, they should appoint an executioner, who should not be me.'[15]

6

When Napoleon went to Malmaison on June 25, General Beker was appointed to take command of his guard. His orders, signed by the President of the Provisional Government, were 'to ensure the safety of the person of Napoleon and the respect that is due to him, and to prevent mischief-makers using his name to stir up trouble'.[1] Bonaparte had become Fouché's prisoner; perhaps his hostage.

Napoleon was worried at the thought of falling into the hands of the enemy. He told Beker as they walked in the garden of Malmaison that first evening that he wanted to leave France, 'to avoid a catastrophe that would bring odium on the whole nation'.[2] Fouché ordered two frigates to be fitted out at Rochefort to take Napoleon to America as soon as permission was obtained from the Allies. He told Davoust to send General Beker with the Emperor to the island of Aix, ten miles from Rochefort, where he was to remain 'until his future and that of his family have been fully decided. Every means will be employed to ensure that the negotiations are completed to his satisfaction'.[3]

When Beker told Napoleon of his instructions, the Emperor promptly refused to budge, suspecting that he would be arrested in Aix far from the support of the *canaille*. He said he did not wish to go to Rochefort, unless he could be certain of leaving there immediately.

Meanwhile Bignon, the Foreign Minister, had received a dispatch sent from Laon on June 26 by the Deputation of Five. They reported that they had failed to get any decision from Blücher but had received permission to continue through the Prussian lines to make contact with the Allied Sovereigns, whose headquarters were last reported to be at Heidelberg. From their conversations with Prussian staff officers they gathered that 'one of the great difficulties will be the Emperor's person. They think that the Powers will insist on guarantees that he will never appear again on the world scene . . . It is our duty to observe that we think that his evasion before negotiations are complete would seriously compromise the safety of France.'[4]

Bignon communicated this at once to the Provisional Government. Fouché had just decided to tell Decrès, the Minister of Marine, to let Bonaparte leave on a frigate without waiting for a passport, if he wished to risk running the British blockade. This was now likely to add another sacrifice to those imposed on France by her insatiate ex-master. Yet there were at least two reasons why he could not be left at Malmaison: there would be lasting disunion in the country if he were captured by the Prussians and Blücher carried out his threat to shoot him out-of-hand; there was the ever present danger of his becoming the rallying point for civil war. He must be sent to the island of Aix and held there until the Allies decided what they wanted. Fouché wrote to Davoust in the afternoon of June 27 that it was imperative that Napoleon should make up his mind to leave. If he did not, he was to be 'kept under observation in such a way that he did not escape'. Beker must be given 'the gendarmerie and troops necessary to guard every avenue leading to Malmaison'.[5]

Next morning Napoleon sent Flahault to Paris to say that he refused to leave Malmaison unless two frigates, then at Cherbourg, were placed unreservedly at his disposal. Flahault was shown into Fouché's room, where he found Davoust standing by the fireplace. He delivered the message. Before Fouché could reply, Davoust swung round and shouted that if the Emperor did not leave he would be arrested – that he would himself arrest him.

Napoleon prepared to leave. His mother and his uncle Fesch, the countess Walewska, Lavalette, Méneval, the actor Talma, the doctor Corvisart and many others came to say goodbye. Late in the evening he received Laffitte who, in return for the Emperor's petty cash and a wagon-load of gold from his secret hoard, gave him letters of credit on American banks to the value of nearly four million francs.

By now Tromelin had returned to Paris. Fouché learned from him that the Allies were insisting that Bonaparte be surrendered to them. Just before midnight he sent a message to Wellington through Marshall, one of the many Englishmen who had remained in Paris after returning there in 1814. Marshall told the Duke that Fouché

'requests to know why the Allied Powers still continue hostilities now that Bonaparte has abdicated the throne, and has no longer a voice in any act of government? What object they propose to themselves to attain by this; and what can be their intention in continuing the war?

To these questions a frank and ingenuous answer is requested. Every possible concession that a free nation can make will be granted; and the duc d'Otrante, in the name of the French Government, pledges himself to deliver up Bonaparte in any way that may be most suitable to the views of the British Government.'[6]

He was willing to deliver him to the British but not to the Prussians. That night he told Decrès to cancel the order that Napoleon must wait for passports. He was free to sail from Rochefort as soon as he wished. It was a gamble, but he had to get the Emperor away from Malmaison, and the odds were that he would not risk capture by the British ships that must by now have closed in all round the coast. Decrès went in person to Malmaison, arriving at dawn on June 29. Napoleon received him, wearing a dressing-gown, and, on hearing his message, gave orders for immediate departure.

Shortly afterwards, a division making its way to new positions at St-Germain halted on the road beside the park and some of the men began to shout *Vive l'Empereur!* The old cry stirred him. He went up to his room, changed into the uniform of the *chasseurs de la garde* and came down with a note which he handed to Beker, asking him to take it urgently to the Provisional Government. It was a request that he should be given command of the army in order to defend Paris.

The honest, simple Beker got short shrift when he delivered this message to Fouché, who angrily asked whether Napoleon took them for fools and why Beker was running errands to Paris when he should be on the road to Rochefort. He sent him back to Malmaison with a note addressed to Maret, saying that the government was unable to accept the proposal 'for reasons which you will be able to appreciate. I beg you . . . to advise him to leave without delay, in view of the fact that the Prussians are marching on Versailles.'[7]

Napoleon received the news placidly. 'Those fellows are losing France,' he said.[8] He changed from uniform into civilian clothes. It was almost half-past-five when he returned to the salon and said farewell to the weeping Hortense, who gave him a diamond necklace worth 200,000 francs that she had sewn into a belt.

While the imperial travelling carriages were being marshalled in front of the house he slipped out into the garden and through a small door in the wall on the south side of the park. Bertrand, Savary and Beker were waiting for him in a yellow barouche, devoid of any armorial bearings, drawn by four post-horses. He did not intend to run the gauntlet of widows and bereaved parents as he had done a year before.

Despite these precautions a small crowd had gathered. They, too, put up scattered shouts of *Vive l'Empereur!* as he set off towards Rambouillet. In the garden a desolate group of servants, aides and relations stood unashamedly sobbing.

In a Brussels hotel, a traveller who had just crossed the plain of Waterloo sat writing a description of the funeral pyres that had been burning there for more than a week. 'It is only human fat that feeds the fires now. Thighs, arms and legs are piled on them. There were about fifty labourers round them, handkerchiefs covering their noses, stirring the fire and bits of bone with long forks.'[9]

7

Napoleon had gone but the ferment in Paris continued. Supported by the mute majority, Fouché was the target for every faction. Napoleon had accused him of being bought by the duc d'Orléans;

Laffitte was convinced he was sold to the King; in fact, nobody knew what he was up to. 'The soldiers are all half drunk, and are crying *Vive l'Empereur!* with the ferocious expression of untameable brutes.'[1] The Jacobins refused to accept the return of the Bourbons. There was a sudden scare of famine, emptying the shops of all provisions. Three members of the Chamber of Deputies burst into Fouché's house when he was dressing and accused him of treason. Continuing shaving, he talked them into leaving peacefully.

As head of the Provisional Government he had a ceremonial cavalry escort; he added a detachment of the National Guard to protect the house in the rue Cerutti. 'You have nothing to fear,' he wrote to Delphine de Custine. 'Rely on me – though I am having to face the storm alone . . . I am thinking only of the country; and the difficulties I encounter come not from material objects but from the men with whom I am associated . . . Depend on my courage.'[2]

The Deputation of Five, refused an armistice by Blücher, was on its way eastward in search of the Allied Sovereigns and discussions of peace. A second deputation – appointed on June 27 and composed of two generals, the deputy Flaugergues, the revered Boissy d'Anglas and La Besnardière, a diplomat in close touch with Talleyrand – was sent to ask Wellington for an armistice. While they were talking with him on June 29 he received a proclamation that Louis XVIII had drawn up on the previous day and proposed to address to the French people. He discussed it with the deputation, listened to their criticisms, and sent a note of them to Talleyrand, who had joined the King at Cambray.

He told Talleyrand he had suggested an armistice was possible 'if Napoleon were given to the Allies, if our advanced guards enter Paris, and if a government were established in France which should conciliate the confidence not only of France but of Europe'. He explained to the deputation that by this he meant they should recall the King 'and that the honour of France required that this should be done without loss of time, and before it could be supposed that the interference of the Allied Powers had occasioned his Majesty's recall'.[3] He was going to consult with Blücher and try to persuade him to agree to an armistice. He met the deputation again that evening at Louvres as they were returning to Paris. His news was disappointing: Blücher was mounting an attack on Aubervilliers and would not call it off; also he refused to suspend operations unless Napoleon was handed over, if he were still in Paris.

The deputation sent a report back to the Provisional Government, but their courier was delayed by the fighting and did not arrive until the evening of the 30th. He returned early in the morning of July 1 with the news that Napoleon had left for Rochefort.

Wellington now agreed that if the French army retreated south of the Loire and the National Guard took over the security of Paris, he would again recommend an armistice to Blücher. But he had scarcely finished speaking when he received a letter from Metternich and Nesselrode at the Imperial Headquarters in Mannheim saying the Allied Sovereigns intended to continue the forward march of their armies and discuss peace terms only when they arrived in Paris. The French Commissioners protested that this was a breach of Wellington's promise; Wellington replied that he had made none, but would still try to win Blücher's support for an armistice. He had by now received a formal request for an armistice from Davoust, as Commander-in-Chief of the French army, and was in the perplexing position that the British Government would not allow him to accord a truce without making a political settlement in favour of Louis, whereas his only excuse for granting an armistice in the face of the objections from the other powers would be that it was a purely military decision.

Every day, every hour and every minute that slid by was vital to Fouché. In a stormy meeting at La Villette on June 30, the officers of Davoust's staff turned on him, denounced his proposal to offer the throne to Louis, and demanded continued resistance to the invaders. Davoust promptly reversed his position and at the meeting of the Provisional Government later in the day announced that he had 70,000 men at his disposal and wished to fight on. Fouché insisted on a detailed report.

Not having received it by eight o'clock the next morning, he wrote to Davoust again, asking him to attend the Council with replies to four specific questions:

> 'Can you defend every approach to Paris, including the left bank of the Seine [which Carnot had pronounced wide open to the enemy]?'
> 'Can you prevent the enemy from entering Paris?'
> 'Can you undertake to fight at every point without compromising the fate of a million men?'
> 'In short how much longer can you guarantee the fate of the capital?'[4]

Davoust stayed away, pleading urgent affairs. Summoned by an official letter from the whole government, he admitted that Paris could not be defended.

'The agitation and violence in which we all lived,' said Pasquier, 'are impossible to describe, continually tossed between fear and hope, dreading the dénouement almost as much as we desired it.' He marvelled at Fouché's

> 'great sang-froid ... Exposed to every hazard, his necessarily ambiguous conduct drew on him the distrust of all parties; and this distrust often went so far as insults and threats, particularly from the Bonapartists and revolutionaries, his former friends. Yet all of them flocked to him; his salons witnessed the most extraordinary gatherings; everybody found a place there, met his friends and adversaries there. As for him, he went from one to the other with the same ease as if he were speaking the same language to them all.'[5]

Fouché was certainly not deluding himself with false hope. 'We were in a desperate state,' he said afterwards. 'The treasury was empty, credit exhausted, the government at bay; and because of the violent collisions of so many different opinions Paris was on top of a volcano. Elsewhere the country was each day being flooded with new waves of foreign troops. If, in those circumstances, the capital were taken by force, we had nothing to hope for – no capitulation, no agreed terms, no concessions.'[6]

He wrote to Wellington, using the Regency as a bargaining counter against the Bourbon restoration that he knew the British desired. 'Our legal situation,' he said, 'is that of a government in which the grandson of the Emperor of Austria is the Head of State ... It is imagined perhaps, that the occupation of Paris, by two of the Allied armies, would promote the views which you may have of reinstating Louis XVIII on the throne. But how can an increase of the misfortunes of war ... be a means of reconciliation? ... Force may replace him on the throne, but it will not maintain him there.'[7]

He begged again for a firm reply to his proposals for an armistice. 'Peace exists already, since the war has no longer any object ... It would be atrocious to fight bloody battles which could not in any way affect the questions which are to be decided.'[8]

Wellington, appalled by the carnage of Waterloo, needed no convincing; but he was having great difficulty in persuading the avenging Blücher and the three monarchs whose countries had suffered the ravages of French armies for so many years. The

Deputation of Five, arriving unexpectedly at Haugenau on June 30, had been refused official recognition and told that the Allied Sovereigns would act only in concert, which could mean a delay of many days, since no representative of Britain had yet joined them. Wellington, unaware of this but conscious of the need to find a solution before the two Emperors and the King of Prussia arrived – to spare lives and to save the Bourbons – spent the whole of July 2 in talks with Blücher and writing notes to the French deputation.

On July 3, Barante, a former prefect in the Vendée, wrote to his wife that the army 'talks of nothing but pillaging, cutting throats, and making a clean sweep of the royalists. They are said to have worked themselves into a passion against Fouché, claiming that he has betrayed them. For the past five days he has run the risk of being denounced in the Chamber.'[9] (There had, indeed, been a strong rumour on July 1 that the Chambers were 'holding a special meeting to receive the accusation against Fouché'.)[10]

That morning the tension broke. Wellington prevailed on Blücher to grant a cease fire on the terms that he had already outlined. It was not – both Wellington and Blücher insisted – an armistice, since they had no powers to grant one. The French army would retire immediately beyond the Loire; the Allied forces would occupy St-Denis, Clichy, and Neuilly on the 4th and Montmartre on the 5th; on the 6th they would take over all the entrances to the city.

8

Fouché successfully insisted that it should be called the Convention of Paris; but it was in fact a capitulation, signed at the Prussian headquarters at St-Cloud in circumstances of such humiliation for the French delegates that it was clear that Blücher hoped to repay not only Napoleon's butchery and rapine but also his arrogance and vulgarity. Fouché's cards were reduced to the disgruntled army now beginning to withdraw southward, the armies in the east that had not been committed at Waterloo, and the potential resistance of the French people – not a strong hand to be played by a man who was eager for peace.

He wrote to Wellington on July 3, asking for an interview at which he was sure they would soon reach agreement. 'The whole of France wishes to be at peace with Europe; she asks only for her independence as a nation and strong institutions to guarantee her liberty.'[1] He sent Maceroni with a verbal message that the King's return would not be opposed if he assured the Chambers that there would be no reprisals against those who had deserted his service for that of Napoleon, and that he would promise reforms.

Wellington was not to be lured into any promises. He received Maceroni in the morning of July 4 in the presence of Talleyrand, Pozzo and Sir Charles Stuart, and dictated a memorandum for Fouché. 'It seems to me that, the Powers having agreed that Napoléon Buonaparte and everything pertaining to him were a usurpation with which they could in no way treat, it is advisable that, as soon as possible, that is to say after the army has left, the two Chambers and the government should declare themselves dissolved . . . I send you a copy of the King's Proclamation of the 28th and I know that the King is disposed to do everything that could be wished to guarantee personal and constitutional liberty.'[2]

This left France entirely at the mercy of the returning royalists. The King, no doubt, meant well, but his first brief term of monarchy had shown that he was incapable of restraining his reactionary supporters. His proclamation, Fouché feared, 'will again upset public opinion'.[3] He sent Tromelin to repeat his request for a meeting. Wellington replied that he would be at Neuilly the following day and would receive him at any time he suggested.

Early in the morning of July 5, Fouché sent Bignon, the Foreign Minister, to Neuilly to tell Wellington that 'the province of Franche-Comté positively refused to obey any royal authority and demands a republican form of government';[4] that the provinces of Burgundy, Champagne and Lorraine were up in arms against the Allies; and that the troops now crossing the Loire intended to join forces with others coming from the south. When Wellington failed to be impressed by these sensational stories, Bignon asked him to receive Fouché that afternoon.

Fouché set out from the Hôtel d'Otrante accompanied by Manuel. In the vestibule, waiting to speak to him, he found Molé, whom he invited to join his party knowing that Molé had already met the Duke of Wellington when he was British Ambassador in 1814. On the stone terrace outside he saw General Valence, a member of the second Deputation of Five that had approached Wellington for an armistice. He told him to get into the carriage as well.

The two men, surprised that even Fouché should so casually pick his companions for a conference that was deciding the fate of France, were still more astonished to find the coachman heading south of the Bois de Boulogne towards St-Cloud instead of north to Neuilly. Fouché had decided to pay a preliminary call on Blücher, no doubt in the hope of playing him off against Wellington. They were frequently halted by sentries and required to identify themselves. It was late afternoon when they arrived at St-Cloud; Fouché's introduction of himself as President of the French Government was received with scarcely concealed contempt. He succeeded, however, in gaining entry to Marie-Louise's boudoir where he was received by Blücher's chief-of-staff, Gneisenau.

The marshal-prince, it appeared, was having an afternoon nap in the Empress's bee-embroidered bedroom and was not to be disturbed. Gneisenau, standing stiffly beside a table on which stood food and wine which he pointedly did not offer to the visitors, replied coldly to Fouché's greetings. The Frenchmen left hastily and drove to Neuilly.

Here, in the attractive country house where Wellington had established his headquarters, instead of 'the commotion and luxury which surrounded the Prussian general', they found only 'simplicity and silence'[5] to such an extent that they wandered around the grounds in the darkness without discovering a single soldier to guide them. At last they penetrated the house and came upon a small room with an English officer in it. Fouché announced himself; the door to a neighbouring salon was at once flung open, revealing Wellington, and behind him Talleyrand, Pozzo, Sir Charles Stuart and von der Goltz, the Prussian envoy.

Wellington came forward, offering his hand to Fouché in a friendly fashion. They sat down and began a discussion which soon concentrated on two points: pardon for those who had supported Bonaparte, and acceptance of the tricolour flag. Wellington's partiality for discipline and castigation set him arguing fiercely against leniency.

'This would be the first time,' he protested, 'that a throne was overturned and re-established, a King betrayed, hounded out and restored, without a single punishment to satisfy the claims of justice and intimidate those who might be tempted to commit similar crimes.'[6]

Talleyrand, the only person present qualified to speak of Louis's intentions, pointed out that the King's proclamation of July 28 pardoned all those who had supported Bonaparte through force of circumstances, and that those who were excluded were few in number and the offence would be difficult to prove. The clause, he said, 'was intended rather as a means of preserving the respect due to public authority than to disquiet or punish'.[7]

This, though a great advance on Wellington's position, did not satisfy Fouché. He stubbornly defended those who had deserted Louis three months before: in particular Marshal Ney, whose impulsive submission to Bonaparte – together with his troops – had made him the arch-traitor in royalist eyes. He repeated that it was in the King's interest to forgive everything and 'spoke of the revolution of March 20 as if it were a mere escapade, a schoolboy prank that had best be forgotten as quickly and completely as possible'.[8]

Leaving the question of retribution undecided they passed on to Fouché's second demand: that the tricolour should remain the national flag. Wellington replied that a year ago he would have supported the proposal but now 'that cockade had become the signal of rebellion [and] the King could not raise the flag under which the usurper had made war on Europe'.[9]

They talked until four in the morning without reaching any conclusions. Fouché promised that he would see what he could do to persuade the Chambers to accept the King and would return to dinner that afternoon, for a further discussion with Wellington and Talleyrand.

After a few hours sleep, he set about doing what he could to strengthen his position for the afternoon's negotiations. In the Chamber of Representatives the place left empty by the removal of the statue of Napoleon was filled with the tricolour flag; outside, the National Guard demonstrated in favour of the blue, white and red. Summoning Marshal Macdonald, at whose house Vitrolles, Pasquier and other royalists usually met, he sent him to find the King (who had now advanced to the château d'Arnouville, near Gonesse) and impress on him the importance of accepting the tricolour. From the flustered Davoust he learned that the original Deputation of Five had returned and were still of the opinion that the Allied Sovereigns were not in favour of the Bourbon restoration. He seized upon this as a possible weapon.

He set out early, planning to catch Wellington alone. But before he left, remembering the tenor of the previous day's conversations, he made out a passport, in a false name, for Marshal Ney. As he drove out through the Etoile barrier, escorted by six gendarmes, he passed crowds of idlers who had come to see the first British troops taking over the guard. On arrival at Neuilly he played his new card immediately. Davoust, he said, had woken him with the report that the Emperor of Russia and King of Prussia 'recognized the impossibility of reinstating Louis XVIII as the ruler of France'.[10] It was only with the greatest difficulty that he had persuaded Davoust not to 'communicate the report he had received to the Chambers and to propose without further delay or ceremony the tender of the crown to the duc d'Orléans'.[11]

He was trying to bluff the wrong man. Wellington replied politely that he found the story difficult to believe. They were interrupted by the arrival of the other dinner guests: Talleyrand, Pozzo and Sir Charles Stuart, and the talk turned to other matters.

Castlereagh arrived after dinner, and Fouché took the opportunity to return to the subject, whereupon Wellington produced a copy of the reply given to the French Plenipotentiaries, sent to him by Castlereagh's brother, Lord Stewart, who had joined the Allied Sovereigns, and added that he had seen a similar report received by Blücher. Neither document contained anything that could support Fouché's suggestion. Fouché, without twitching an eyelid, expressed his astonishment that the Deputation had failed to pass on to him so important a document. He asked for a copy to show to his colleagues.

He returned to the question of a universal pardon. He argued that 'even if Bonaparte had not returned there would still have been a crisis'.[12]

Talleyrand leaned forward. 'The King offers you a full and complete amnesty,' he said. Then he added: 'At the same time he offers you the Ministry of Police. Do you accept?'

Fouché looked at him, his face entirely devoid of expression.

'Yes,' he said.[13]

Notes to Part VI

Chapter 1

1 Despatys, *Ami*, 329
2 Pasquier, III, 170
3 *Ibid.*, 171
4 Wertheimer, 192(1)
5 Carnot, II, 462
6 Hobhouse, II, 18
7 Nap. I, *Corresp.*, XXVIII, 77(21769)
8 Despatys, *Ami*, 332

Chapter 2

1 Brotonne, 579(1438)
2 Laffitte, 67
3 Las Cases, I, 503
4 Fouché, *Mémoires*, 344
5 Metternich, II, 602
6 Despatys, *Ami*, 346
7 Lavallette, II, 181–2
8 Metternich, II, 601
9 Villemain, II, 222–4
10 Méneval, *Mémoires*, III, 524
11 *Ibid.*
12 Despatys, *Ami*, 349–50
13 Wellington, *Supp. Desp.*, X, 61
14 *Ibid.*, 80
15 PRO, FO 27/116

Chapter 3

1 Daudet, *Police*, 347
2 Pasquier, III, 230
3 Hobhouse, I, 245
4 Chénier, II, 511
5 Carnot, II, 461
6 Hobhouse, II, 157–8

Chapter 4

1   Marchand, I, 167
2   Fouché, *Mémoires,* 492
3   Boulay de la Meurthe, *Boulay,* 281
4   Villemain, II, 257
5   Taine, 48
6   Noailles, I, 227
7   Bertrand, II, 364
8   Gourgaud, II, 321
9   Noailles, I, 225
10 Fleury de Chaboulon, II, 169
11 Hobhouse, II, 13
12 Fleury de Chaboulon, II, 176
13 Noailles, I, 226
14 Villemain, II, 266
15 Bertrand, II, 96
16 Fleury de Chaboulon, II, 181
17 *Moniteur,* 23 June 1815, p. 717
18 Pasquier, III, 253

Chapter 5

1   Bertrand, I, 245
2   Noailles, I, 234
3   *Moniteur,* 24 June 1815, p. 725
4   Ernouf, *Capitulation,* 173
5   Carnot, II, 521(1)
6   *Ibid.*
7   Hobhouse, II, 61–3
8   *Ibid.*
9   PRO, WO 1/205
10 Wellington, *Supp. Desp.,* X, 590–1
11 *Ibid.,* **X,** 610
12 Carnot, II, 530
13 *Ibid.,* 623
14 Chénier, II, 624–5
15 Castlereagh, X, 386

Chapter 6

1   Fleury de Chaboulon, II, 210–11
2   Martha-Beker, 62

3   Las Cases, I, 811
4   Ernouf, *Capitulation*, 192–3
5   Wellington, *Supp. Desp.*, X, 601
6   *Ibid.*
7   Marchand, I, 191
8   *Ibid.*
9   Houssaye, III, 136(4)

Chapter 7

1   Scott, lviii
2   Bardoux, 243–4
3   Wellington, *Supp. Desp.*, XIV, 564
4   Chénier, II, 650
5   Pasquier; III, 308–10
6   Fouché, *Mémoires*, 506
7   Wellington, *Supp. Desp.*, X, 641–2
8   *Ibid.*
9   Barante, II, 164–5
10 Scott, lx

Chapter 8

1   Wellington, *Supp. Desp.*, X, 653
2   PRO, FO 146/4
3   Bardoux, 245
4   PRO, FO 146/4
5   Noailles, I, 259–60
6   *Ibid.*, 266
7   Polovtzov, 285
8   Noailles, I, 266
9   Polovtzov, 286
10 *Ibid.*
11 PRO, FO 146/4
12 Fouché, *Mémoires*, 511
13 Despatys, *Ami*, 417–18

PART VII

Minister of Police
1815-1820

I

It came as a triumph, but not a great surprise. The many messengers Fouché had sent to the King's headquarters as it cautiously advanced from Ghent to Gonesse had all presented him as the only man who could guarantee a smooth restoration. Wellington, who according to Talleyrand 'had had his head turned by Fouché', declared after his first meeting with him that 'this was the only man who could guarantee the submission of the capital and therefore of France', and went personally 'to urge the King not to refuse to admit him to his council'.[1] As soon as the capitulation made movement possible, the aristocrats of the faubourg St-Germain came flocking to the château d'Arnouville to pay their respects to Louis and assure him that 'without Fouché there is no security for the King, no safeguard for France; he alone has saved the country, and he alone can complete the task'.[2]

These royalist enthusiasts were not solely Fouché's friends and acquaintances. The comte d'Artois, delighted that Fouché had saved his close friend, the brave, handsome, conceited, lying Vitrolles, was pleading his case. The elderly bailli de Crussol, former bodyguard to Louis XVI, more royalist than the King, 'the last of our *chevaliers*, the prototype of fidelity', claimed a private interview in the King's study to tell him that Fouché 'has saved us all . . . Who in France are the real enemies of the Royal Family? The Jacobins? Well, Fouché has them under his thumb, and as soon as he is on the King's side we can sleep safe in our beds at night.'[3]

When the possibility of taking the regicide into his ministry was first mentioned, Louis told Talleyrand sharply never to raise the matter again. But under continual pressure from 'royalists and liberals, French generals and foreigners',[4] and the threat that he might not otherwise be able to return to his throne, he began to have second thoughts. Unlike his elder brother, he was not a man who believed in sacrificing himself to his principles. When Talleyrand importuned him after the first conference at Neuilly on July 5, he replied: 'Go back to Wellington and the duc d'Otrante and act in my best interest. You have *carte blanche*, but spare me as much as you can.'⁵

Talleyrand concluded that there was nothing he could be spared. Castlereagh confirmed this opinion when he wrote to Liverpool the following day: 'I consider the King's decision to employ Fouché a great point gained, and his means of acting to have been essential to His Majesty's restoration.'⁶

The new Minister lost no time in setting about his work. Still seated at Wellington's dining-table, he called for a pen and paper and roughed out the measures he proposed to take next day: a letter to the King from the Provisional Government announcing that it considered itself dissolved; a similar message to the Chambers; plans for persuading the Chambers to dissolve themselves voluntarily; the appointment of a new commander for the National Guard and the reinstatement of those officers who had been dismissed for royalist sympathies. He agreed these points with Talleyrand and then, at 9 p.m., set off with him to be informally presented to the King.

There are conflicting accounts of this first meeting between the King and the man who voted for his brother's death. It was believed at the time that Fouché again urged Louis to adopt the tricolour: 'Henry the Great had swallowed a Mass, it could be but a trifling sacrifice in His Majesty to swallow a ribbon'⁷ – and that Louis replied that he had no objection personally, but the whole of the rest of his family would go back to Hartwell if he did. Fouché reported only that he had himself been 'natural, modest' and the King 'paternal'.

In the presence of his acting secretary, Beugnot, Louis gave a more dramatic performance. Beugnot set before him the warrant appointing Fouché to the Ministry of Police.

> 'The King glanced at it and let it fall on the desk; the pen slipped from his fingers; the blood rose to his face; his eyes became sombre and he sank back as if weighed down by some deadly thought. A gloomy silence descended on our conversation that had been easy and pleasant a moment before. This silence lasted several minutes; then the King said to me, with a deep sigh: "If we must, then let us do it!"
>
> 'He picked up his pen, paused once more before tracing the letters of his name, and uttered these words: "Oh! my unfortunate brother! If you can see me, you will have forgiven me!"

'At last he signed, but as he did so, painfully and with trembling hand, large teardrops fell from his eyes and moistened the paper.'[8]

Fouché meanwhile was informing his fellow-members of the Provisional Government of the result of his mission. He admitted that he had failed to get the guarantees of a more liberal policy he had hoped for, but claimed that 'though there was no remedy for the ill, it was possible to palliate it by my presence in the council'.[9] His *governomania* and self-confidence were as strong as ever. Carnot urged that the government should retire beyond the Loire with the army and fight on. Fouché replied that this would merely add to the people's sacrifice without altering the outcome. The government ought not to quit Paris; and it was better that it should dissolve itself than be forcibly dismissed.

While they argued, Prussian troops began their entry into the city. They occupied the Luxembourg Palace, thus putting an end to the deliberations of the Chamber of Peers. Their infantry and artillery took up positions in the Place du Carousel. An officer strode into the Tuileries and presented the five Commissioners of the Provisional Government with a demand from Blücher for 100,000,000 francs as reparation.

Fouché did not need to persuade them any more. Carnot drew up a statement which they agreed to send to the Chamber of Representatives, whose session at the Palais-Bourbon had not yet been interrupted.

'Until now we have been led to believe that the Allied Sovereigns were not unanimous in their choice of the prince who should reign over France ... However, the ministers and generals declared yesterday ... that all the Sovereigns had undertaken to replace Louis XVIII on the throne. Foreign troops have occupied the Tuileries, the seat of government ... No longer free to deliberate, we consider it our duty to disband.'[10]

Fouché left the palace and made his way towards St-Denis, where he was to be presented formally to the King in company with the other members of the new ministry. The famous avenue of elms had been sadly hacked and lopped to provide barricades, now dragged aside. His carriage rattled over planks thrown across the wide ditches cut into the road to let the canal water form a succession of moats, flanked by heavy cannon. On either side the walls of gardens and houses were perforated to make musketry loopholes.

The King had moved overnight from Arnouville to the great Benedictine abbey at St-Denis. His new ministry, with Talleyrand as Foreign Minister and President of the Council, included Pasquier (Justice), Jaucourt (Marine), baron Louis (Finance) and Gouvion Saint-Cyr (War). Chateaubriand, in one of the ante-rooms, watched as the lame Talleyrand, supported on Fouché's arm, entered the King's study. 'Vice leaning on the arm of crime ... the trusty regicide, kneeling, placed the hands that brought death to Louis XVI between the hands of the brother of the martyr King; and the apostate bishop stood surety for the oath.'[11]

Fouché's immediate business was to arrange the time for the King's entry into Paris. He suggested three o'clock in the afternoon, and Louis accepted this. It was past ten o'clock and the Minister of Police had arrangements to make. He bowed himself out of the royal presence, leaving behind a letter of advice for his royal master.

It was a survey of the state of feeling in the realm on which Louis was about to renew his shaky grasp. It was also a lecture in the sharp tones of a master to an idle pupil.

> 'Everybody knows that Your Majesty lacks neither knowledge nor experience; you know France and the age you live in; you know the power of public opinion; but your benevolence has too often given ear to the claims of those who followed you in adversity ...
>
> 'If the same policy is repeated, and if Your Majesty, basing all his powers on heredity, recognizes no other rights for the people than those that come from the throne, France, as on the first occasion, will ... hesitate between its love for the country and its love for the Prince ...
>
> 'The French people today attach as much importance to liberty as to life ... Today concessions would ... pacify, and give strength to the royal authority; at a later period concessions would prove its weakness.'[12]

So that the King should have the feeling that he returned on sufferance, Fouché kept the barriers closed on the St-Denis side until shortly before the royal cortège arrived, with the result that there were few to cheer Louis on his way to Paris. Yet he seemed very well pleased with his reception, and grateful for Fouché's exertions.

That evening, as the Minister of Police stood in the throne room of the Tuileries, crowded with aristocrats, émigrés, *chouans* and the devout, the double doors were thrown open to admit the comte d'Artois. Catching sight of Fouché, he strode towards him and shook him warmly by the hand. 'Sir,' he said, 'you see me very happy, very satisfied; the entry was admirable, and we are most obliged to you for it.'[13]

He turned to the rest of the company, bowed and went out. Half an hour passed. An usher entered and announced that the King wished to speak with the Duke of Otranto. His Majesty was tired and would not be receiving anybody else.

The courtiers retired in mortified silence 'leaving to Fouché alone the honour of conversing that night with the son of St Louis. It was the attentions of *Monsieur* in particular that petrified the assembly . . . How could he shake that man's hand without being forced to?'[14]

2

He was almost entirely on his own. Wellington, Castlereagh and Pozzo had called on Talleyrand earlier in the day 'to draw his attention to Fouché's barefaced deception'[1] in signing the statement to the Chambers that Louis owed his return to the insistence of the Allied Sovereigns. Talleyrand agreed with them, heartily condemned him, and then added that Fouché would undoubtedly answer. 'Haven't I done what you wished? Why inquire as to the means?'[2]

This was exactly what Fouché did reply: that he had brought the King back; and that he could not have persuaded the Provisional Government to resign without signing Carnot's statement. In any case, as he said to Gaillard, the King could not dismiss him: 'having only just been appointed . . . the effect would have been disastrous'.[3] Which was almost exactly what Castlereagh wrote to Liverpool: 'It is a most unjustifiable transaction, but not one which ought to induce us, having prevailed on the King to use Fouché, now to quarrel with him.'[4]

Molé, amazed but far from admiring, studied him with a sort of horrified fascination.

'He had neither birth nor family to support him. Even those who helped him to the ministry deplored having been reduced to such a sad necessity. But he had managed to make himself indispensable to both parties. The royalists feared massacre if he did not keep an eye on their enemies; the revolutionaries asked for his protection against increasing reaction. Which did not prevent the first from regarding him as a villain worthy of the worst torments, and the second as a traitor whom they would send to his just deserts as soon as they could do without him.'[5]

There were still the startling contradictions between his past, his appearance, his reputation and his private character. 'He is tall, thin limbed, dry complexioned, swift in his movements, fine featured, his eyes bloodshot yet piercing, his hair that of an albino; there is something ferocious, elegant, agile that makes him resemble a panther.' Yet seen from close at hand, 'a good husband, very affectionate father, good friend and above all good comrade, given neither to hatred nor revenge, one cannot explain the excesses that blotted his career'.[6]

It was difficult, indeed, to distinguish him as the same man from one day to the next, though usually the disparity lay in the eye – and attitude – of the beholder. At one moment Molé described him as 'indiscreet, idle , a gossip and a liar',[7] and at another as 'always busy; it was his system to do much of his business by conversation, but he never talked except with that object and seemed devoured by a nervous activity which would not let him rest'.[8] His only relaxation was walking, or enjoying the company of his children. These were allowed to enter his study at any time: 'they were constantly in and out, to kiss him, ask him how he was, to bring him a glass of orangeade, or beg him not to tire himself'.[9]

Hobhouse, a less biased observer, refused to believe 'that ambition or meaner avarice has prompted this celebrated person to accept a post in which there is so little chance of aggrandisement, either of character or fortune, and which, without any of the charms of distinction, must draw upon him not only the redoubled hatred of his former enemies but the suspicion of his friends'.[10] But in this Hobhouse was probably putting too narrow a definition on ambition. Fouché had never underrated his own abilities, never lacked sinful pride. He firmly believed that he could succeed where others failed.

Supported by that belief he was prepared to accept the increasing coldness and incivility that he encountered at court among the returned émigrés 'who talk of *les Français* as if they were foreigners to them, unallied, unconnected, the objects of disgust and fear'.[11] Only occasionally did he strike back, as when he walked up to one nobleman whom he had formerly employed, and said: 'Ah, duke! I see I am no longer a friend of yours. But there – we live in better times; the police no longer need to pay great personages to keep observation on the King at Hartwell.'[12]

His immediate task – of persuading the country to accept Louis without disorder – was made very difficult by the excesses committed by the Prussian troops. In the countryside they continued unchecked a policy of revenge by rape and robbery. In Paris, Blücher's first move was to send his engineers to blow up the pont d'Iéna, which perpetuated the name of a battle at which he had been defeated.

Wellington and Castlereagh talked with Blücher in the morning of July 9, arguing against the destruction of the bridge, pointing out that this, and the demand for 100,000,000 francs that he had served on the Provisional Government and was now demanding from the King, were a breach of the convention signed at St-Cloud. Blücher replied that blowing up the bridge was a matter of national pride. 'If the general commanding British troops at Washington in the recent war with America,' he said with more pertinence than politeness, 'had found a bridge named Saratoga, and had failed to destroy it, wouldn't he have deserved the reproaches of the British nation?'[13] He refused to delay dealing with what Wellington tactfully referred to as 'the last bridge in Paris on the Sèvres side' but, whether from inefficiency or second thoughts, the charges his engineers used were too feeble to bring it down. Next day it was reprieved by the arrival of the Allied Sovereigns.[14]

Fouché complained to Stuart that the Prussian excesses were causing much resentment in the French army which he was trying to disband peacefully, and warned him that France would not long submit to such treatment. 'Besides 80,000 men perfectly accustomed to war which compose this force of the Army beyond the Loire, the addition of 20,000 *chouans* will place 100,000 men animated with a very determined spirit of resistance at the disposal of the King, if the Outrages we daily witness continue longer.'[15]

He was not exaggerating. Wellington, who issued and enforced stringent orders against looting and other misbehaviour, was increasingly concerned by 'the useless and . . . ridiculous oppression practised upon the French people'. He predicted that 'we shall immediately set the whole country against us, and shall excite a national war . . . if the troops of the several armies are not prevented from plundering the country, and the useless destruction of houses and property.'[16]

Liverpool anxiously surveying the scene from London agreed that strengthening Louis's government would be 'an Herculean task ... For what is a King, unsupported by opinion, by an army, or by a strong national party? I am glad, upon the whole, that he has determined to employ Fouché. He may betray him; but he may likewise feel it his best interest to save him. In a desperate state of affairs, we must try desperate remedies.'[17]

Would Fouché betray Louis as he had betrayed Napoleon? It was entirely possible. At this moment he was complaining because the Prussians were supporting the claims of the duc d'Orléans to the throne – though he himself had supported them only a few weeks before. 'You will have seen the message of the Provisional Government to the Chambers, stating what passed in the conference at Neuilly,' he said to Stuart. 'Well, there was not a word of truth in it. A falsehood was necessary to prevent the progress of intrigue fomented by Prussia in favour of the duc d'Orléans. You have, of course, taken an early opportunity to contradict it, and you are justified in so doing.'[18]

Stuart was impressed by his 'air of confidence and frankness,'[19] and not unduly surprised by his change of attitude to the duc d'Orléans. The French, obsessed by loyalties to persons and families – Bourbonists, Orleanists, Bonapartists – were less likely than the British to appreciate that a man might betray a person without betraying his country: particularly a man who still, beneath the cynicism and deceptive chatter, held fast to the Jacobin enthusiasms of his early manhood, yet cherished a concern for tolerance unexpected in one who had been the chief policeman in a totalitarian state, a love of *patrie* that was suspect in partisan France.

'Fouché, I understand,' Castlereagh wrote to Liverpool on August 3, 'is horribly unpopular in England. I don't wonder at it, as far as the mass are concerned; but those who know how impossible it is to find men of character in France who can be employed ought to be very cautious about encouraging this clamour. I am always abusing him for not executing with more vigour his own decrees; and yet I doubt whether the King could do without this man.'[20]

3

There were many who believed that Louis could, and should, do without him. They were in the majority at court and their leaders were the Artoîs and the duchesse d'Angoulême. They loathed the Revolution and whatever Napoleon had spared of its reforms; they hated all who had played an active part in it; they felt humiliated by Fouché's presence in the ministry, unable to raise their heads until he was brought down.

They had a valuable ally within the Ministry of Police – the handsome Elie Decazes, whom Fouché had unwillingly accepted as Prefect of Police, knowing that he was to spy on him; though he was well aware that a dozen other spy organizations were paying him special attention – the Allied military police, the King's police, *Monsieur's* police, the police of several ministers and court officials. Decaze's agents, loitering around the Hôtel de Juigné and the Hôtel d'Otrante, bribing servants and buying drinks for messengers, were under the control of Foudras, appointed Inspector-General of the prefecture police in succession to Veyrat and eager to atone for his failure to arrest Fouché four months before.

It was a difficult job, for though information was available it was hard to know which of it to believe. Within a week of his appointment Fouché was telling friends that 'every means was being used to discourage him'.[1] 'Don't laugh at fools,' he wrote ruefully to Delphine. 'They are a power in times of crisis.'[2] Benjamin Constant noted that 'he has the feeling that he is finished'.[3] It certainly did not show in his actions, for he was already clashing head-on with the extremists, ordering Decazes to stop provocative royalist demonstrations in the Tuileries gardens, recalling the special commissioners who were encouraging a White Terror in the provinces.

He caused alarm by spending a long time with the Tsar of Russia, possibly discussing with him the *Note on the State of France* which he circulated to the four Allied Powers on July 20. This long review of the causes of the failure of the first restoration and the success of Bonaparte's return was the result of the pressure he was under to prepare a list of Bonaparte's supporters to be brought to trial. He pleaded for discreet forgetfulness and warned that 'prosecutions against a faction serve only to give rise to other factions'.[4] He argued that not more than eight or ten of the people involved in Bonaparte's return were still dangerous and these would 'retire of themselves'[5] if left alone.

He made little impression on the Tsar Alexander, and none at all on the Prussians, but Wellington continued to see a great deal of him and to support his policy of reconciliation. He dined with Wellington on July 23; Wellington came to his formal banquet for the Allied generals and ministers the following day, and to an informal dinner on July 29; and he was a guest at the ball given by Wellington on

July 31, where Lady Granville gazed fascinatedly at him: 'a little, spare, shallow, shrewd-looking man' (it was evidently not one of his days for looking tall, or ferocious, elegant and agile as a panther). 'He is, I conclude, the worst and the most useful man that the King could have found in his whole dominions.'6

Wellington's view was a great deal more approving. 'I advised the King to take Fouché into his service so as to be able to return with dignity and without effort on the part of the Allies; and I am perfectly certain that he owes his peaceful and dignified restoration to that advice. I also believe that the courtiers – vile, useless and even harmful to the King – were satisfied, and applauded the arrangement as much on the day it was adopted as they blamed it immediately they had benefited from its effects. They immediately began to intrigue against Fouché and the whole ministry.'7

Fouché, struggling with his lists and unusually sensitive to criticisms in the English newspapers – where he had been an enigmatic and usually sinister figure ever since his first appearance in *The Times* in 1793 – was churlish, impatient and nervy, according to the servant L** who was supplying Foudras with domestic information. He presented the Council of Ministers with 'two enormous lists containing three or four times as many names as were necessary'8 and then 'argued in a specious way that the measure would be of no use unless it were carried out on that scale. He hoped in this way to get it completely abandoned'.9

The Council was too scared. He whittled the list down to nineteen officers to be brought to trial by court-martial and thirty-eight soldiers and civilians to leave Paris within three days and reside wherever ordered by the Minister of Police until the Chambers decided whether they should be prosecuted. The King signed the edict on July 24; on the same day a reliable informant reported to Foudras that '*M. Fouché is convinced that the court wants to get rid of him. He is not loath to go*', but when Foudras himself met the minister, he told him '*he simply could not understand the fury that had been directed against him; but it had at least served to reveal the strength of public opinion in his favour*'.10

Foudras was quite incapable of interpreting the constant flow of contradictory confidences that came from the minister; and equally unable to penetrate the mysteries of his correspondence with the Russian Nesselrode or the Austrian Metternich, whom he saw at Madame Junot's house in the rue des Champs-Elysées. '*The Duke appears calm and sometimes gay*,' he reported, '*but it is not natural, and those who are in the best position to observe him at home have never seen him so sad and preoccupied.'*[11]

The lassitude was not reflected in his work. Disregarding the clamour for reprisals, he sent an instruction to all prefects that the King's wish was that the past should be forgotten; only in unity would the nation find security and honour. Learning that Decazes had not cleared the royalist demonstrators away from the Tuileries, he arranged for the appearance of a rival mob which answered every shout of *Vive le Roi!* with *Vive l'Empereur!* The King himself gave Decazes instructions to prevent all manifestations.

The baffled Foudras noted that of the thirty-eight persons named in Fouché's list of proscriptions, most were still in the city or had gone only as far as Versailles and 'practically all have been to see the duc d'Otrante and came out generally satisfied'.[12] Taxed with open neglect to carry out a royal command, Fouché sent orders to Decazes to arrest them all within twenty-four hours. 'You will let me know, at the end of the same period, the places they have chosen to go to. His Majesty's intention is that they should retire to a distance of thirty miles.'[13] The first person arrested by Decazes's men was Boulay de la Meurthe. Fouché promptly ordered him to be set free and for all the others to be given a further twenty-four hours' grace.

His unwillingness to take action against the Bonapartists contrasted sharply with the eagerness of Decazes, who arrested Labédoyère in Paris and then, greatly exceeding his authority, tracked down Ney in the uplands of the Cantal. In those provinces which had remained unaffected by the Allied advance and had never known the fear that forced others to turn to Fouché for protection, feeling was hardening against him. The members of the Council of Ministers stirred uneasily. Fouché's inclusion in the government had been intended to reassure the Jacobins and Bonapartists but now, as Pasquier said, 'it turned out they were almost immediately reduced to silence, while the opposing interests, whom his presence irritated to the last degree, gained a strength for which they were not prepared'.[14]

But for those who believed his position was undermined, he had a startling surprise in store: he married for the second time on August 1 – and the King paid him the rare royal honour of signing the marriage contract. His second wife, Gabrielle-Ernestine de Castellane-Majastres, whom he had met during his exile in Aix five years before, was very different from the ugly, mean, yellow-wigged Bonne-Jeanne whom he had loved so dearly. 'Young, intelligent, beautiful, rich and of a great family', she shocked her aristocratic friends by her union with 'this unfrocked ex-conventional and regicide'. They could only assume that, though rich, she was not rich enough to withstand the temptation of 'the monster's many millions'; and that he was interested in finding a hostess who could 'do the honours with ease and grace to the Duke of Wellington, the ambassadors and all the great personages whom he enjoyed entertaining'.[15]

They were married at midnight in the chapel of the Abbaye-aux-Bois, she twenty-six and he some thirty years older. They returned to the bride's mother's house for the reception and then, a little after two o'clock, went to the Hôtel de Juigné. '*The Duke behaved quite gallantly with his new bride,*' tittered Foudras. '*He retired to bed with her and gave instructions that nobody should disturb him before ten in the morning.*'[16]

4

A royalist from the provinces, outraged by the King's condescension to one of his brother's murderers, deplored that 'until now, Fouché has been King of France; he has decided appointments and entirely controlled the ministry. The royalists are eating their hearts out in silence; but they are all planning a revolution which the King has made all the more necessary by his weakness.'[1] It was not true that Fouché controlled the Council, but it was certain that it in no way controlled him. At a meeting presided over by the King in mid-August, with no preliminary notification to his colleagues, Fouché presented a report bitterly attacking the Allied occupation forces – in particular those of Prussia – for brutality and pillage. In a memoir a few days later, he gave warning that a civil war was being precipitated by royalist excesses.

It was a remarkable double document for any minister to address to his sovereign, 'combining the most sombre forebodings with admonitions stern enough to sound like threats'.[2] In the *Rapport* he spoke of peasants 'in flight from undisciplined soldiers, the woods filled with unfortunates seeking a last refuge'.[3] He admitted that French armies had ravaged Europe, 'but must that be imitated? . . . There will never be an end to the ills of mankind, if alternate vengeance becomes the rule of war.'[4] He predicted that 'on the day that the inhabitants have lost everything and their ruin is complete . . . a blind fury will take the place of resignation . . . and France will find it less dishonourable to destroy herself than to allow herself to be destroyed by foreign hordes.'[5]

In places this reaction had already begun, led by the dismissed officers whom an English visitor noticed hanging about the Paris cafés in plain clothes, 'easily distinguished by their large mustachios, ferocious countenances, and sullen, discontented air . . .'[6] Yesterday five Prussian soldiers were taken out of the River Seine, their bodies mangled most dreadfully; and some of the Allied troops are constantly found missing from their quarters; from which there is too much reason to apprehend that murders are perpetrated by the dispersed French soldiery.'[7]

Fouché's criticism of the foreigners was mild in comparison with the attack that he launched in the *Mémoire* against the *ultra-royalistes*. 'France is at war with herself,'[8] he said. In the West, for twenty years, 'they have confused the royalist cause with the cause of the *ancien régime*'.[9] In the Midi the towns and countryside alike were terrorized by royalist bands waging a war of revenge and religion against the Revolutionaries, Bonapartists and Protestants. In the East there was danger of another kind – revolt against royal authority because of the hardships of the occupation and the fear of confiscation of the former *biens nationaux*.

'You would find,' he continued in words of striking outspokenness, 'scarcely a tenth of the French people who would willingly return to the *ancien régime*, and scarcely a fifth who are genuinely devoted to the legitimate authority.'[10] He warned of the dangers of dismissing too many of Bonaparte's officers and soldiers: 'The fewer there are in the new regiments that are being formed, the more there will be among the ranks of the malcontent and seditious.'[11] As for the King's prospects of survival in the event of a civil war: 'The absolute royalists would predominate in ten departments; the parties would be evenly balanced in fifteen others; in the whole of the rest of France [the remaining fifty-eight departments] there would be only a handful of royalists to oppose the mass of the people . . .'[12]

'One cannot govern without physical strength and moral strength. The one cannot do without the other – and we lack both . . .'[13] For the creation of moral strength Your Majesty must take a firm and unshakeable resolve: to proceed on the principle that public opinion has become a factor in the art of government and that it has altered its entire balance. France can no longer be governed except under a constitutional régime . . .'[14]

He would not have been Fouché had he failed to conclude with a homily on his own wisdom and the King's obtuseness. 'The various ideas which I have the honour to submit to Your Majesty differ very little from those which would have been more easily adopted in 1814, and the whole world may judge the difference that such a policy would have made to our situation and to that of all Europe. How many misfortunes might have been prevented!'[15]

Fouché handed both documents to the King – who put them in his pocket and did not mention them again. A few days later, Pasquier received a manuscript copy of both papers, sent to him by the pro-curator of Moulins who had found them being circulated secretly in the town. It was generally assumed that Fouché had deliberately disseminated them in order to bring pressure on his colleagues and the King. Wellington stated that 'on the contrary, I know it was the courtiers who published them'.[16] But when he sent a draught of the report to Delphine in the first week of August Fouché had said, 'I want to present a picture that will enlighten the rulers and peoples on their future.'[17] There is no doubt that he intended publication.

Certainly the courtiers made the most capital out of the affair: 'If the fate of Louis XVI had been visited on his successor, this document would have provided the indictment of the monarch, entirely drawn up by one of his ministers.'[18] Pasquier passed it to Talleyrand, who was already willing to get rid of a colleague who showed such disturbing activity. The pair of them persuaded the Council – without great difficulty – to advise the King to appoint a new Minister of Police.

Louis received the suggestion with great relief. 'God be praised!' he sighed. 'The poor Duchess [of Angoulême] will no longer be in danger of meeting that odious face!'[19]

Fouché learned that Pasquier was preparing the necessary docu-ments for the King to sign the following morning. Without alerting his opponents by leaving his home, he got a message to the princesse de Vaudémont, who at once passed the news to Wellington.

The field-marshal showed less contempt for the Duke of Otranto than he did for most of his fellow beings and almost all foreigners. 'Fouché has perhaps behaved badly in certain circumstances,' he said, 'but not half as badly as people say and believe.'[20] By eight o'clock the following morning he was closeted with the unhappy King, reading him yet another lecture.

'He is the only link that exists between you and a great part of your people,' Wellington reminded him. 'They regard him as the sole guarantee of their personal safety. If Your Majesty dismisses him they will fall into anxiety which might lead to despair. On the other hand, the royalist party, which already shows little inclination to listen to reason, will become impossible to control.'[21]

Louis, unconvinced but wary of biting the hand that had set him back on the throne, told Pasquier that he had changed his mind. 'Thus,' said the discomforted Minister of Justice, 'our situation was as painful as could be. Henceforward we had to sit in the Council face to face with a man who could not be ignorant that we had done everything we could to expel him, and in whose presence we could not express our thoughts with confidence.'[22]

He had fought off this attack, but there were more storms ahead. One of the more threatening clouds became apparent with the results of the elections to the two Chambers that had extended through the month of August. Fouché was returned as a deputy for the department of the Seine (which he chose to represent) and also for Corrèze and Seine-et-Marne. Most of the successful candidates – chosen by 15,000 electors out of a population of some twenty-five million – were far over to the right. He had made little attempt to swing the elections as he had done on previous occasions, probably recognizing that there was no future for him in a Bourbon ministry.

He spoke quite openly of the plot to get rid of him and claimed equally openly that 'he had a very strong party in the country' who would support him. Lady Malmesbury, who met him at his mother-in-law's house (and found he had 'not a bad countenance – pale and sensible'), expressed the common official British feeling that his dismissal would be 'in the present State of Things an act of the greatest folly. If he is honestly disposed, the King should keep him. If otherwise, he can do much more mischief *out* of office than in it. All the reasonable people are for keeping him, and when the Report got to the Bank the *funds fell directly*.'[23]

He had a private audience with the King on September 6 which reassured neither of them. The following day Foudras reported that: 'He is building himself a powerful and numerous party. On all sides one hears it said that the day he is dismissed will be a day of mourning, that government stocks will drop considerably, that it will be the signal for reaction, that many people will quit Paris, etc.'[24] More alarming than this was the belief that Fouché proposed to place the duc d'Orléans on the throne.

He gave a dinner for the Duke of Wellington on September 7, including among his guests the Whig peer, Lord Kinnaird, who had arrived in Paris ten days earlier and was known to have been in touch with Lafayette and various other liberals. 'There can be no doubt,' Foudras commented, 'that Lord Kinnaird is the principal agent for the duc d'Orléans.'[25]

On the evening after Fouché's dinner, Kinnaird entertained several important guests in the lodgings he had rented from the duc de Bassano – among them Metternich, Lady Shelley, and William Hamilton, British Under-Secretary for Foreign Affairs. 'The duc d'Otrante was praised to the skies,' said the agitated Foudras, 'and they eulogized the duc d'Orléans.'[26] By September 10 he had discovered more evidence that 'the duc d'Otrante is strongly supported by the English. Again yesterday Lord Hamilton was praising him in the warmest terms at Lord Castlereagh's. He said he was a great statesman, cool-headed, and inspired by the highest sentiments.'[27]

So widespread was the suspicion of Fouché's Orléanist leanings that one Catholic group, led by a lawyer named Agier, went to the trouble of infiltrating the masonic movement – to which Fouché and many other Jacobins and Bonapartists belonged – for the purpose of thwarting his supposed plot.[28] If he did have any thoughts of effecting a change of regime he was inclined more towards a regency, which he could again hope to control, but in fact he decided, as he had so often advised others, to stay in the game to the end. Stuart, who told Castlereagh on September 7 that 'the King's determination to remove M. Fouché from his counsels appears to be no longer doubtful' reported on September 11 that 'the publication of M. Fouché's Reports has produced no more serious result than a strong reprimand and a caution recommending greater discretion in the future'.[29]

On September 12, well knowing that his words would be carried back to Decazes's office in the rue de Jérusalem, Fouché told Fauchet, the former Prefect of Bordeaux, that everything was going well and would go better; that he had no fear of the new Chambers then assembling; that he knew who his enemies were and they could not get the better of an old hand like himself; that he had received secret approaches from *Monsieur* and could form an alliance with him whenever he wished. The prefect 'had never seen him so gay'.[30]

It was very much an assumed gaiety. He saw the forces at court, in the Council and in the Chambers massing against him. Castlereagh, writing to Liverpool on September 14, predicted that 'the Court, that is *Monsieur* and the duchesse d'Angoulême, will probably excite the Royalist members [of the Chambers] to run first at Fouché, as the most odious object, and next at the government generally. In both these efforts they will be assisted by the Jacobins, who wish nothing so much as to see the Royalists committed in the government, which will soon concentrate all the weight of the Revolution against the Court, and thus render their chance of overturning the Bourbons infinitely greater.'[31]

It was a situation that Fouché had so often warned against. But there was no virtue in being right when nobody wanted to listen, no future for a moderate when the two extremes were seeking battle. He may well have been right in believing that the mass of the people supported him, but the mass of the people had no voice. In addition, the Duke of Wellington's patronage had now lost much of its value at court.

The end of the special relationship between Wellington and Louis XVIII was brought about by a dispute over the art treasures which Napoleon had looted or extorted from all over Europe and deposited in the Museum of the Louvre. In 1814 the Allies, preferring not to embarrass the restored King and perhaps even a little impressed by the French argument that it was such a boon to the student and the tourist to have so many works of art handily gathered in one place, did not insist on restitution of the stolen goods. In 1815 they were in a quite different mood. The Prussians made it clear that they intended to take all their former property back with them, and the King of the Netherlands appealed to Wellington (in whose army his troops had served) to help him regain the many works by Dutch masters that had been taken from Holland. In the face of shrill protests in public and several insults in private, the Duke made it clear that he supported the Netherlands claim, intended to take the pictures from the museum. and would employ armed British troops to do it if necessary. Henceforward his patronage of Fouché was as much a hindrance as a help.

Talleyrand, trying to form a new ministry that might make him more popular with the new chambers, found that none of the men he approached was willing to sit in the same council as Fouché. The King was more ready than ever to get rid of him. Royalist pamphleteers openly attacked him: 'Whatever may be his services [to the King] they could never be greater than his crimes, they could at best earn him a pardon but could never give him any claim to His Majesty's favour.'[32] The problem was what to do with him after he was dismissed. As Vitrolles remarked, it was impossible to 'leave him in Paris amid his comrades and friends . . . like a tricolour flag flying in the Place de la Bastille'.[33]

As early as September 6, Hamilton told Lord Bathurst that 'there is an idea of sending him as Minister to America'.[34] Gaillard was sounded on the possibility of Fouché's accepting the post. On September 14, before the council meeting, Talleyrand and Pasquier went through a childish charade of discussing the appointment in Fouché's presence and praising its attractions. 'I don't know of anything more desirable in the present state of Europe, with all this upheaval,' said Talleyrand. 'What better could one wish for one's closest friend?'[35] Fouché smiled and said nothing.

That evening the whole Council with the exception of Fouché took dinner at Jaucourt's house. 'The Chamber is hostile to us,' said Talleyrand when the dessert had been brought in and the servants left. 'The duc and duchesse d'Angoulême have great influence there. We must gain the goodwill of their royal highnesses. My dear colleagues, you know how it must be done.'[36]

Next morning, at the request of his Council, Louis XVIII appointed Fouché as his Ambassador to the Court of Saxony.

5

He sent his formal letter of resignation to the King immediately but, since no successor was appointed for several days, did not move from his official quarters in the Hôtel de Juigné to his home in the Hôtel d'Otrante until September 20. He accepted his dismissal with dignity. 'He seemed to me to bear no grudge, not even bitterness, against his colleagues,' said Molé. 'But he already felt the boredom and sorrow of exile.'[1] He had never been on anybody's side. He could not now expect many to be on his.

Among his friends he put it about that Castlereagh and Wellington were urging him 'to remain in France where his presence might still be very necessary'; and gave it as his own opinion that 'the present state of affairs cannot last six weeks'.[2] But by September 27 he was on his way to Dresden, escorted on the first part of his journey by a British officer.

In a farewell note to Delphine, he said: 'I have not had the success I wished for. I spoke the language of reason to men who wanted to hear only that of the passions.'[3]

He wrote from Brussels on October 3 to thank Wellington for the escort and 'for the courageous friendship that you have shown to me; it has brought you some injustice, but the nation's esteem will avenge you and the future will justify your feelings for me'.[4] The fall of Talleyrand's ministry followed closely on his own dismissal and he stayed in Brussels for some days, evidently nursing the slender hope that he might be recalled. On October 16 he set off. He arrived in Dresden on October 28, and was very affably received by the King who remembered his considerate behaviour two years before.

In Paris Decazes had stepped into his shoes at the ministry and lost little time in searching the files for correspondence which he offered to Pozzo di Borgo as proof that Fouché had been conspiring with the English, and to Wellington to show that he had been plotting with the Russians. The pamphleteers were attacking him in the streets and the new deputies in the Chamber, where, by November, there was already a move on foot to impeach him.

It was not necessary. The amnesty which Louis had promised on his return came up for debate in the Chamber of Deputies at the beginning of January. The extremists proposed an amendment that all regicides who had voted for Napoleon's *Acte Additionel* or taken office during the Hundred Days should be deprived of citizenship and banished for life.

Foreseeing his fate, Fouché sent Wellington an apologia of amost 30,000 words, claiming that 'when Louis returned for the second time my entry into public affairs was an act of devotion . . . It would have been safer for me to retire . . . but there was more grandeur in facing events.' Of the returning royalists, he asserted 'time, which destroys all, has not destroyed their prejudices . . . We know where reaction begins: we do not know where it ends. Its first fury at least was almost exhausted on me alone; it has developed and spread only since my departure from Paris.'⁵

His habit of blowing his own trumpet was perhaps more permissible by French standards than by British, but Wellington must have warmed a little to this Frenchman who chose so unrewarding a moment to speak well of Bonaparte. Condemning those who now denied their association with the Empire, Fouché declared that 'everything was wonderful at the beginning of his reign . . . At what period did France have greater splendour and more power than at the moment when every Sovereign recognized Napoleon?'⁶

The old triumphs took on a greater glory viewed from an exile which he now realized would be permanent. The Chamber of Peers accepted the *loi d'amnistie* that the Deputies passed by a jubilant majority of more than ninety per cent. The King deprived him of his post of ambassador. The letter withdrawing his credentials was brought to him by one of his former secretaries, Fabry, who was thus able to take back Fouché's instructions on his private affairs.

In February he wrote to Metternich, asking for permission to live in Austria. He mentioned that he intended to write his Memoirs – a hint, perhaps, that his opponents still had something to fear from him. In a postscript he protested that:

> 'I am included by the generalization of the law among those exiled for having taken office under Napoleon. But since that time I have been called by the King to the Ministry of Police; I have received from him a letter of recognition for my services.
>
> 'My mission to Dresden was not a favour but a new appointment by the King; my election to the Chamber of Deputies by the most numerous of the electoral colleges – that of Paris – is a nomination by the people. All these titles place me in an exceptional position, so solemn and so inviolable that the King cannot possibly apply the law to me.'[7]

It was a strong argument, but this was not a time when the French Government listened to pleas of reason, nor Louis to those of honour. Fouché had, in any case, been playing the game long enough to be familiar with the rules.

He sent a similar letter to Castlereagh four days later, asking for 'the passports necessary for me to travel with my wife and children in England and Scotland',[8] accompanied by the pleasantly named Mlle Bienassis, who had succeeded Mlle Ribou as governess. He repeated the request in April, enclosing a copy of the letter he had written to Wellington.

Metternich consulted the French Government who were well satisfied to have Fouché safely under the eye of the efficient Austrian secret police. Harassed by the Prussians, who put pressure on the King of Saxony to get rid of him, and worried about his wife's health, which seemed to be suffering from the Dresden climate, he made a visit to Prague in July, and obtained Metternich's permission to settle there. 'Be sure to tell my friends in Paris that my love for my country will not grow cold because I am three hundred leagues away,' he wrote to Delphine.[9]

Europe was now lightly peppered with French exiles, some of whom – Fouché, for instance, and members of the Bonaparte family – were discouraged from living in countries which had common frontiers with France. For this reason Metternich refused him permission to spend the winter of 1816–17 in Tuscany; and perhaps also because he was suspected of being involved in an attempt to get messages to St Helena. These took the form of advertisements in an English periodical, written in a code which the Austrian experts soon deciphered. Metternich was convinced that they were addressed to Napoleon and would be used for an escape attempt.

One of them, published in November 1816, included the sentences: 'The rumour that you have sold your silver has caused a sensation here. This is a big blunder on your part; for Joseph has promised us he will provide for your needs.'[10] On being shown this, Metternich wrote to the Austrian Ambassador in London, Prince Esterhazy, 'Only Hortense, Fouché or Lavalette would take the liberty of addressing Napoleon as a blunderer.'[11] But the riddle remained unsolved. The editor, Lewis Goldsmith, was questioned by British and Austrian officials. He told them the advertisements arrived anonymously, accompanied by the fee of four guineas. As soon as the inquiry began the advertisements ceased.

Fouché was making tentative moves towards composing his reminiscences; sentimentalizing a little about the past, still refusing to accept that there was no future. 'You will see what I say in my *Mémoires* about the Oratory,' he wrote to a friend in Paris. 'I have let myself dwell at length on the years I spent there – I still have lively and pleasant feelings for them.'[12]

He kept in touch with his sister and his nephews and nieces at Nantes. Nearly twenty years before, when he was appointed by the Directory to the Ministry of Police, one of his first actions was to secure the return of one of the Broband boys – a prisoner of war in England – and to provide him with a job in the ministry. He placed a younger nephew in a branch of the Ministry of Finance in the Midi. 'I have recommended him to the care of the Mayor of Marseilles, a respectable man,' he assured his sister, 'he keeps a close eye on him and reports to me every month on his way of life.'[13] In the same letter he offered words of advice on the upbringing of his nieces: 'Recommend to them great reserve in their speech and strictness in their deportment. The most sought-after women in society are those who grant the least to the men.'[14]

It grieved him that he could no longer help them in their careers but, as he wrote to Brillaud de Laujardière, a Nantes councillor whose daughter was engaged to a Broband, 'I can provide whatever my nephew lacks to conclude the marriage to which I consented when he occupied an advantageous post and had the expectation and right to retain it. I am very happy to take the responsibility of making him the same allowance as you give to your daughter until he finds employment which is at least equivalent to that allowance.'¹⁵ He regretted being unable to attend the wedding but sent them from Prague his congratulations, assurances that he would make them as comfortable as he could, and a brief avuncular homily: 'Make each other happy; you, Broband, by attentions and unfailing consideration, and you, Alexandrine, by invariable gentleness, by the domestic virtues which confer such dignity in later years. Copy your fathers and your mothers; they offer a useful lesson. After long years of marriage their love still continues because they respect each other. There are no lasting sentiments except those which are based on respect.'¹⁶

In Prague they had the company of the Thibaudeau family – a tenuous friendship based on a common revolutionary past but impaired by the memory that Fouché had placed Thibaudeau on the list of proscriptions that he drew up in July 1815. When local gossips began to talk of the attentions that the Duchess of Otranto was receiving from Thibaudeau's son Adolphe – and the scandal was picked up by newspapers in several countries – Fouché decided to move again.

He travelled around Austria with his son Joseph, looking for a town in which his young wife would not feel too cloistered after the gaiety of Paris. He had asked Metternich if positions could be found in the Austrian service for Joseph and his brother Armand. Metternich answered that this would be possible only if Fouché himself renounced his French nationality – which he refused to do. In May 1818 the local commissioner of police notified Vienna that Fouché 'was thinking of buying property in Linz'.¹⁷ First he took his wife to Karlsbad: 'the wildest, most rustic and prettiest hole in the world', as she delightedly wrote to her sister.¹⁸

The duchess's mood changed sharply when they moved to Linz. Local society and even the officers of the garrison refused to have anything to do with the regicide and his wife. 'What is the use of being in this world,' she lamented, 'if one lives as we do?'¹⁹ Early in 1819 they decided to move to Munich, where they counted on a welcome from Eugène de Beauharnais; but Metternich forbade this because Hortense, the most enthusiastic of all Bonapartists, was staying at Augsburg.

He consulted Gaillard on the possibility of settling in Brussels but, even if he could have obtained permission to live so near to France, he would, Gaillard advised him, not feel comfortable there – the city was a home for several of those he proscribed in 1815, and who still kept the feud very much alive. He continued to publish open letters and explanations, hoping that some change of government in Paris would open the way to his return. Richelieu's ministry resigned in December 1818 and Fouché was delighted to see Lafayette and Manuel among the new deputies. In May 1819, the Chambers debated an amnesty for the exiled *votants*. With the defeat of the motion all Fouché's hopes died.

He was becoming increasingly irked by police supervision, blaming it for the continued ostracism in Linz. 'It is the exile's fate to be a contagious thing to all who approach him,'[20] he wrote bitterly to Metternich. His health was showing the strain of repeated disappointments. He applied for permission to reside in the milder climate of Trieste, where Elisa Bonaparte had helped him find a house. He arrived in January 1820.

There was company here: Elisa, now comtesse de Campignano, at the Villa Vicentina at Sant'Andrea, on the road to Udine, and her brother Jérôme who lived at Campo Marzo with his wife Catherine of Württemberg under the title of comte and comtesse de Montfort. Fouché saved Jérôme from capture in 1815 and had been in correspondence with him frequently since then. 'I wish I could divide that man into two persons,' Jérôme said, 'so that I could have the politician hanged and cherish the creature who rescued me.'[21] Fouché took his wife and children to visit them; received them in his own fine house, the Vico Palace in the via Cavana; and stood with Jérôme and Catherine at Elisa's bedside when she died in August 1820.

There were no hardships. He was a wealthy man. He lacked for nothing except an interest in life; behind the hooded eyes the bright sardonic gleam was fading. Ten days before Christmas he caught a chill while out walking. The affection went to his weak chest; when Jérôme visited him on December 20 he was unable to talk.

He died on December 26, 1820. There was talk of his having made his peace with the Church at the end, of his having asked for the sacraments. The family gave him a stately funeral, with a ceremony in the cathedral according to the 'superstitious and hypocritical cults'[22] that he had once denounced. The coffin conspicuously lacked the pall inscribed *Death is an eternal Slumber* that he had once invented.

Whether because of this or despite it, as the funeral procession made its way in a snow storm to the cathedral of San Giusto, a great single gust of wind suddenly sprang up and overturned the hearse.

Notes to Part VII

Chapter 1

1 Pasquier, III, 330
2 Chateaubriand, *Outre-Tombe*, VI, 42
3 Beugnot, 600–1
4 Barante, *Souvenirs*, II, 168
5 *Ibid.*
6 Wellington, *Supp. Desp.*, X, 676
7 Hobhouse, II, 1–2
8 Beugnot, 603
9 Fouché, *Mémoires*, 511
10 *Moniteur*, 7 July 1815 (Supp.), p. 776 bis
11 Chateaubriand, *Outre-Tombe*, VI, 41
12 Fouché, *Mémoires de la vie publique*, 113–15
13 Beugnot, 610
14 *Ibid.*

Chapter 2

1 Polovtzov, 287
2 Castlereagh, X, 418
3 Despatys, *Ami*, 420
4 Castlereagh, X, 419
5 Noailles, I, 276–7
6 *Ibid.*
7 *Ibid.*, 277
8 *Ibid.*
9 *Ibid.*, 289
10 Hobhouse, II, 186
11 *Ibid.*
12 Capefigue, III, 114
13 Wellington, *Supp. Desp.*, XI, 21
14 *Ibid.*, 22
15 PRO, FO 27/118
16 Wellington, *Dispatches*, VIII, 207–8
17 Castlereagh, X, 422
18 PRO, FO 27/118
19 *Ibid.*
20 Castlereagh, X, 451

Chapter 3

1 Forgues, 19
2 Bardoux, 419
3 Constant, *Journal*, 356
4 Fouché, *Sketch*, 138
5 *Ibid.*, 141
6 Granville, I, 67
7 Wellington, *Dispatches*, VIII, 271
8 Pasquier, III, 368
9 Barante, *Souvenirs*, II, 190
10 Forgues, 31–2
11 *Ibid.*, 42
12 *Ibid.*, 40
13 Langeron, 40
14 Pasquier, III, 358
15 Cussy, I, 58
16 Forgues, 47

Chapter 4

1 Géraud, 270
2 Noailles, I, 326
3 Fouché, *Rapport au Roi*, 5
4 *Ibid.*, 12
5 *Ibid.*, 13
6 Fellowes, 111
7 *Ibid.*, 142
8 Fouché, *Mémoire* [in *Rapport fait au Roi*], 15
9 *Ibid.*, 18
10 *Ibid.*, 21
11 *Ibid.*, 23
12 *Ibid.*, 21
13 *Ibid.*, 43
14 *Ibid.*, 46
15 *Ibid.*, 48–9
16 Wellington, *Dispatches*, VIII, 271
17 Bardoux, 259
18 Noailles, I, 327
19 Pasquier, III, 392
20 Wellington, *Dispatches*, VIII, 271
21 Pasquier, III, 390
22 *Ibid.*, 393
23 PRO, PRO30 43/29

24 Forgues, 62–3
25 *Ibid.*, 63
26 *Ibid.*
27 *Ibid.*, 64
28 The pastime of seeking a freemason under every revolutionary bed is as old as the Revolution itself. Occasional attempts to explain Fouché's policies in terms of favouring the freemasons in order to protect the Jacobins, or vice versa, fail to explain why he should have been so bitterly opposed by other freemasons such as Cambacérès or the prefect of police, Dubois, or Joseph Bonaparte, Grand Master of the Grand Orient and head of all French freemasonry. The fact is that freemasonry had adherents in all classes and all parties, and even in both sexes: for example, that very unjacobinical member of the Ste-Catherine lodge, the princesse de Vaudémont. For a recent discussion of Freemasonry and the Revolution, see *Annales Historiques de la Révolution Française*, No. 197 (July–Sept. 1969).
29 PRO, FO 146/4
30 Forgues, 65
31 Castlereagh, XI, 15–16
32 Massacré, 4
33 Vitrolles, III, 198
34 Bathurst, 385
35 Pasquier, III, 420
36 Despatys, *Ami*, 430

Chapter 5

1 Noailles, I, 340
2 Forgues, 76
3 Bardoux, 272 (Dated Paris, 4 October – see next)
4 Wellington, *Supp. Desp.*, XI, 185 (Dated Brussels, 3 October – see previous entry)
5 Castlereagh, XI, 220–1
6 *Ibid.*, 234
7 Schlitter, 211
8 Castlereagh, XI, 175
9 Bardoux, 421
10 Schlitter, 23
11 *Ibid.*, 24
12 Wertheimer, 206(1)
13 Caillé, 12
14 *Ibid.*, 13
15 *Ibid.*, 14
16 *Ibid.*
17 Schlitter, 229
18 Wertheimer, 222(4)
19 *Ibid.*, 230
20 Wertheimer, 239(1)
21 *Ibid.*, 240(1)
22 Martel, *Fouché*, 161

*Sources
Index*

Sources

This list comprises only those sources from which I have drawn material for this book.

Apart from Martel's unfinished work, the first, and still the fullest and greatest, biography of Fouché is Madelin's, published in 1901. There have been subsequent studies in French, German and Swedish: Jean de Brébisson (1906), Hans von Hentig (1919), Nils Forssell (1928), Stefan Zweig (1929), Jean Savant (1955), Henry Buisson (1968). This is the first to be written originally in English.

Fouché's own *Mémoires*, ghosted by A. de Beauchamp and first published in 1824, were successfully branded as spurious in a lawsuit brought by the Fouché family; but Madelin has shown (in his preface to the 1945 edition and *La Révolution française*, September 14, 1900) that they are largely authentic and accurate. Subsequent research has confirmed rather than contradicted this view.

In the seventy years since Madelin's two-volume work, a great many of the French manuscript sources have been published: e.g. Gaillard's papers by Baron Despatys, the Ministry of Police Bulletins by Ernest d'Hauterive.

The considerable amount of material relating to Fouché in the Public Record Office has been hitherto neglected, except for the limited extracts published by P. Coquelle, whose book is tangential to this subject, and the comte de Martel, whose dislike of Thiers distracted him from completing his attack on his other *bête noire*, Fouché. I have given some prominence to this material, and to eyewitness accounts by British, German and Russian contemporaries, in the belief that their prejudices, if national, are less personal.

I am very grateful to Lord Northbrook for permission to consult his family papers, which throw new light on the Labouchère negotiations.

Manuscripts

The Northbrook papers: A.20
Public Record Office: FO 27/54–122, 33/26, 146/1–4, 323/4; PRO 30.
43/29; WO 1/205

Books and Periodicals

Abrantès, Laure Junot, duchesse d', *Histoire des salons de Paris* (Paris, 1837–8).
——, *Mémoires* (Paris, 1905–13).
Annales historiques de la révolution française, see Dautry, Rudé.
Annales de la Religion, X.
Annales révolutionnaires, see Vauthier.
Annual Register, The, LVIII.
Annuaire nécrologique, 1820.
Archives parlementaires de 1787 – [ed. Mavidal, Laurent, etc.] (Paris, 1879–).
Arjuzon, Caroline d', *Hortense de Beauharnais* (Paris, 1897).
Arnault, Antoine-Vincent, *Souvenirs d'un sexagénaire* (Paris, 1833).
Artaud de Montor, Alexis-François, *Histoire de la vie et des travaux politiques du comte d'Hauterive* (Paris, 1839).
Audiat, Louis, *La Terreur en Bourbonnais* (Paris, 1873).
Aulard, François-Victor-Alphonse, *Le culte de la raison et le culte de l'être suprême, 1793–1794* (Paris, 1909, 3rd ed.).
——, *L'état de la France en l'an VIII et en l'an IX* (Paris, 1897).
——, *Histoire politique de la Révolution* (Paris, 1901).
——, *La Société des Jacobins* (Paris, 1889–97).
Avrillon, Mlle [pseud.], *Mémoires* (Paris, 1896).
Babeau, Albert, *Histoire de Troyes pendant la Révolution* (Paris, 1873-4).
Bailleu, Paul [ed.], *Preussen und Frankreich von 1795 bis 1807. Diplomatische Correspondenzen* (Leipzig, 1881).
Balleydier, Alphonse, *Histoire politique et militaire du peuple de Lyon pendant la Révolution française* (Paris, 1845–6).
Barante, Aimable-Guillaume-Prosper Brugière, baron de, *Histoire de la Convention* (Paris, 1853).
——, *Histoire du Directoire* (Paris, 1855).
——, *Souvenirs* (Paris, 1890–1901).
Bard, J., *Tableau de Lyon,* in *Revue du Lyonnais,* I.
Bardoux, Agénor, *Madame de Custine* (Paris, 1891).
Barère, Bertrand, *Mémoires* (Paris, 1842–4).
Barras, Paul-François-Jean-Nicolas de, *Memoirs* (London, 1895).
Bathurst, Report on the Manuscripts of Earl, (London, 1923).
Baudot, Marc-Antoine, *Notes historiques sur la Convention nationale, le Directoire, L'Empire et l'Exil des votants* (Paris, 1893).
Berry, Mary, *Extracts of the Journals and Correspondence* (London, 1865).
Bertier de Sauvigny, Guillaume, *Ferdinand de Bertier* (Paris, 1948).
Bertrand, Henri-Gratien, comte, *Cahiers de Sainte-Hélène* (Paris, 1949–59).
Beugnot, Jacques-Claude, comte, *Mémoires* (Paris, 1889, 3rd ed.).
Biographie bretonne [ed. P-J. Levot] (Paris, 1852-7).

Bignon, Louis-Pierre-Edouard, baron de, *Histoire de France depuis le 18 brumaire jusqu'à la paix de Tilsit* (Paris, 1829–50).

Billard, Max, *La Conspiration de Malet* (Paris, 1907).

Biographie des ministres français depuis juillet 1789 jusqu'à ce jour (Brussels, 1826).

Blanchard, *Mémoires,* in *Revue de la Révolution,* IV.

Blücher, Gebhard Leberecht von, *Blücher in Briefen aus den Feldzügen, 1813–1815* [ed. E. von Colomb] (Stuttgart, 1876).

Boigne, Charlotte-Louise-Eléonore-Adélaïde, comtesse de, *Mémoires* (Paris, 1907).

Bonaparte, Louis, *Réponse à Sir Walter Scott sur son Histoire de Napoléon* (Paris, 1829).

Bonnal, Edmond, *Manuel et son temps* (Paris, 1877).

Bord, Gustave, *Etablissement d'un contre-police royaliste* in *Revue de la Révolution,* XI (Feb. 1888).

Bouillé, Louis-Joseph-Amour, marquis de, *Souvenirs et Fragments,* (Paris, 1906–11).

Boulay de la Meurthe, comte Alfred, *Documents sur la négociation du Concordat* (Paris, 1891–1905).

——, *Boulay de la Meurthe* (Paris, 1868).

Bourrienne, Louis-Antoine-Fauvelet de, *Mémoires* (Paris, 1829).

Broglie, Achille-Charles-Léonce-Victor, duc de, *Souvenirs* (Paris, 1886).

Brotonnne, Léonce de [ed.], *Lettres inédites de Napoléon Ier* (Paris, 1898).

Browning, Oscar [ed.], *England and Napoleon in 1803* (London 1887).

Buonaparte et de Bourmont, Précis de la conversation de, in *Le Carnet historique,* VIII.

Buchez, Philippe-Joseph-Benjamin, and Roux-Lavergne, Pierre-Célestin, *Histoire parlementaire de la révolution française* (Paris, 1834–8).

Bulletins quotidiens adressés par Fouché à l'Empereur. La police secrète du Premier Empire [ed. Ernest d'Hauterive] (Paris, 1809–63).

Burney, Frances, *Diary and letters* (London, 1904–5).

Burr, Aaron, *Private Journal,* [ed. W. K. Bixby] (Rochester, N.Y., 1903).

Cadoudal, Louis-Georges de, *Georges Cadoudal* (Paris, 1887).

Caillé, Dominique, J. *Fouché d'après une correspondance privée inédite,* in *Revue de Bretagne, de Vendée et d'Anjou,* XI.

Canuel, Simon, baron, *Mémoires sur la guerre de la Vendée en 1815* (Paris, 1817).

Capefigue, Baptiste-Honoré-Raymond, *Histoire de la Restauration* (Paris 1831–3).

Caprin, Giuseppe, *I Nostri Nonni* (Trieste, 1888).

Carnet historique, Le, see *Buonaparte et de Bourmont.*

Carnot, Hippolyte, *Mémoire sur Lazare Carnot par son fils* (Paris, 1907).

Carr, Sir John, *The Stranger in France* (London, 1803).

Castellane, Esprit-Victor-Elisabeth-Boniface, comte de, *Journal* (Paris, 1895–7).

Castlereagh, Robert Stewart, Viscount [2nd Marquess of Londonderry], *Correspondence, despatches and other papers* (London, 1848–53).

Chaptal, Jean-Antoine, comte de Chanteloup, *Mes souvenirs sur Napoléon* (Paris, 1893).

Charles-Roux, François, *Rome, asile des Bonapartes* (Paris, 1952).

Charrier, Jules, *L'histoire religieuse du département de la Nièvre pendant la Révolution* (Paris, 1926).

Chassin, Charles-Louis, *Les pacifications de l'Ouest* (Paris, 1896–9).

——, *La préparation de la Guerre de Vendée* (Paris, 1892).

Chastenay, Louise-Marie-Victorine, comtesse de, *Mémoires* (Paris, 1896).

Chateaubriand, François-René, vicomte de, *Mémoires d'outre-tombe* [ed. Biré and Moreau] (Paris, 1947).

Chénier, Louis-Joseph-Gabriel de, *Histoire de la vie du maréchal Davout* (Paris, 1866).

Chuquet, Arthur, *Études d'histoire* (Paris, n.d.).

——, *Inédits napoléoniens* (Paris, 1913–19).

Clary-et-Aldringen, prince Charles de, *Souvenirs* (Paris, 1914).

Claudon, Ferdinand [ed.], *Journal d'un bourgeois de Moulins*, in *Curiosités bourbonnaises*, No. 13, 1898.

La clef du cabinet des souverains, No. 1235, primidi 21 prairial, an VIII.

Cobb, Richard Charles, *L'armée révolutionnaire parisienne à Lyon et dans la région Lyonnaise* (Lyon, 1952).

——, *Les armées révolutionnaires* (Paris, 1961–3).

Cochelet, Louise, *Mémoires sur la reine Hortense et la famille impériale* (Paris, 1837–8).

Collot d'Herbois, Jean-Marie. *Convention Nationale – Rapport fait au nom du Comité de salut public sur la situation de Commune-Affranchie . . . le 1er nivôse* (Paris, An II).

Consalvi, cardinal Ercole, *Mémoires* (Paris, 1895).

Constant, Benjamin, *Journal intime* [ed. J. Mistler] (Monaco, 1946).

——, *Lettres à Mme Récamier* [ed. A. Lenormand] (Paris, 1882).

——, *Mémoires sur les Cent Jours* (Paris, 1820–2).

Coquelle, P., *Napoleon and England* (London, 1904).

Cornillon, Jean, *Le Bourbonnais sous la Révolution française* (Vichy, 1888–95).

Courtois, Edmé-Bonaventure, *Papiers inédits trouvés chez Robespierre, Saint-Just, Payan, etc., supprimés ou omis par Courtois; précédés du rapport de ce député à la Convention Nationale* (Paris, 1828).

Creevey, Thomas, *The Creevey papers* [ed. H. Maxwell] (London, 1912).

Crouzet, François, *L'économie britannique et le blocus continental, 1806–13* (Paris, 1958).

Curiosités bourbonnaises, see Claudon.

Cussy, baron Ferdinand de, *Souvenirs*, (Paris, 1909).

Daudet, Ernest, *La police et les chouans* (Paris, 1895).

——, *Histoire de l'émigration* (Paris, 1905–7).

Dautry, Jean, *La véracité de Barras et les comptes de la police secrète* in *Annales historiques de la révolution française,* année 23, 1951.

Dautry, Jean, *Saint-Simon et les anciens babouvistes de 1804* in *Babeuf*; *Buonarroti* (Nancy, 1961).

Debibour, Antonin, *Recueil des actes du Directoire exécutif* (Paris, 1910).

Delandine, Antoine-François, *Tableau des prisons de Lyon* (Lyon, 1797).

Des Echerolles, Alexandrine-Etiennette-Marie-Charlotte, *Une famille noble sous la Terreur* (Paris, 1879).

Desmarest, Pierre-Marie, *Quinze ans de haute police sous le consulat et l'empire* [ed. L. Grasilier] (Paris, 1900).

Despatys, Pierre-Camille-Augustin-Omer, baron, *Un ami de Fouché, d'après les mémoires de Gaillard* (Paris, 1911).

——, *La Révolution, La Terreur, le Directoire, d'après les mémoires de Gaillard* (Paris, 1909).

Divoff, Elisabeth, *Journal et souvenirs* (Paris, 1929).

Donot, Pierre, and Neufbourg, *Le Forez pendant la Révolution* (Lyon, 1888).

Dostal, Joseph, *Le passage de Fouché en Bohême en 1813,* in *La Révolution Française,* 1936.

Druy de Constant-Scribé, *La vie du général baron Ramel* (Paris, 1912).

Durand, Sophie Cohonset, *Mémoires sur Napoléon et Marie-Louise* (Paris, 1886).

Duvergier de Hauranne, Prosper, *Histoire du gouvernement parlementaire en France, 1814–1848* (Paris, 1857–71).

Duveyrier, Honoré, baron, *Anecdotes historiques* (Paris, 1907).

Enghien, Louis-Antoine-Henri de Bourbon-Condé, duc d', *Correspondence* [ed. Boulay de la Meurthe] (Paris, 1904–13).

Ernouf, baron Alfred-Auguste, *Histoier, de la dernière capitulation de Paris* (Paris, 1859).

——, *Maret, duc de Bassano* (Paris, 1878).

Esquisse historique et fragments inédits sur les Cent-Jours (Paris, 1819).

Fabre (de l'Aude), Jean-Pierre, comte, *Histoire secrète du Directoire* (Paris, 1832).

Fabry, Jean-Baptiste-Germain, *Itinéraire de Bonaparte, depuis son départ de Doulevent . . . jusqu'à son embarquement à Fréjus . . . 1814* (Paris, 1814).

Fauche-Borel, Abram-Louis, *Mémoires* (Paris, 1829).

——, *Précis historique des différentes missions dans lesquelles M. L. Fauche-Borel a été employé pour la cause de la monarchie* (Paris, 1815).

Fauriel, Claude-Charles, *Les derniers jours du consulat* (Paris, 1886).

Fellowes, William Dorset, *Paris during the interesting month of July 1815* (London, 1815).

Ferrand, Antoine-François-Claude, comte, *Mémoires* (Paris, 1897).

Fescourt, *Histoire de la double conspiration de 1800* (Paris, 1819).

Fiévée, Joseph, *Correspondance et relations . . . avec Bonaparte, premier consul et empereur pendant onze années* (Paris, 1836).

Firmin-Didot, Georges, *Royauté ou Empire, la France en 1814, d'après les rapports inédits du comte Anglès* (Paris, 1898).

Fleury de Chaboulon, Pierre-Alexandre-Edouard, baron, *Mémoires . . . avec annotations manuscrites de Napoléon Ier* (Paris, 1901).

Forgues, Eugène, *Le dossier secret de Fouché, juillet-septembre 1815* (Paris, 1908).

Fortescue, *Report on the manuscripts of John Bevill* (London, 1892–1927).

Fouché, Joseph, duc d'Otrante *Authentic memoirs* [or *Sketch*] *of the public life of M. Fouché, Duke of Otranto* (London, 1818).

——, *Défense ou réflexions de Fouché de Nantes sur les calomnies répandues contre lui, prairial an III* (Paris, 1795).

——, *Fête civique pour honorer la valeur et les moeurs, arrêtée par le citoyen Fouché, représentant du peuple* (Nevers, an II).

——, [ed. L. Madelin], *Mémoires* (Paris, 1945).

——, *Mémoires de la vie publique de M. Fouché, duc d'Otrante, contenant sa correspondance avec Napoléon, Murat, le comte d'Artois, le duc de Wellington, le prince Blücher, S. M.. Louis XVIII, le comte Blacas, etc.* (Paris, 1819).

——, *Le Ministre de la Police Générale aux administrations centrales et municipales de la République, 6 frimaire an VIII* (Paris, 1799).

——, *Un mot de Fouché sur la dénonciation déposée contre lui* (Paris, 1795).

——, *Notice sur le duc d'Otrante, extraite et traduite de l'ouvrage allemand . . . Zeitgenossen* (London, 1816).

——, *Première lettre de Fouché de Nantes à la Convention nationale, 25 Thermidor an III* (Paris, 1795).

——, *Rapport de Fouché au 1er Consul, 1799,* in *Revue des documents historiques,* 6e année (1879).

——, *Rapport de Fouché (de Nantes), envoyé dans les départements de la Mayenne et de la Loire-Inférieure* (Paris, 1793).

——, *Rapport de Fouché (de Nantes) sur la situation de Commune-Affranchie, 6 germinal an II* (Paris, 1794).

——, *Rapport et project de decret présentés au nom des comités d'instruction publique et finances* (Paris, March 8, 1793).

——, *Rapport fait au Roi . . . le 15 août 1815; Mémoire présenté au Roi dans le même mois; attribué au duc d'Otrante. Observations critiques par M. de Lanoë* (Paris, 1815).

——, *Réflexions de Fouché de Nantes, représentant du peuple, sur l'éducation public* (Paris, 1793).

——, *Réflexions de Fouché sur le jugement de Louis Capet* (Paris, 1793).

——, *Supplément aux rapports de Fouché (de Nantes) sur les diverses missions qu'il a remplies, pluviôse an III* (Paris, 1795).

Foucher, Pierre, *Souvenirs* (Paris, 1929).

Fox, Henry Edward, Baron [Lord Holland], *Journal* (London, 1923).

Gautherot, Gustave, *Un gentilhomme de grand chemin: le maréchal de Bourmont* (Paris, 1926).

Géraud, Edmond, *Un témoin des deux Restaurations* (Paris, n.d.).

Girardin, Louis-Stanislas-Cecile-Xavier, comte de, *Journal et Souvenirs, Discours et Opinions* (Paris, 1828).

Glenbervie, Sylvester Douglas, Lord, *Diaries* [ed. F. Bickley] (London, 1928).

Godechot, Jacques-Léon, *Les Commissaires aux armées sous le Directoire* (Paris, 1937).

——, *Les institutions de la France sous la Révolution et l'Empire* (Paris, 1951).

Gohier, Louis-Jérôme, *Mémoires* (Paris, 1824).

Gonon, Pierre-Marie, *Bibliographie historique de la ville de Lyon* (Lyon, 1844).

Gourgaud, baron Gaspard, *Journal* (Paris, 1899).

Granville, Harriet Elizabeth Leveson, Countess, *Letters* (London, 1894).

Greer, Donald Malcolm, *The Incidence of the Terror during the French Revolution* (Cambridge, Mass., 1935).

Guépin, Ange, *Histoire de Nantes* (Nantes, 1839).

Guérin, Daniel, *La lutte de classes sous la première République* (Paris, 1946).

Guiche, Aglaé, duchesse de, *Voyage en France en 1801*, in *Revue des Deux Mondes*, CLII.

Guillaume, James, [ed.], *Procès-verbaux du comité d'instruction publique de la Convention Nationale* (Paris, 1891–7).

Guillon, Edouard, *Les complots militaires sous le Consulat et l'Empire* (Paris, 1894).

——, *Les Complots militaires sous la Restauration* (Paris, 1895).

Guillon de Montléon, Aimé, *Mémoires pour servir à l'histoire de la ville de Lyon pendant la Révolution* (Paris, 1824).

Guizot, François-Pierre-Guillaume, *Mémoires pour servir à l'histoire de mon temps* (Paris, 1858–67).

Hamel, Charles, *Histoire de l'abbaye et du collège de Juilly* (Paris, 1868).

Hampson, Norman, *A social history of the French Revolution* (London, 1963).

Hauterive, Ernest d', *La contre-police royaliste en 1800* (Paris, 1931).

——, *L'enlèvement d'un diplomate*, in *Revue de Paris*, XLII.

——, *L'enlèvement du sénateur Clément de Ris* (Paris, 1926).

——, *Napoléon et sa police* (Paris, 1944).

Hautpoul, marquis Amand d', *Souvenirs sur la Révolution, l'Empire et la Restauration* (Paris, 1904).

Héricault, Charles de Ricaud d', *La révolution de Thermidor* (Paris, 1878).

Herriot, Edouard, *Lyon n'est plus* (Lyon, 1937).

——, *Madame Récamier et ses amis* (Paris, 1904).

Hobhouse, John Cam [Lord Broughton], *Recollections of a Long Life* (London, 1909–11).

——, *The substance of some Letters written by an Englishman resident at Paris during the last reign of the Emperor Napoleon* (London, 1816).

Hortense [de Beauharnais], Queen of Holland, *Mémoires* (Paris, 1927).

Houssaye, Henri, *1815*, III (Paris, 1909, 44th Ed.).

Hyde de Neuville, Jean-Guillaume, baron, *Mémoires et souvenirs* (Paris, 1888).

Iung, Théodore, *Lucien Bonaparte et ses Mémoires* (Paris, 1882).

Jackson, Sir George, *The Bath Archives* (London, 1873).

——, *Diaries* (London, 1872).

Jal, Auguste, *Souvenirs d'un homme de lettres* (Paris, 1877).

Jaucourt, Arnail-François, comte de, *Correspondance avec le Prince de Talleyrand pendant le Congrès de Vienne* (Paris, 1905).

Jaurès, Jean, *Histoire socialiste de la Révolution française* [ed. A. Mathiez] (Paris, 1922).

Jérôme [Bonaparte], King of Westphalia, *Mémoires et correspondance du roi Jérôme et de la reine Catherine* (Paris, 1861–6).

[Jullian, Pierre-Louis-Pascal de], *Considérations politiques sur les affaires de France et d'Italie pendant les trois premières années du rétablissement de la Maison de Bourbon sur le trône de France. Par M. de **** (Brussels, 1817).

Kleinclausz, Arthur, *Histoire de Lyon* (Lyon, 1948).

Labouchère, Georges, *Un Financier diplomatique au dernier siècle*: *P. C. Labouchère,* in *Revue d'histoire diplomatique,* 1913.

La Chapelle, A. Salomon de, *Histoire des tribuneaux révolutionnaires de Lyon et de Feurs* (Lyon, 1879).

——, *Documents sur la Révolution* (Lyon, 1885).

Lacretelle, Jean-Charles-Dominique de, *Dix années d'épreuves pendant la Révolution* (Paris, 1842).

Laffitte, Jacques, *Mémoires, 1767–1844* (Paris, 1932).

Lallemand, Paul, *Histoire de l'éducation dans l'ancien Oratoire de France* (Paris, 1888).

Lallié, Alfred, *La Diocèse de Nantes pendant la Révolution* (Nantes, 1893).

——, *La justice révolutionnaire à Nantes* (Nantes, 1896).

——, *Minée et son épiscopat,* in *Revue de la Révolution,* II.

Langeron, Roger, *Decazes, ministre du roi* (Paris, 1960).

Lansdowne, Henry William Edmund Petty-Fitzmaurice, 6th marquis of, *The First Napoleon* (London, 1925).

Lanzac de Laborie, Léon de, *La domination française en Belgique* (Paris, 1895).

Larévellière-Lépeaux, Louis-Marie de, *Mémoires* (Paris, 1895).

Las Cases, Marie-Joseph-Emmanuel-Auguste-Dieudonné de, *Mémorial de Sainte-Hélène* [ed. M. Dunan] (Paris, 1951).

Lavallette, Antoine-Marie Chamans, comte de, *Mémoires* (Paris, 1831).

Lecestre, Alexandre-Léon [ed.] *Lettres inédites de Napoléon Ier* (Paris, 1897).

Lechat, Jean-Claude, *Journal,* in *Nouvelle Revue Retrospective,* XIV.

Le Coz, Claude, *Correspondance* (Paris, 1903).

Le Herpeur, Michel, *L'Oratoire de France* (Paris, 1926).

Lenotre, Georges, *L'affaire Perlet* (Paris, 1923).

Levasseur, René, *Mémoires* (Brussels, 1830–2).

Lombard de Langres, Vincent, *Mémoires* (Paris, 1823).

Louis [Bonaparte], King of Holland, *Documens historiques et réflexions sur le gouvernement de la Hollande* (London, 1820).

——, *Observations de Louis Bonaparte, comte de St. Leu, sur l'histoire de Napoléon, par M. de Norvins* (Paris, 1834).

M***, *Des révolutionnaires* (London, 1815).

Macdonald, maréchal Etienne-Jacques-Joseph-Alexandre, duc de Tarante, *Souvenirs* (Paris, 1892).

Maceroni, Francis, *Memories of the Life and adventures of colonel Maceroni* (London, 1838).

Madelin, Louis, *Fouché* (Paris, 1901).

Marchand, Louis-Joseph-Narcisse, *Mémoires* (Paris, 1952-5).

Marmottan, Paul, *La Grande Duchesse Elisa et Fouché,* in *Revue d'histoire diplomatique,* XL. ——————

Martel, Aimé-Denis du Porzou, comte de, *Etude sur Fouché et le communisme dans la pratique en 1793* (Paris, 1873-9).

——, *Les historiens fantaisistes* (Paris, 1883-7)

Martha-Beker, Félix, *Le général Beker* (Paris, 1876).

Massacré, Léopold de, *Du Ministère* (Paris, 1815).

Masuyer, Valérie, *Mémoires, lettres et papiers* (Paris, 1937).

Mathiez, Albert-Xavier-Emile, *Autour de Robespierre* (Paris, 1926).

——, *Contribution à l'histoire religieuse de la Révolution française* (Paris, 1907).

——, *Le Directoire* (Paris, 1934).

——, *La Théophilanthropie et le culte décadaire* (Paris, 1904).

Mautouchet, Paul, *Le gouvernement révolutionnaire* (Paris, 1912).

Meillan, Arnaud-Jean de, *Mémoires* (Paris, 1828).

Mellinet, Camille, *La commune et la milice de Nantes* (Nantes, 1840-4).

Méneval, Claude-François, baron de, *Mémoires pour servir à l'histoire de Napoléon Ier* (Paris, 1894).

——, *Napoléon et Marie-Louise* (Brussels, 1843).

Ménière, Prosper, *Journal* (Paris, 1903).

Metternich-Winneburg, Klemens Lothar Wenzel, fürst von, *Memoirs* (London, 1880).

Metzger, Albert, *Révolution française: Lyon en 1789-95* [Ed. J. Vaesen] (Lyon, 1882-6).

Meunier, Paul, *La Nièvre pendant la Convention* (Nevers, 1895-8).

Michelet, Jules, *Histoire de la révolution française* [ed. G. Walter] (Paris, 1961-2).

Miles, William Augustus, *Correspondence on the French Revolution* (London, 1890).

Mirabeau, Honoré-Gabriel Riquetti, comte de, *Correspondance entre le comte de Mirabeau et le comte de la Marck* (Paris, 1851).

Molé, Mathieu, *Souvenirs d'un témoin de la Révolution et de l'Empire* (Geneva, 1943).

Moniteur, Le [for the period 1789–99: *Réimpression* (Paris, 1847–58).]

Montarlot, Paul *Un agent de la police secrète (1800–17), Jean-Marie François,* in *Revue des questions historiques,* XCIV.

——, and L. Pingaud, *Le Congrès de Rastatt* (Paris, 1913).

Montbel, Guillaume-Isidore, comte de, *Souvenirs* (Paris, 1813).

Montholon, Albine-Hélène de Vassal, comtesse de, *Souvenirs de Sainte-Hélène* (Paris, 1901).

Montholon, Charles-Jean-François-Tristan de, *Récits de la captivité de l'empereur Napoléon à Sainte-Hélène* (Paris, 1847).

Moulin, A. E., *Les tribulations de Fouché à Prague* in *Revue de France,* VI.

Murat, Joachim, *Lettres et documents pour servir à l'histoire de* [ed P. Le Brethon] (Paris, 1908–14).

Napoléon 1er, *Correspondance* (Paris, 1858–69).

Nesselrode, Carl-Robert, comte de, *Lettres et papiers du Chancelier* (Paris, 1904–11).

Noailles, Emmanuel-Henri, marquis de, *Le comte Molé, sa vie, ses mémoires* (Paris, 1922–30).

Nodier, Charles, *Eloquence de la Tribune – Robespierre,* in *Revue de Paris,* VI.

——, *Souvenirs de la Révolution et de l'Empire* (Paris, 1872).

Nolte, Vincent, *Fifty Years in Both Hemispheres, or Reminiscences of a Merchant's Life* (London, 1854).

Norvins, Jacques Marquet, baron de Montbreton de, *Fouché à Rome,* in *Revue de Paris,* LVII.

Nouvelle revue retrospective, see Lechat.

Ouvrard, Gabriel-Julien, *Mémoires* (Paris, 1826-7).

Pasquier, Etienne-Denis, duc, *Histoire de mon temps* (Paris, 1894).

[Paul, Sir John Dean], *Journal of a Party of Pleasure to Paris, in the month of August, 1802* (London, 1802).

Picard, Ernest, *Bonaparte et Moreau* (Paris, 1905).

Pingaud, Léonce, *Un agent secret sous la Révolution et l'Empire: le comte d'Antraigues* (Paris, 1893).

——, *Bourmont et Fouché,* in *Revue de Paris,* IV.

Polovtzov, Aleksandr Aleksandrovich [ed.], *Correspondance diplomatique, 1814–16* (St Petersburg, 1901).

Pontécoulant, comte Gustave, *Souvenirs historiques et parlementaires* (Paris, 1861–5).

Pozzo di Borgo, comte Charles-André, *Correspondance diplomatique* (Paris, 1890).

Proudhon, Pierre-Joseph, *Commentaires sur les Mémoires de Fouché . . .* (Paris, 1900).

Rambuteau, Claude-Philibert, comte de, *Memoirs,* (London, 1908).

Réal, Pierre-François, *Anecdotes de l'Empire et de la Restauration* [ed. Musnier-Desclozeaux] (Brussels, 1839).

Remacle, comte L, *Bonaparte et le Bourbons. Relations secrètes des agents de Louis XVIII à Paris sous le Consulat* (Paris, 1899).

Réponses des membres des deux anciens comités de salut public et de sûreté général.
    [Barère, Billaud-Varennes, Collot d'Herbois and Vadier] (Paris, an III).
La Révolution française, see Dostal.
Revue de Bretagne, de Vendée et d'Anjou, see Caillé.
Revue de France, see Moulin.
Revue de la Révolution, see Blanchard, Bord, Lallié.
Revue de Paris, see Hauterive, Nodier, Norvins, Pingaud.
Revue des Deux Mondes, see Guiche, Taine
Revue des documents historiques, see Fouché, *Rapport au 1er consul.*
Revue des questions historiques, see Montarlot.
Revue d'histoire diplomatique, see Labouchère, Marmottan.
Revue du Lyonnais, see Bard.
Richard, Camille, *Le comité de salut public et les fabrications de guerre sous la Terreur* (Paris, 1921).
Riffaterre, C., *Le mouvement anti-jacobin et anti-parisien à Lyon et dans le Rhône-et-Loire en 1793* (Lyons, 1912–28).
Rivière, Charles-François, duc, *Mémoires posthumes* (Paris, 1829).
Robespierre, Marie-Marguerite-Charlotte, *Mémoires* [ed. H. Fleischmann] (Paris, 1909).
Rocquain, Félix, *Napoléon 1er et le roi Louis* (Paris, 1875).
Roederer, comte Pierre-Louis, *Oeuvres* (Paris, 1853–9).
Romberg, Edouard, and A. Malet, *Louis XVIII et les Cent-Jours à Gand* (Paris, 1898–1902).
Roustam, Raza, *Souvenirs* (Paris, 1911).
Rudé, George, *Correspondance de Fouché à la veille du 9 Thermidor,* in *Annales historiques de la Révolution française, XXXIV.*
[Saint-Elme, Ida], *Mémoires d'une contemporaine* (Paris, 1827–9).
Saladin, Jean-Baptiste-Michel, *Rapport au nom de la Commission des Vingt-un* . . . (Paris, an III).
Salut Public, Recueil des actes du comité de, [ed. F. Aulard] (Paris, 1889).
Sarrazin, Jean, *Confession du général Buonaparte à l'abbé Maury* (London, 1811).
Savary, Anne-Jeanne-Marie-René, duc de Rovigo, *Mémoires* (Paris, 1828).
Schlitter, Hans, *Kaiser Franz I und die Napoleoniden* (Vienna, 1888).
Sciout, Ludovic, *Le Directoire et la République Cisalpine,* in *Revue des questions historiques, LVI.*
Scott, John, *A Visit to Paris in 1814* (London, 1815).
Sénart, Gabriel-Jérôme, *Révélations puisées dans les cartons des comités de Salut Public et de Sûreté Général, ou Mémoires inédits* . . . (Paris, 1828).
Soboul, Albert, *Les sans-culottes parisiens de l'an II* (Paris, 1962).
Sorel, Albert, *Lectures historiques* (Paris, 1894).
Sotheby and Co., Sale catalogue, 28 March 1960.
Souvenirs et Mémoires, III (July-Dec., 1899).

Staël-Holstein, Anne-Louise-Germaine, baronne de, *Dix ans d'exil* [ed. S. Balayé] (Paris, 1966).

Stendhal [Marie-Henri Beyle], *Napoléon* [ed. J. de Mitty] (Paris, 1897).

Taillandier, Alphonse-Honoré, *Documents biographiques sur P. C. F. Daunou* (Paris, 1841).

Taine, Hippolyte-Adolphe, *Napoléon Bonaparte,* in *Revue des Deux Mondes,* LXXX (1 March 1887).

Talleyrand-Périgord, Charles-Maurice de, prince de Benévénte, *Lettres inédites à Napoléon* (Paris, 1889).

——, *Mémoires* (Paris, 1891–2).

Thibaudeau, comte Antoine-Claire, *Le Consulat et l'Empire* (Paris, 1834).

Thiers, Louis-Adolphe, *Histoire de la révolution française* (Paris, 1846–66).

——, *Histoire du Consulat et de l'Empire* (Paris, 1845).

Thiry, Jean, *La première Restauration* (Paris, 1941).

The Times.

Touchard-Lafosse, Georges, *Souvenirs d'un demi-siècle* (Paris, 1836).

Trénard, Louis, *Lyon, de l'Encyclopédie au préromantisme* (Paris, 1958).

Truchess von Waldburg, Ludwig Friedrich, graf, *A narrative of Napoléon Bonaparte's journey from Fontainebleau to Fréjus in April 1814* (London, 1816).

[Underwood, Thomas Richard], *A Narrative of memorable events in Paris, preceding the Capitulation and during the Occupancy of that City by the Allied Armies in the Year 1814 . . ., etc.* (London, 1828).

Vandal, Albert, *L'avènement de Bonaparte* (Paris, 1903).

Vauthier, Gabriel, *Une circulaire de Fouché aux évêques,* in *Annales révolutionnaires, XV.*

Verger, F.-J., *Archives curieuses de la ville de Nantes* (Nantes,1838–40).

Vialles, Pierre, *L'Archichancelier Cambacérès* (Paris, 1908).

Vidocq, François-Eugène, *Mémoires* (Paris, 1828–30).

Villèle, Joseph, comte de, *Mémoires et correspondance* (Paris, 1889–90).

Villemain, Abel-François, *Souvenirs contemporains d'histoire et de littérature* (Paris, 1854).

Vitrolles, Eugène-François-Auguste d'Arnaud, baron de, *Mémoires* (Paris, 1884).

Wallon, Henri-Alexandre, *Les représentants du peuple en mission* (Paris, 1889).

Walter, Gérard, *Histoire des Jacobins* (Paris, 1946).

——, *Robespierre* (Paris, 1946).

Warren, Rev. Dawson, *The Journal of a British Chaplain in Paris during the Peace negotiations of 1801-2* (London, 1813).

Weil, M. H., *Le Prince Eugène et Murat, 1813–1814* (Paris, 1902).

Wertheimer, Eduard, *Die Verbannten des ersten Kaiserreichs* (Leipzig, 1897).

Wellington, Arthur Wellesley, Duke of, *The dispatches of Field Marshal the Duke of Wellington* [ed. J. Gurwood] (London, 1834–9).

——, *Supplementary despatches and memoranda* [ed. 2nd Duke of Wellington] (London, 1858–72).

Index